SURNAME INDEX
TO
SIXTY-FIVE VOLUMES OF
COLONIAL AND REVOLUTIONARY
PEDIGREES

by

G(eorge) Rodney Crowther, III

Member National Genealogical Society

Foreword by

Milton Rubincam, F.N.G.S., F.A.S.G., F.G.S.P.

published by
National Genealogical Society
1921 Sunderland Place, N.W.,
Washington, D.C. 20036
1964

Second Printing 1965
Third Printing 1977

FOREWORD

Donald Lines Jacobus has commented in one of his reviews that many pedigrees are "buried" in printed collections of genealogies. Library card catalogues do not pick up individual families treated in works such as the Colonial and Revolutionary Lineages of America. For that reason, Mr. Jacobus included in volume III of his Index to Genealogical Periodicals a section entitled "My Own Index" — his private listing, in alphabetical order, of the families discussed in printed genealogical collections.

Mr. Crowther has followed the same plan in the present compilation. His index of families discussed in 17 works (totalling 65 volumes) is a ready reference to the pedigrees that have appeared in the collections consulted by him.

Too much emphasis can not be placed on his section entitled "Caution". Mr. Crowther quite properly notes that all pedigrees must be used only as a guide or lead to further investigation. None of these works may be considered as authoritative; their statements must be treated with care. The information concerning their ancestry is provided by members of the families included therein, and it may or may not be based on researches among primary source materials. Very often the data are taken from family traditions or from inferior printed works without the benefit of independent investigation. For example, Burke's The Prominent Families of the United States of America (1908) does not provide for documentation of its pedigrees. As a case in point, it traces the Cope family of Pennsylvania back to John Cope (1355-1415), of Deanshangar, county Northampton, and Hausted, county Buckingham, without citing any sources. The lineage was prepared by James Biddle Cope who, yearning for ancestral honors, went to England in the hope of obtaining a knighthood or a peerage, but, failing in his objective, removed to Italy whose monarch gratified his desires — or his vanity — by creating him Baron Cope di Valromita, certainly an aristocratic title for the scion of a modest Quaker family! There is no satisfactory evidence (that I have seen) for the English lineage with which the noble American-Italian baron bedecked himself, and it should not be accepted without verification.

As another illustration, Adams and Weis' The Magna Charta Sureties, 1215, while better than some productions we have seen, contains errors which have been picked up by reviewers of the book. It, too, is useful as a guide but must not be considered authoritative.

The National Genealogical Society does not endorse any of the seventeen works indexed in the present volume. It believes, however, that a public service is being rendered by its publication. Mr. Crowther is to be congratulated for taking the initiative in preparing this index and on his assiduity in carrying the project to its completion.

Milton Rubincam

INTRODUCTION

This volume had its origin in a year-long search through scores of volumes for information about a number of Colonial families. What began as a sort of by-product of the research — a list of surnames for my guidance through the intricacies of the genealogical information — gradually developed into a major enterprise of its own. Researching had not been long under way before I realized in leafing through one after another of the volumes containing Colonial and Revolutionary pedigrees that some master index to the volumes would prove helpful to other persons engaged in genealogical research. The seed was nourished by the staff of the Maryland Historical Society who expressed continued interest in seeing such an index completed.

Without the assistance and encouragement of the Library of Congress, it would have been difficult to make the page by page searches which made this volume possible. The works indexed here are to be found in the collection of the Library of Congress, Washington 25, D.C., although several volumes, missing temporarily from the shelf or in the bindery, were used at the Maryland Historical Society, 201 West Monument Street, Baltimore 1, Maryland, and the New York Public Library, Fifth Avenue and 42nd Street, New York 18. A search of the National Union Catalog was made and a brief list of additional libraries is given after each volume in the KEY. No effort has been made to give a "complete" listing for each volume for in several cases such a list would be unreasonably long, but is intended to give a second or third location for a given volume should the searcher experience delays.

In now offering this completed surname index to 65 volumes of historical data on American families, it is my hope that it will prove useful to many who may hereafter seek out the pedigree of their own, or some other, family.

The surnames listed alphabetically in this index are those of all the families to be found in the 27 volumes of <u>Colonial Families of America</u>, the 20 volumes of <u>Colonial and Revolutionary Lineages of America</u>, and a dozen-and-a-half individual volumes giving background data about families who have helped to make America.

You will note several corrections to pedigrees, pp. 25, 49, 55 and 98, which are to the author's own family. I could not very well allow known errors to pass uncorrected. There are certainly other errors in many families unresearched by me.

This index is designed to do what none of the indexes to the 65 individual volumes can do: namely, tell you, for a given family name, in which of the 65 volumes data about that family may be found. For example, if you should wish data about the pedigree of, say the Byrd family, you would begin by looking for BYRD under the alphabetical listing: (page 21)

BYRD   Eng.   Va.   Arms:-   CFA17------347

Key   This is the distinguished Byrd family of Virginia showing their ancient origin in England. Arms are blazoned only. The pedigree is to be found in Colonial Families of America CFA , by Ruth Lawrence, volume 17 (1937), page 347 (f.).

Every success in your search.

Chevy Chase, Maryland   G. Rodney Crowther, III
Fall, 1963

CAUTION

Verification of a pedigree rests with you. It will behoove the casual searcher to seek out all accreditation references given in any pedigree and check with care any other-than-primary source documents. Use all pedigrees as a guide or lead to further investigation. If an accreditation is nothing more than 'family information' you will have to contact that family or start from the bottom.

And it does not necessarily follow that just because you are here you or your family are entitled to bear existing coat armor. The only person who can tell you "this is your Coat-of-Arms" is the "patentee" (ancient or modern) from whom you must descend in an unbroken line. See Armorial Families: (London, 1929), compiled and edited by Arthur Fox-Davies, pp. xiii-xxxiv, sub. "The Abuse of Arms."

G. R. R. C.

K E Y

All volumes are at the Library of Congress as well as other libraries,
some listed after each volume. Abbreviations are described at end of Key.

CFA.......Colonial Families of America (New York, 1928-48), edited by Ruth Lawrence; published by National Americana Society; National Americana Publications, Inc. 27v.

MdHi (vols. 1-16 only), MH, MWA, N, NN

CRLA......Colonial and Revolutionary Lineages of America (New York, 1939-59), published by
the American Historical Company, Inc. 20v.(pub. to date).

MB, MH, NN (vols. 1-18 only), PP (vols. 14-15

only), PPAmSwM, WHi(vols.1-3,5,8,10-12,14-20)

ACF.......American Colonial Families (New York, 1930), by L. Effingham De Forest.

NN

AF*.......American Families: (New York, 1928?), published by the American Historical Society, Inc.

AF**......American Families: (New York, 1932?), published by the American Historical Society, Inc.

AF***.....American Families: (New York, 1932), published by the American Historical Society, Inc.

AF****....American Families: (New York, 19__), by William Richard Cutter; published by the
American Historical Society.

MH, OClWHi

AFA1......American Family Antiquity: (New York, 1880), by Albert Welles, volume 1

MH, MWA, NBuG, NN, OClWHi, PBL, PHi, WHi
AFA2......Ibid., volume 2(1881)
                                          (To be used with care)
AFA3......Ibid., volume 3(1881)

AFA4......Ibid., volume 4(1881)

AFA***....Armorial Families of America (Philadelphia, Bailey, Banks and Biddle Co., 1929),
edited by Ernest Spofford.

MB, NN, PHi

ARSC......Ancestral Roots of Sixty Colonists Who Came to New England Between 1623 and 1650
(Lancaster, Mass., 1951), by Frederick Lewis Weis.

MiD

HFA.......Historic Families of America: (New York, 1907), edited by Walter W. Spooner.

MB, PKsL, TxU

MCS.......The Magna Charta Sureties, 1215, . . . and Some of Their Descendents Who Set-
tled in America 1607-1650 (Boston, Mass., 1955), by Arthur Adams and Frederick
Lewis Weis.

ICN, MB, MsSM, NjR, NN, PHi, WHi

PBAF......Patten, Buchanan, and Allied Families: (New York, 1934), published by the American Historical Society, Inc.

OClWHi

KEY

FPU.......The Prominent Families of the United States of America (London, The Sackville
Press, Ltd., 1908), by Arthur M. Burke, volume 1(only one pub.),

CU, CtY, MB, MWA, OClWHi, OO, PHi, PP, ViU

PPA.......The Poets and Poetry of America (Philadelphia, Parry and McMillan, 1855), by
Rufus Wilmot Griswold.

CSmH, ICU, MB, OCl, PPD, PPL-R, PV

SDI.......The Story of the Declaration of Independence (New York, Oxford University Press,
1954), by Dumas Malone. Still available for purchase, $10.00.

TNEF...... . . . Tercentenary of New England Families 1620-1922 (Boston, New York /etc./,
1922), issued under the auspices of the American Historical Society.

NN, OClWHi

(17 titles in 65 volumes)

ABBREVIATIONS

CU.......University of California, Berkeley.

CSmH......Henry E. Huntington Library, San Marino, California

CtY.......Yale University, New Haven, Connecticut.

ICN.......Newberry Library, Chicago, Illinois.

ICU......University of Chicago, Chicago, Illinois.

MB.......Boston Public Library, Boston, Massachusetts.

MdHi......Maryland Historical Society, Baltimore.

MH.......Harvard University, Cambridge, Massachusetts.

MiD......Detroit Public Library, Detroit, Michigan.

MsSm......Mississippi State University, State College, Mississippi.

MWA.......American Antiquarian Society, Worcester, Massachusetts.

NBuG......Grosvenor Reference Division, Buffalo and Erie County Public
Library, Buffalo, New York.

N.........New York State Library, Albany.

NN........New York Public Library.

NjR.......Rutgers University, New Brunswick, New Jersey.

OCl.......Cleveland Public Library, Cleveland, Ohio.

OClWHi....Western Reserve Historical Society, Cleveland, Ohio.

OO........Oberlin College, Oberlin, Ohio.

PBL.......Lehigh University, Bethlehem, Pennsylvania.

PHi.......Historical Society of Pennsylvania, Philadelphia.

PKsL......Longwood Library, Kennett Square, Pennsylvania.

PP........Free Library of Philadelphia.

PPAmSwM...American Swedish Historical Foundation, Philadelphia.

PPL-R.....Library Company of Philadelphia, Ridgeway Branch.

PPD.......Drexel Institute of Technology, Philadelphia.

PV........Villanova College, Villanova, Pennsylvania.

TxU.......University of Texas, Austin.

ViU.......University of Virginia, Charlottesville.

WHi.......State Historical Society of Wisconsin, Madison.

———

SYMBOLS

Arms:-....Armorial Bearings are blazoned only, i. e. verbally described.

*.........An achievement of arms, i. e. a complete illustration, is facing or nearby.

de........In most families requiring it, this prefix has been placed after the surname; thus "de Beauchamp" will be found in -B- as "Beauchamp (de)" (Armorial Général: ((Paris, 1884)), by Louis Pierre d'Hozier). However, a few surnames of the lesser than great Norman houses, etc., such as De Wit, where the prefix is necessary in locating the name in its American usage, have been placed by the author under -D- in this index.

?.........Reference material states only that original settler was "probably from_____" or "may have been born in_____."

=.........Indicates an alliance by marriage or, in rare instances, a variation in spelling of the same name.

SOME COMPLEMENTARY INDEXES AND GUIDES

Genealogical Research Methods and Sources (Washington, D. C., 1960), by the American Society of Genealogists.

Search and Research: (Salt Lake City, Utah, Deseret Book Company, 1959), by Noel C. Stevenson.

American and English Genealogies in the Library of Congress (Washington, D. C., Government Printing Office, 1919), by J. C. M. Hanson.

Index to American Genealogies: (Albany, N.Y., Joel Munsell's Sons, 1900), edited by Daniel S. Durrie.

The Genealogist's Guide (Guilford, 1903), by George W. Marshall.

A Genealogical Guide: (London, Walford Brothers, 1953), compiled by J. B. Whitmore (A continuation of Marshall, above).

The American Genealogical-Biographical Index to American Genealogical, Biographical and Local History Materials (Middletown, Conn., Godfrey Memorial Library, 1952-   ), edited by Fremont Rider.

The Genealogical Index of the Newberry Library Chicago (Boston, Mass., G. K. Hall & Co., 1960.

Americana (Illustrated), formerly The American Historical Magazine (New York, 1906-43), published by the Americana Society: the American Historical Co., Inc. 37v. An index to this set may be found in Index to Genealogical Periodicals (New Haven, Conn.), by Donald Lines Jacobus, volumes 1 (1932) and 2 (1948). See also his Index:, volume 3 (1953).

Genealogical Guide to the Early Settlers of America (New York City, Spirit of '76 Press, 1898-99), compiled by Henry Whittemore.

American Genealogy: (Albany, J. Munsell, 1848), by Jerome B. Holgate.

Living Descendants of Blood Royal: (London, World Nobility and Peerage, 1959), edited by Arthur Adams and Count d'Angerville, volume 1 (only one published).

America Heraldica (New York, 1886), edited by E. De V. Vermont.

Burke's Distinguished Families of America: (Burke's Peerage Limited, 1948), as well as Sir (John) Bernard Burke's 2 volumes, A Genealogical and Heraldic History of the Colonial Gentry (1891-95).

SOME COMPLEMENTARY DEPOSITORIES

The National Archives of the United States, Pennsylvania Avenue at 8th Street, N.W. Washington, D. C. 20408.

Genealogical Society of the Church of Jesus Christ of Latter-Day Saints, 107 South Main Street, P. O. Box 749, Salt Lake City 11, Utah.

Daughters of the American Revolution, 1776 D Street, N.W., Washington, D. C. 20006

Library of Congress, Local History and Genealogy Room, Family Name Card Indexes;and Microfilm Reading Room - Principal Collections: a- Early State Records(Colonies, States and Territories). Filmed 1941-50 by the Library of Congress in association with the University of North Carolina. b- British Manuscripts Project Filmed 1941-45 for the American Council of Learned Societies (which includes Colonial Office documents held by the Public Record Office; also includes important manuscript collections from the National Library of Wales, Aberystwyth; and privately held collections). c- Irish Genealogical Records from the National Library of Dublin - 127 reels. d- Continually expanding collection on film of Deteriorating and Mutilated Items From the Library's Book Collection. e- Card Catalog - sub. "Genealogy".

SURNAME INDEX
TO
SIXTY-FIVE VOLUMES OF
COLONIAL AND REVOLUTIONARY
PEDIGREES

FAMILY NAME	ORIGIN	COLONY OR STATE OF RESIDENCE	ARMS	VOLUME	PAGE

- A -

FAMILY NAME	ORIGIN	COLONY OR STATE OF RESIDENCE	ARMS	VOLUME	PAGE
ABBOT	————	————	*(only)	CRLA12	88
ABBOTT	Eng.?	Mass.	Arms:-*	CFA4	263
ABBOTT	Eng.	Mass.	Arms:-*	CFA12	84
ABBOTT	Eng.	N.J.		CRLA11	249
ABBOTT	Eng.	Pa.		CRLA15	240
ABBOTT	Eng.?	Mass.	Arms:-*	AF***	20
ABELL	Eng.	Mass./Md.	Arms:-*	CRLA9	524
ABELL	Eng.	Mass./Md.		CRLA12	136
ABERCROMBIE	Scotland	Mass.	Arms:-*	CFA8	66
ABNEY	Eng.	Va.	Arms:-*	PFU	278
ABORN	————	R.I.		CFA5	48
ABRAHAM	Wales	Pa.		CRLA9	250
ABRAMS	————	Ohio		CRLA12	192
ACKERMAN	————	N.Y.		CRLA18	216
ACKERSON	————	————		CFA4	175
ADAMS	Wales	Mass.	Arms:-*	CFA6	57
ADAMS	Eng.	Mass.		CFA7	159
ADAMS	Eng.	Mass.		CFA8	111
ADAMS	————	Mass.		CFA9	317
ADAMS	Eng.	Mass.	Arms:-*	CFA10	15
ADAMS	Eng.	Mass.		CFA11	176
ADAMS	Eng.	Mass.		CFA11	214
ADAMS	Eng.	Mass.	Arms:-*	CFA12	49
ADAMS	Wales/Eng.	Mass.	Arms:-	CFA13	367
ADAMS	Eng.	Mass.		CFA14	98
ADAMS	————	Mass.		CFA15	351
ADAMS	Eng.	Mass.	Arms:-	CFA16	272
ADAMS	Eng.	Mass.	Arms:-*	CFA18	74
ADAMS	Eng.	Mass.	Arms:-*	ACF	49
ADAMS	Eng.	Mass.	Arms:-*	CRLA7	33
ADAMS	————	Mass.		CRLA7	167
ADAMS	Scotland	Mass./N.H./S.C.		CRLA8	55
ADAMS	————	Conn.	Arms:-	CRLA10	282
ADAMS	Germany	Pa.		CRLA12	335
ADAMS	————	Conn.	Arms:-*	CRLA13	440
ADAMS	Eng.	Mass.	Arms:-*	CRLA15	90
ADAMS	————	Conn.	Arms:-*	CRLA15	473
ADAMS	Eng.	Conn.		CRLA15	598
ADAMS	Eng.	Mass.	Arms:-	CRLA16	114
ADAMS	Eng.	Mass.		CRLA16	184
ADAMS	————	Va./Ky.		CRLA16	219
ADAMS	Eng.?	Maine	Arms:-*	CRLA17	542,555
ADAMS	————	Pa.		CRLA18	597
ADAMS	Eng.	Mass./Conn.		CRLA18	606
ADAMS	Eng.	Mass.	Arms:-*	CRLA19	44
ADAMS	Eng.	Mass.		CRLA19	260
ADAMS	Eng.	Mass.	Arms:-*	CRLA20	91
ADAMS	————	Mass.		CRLA20	168

Surname	Origin	Location	Arms	Reference
ADAMS	———	Mass.		PPA--------------68
ADAMS	Eng.	Mass.	Arms:-	TNEF------------196
ADAMS, John	———	Mass.		SDI---------105,112
ADAMS, Samuel	———	Mass.		SDI---------105,111
ADAMSON	Scotland	La.		CRLA13----------202
ADAMSON	———	Tenn.		CFA11-----------247
ADEE	Scotland/France	R.I.	Arms:-	CFA26------------83
ADGATE	Eng.	Conn.		CFA23------------94
AELTHRYTH, daughter to Alfred the Great, Royal line from Cedric de Warren descent				TNEF------------95
AGLIONBY	Eng.	Va.	Arms:-*	PFU-------------252
AGRY	———	Mass.		CFA13-----------362
AIGUIER	———	N.Y.		CRLA10----------374
AILES	Wales?	Pa.	Arms:-*	CRLA17-----------48
AINSWORTH	Eng.	Mass.	Arms:-	AF**------------213
ALBEE	———	Mass.		CFA10------------88
ALBERT	———	Pa.		CFA17-----------299
ALBERTSON	Holland	N.Y.	Arms:-*	CRLA11----------447
ALBINI (de), see: ARUNDEL, Earls of				
ALBRIGHT	Germany	N.Y./Pa.	Arms:-*	AFA***----------379
ALBRO	———	———	Arms:-*	CRLA13------407,409
ALCOTT	Eng.		Arms:-*	CRLA13----------133
ALDEN	Eng.	Mass.		CFA5------------251
ALDEN	———	Mass.		CFA7------------179
ALDEN	Eng.	Mass.	Arms:-*	CFA9------------214
ALDEN	Eng.	Mass.	Arms:-	CFA10-----------375
ALDEN	Eng.	Mass.		CFA11-----------178
ALDEN	Eng.	Mass.		CFA12------------76
ALDEN	Eng.	Mass.		CFA12-----------226
ALDEN	Eng.	Mass.		CFA13-----------361
ALDEN	Eng.	Mass.		CRLA7------------77
ALDEN	Eng.	Mass.		CRLA10----------342
ALDEN	Eng.	Mass.		CRLA12-----------65
ALDEN	———	Mass.		CRLA17----------262
ALDEN	Eng.	Mass.		CRLA19----------150
ALDEN	Eng.	Mass.	Arms:-*	CRLA20-----------49
ALDEN	Eng.	Mass.	Arms:-	AF**-------------81
ALDEN	———	Mass.	Arms:-	AF**------------454
ALDEN	———	———	*(only)	TNEF---------opp.78
ALDEN, see: PILGRIMS				
ALDRICH	Eng.	Mass.		CFA10------------25
ALDRICH	Eng.	Mass./R.I.		CFA22-----------256
ALDRICH	———	N.Y.		PPA-------------453
ALENCON, Counts of	Yves or Ives de Creil, d. ca. 997			CRLA5-----------201
ALEXANDER	Scotland	N.Y.		CFA11------------22
ALEXANDER	———	Pa./Va.		CRLA3-----------411
ALEXANDER	———	Md./Va./N.C.		CRLA8-----------160
ALEXANDER	Scotland	Va.		PFU-------------409
ALFANSO IX -1214, see: CASTILE, House of				
ALFRED THE GREAT, Descent from				CFA24------------21
ALFRED THE GREAT, Descent from				CRLA1-----------463
ALFRED THE GREAT, Descent from		Lawrence descent		CRLA19----------331
ALFRED THE GREAT, Descent from		de Warren descent		TNEF------------95
ALGER	———	Mass.		CFA6------------195
ALGER	———	Mass.		CFA12-----------372
ALGER	———	Mass.		CFA13-----------157
ALLEN	Eng.	Mass.	Arms:-*	CFA1------------147
ALLEN	———	Maine		CFA2------------176
ALLEN	Eng.	Pa.		CFA7------------396
ALLEN	———	Conn.		CFA9------------325
ALLEN	Eng.	Mass.		CFA12------------78
ALLEN	———	N.J./R.I./Mass.		CFA12-----------121
ALLEN	Eng.	Mass./Conn.	Arms:-	CFA15-----------337
ALLEN	Eng.	Mass.	Arms:-	CFA17-----------150
ALLEN	Scotland?	Mass./Conn.		CFA18-----------132
ALLEN	Eng.	Mass./Conn.	Arms:-*	CFA22------------22
ALLEN	Eng.	Mass.	Arms:-*	CFA23------------32

ALLEN	Eng.	Mass./Conn.		CFA24----------158
ALLEN	Eng.	Pa.	*(only)	CRLA2----------422
ALLEN	------	N.C.		CRLA4----------118
ALLEN	Eng.	Va.	Arms:-*	CRLA11-,-------285
ALLEN	Eng.	Mass.	Arms:-*	CRLA18----------571
ALLEN	Eng.	Mass.		CRLA19----------64
ALLEN	------	Mass.	Arms:-*	CRLA20----------8
ALLEN	------	R.I.	Arms:-	AF*------------395
ALLEN	------	N.J.		AF**-----------467
ALLEN	------	N.J./Mass.		TNEF------------145
ALLEN	------	------	*(only)	TNEF--------opp.78
ALLEN, see: PILGRIMS				
ALLERTON	Eng.	Mass.		CFA7-----------143
ALLERTON	Eng.	Conn.	Arms:-*	CRLA7----------360
ALLERTON	Eng.	Mass./Conn.		CRLA16----------143
ALLERTON	Eng.	Conn.	Arms:-*	CRLA17----------28
ALLERTON	------	Mass./N.Y.		PFU------------37
ALLEY	Eng.	Mass.		ACF------------80
ALLING	Eng.	Conn.	Arms:-*	CRLA14----------160
ALLISON	Ireland	Pa.		CRLA1----------132
ALLSTON	------	S.C./Mass.		PPA------------86
ALLYN	Eng.			CRLA1----------182
ALLYN	------	Conn.		CRLA6----------402
ALLYN	Eng.	Conn.		CRLA7----------98
ALLYN	------	Mass./Conn.		CRLA17----------477
ALMY	Eng.	Mass.	Arms:-*	CFA8-----------162
ALMY	Eng.	Mass./R.I.	Arms:-*	CFA14----------33
ALMY	Eng.	Mass.	Arms:-*	CFA18----------42
ALMY	------	------	*(only)	TNEF-------btn.78-9
ALMY, see: PILGRIMS				
ALSOP	Eng.	L.I.,N.Y.		CFA1-----------203
ALSOP	------	Conn.		PPA------------64
ALSTON	Eng.	Va./N.C.	Arms:-*	CFA1-----------161
AMBLER	Eng.	N.J./Pa.	Arms:-*	CRLA17----------363
AMES	------	Mass.	Arms:-*	CFA4-----------152
AMES	------	Mass.		CFA5-----------309
AMES	Eng.	Mass.	Arms:-*	TNEF------------73
AMORY	Eng.	S.C./Mass.		CFA4-----------45
AMORY	Eng.	S.C.		CFA18----------271
AMORY	Eng.	Mass./S.C.	Arms:-*	CRLA8----------7
AMYCE	Eng.		Arms:-*	CRLA5----------86
ANDERSON	Scotland	N.Y.		CFA15----------80
ANDERSON	Eng.?	Va.		CFA21----------89
ANDERSON	Ireland	Md.		CRLA4----------328
ANDERSON	------	Va.		CRLA4----------389
ANDERSON	------	N.Y./N.J.		CRLA11----------260
ANDERSON	------	Del.		CRLA15----------575
ANDERSON	------	Va.		CRLA10----------29
ANDERSON	Scotland	Va.		PFU------------59
ANDRAE	Europe	Pa.	Arms:-*	CRLA8----------264
ANDREW (or) ANDREWS	------	Mass./Maine		CFA14----------282
ANDREWS	Ireland	Md.		CFA3-----------301
ANDREWS	Eng.	Mass.		CFA7-----------80
ANDREWS	Eng.	Mass.		CFA7-----------122
ANDREWS	Eng.	------		CFA7-----------322
ANDREWS	Eng.	Mass.		CFA18----------141
ANDREWS	Ireland	Md.		CFA20----------214
ANDREWS	Eng.	Md.	Arms:-*	CRLA8----------214
ANDREWS	Eng.	Mass.		CRLA18----------41
ANDREWS	Eng.	Md.	Arms:-*	CRLA19----------6
ANDREWS	------	Mass.		CRLA19----------47
ANDREWS	------	Mass.	Arms:-*	CRLA20----------77
ANDRIESSEN	Holland	N.Y.	Arms:-*	CRLA20----------68
ANGARICA	Cuba	------		ACF------------93
ANGELL	------	Mass.		CFA8-----------357
ANGELL	Eng.	Mass.	Arms:-*	CFA10----------20
ANGELL	Eng.	Mass.		ACF------------83

ANGELL	——	——	*(only)	TNEF------btn.70-1
ANGOULEME, Counts of	France			CRLA1-----------333
ANGOULEME, Counts of	France	Taillefer	Peck=Bowen desc.	CRLA2------------33
ANGOULEME, Counts of	France		Ludlow=Brewster desc.	CRLA2-----------340
ANGOULEME, Counts of	France	Taillefer		CRLA2-----------509
ANGOULEME, Counts of		Wulgrin I, d. 866	Arms:-*	CRLA5-----------204
ANGOULEME, Counts of	France		Haskell descent	CRLA8------------75
ANGOULEME, Counts of	France		Hinton descent	CRLA8-----------467
ANGOULEME, Counts of	France		Blackiston desc.	CRLA11----------416
ANGOULEME, Counts of	France		Cooley=Twining desc.	CRLA18----------101
ANGUS	Scotland	Va.		CFA10------------76
ANJOU, Counts of	France			CRLA1-----------340
ANJOU, Counts of	France		Gaunt=French desc.	CRLA1-----------551
ANJOU, Counts of	France	Peck=Bowen desc.	*(only)	CRLA2------------35
ANJOU, Counts of	France		Warren=Belknap desc.	CRLA2-----------180
ANJOU, Counts of	France		Fulk I -938	CRLA2-----------516
ANJOU, Counts of	France		Fulk I-Geoffrey V	CRLA2-----------361
ANJOU, Counts of	France	Tertule	Arms:-*	CRLA5-----------207
ANJOU, Counts of	France			CRLA7-----------215
ANJOU, Counts of	France		Haskell descent	CRLA8------------77
ANJOU, Counts of	France		Hinton descent	CRLA8-----------468
ANJOU, Counts of	France		Cooley=Twining desc.	CRLA18----------103
ANKENY	France/Germany	Pa./Md.	Arms:-*	CRLA11-----------14
ANKENY	Belgium	Pa.	Arms:-*	CRLA10----------359
ANNE	Eng.		*(only)	CRLA2------------11
ANSON	——	N.Y.	Arms:-*	CRLA20----------154
ANTHONY	Eng.	R.I.	Arms:-*	TNEF------------13
ANTRIM	——	N.J.		CRLA17-----------79
APPLEBY		N.J./N.Y.		CRLA9-----------423
APPLETON	Eng.	Mass.	Arms:-*	CFA13-----------289
APPLETON	Eng.	Mass.	Arms:-	CFA21-----------234
APPLETON	Eng.	Mass.	Arms:-	CFA22-----------191
APPLETON	Eng.	Mass.	Arms:-	CFA24-----------130
APPLETON	——	Mass.		MCS-------------113
APTHORP	Eng.	Mass.		CFA13------------38
AQUITAINE, Dukes of	France			CRLA1-----------336
AQUITAINE, Dukes of	France		Gaunt=French desc.	CRLA1-----------553
AQUITAINE, Dukes of	France		Warren=Belknap desc.	CRLA2-----------184
AQUITAINE, Dukes of	France		Bernard I, ano. 844	CRLA2-----------512
AQUITAINE, Dukes of	France		Bernard I-Eleanor of, m. Henry II, Eng.	CRLA5-----------211
AQUITAINE, Dukes of	France			CRLA7-----------216
AQUITAINE, Dukes of	France		Haskell descent	CRLA8------------80
AQUITAINE, Dukes of	France		Hinton descent	CRLA8-----------470
AQUITAINE, Dukes of	France			CRLA9-----------376
AQUITAINE, Dukes of	France			CRLA15-----------95
AQUITAINE, Dukes of	France		Bernard I	CRLA17----------155
ARAGON, Kings of	Spain		Ramirez I, d. 1063	CRLA5-----------214
ARAGON, Kings of	Spain		Ramirez I	CRLA17----------156
ARAGON, Kings of	Spain		Cooley=Twining desc.	CRLA18----------105
ARCHBALD	Scotland	Pa.		CRLA10----------270
ARCHER	——	Pa.		CRLA8-----------324
ARCHER	——	Md.	Arms:-*	CRLA17----------416
ARCHIBALD	Ireland	Nova Scotia		CFA23-----------161
ARDENNES, Counts of	France		Drogo, d. 708	CRLA5-----------217
ARDERNE (Arden)	Eng.	Eustace, alias Watford	Arms:-*	CRLA5-----------218
ARETS	Germany	Pa.		CRLA9-----------159
AREY	——	Mass.		CRLA18-----------73
ARGALL	——	Va.		MCS-------------110
ARMITAGE	Eng.	Pa.	Arms:-*	CRLA1------------78
ARMITAGE	Eng.	Pa.		CRLA9-----------323
ARMITAGE	Eng.?	Mass.		CRLA17----------341
ARMS (Armes)	Eng.	Mass.	Arms:-	AF***-----------421
ARMSTRONG	Ireland	Pa.	Arms:-*	CRLA9-----------486
ARMSTRONG	No family data		Arms:-*	CRLA19------opp.226
ARMSTRONG	——	N.C.	Arms:-*	AF**------------304
ARNOLD	Wales	R.I.		CFA1------------199

AUDLEY (de)	Eng.			CRLA15----------107
AUSTIN	——	Mass.		CFA12-----------215
AUSTIN	——	Conn.		CFA20-----------110
AUSTIN	Eng.	Pa.	Arms:-*	CRLA13----------128
AUSTIN	Eng.	Mass.		CRLA19-----------44
AUSTIN	——	N.C.		CRLA19----------388
AUSTIN	——	Conn./Va.		TNEF-----------203
AUZIAS DE TURENNE	France	Canada/America	Arms:-	CFA22-----------248
AVERELL	Eng.	Mass.	Arms:-*	CFA1------------210
AVERELL	Eng.	Mass.	Arms:-*	CFA11-----------376
AVERELL	——	Mass.		CRLA9-----------266
AVERILL	Eng.	Mass.		CFA21-----------241
AVERY	Eng.	Conn.	Arms:-*	CFA1--------------8
AVERY	——	Oregon		CFA11-----------248
AVERY	Eng.	Mass./Conn.		CFA19-----------65
AVERY	Eng.	Conn.	Arms:-*	CFA19-----------227
AVERY	Eng.	Mass./Conn.		CFA22-----------219
AVERY	Eng.	Mass./Conn.	Arms:-*	CRLA17----------465
AVERY	Eng.?	Mass.	Arms:-*	CRLA17----------523
AVERY	——	N.H./Mass.	Arms:-*	CRLA17----------575
AVERY	——	Mass./Conn.		CRLA20----------173
AVERY	Eng.	Mass.	Arms:-*	AF*-------------71
AWBREY	Wales	——	Arms:-*	CFA20-----------96
AYER	Eng.	Mass.		CFA21-----------193
AYER	Eng.	Mass.	Arms:-*	CFA27----15,148cht.
AYER	Scotland	S.C.		CRLA17-----------11
AYLSWORTH	——	R.I.	Arms:-*	CRLA19----------284
AYRE=AYRES=EYRES	——	Va./Md.	Arms:-*	CRLA15----------317
AYRES (Eyres)	——	Md.	Arms:-*	CRLA2-----------127
AYRES	Eng.?	Mass.	Arms:-*	CRLA2-----------247
AYRES	——	Va./Md.	Arms:-*	CRLA11-----------28
AYRES	——	Md.		CRLA16-----------45

- B -

BABBITT	——	Mass.		CFA1------------243
BABBITT	Wales	Mass.		CFA26-----------22
BABCOCK	Eng.	R.I.		CFA9------------14
BABCOCK	Eng.	R.I.		CFA10-----------277
BABCOCK	Eng.	R.I.		CFA19-----------237
BABCOCK	Eng.	R.I.	Arms:-*	CFA23-----------106
BABCOCK	——	R.I.		CRLA20----------174
BABCOCK	Eng.?	R.I./Conn.	Arms:-*	CRLA20----------356
BABCOCK	Eng.	Mass./R.I.	Arms:-*	AFA3------------195
BABSON	Eng.?	Mass.		CFA6------------168
BABST	France	N.Y.	Arms:-*	CFA24-----------22
BACHILER	Eng.	Mass.		CRLA14----------157
BACHILER	No family data		Arms:-*	CRLA18----------353
BACKUS	Eng.	Conn.		CFA4------------169
BACKUS	——	Conn.	Arms:-*	CRLA3-----------275
BACON	Eng.	Mass.	Arms:-	CFA2------------153
BACON	Eng.	Mass.	Arms:-	CFA4-------------16
BACON	——	Mass.		CFA6------------349
BACON	——	Mass.		CRLA6------------36
BACON	Eng.	Mass.		CRLA7-----------516
BACON	Eng.	Mass.		CRLA10----------261
BACON	Eng.	Mass.	Arms:-*	CRLA15-----------30
BACON	——	Va.	Arms:-*	CRLA17----------219
BACON	Eng.	Mass.	Arms:-*	CRLA20----------215
BADLESMERE	Eng.			CRLA2-----------476
BADLESMERE	Eng.		Arms:-*	CRLA5-----------227
BADLESMERE	Eng.		Hinton descent	CRLA8-----------472

BAGLEY	Eng.	Mass.		CRLA6----------524
BAGLEY	Eng.	Mass.		CRLA13----------268
BAILES (Bayles)	-------	N.Y.	Arms:-*	CRLA20-----------23
BAILEY	Eng.	Maine/Mass.	Arms:-*	CFA5------------175
BAILEY.	-------	Conn./Mich.		CRLA6----------486
BAILEY.	-------	N.Y.		CRLA9----------436
BAILEY	-------	Mass.	Arms:-	AF**-----------172
BAILEY	Eng.	Pa.	Arms:-	AF***----------104
BAILEY.	-------	Maine		TNEF------------134
BAILY	-------	Pa.		CRLA15----------239
BAINBRIDGE	Eng.	N.J.		CFA12----------170
BAKER	Eng.	Mass.		CFA3------------239
BAKER	Eng.	Mass.	Arms:-	CFA11----------232
BAKER	Eng.	Mass.		CFA21----------236
BAKER	-------	Va.		CRLA4----------456
BAKER	-------	Pa.		CRLA8----------242
BAKER	-------	-------	*(only)	CRLA12-------opp.88
BAKER	-------	Conn./N.Y.		CRLA12----------153
BAKER	Eng.	Mass.		CRLA13----------259
BAKER	Eng.	Mass.	Arms:-*	CRLA15--------44,58
BAKER	No family data		Arms:-*	CRLA15----btn.342-3
BAKER	Eng.	Mass.	Arms:-*	CRLA18----------534
BAKER	-------	Maine		AF**-----------171
BAKER	-------	N.Y./Ohio	Arms:-	AF***------+----336.
BAKER	-------	-------	*(only)	TNEF------------48
BALDWIN	-------	Conn.		CFA10----------201
BALDWIN	-------	N.Y.		CFA11----------262
BALDWIN	Eng.	Conn.	Arms:-	CFA19-----------21
BALDWIN	Eng.	Conn.	Arms:-*	CFA27-----13cht.,17
BALDWIN	Eng.	Conn.	Arms:-*	CRLA2----------278
BALDWIN	Eng.	Mass.		CRLA7----------520
BALDWIN	-------	Md.		CRLA8----------163
BALDWIN	Eng.	Conn.	Arms:-*	CRLA10-----68,79
BALDWIN	Eng.	Conn.		CRLA12-----------53
BALDWIN	-------	-------	*(only)	CRLA12-------opp.88
BALDWIN	Eng.	Conn.		CRLA19----------83
BALDWIN	Eng.	Conn.	Arms:-*	AF****----------165
BALDRY=BALDERO=BALDREY	No family data		Arms:-*	CRLA13------opp.130
BALL	Eng.	-------	Arms:-*	CFA4-------------1
BALL	-------	Mass.		CFA6------------116
BALL	-------	R.I.		CFA13----------144
BALL	Eng.?	Conn?/N.Y.	Arms:-*	CFA17------229,230
BALL	Eng.	Va.		CFA23----------187
BALL	Eng.	Va.		CRLA1----------264
BALL	Eng.	Mass.	Arms:-*	CRLA12------8,12,43
BALL	-------	Va.		CRLA12----------170
BALL	Eng.	Mass.	Arms:-*	CRLA15----------66
BALL	Ireland	Pa.	Arms:-*	AFA***----------71
BALLARD	-------	Mass.		CFA7-------------68
BALLARD	Eng.	Mass.		CFA19----------294
BALLARD	-------	Mass.	Arms:-*	CRLA6----------413
BALLARD	-------	-------	*(only)	CRLA12-------opp.88
BALLARD	Eng.	Mass.	Arms:-	AF***----------378
BALLANTYNE	Eng.	Ill.	Arms:-*	AF***-----------36
BALLINGER	-------	N.J.		CRLA16----------214
BALLOU	Eng.	R.I.		CFA10------------7
BALLOU	-------	-------		ACF-------------89
BANCKER	Holland	N.Y.	Arms:-*	CRLA14-----------28
BANCROFT	Eng.	Mass.	Arms:-*	CFA6------------145
BANCROFT	-------	Mass.		CFA8------------250
BANCROFT	Eng.	Del.	Arms:-*	ACF-------------26
BANCROFT	Eng.	Mass.	Arms:-*	CRLA12----------23
BANCROFT	Eng.	Del.	Arms:-*	AFA***-----------7
BANCROFT	-------	Mass.		PPA------------273
BANGS	Eng.	Mass.		CFA3------------125
BANGS	-------	Mass.		CFA8------------138
BANGS	Eng.	Mass.	Arms:-	CFA11----------271

BANGS	Eng.	Mass.		ACF------------98
BANGS	Eng.	Mass.	Arms:-*	CRLA2-----------309
BANKS	-------	Maine		CRLA4-----------342
BANNING	-------	Md.;Conn.;Del.;etc. Arms:-*		TNEF-----------118
BANTA	Holland	N.Y.		CFA16----------66
BANTZ	-------	Md.		CFA2-----------50
BARBER	Eng.	Conn.	Arms:-	CFA17----------153
BARBER	-------	R.I.		CRLA12----------71
BARBER	Eng.			CRLA13----------432
BARBER	Eng.	Pa.	Arms:-*	CRLA14----------47
BARBER	-------	N.J.		CRLA15----------546
BARBOUR	Eng.	Mass.		CFA10----------104
BARBOUR	Scotland	Va.		CFA10----------114
BARBOUR	-------	Conn.		AFA***----------116
BARCELONA, Counts of	Spain			CFA27----------235
BARCLAY	Scotland	Mass./N.Y.C.		CFA25----------102
BARCLAY	Scotland?	Del./Md.	Arms:-*	ACF------------60
BARCLAY	-------	N.J.		MCS------------76
BARCLAY	Eng./Scotland	N.J.	Arms:-*	CRLA8----------385
BARCLAY	-------	N.Y.		PFU------------343
BARD	France	N.J.		CFA9-----------132
BARHAM	-------	Va.		MCS------------110
BARKER	-------	Mass.	Arms:-*	CFA27----20,148cht.
BARKER	-------	Mass.	Arms:-*	CRLA6----------306
BARKER	Eng.	Mass./R.I.		CRLA15----------290
BARKER	Eng.?	R.I.		CRLA19----------14
BARKER	Eng.?		Arms:-*	CRLA20----------104
BARKER	-------	R.I.	Arms:-	AF****----------85
BARKEY	-------	Pa.		CRLA6----------469
BARLOW	-------	Conn.		PPA------------57
BARNARD	Eng.	Mass.	Arms:-	CFA16----------337
BARNARD	-------	Mass.	Arms:-*	CRLA3-----------17
BARNARD	Eng.	Mass.		CRLA7----------431
BARNARD	-------	Mass.		CRLA12----------258
BARNARD	-------	Mass.		CRLA18----------621
BARNARD	Eng.	Pa.		CRLA19----------293
BARNARD	Eng.	Mass.	Arms:-*	CRLA20----------384
BARNARD	Eng.	Pa.	Arms:-*	AFA***----------201
BARNARD	Eng.	Mass.		PFU------------62
BARNARD	Eng.	Mass.	Arms:-*	TNEF-----------36
BARNES	-------	-------		CFA9-----------86
BARNES	-------	Mass.		CFA19----------273
BARNES	-------	Mass.	Arms:-*	CRLA15----------14
BARNES	Eng.	Conn.	Arms:-*	AF**-----------391
BARNES	Eng.	Conn.	Arms:-*	AF**-----------543
BARNET	-------	Pa.		CRLA15----------572
BARNEY	Eng.	Mass.		CFA6-----------319
BARNEY	Eng.	Mass.		CFA7-----------296
BARNWELL	Ireland	S.C.		PFU------------326
BARR	Scotland	Pa.	Arms:-*	AFA***----------205
BARRETT	Eng.	Mass.	Arms:-*	CFA11----------204
BARRETT	Eng.	Mass.		CRLA10----------145
BARRETT	-------	Mass.	Arms:-*	AFA***----------247
BARRINGER	Germany	Pa./N.C.		CRLA13----------218
BARRON	Ireland	Mass.	Arms:-	CRLA2----------147
BARRON	-------	Mass.	Arms:-*	CRLA15----------83
BARRON	-------	Mass.		CRLA20----------168
BARRON (Fitzgerald)	France/Ireland	Mass.	Arms:-*	AFA1-----------25
BARSTOW	Eng.	Mass.		CFA5-----------311
BARTLETT	Eng.	Mass.		CFA5-----------118
BARTLETT	Eng.	Mass.		CFA7-----------157
BARTLETT	-------	Mass.		CFA9-----------209
BARTLETT	-------	Mass.	Arms:-*	CRLA6----------509
BARTLETT	Eng.?	Mass.		CRLA13----------261
BARTLETT	Eng.	Mass.	Arms:-*	CRLA16----------10
BARTLETT	Eng.	N.J.		CRLA17----------502
BARTLETT	-------	Conn./Mass.	Arms:-	AF*------------41

BARTLETT	———	Mass.	TNEF------------111
BARTLETT, Josiah	———	Mass./N.H.	SDI-----------97,98
BARTON	Eng.	Mass.	Arms:-*	CFA14-----------117
BARTON	———	N.Y.	CRLA19-----------23
BARTRAM	Eng.	Pa.	Arms:-*	AFA***----------161
BARTOW	Eng.	N.Y.	Arms:-	CFA5------------22
BARTOW	Eng.	N.Y.	Arms:-*	CFA24-----------107
BASS	Eng.	Mass.	CFA6------------246
BASS	———	Mass.	CFA7------------178
BASS	———	Mass.	CFA7------------179
BASS	———	Va./Ky.	Arms:-*	CFA10-----------235
BASS	Eng.	Mass.	Arms:-	CFA10-----------374
BASS	Eng.	Mass.	CFA11-----------178
BASS	Eng.	Mass.	CFA13-----------360
BASS	Eng.	Mass.	CRLA12-----------63
BASS	Eng.	Mass.	Arms:-*	CRLA15-----------88
BASSET	Eng.	Arms:-	CRLA5-,---------228
BASSETT	Eng.	Mass.	CFA3------------128
BASSETT	Eng.	Mass.	Arms:-*	CFA6------------190
BASSETT	———	Conn.	Arms:-*	CFA8------------307
BASSETT	Eng.	Mass.	Arms:-*	CFA12-----------368
BASSETT	Eng.	Mass.	CFA13-----------160.
BASSETT	Eng.	Mass.	ACF-------------100
BASSETT	Eng.	Mass.	CRLA5------------15
BASSETT	———	Mass./Conn.	CRLA20----------187
BATCHELDER	Eng.	Mass.	CRLA7----------387.
BATCHELDER	Eng.	Mass.	Arms:-*	CRLA8------------60
BATCHELDER	Eng.	Mass.	CRLA12----------264
BATES	Eng.	Mass.	CFA14-----------42
BATES	Eng.	Mass.	Arms:-*	AF*------------199
BATH, Order of the	Eng.	Schull descent	CRLA5----------173
BATHURST	Eng.	Va.	CRLA4----------142
BATT	Eng.	Mass.	Arms:-*	CFA18-----------127
BATTE	———	Va.	MCS-------------91
BATTELLE	Eng.	Mass.	Arms:-*	CFA1------------144
BATTELLE	Eng.	Mass.	Arms:-	AF**------------88
BATTLE	Eng.	Mass.	Arms:-	CFA5------------220
BAUER	———	Pa.	CRLA9----------452
BAXTER	———	Mass.	CFA9------------242
BAXTER	———	Mass.	CRLA18----------539
BAYARD	France/Eng.	Arms:-*	CFA13-----------20
BAYARD	Eng.	N.Y./Md.	CFA15-----------294
BAYARD	France/Holland N.Y.	Arms:-*	CFA25-----------116
BAYARD	———	Pa./Del.	Arms:-*	CRLA15----------244
BAYFORD	———	———	*(only)	CRLA12-------opp.88
BAYLEY	Eng.	Mass.	Arms:-*	CFA8------------242
BAYNE	Eng.	Md.	Arms:-*	CRLA15----------324
BAYNE	———	Md.	Arms:-*	AF*-------------98
BAZILIE (Bazalee)	Eng.	Pa.	Arms:-*	AFA***----------365
BEACH	———	Conn.	CFA11-----------184
BEACH	Eng.	Conn.	CFA19-----------190
BEAL	———	Mass.	CFA10-----------267
BEAL	———	Maine	CRLA3----------207
BEALE	Eng.	N.Y./Pa.	CRLA17----------613
BEALE=McILWAIN	———	Pa./Va.	CRLA9----------511
BEALL	Scotland	Md.	Arms:-	CFA15-----------171
BEALL	Scotland	Md.	Arms:-	CFA16-----------79
BEALL	Scotland	Md.	CRLA3----------289
BEALL	Scotland	Md.	CRLA6----------431
BEALS (Beal)	Eng.	Mass.	CRLA6----------434
BEAMSLEY	———	Mass.	CFA14-----------39
BEARD	———	Pa./N.Y.	CRLA8----------376
BEARD	———	N.C.	CRLA9----------429
BEARD	Germany	N.Y.	CRLA20----------143
BEARDSLEY	Eng.	Conn.	CFA17----------293
BEATTY	———	N.Y.	Arms:-	CRLA3-----------48
BEATTY	Scotland/Ireland Pa.	Arms:-*	AFA***----------119

Surname	Origin	Location	Notes	Reference
BEAUCHAMP (de)	Eng.		Chaworth descent	CRLA2-----------351
BEAUCHAMP (de)	Eng.	Jones=Paul=Knight desc. *(only)		CRLA2-----------547
BEAUCHAMP (de)	Eng.			CRLA2-----------565
BEAUCHAMP (de)	Eng.		Arms:-*	CRLA5-----------229
BEAUCHAMP (de)	Eng.		Arms:-*	CRLA10-----btn.78-9
BEAUCHAMP (de)	Eng.			CRLA11-----------73
BEAUCHAMP (de)	Eng.		Arms:-*	CRLA17------175,177
BEAUCHAMP (de)	Eng.		Cooley=Twining desc.	CRLA18-----------129
BEAUCHAMP (de), see: D'ABITOT				
BEAUCHAMP (de), see: MAUDUIT				
BEAUMONT (de)	Eng.			CRLA1-----------371
BEAUMONT (de)	Eng.		Arms:-*	CRLA5-----------231
BEAUMONT (de)	Normandy			CRLA7-----------236
BEAUMONT (de)	Eng.			CRLA11-----------76
BEAUMONT (de)	Eng.			CRLA11-----------161
BEAUMONT (de)	Eng.			CRLA15-----------108
BEAUMONT (de)=TORVILLE	Normandy, bfr. Conquest			AF*-------------43
BEAUPRE	Eng.	——	Arms:-*	CFA18------------25
BECHDEL	——	Pa.		CRLA19---------339
BECK	Germany	Pa.	Arms:-*	CRLA1-----------33
BECKFORD	——	Mass.	Arms:-*	CRLA15-----------18
BECKWITH	——	Conn.	Arms:-	CRLA3------------86
BECKWITH	Eng.	Conn.	Arms:-*	CRLA6-----------398
BECKWITH	Eng.	Conn.	Arms:-*	CRLA14---------119
BECKWITH	Eng.	Conn.		CRLA19---------304
BECKWITH	——	Conn.		CRLA20-----------169
BECKWITH (Malebisse)	Eng.	Conn.	Arms:-	AF****----------67
BEDFORD	——	N.J.		CRLA8-----------284
BEEBE	Eng.	Conn.	Arms:-*	CRLA12-----------127
BEEBEE	Eng.	Mass.		CFA7------------245
BEEBEE	Eng.	Conn.		CRLA16-----------166
BEEKMAN	Germany	N.Y.		CFA20-----------319
BEEKMAN	Germany	N.Y.		CFA25------------46
BEEKMAN	Germany	N.Y.		CRLA8-----------225
BEEKMAN	——	N.Y.		PFU-------------400
BEERS	——	Mass.		CFA15-----------245
BEESON	Eng.	Pa.	Arms:-*	CRLA3-----------142
BELSHER	Eng.	Mass.		CFA7------------140
BELCHER	Eng.	Mass.		CRLA6-----------270
BELCHER	——	Mass.		CRLA12-----------67
BELCHER	——	Mass.	Arms:-*	CRLA20-----------114
BELDEN	Eng.	Conn.	Arms:-	AF****----------37
BELKNAP	Eng.	Mass.	Arms:-*	CRLA2-----------132
BELL	——	Conn.		CFA9------------59
BELL	Ireland	N.Y.C.		CFA10-----------207
BELL	——	Iowa		CRLA3-----------219
BELL	Eng.	Pa.		CRLA13---------418
BELLEW (Bellou)	——	R.I.	Arms:-*	PBAF-------------47
BELLINGHAM	Eng.		Arms:-*	CRLA14------opp.129
BELLOT	——	——	*(only)	TNEF-------------44
BELT	——	Md.		CRLA6-----------422
BELTOFT=BELKNAP	Eng.	Mass.		CFA19-----------287
BEMIS	——	Conn.		CFA1-------------10
BEMIS	Eng.	Mass.		CFA8------------93
BEMIS	Eng.?	Mass.		CFA17-----------249
BEMIS	Eng.	Mass.	Arms:-*	CRLA15-----------87
BEMIS	——	Mass.		TNEF------------241
BENBOW	——	N.C.		CRLA17-----------47
BENEDICT	Eng.	Mass.		CFA10-----------288
BENEDICT	Eng.	Mass.		CFA21------------24
BENEDICT	Eng.	Mass.		CFA22-----------122
BENEDICT	Eng.	Mass./Conn.		CFA27------------23
BENEDICT	Eng.	Mass.		CRLA13---------176
BENEDICT	Eng.	Mass./N.Y.		CRLA16---------176
BENHAM	——	Mass.		CRLA17---------526
BENJAMIN	Eng.	Mass.		CFA11-----------143
BENJAMIN	Wales	Conn.		PPA-------------435

BENNET	——	——		CFA4------------174
BENNET	Eng.?	L.I.,N.Y.	Arms:-	AF**------------105
BENNETT	——	Mass.		CFA21-----------223
BENNETT	——	Mass./Conn.	Arms:-*	CFA27----29,148cht.
BENNETT	——	N.Y.		AF***-----------200
BENSON	Holland	N.Y.		CFA6--------------4
BENSON	Holland	N.Y.		CFA13-----------249
BENSON	Holland	N.Y.		CFA21------------55
BENSON	Eng.			CRLA9------------17
BENSON	Eng.	Md.	Arms:-*	CRLA10----------293
BENT	Eng.	Mass.		CFA7------------140
BENT	Eng.	Mass.	Arms:-*	CFA24-----------39
BENT	Eng.	Mass.		CRLA1-----------198
BENTLEY	Eng.	R.I.		CFA17-----------143
BENTON	Eng.	Conn.	Arms:-*	CRLA3------------29
BERCHAUD	France	S.C.		CFA13-----------230
BERENGER, see: NAMUR, Counts of				
BERESFORD	Eng.			CRLA5------------43
BERGEN	Norway	N.Y.		CFA7------------226
BERGEN	Norway	N.Y.		CRLA13----------400
BERGEN	——	N.Y.		CRLA20-----------23
BERKELEY (de)	Eng.		Dudley descent	CRLA1-----------410
BERKELEY	——	Va.		MCS--------------57
BERKLEY	——	Va.		CRLA17----------425
BERL	——	Del./Calif.		CRLA19----------343
BERNARD	——	Va.		MCS--------------41
BERNARD I, see: AQUITAINE, Dukes of				
BERNON	Eng.	Mass./R.I.	Arms:-	CFA22-----------176
BERNON	——	——	*(only)	TNEF--------opp.78
BERNON, see: PILGRIMS				
BERRIEN	Holland	N.Y.		CFA5-------------15
BERRIEN	——	N.Y.		CFA9------------305
BERTHOLF	Holland	N.J.		CFA16------------70
BERRITT	——	N.Y.		CRLA12----------432
BERRY	——	Pa.		CRLA8-----------406
BERRY	Eng.	Mass.		CRLA18----------536
BERTRAM	Eng.		Arms:-*	PBAF------------210
BESSON	Eng.	Va./Md.	Arms:-	CFA2-------------38
BETHUNE	——	N.Y.		PPA-------------327
BETTS	Eng.?	Mass./N.Y.	Arms:-*	CRLA18----------563
BEVAN	——	Pa.		AFA***-----------40
BEVAN	——	Pa.		AFA***----------168
BEVERIDGE	Scotland	N.Y.	Arms:-*	PBAF-------------25
BEVERLEY	Eng.	Va.		CRLA1-----------255
BICKEL	——	Pa.		CRLA8-----------434
BICKLEY	France/Germany	Md.	Arms:-*	CRLA11-----------17
BICKLEY, see: WHARTON=BICKLEY				
BICKNELL	Eng.	Mass.		CFA12-----------124
BICKNELL	Eng.	Mass.	Arms:-*	CRLA18-----------66
BIDDLE	Eng.	N.J.	Arms:-*	CRLA1-----------464
BIDDLE	Eng.	N.J.		CRLA8-----------424
BIDDLE	Eng.	N.J.		CRLA13----------231
BIDDLE	Eng.	Pa.		CRLA17----------709
BIDDLE	Eng.	N.J.		PFU-------------199
BIDWELL	——	Conn.		CFA19------------59
BIGELOW	——	Mass.		CFA15-----------356
BIGELOW	——	Mass.	Arms:-*	CRLA15-----------69
BIGELOW	Eng.	Mass.		CRLA18----------382
BIGOD	Eng.		Arms:-*	CRLA5-----------234
BIGOD	Eng.		Wales descent	CRLA13----------101
BIGOD	Eng.			CRLA15-----------97
BIGOD	Eng.		Bray descent Arms:-*	CRLA17----------148
BIGOD	Eng.		Cooley=Twining desc.	CRLA18----------107
BIGOD	Eng.		Titus descent	CRLA18----------501
BILL	Eng.	Mass.		CFA10-----------297
BILLINGS	——	Mass.		CFA21-----------215
BILLINGS	——	Mass.	Arms:-*	CRLA15-----------58

BILLINGS	———	Mass.	Arms:-*	CRLA15----------479
BILLINGS	———	Mass.		ARSC------------58
BINGHAM	Eng.	Conn.	Arms:-*	CFA1------------57
BINGHAM	Ireland/Eng.	N.C.		AFA***----------37
BINNEY	Eng.?	Mass.		CRLA17----------559
BIOREN	———	Pa.		CRLA17----------556
BIRCH	———	Calif.		CRLA10----------346
BIRGE	———	Mass.		CRLA13----------48
BIRD	Eng.	N.Y.C.		CFA23-----------125
BIRD	———	Conn.	Arms:-*	CRLA10----------306
BISBING	Germany	Pa.		CRLA8-----------563
BISHOP	Eng.	Mass.		CFA16-----------247
BISHOP	———	Mass.		CFA21-----------168
BISHOP	Eng.	Conn.		CFA27-----------33
BISHOP	———	Mass.		ACF-------------82
BISHOP	Eng.	Mass./Conn.	Arms:-*	AF***-----------30
BISPHAM	Eng.	Pa./N.J.		CRLA8-----------149
BISPHAM	Eng.	N.J.		CRLA8-----------356
BISPHAM	Eng.	N.J.		CRLA11----------537
BISSELL	———	Conn.		CRLA10----------136
BITTEL	Germany	N.Y.		CRLA15----------396
BIXBY	Eng.	Mass.	Arms:-	AF***-----------272
BLABON	France	Maine	Arms:-*	AFA***----------145
BLACHLY	Eng.	Mass.		AF***-----------50
BLACK	———	Mass.		CFA9------------185
BLACK	Ireland	Pa.		CRLA17----------625
BLACKBURN	Eng.	Mass.		CFA4------------301
BLACKINGTON	———	Mass.		CFA9------------256
BLACKISTON	Eng.	Md.	Arms:-	CFA15-----------158
BLACKISTON	Eng.	Md.		CRLA11----------368
BLACKMAN	———	Mass.		CRLA20----------210
BLACKMAR	———	Conn./Vt.		CRLA16----------136
BLACKSHAW	Eng.	Md./Pa.		CRLA9-----------158
BLACKSHAW	———	Pa.		CRLA17----------292
BLACKWELL	———	Mass.	Arms:-*	CRLA10----------296
BLAGDON	———	N.H./Maine		CRLA15----------17
BLAIR	Scotland	N.J.	Arms:-*	CFA16-----------116
BLAIR	Scotland/Eng.		Arms:-*	CFA24-----------3
BLAIR	Eng.	Va.	Arms:-*	CRLA4-----------127
BLAKE	Eng.	Mass.	Arms:-*	CFA6------------106
BLAKE	Eng.	Mass.		CFA7------------133
BLAKE	———	———		CFA17-----------376
BLAKE	Eng.	Mass.		CRLA13----------37
BLAKE	Eng.	Mass.	Arms:-*	CRLA13----------335
BLAKE	Eng.		Arms:-*	CRLA20----------380
BLAKE	Eng.	S.C.	Arms:-*	PFU---------79,455
BLAKELEY	Eng.	Pa.		CRLA11----------482
BLAKEMAN	Eng.	Conn.		CFA9------------226
BLAKESLEE	———	Mass./Conn.		CRLA19----------271
BLAKESLEE (Blakley)	Eng.	Mass./Conn.	Arms:-*	AF*-------------279
BLANCHAN	France/Germany	N.Y.		CRLA12----------431
BLANCHAN	France	N.Y.		CRLA20----------67
BLANCHARD	Eng.	Mass.		CFA9------------74
BLANCHARD	France/Eng.	Mass.		CFA14-----------7
BLANCHARD	———	Mass.		CFA21-----------223
BLANCHARD	———	N.H.	Arms:-*	CRLA3-----------9
BLANCHARD	Eng.	Mass.		CRLA15----------293
BLANCHARD	France/Eng.	Mass.	Arms:-	AF**------------176
BLAND	Eng.	Va.		CRLA3-----------239
BLANEY	———	Mass.	Arms:-*	CFA7------------121
BLANKENBAKER	———	Va.		CRLA6-----------309
BLEECKER	Holland	N.Y.	Arms:-	CFA16-----------302
BLEECKER	Holland	N.Y.		CRLA17----------562
BLEWETT	———	Ky.		AF***-----------292
BLISS	Eng.	Mass./Conn.	Arms:-*	CFA5------------217
BLISS	Eng.	Conn.		CFA7------------409
BLISS	Eng.	Mass.		CFA8------------52

BLISS	Eng.	Mass.		CFA12-----------349
BLISS	Eng.	Mass.	Arms:-*	CFA14-----------78
BLISS	Eng.	Mass.		CFA15-----------344
BLISS	Eng.	Mass./Conn.		CRLA19----------72
BLODGETT	Eng.	Conn.	Arms:-*	CFA3-----------220
BLODGETT	Eng.	Mass.	Arms:-	CFA9-----------261
BLODGETT	Eng.	Mass./Conn.	Arms:-	CFA17----------117
BLODGETT	Eng.	Mass.		CFA19----------81
BLODGETT	Eng.	Mass.	Arms:-	CFA19----------277
BLOIS	Eng.		Arms:-*	CRLA13---------455
BLOIS	Eng.		Arms:-*	CRLA15---------493
BLOOD	Eng.?	Mass.	Arms:-	CFA4-----------15
BLOOD	———	Mass.		CFA21----------224
BLOOD	Eng.	Mass.		CRLA20---------166
BLOOD	Eng.?	Mass.	Arms:-*	AF*------------222
BLOODGOOD	Holland	L.I.,N.Y.		CFA3-----------336
BLOODGOOD	Holland	N.Y.		CRLA20---------346
BLOODGOOD	———	N.J.		AFA***---------46
BLOOMER	———	N.Y.		CFA16----------289
BLOOMFIELD	———	Mass./N.J.		CRLA6----------126
BLOOMFIELD	———	Conn.	Arms:-*	CRLA18---------562
BLOSS	Eng.	Mass.	Arms:-	AF***----------357
BLOTT	Eng.	Mass.		CFA15----------340
BLOTT	Eng.	Mass.		CFA18----------82
BLOUNT	Eng.	N.C.	Arms:-	CFA5-----------266
BLOUNT	Eng.	Va./N.C.	Arms:-*	CRLA4-------457,476
BLUMER	Switzerland	Pa.		CRLA11---------344
BLUNT	———	Mass.		TNEF-----------238
BOARDMAN	Eng.	Conn.	Arms:-*	CFA9-----------196
BOARDMAN	Eng.	Mass.		CFA20----------274
BOARDMAN	Eng.	———	Arms:-*	CFA20----------306
BOARDMAN	———	N.J./N.Y.		CFA20----------315
BOARDMAN	Eng.	Mass./Conn.		CRLA19---------120
BOARDMAN	———		*(only)	TNEF--------opp.82
BOARMAN	———	Md.	Arms:-*	CRLA2----------67
BOARMAN	Eng.	Md.	Arms:-	AF***----------440
BOATMAN	———	Pa.		CRLA19---------342
BODDIE	Eng.	Va.		CRLA4----------80
BODINE	France/Eng.	N.Y.		CRLA9----------547
BODLEY	Eng.			CRLA9----------14
BODLEY	———	———	Arms:-*	CRLA15------opp.333
BOELE	No family data		Arms:-*	CRLA18------opp.560
BOELE	Holland		Arms:-*	CRLA20---------67
BOGARDUS	Holland	N.Y.		AF*------------319
BOGARDUS	Holland	N.Y.	Arms:-*	AFA***---------97
BOGART (or) BOGERT	Holland	N.Y.	Arms:-*	CFA15----------78
BOHEMIA, Rulers of	Europe	Borivij	Arms:-*	CRLA17---------159
BOHEMIA, Rulers of	Europe	Cooley=Twining desc.		CRLA18---------109
BOHEMIA, Royal descents	Europe	Vou descent		CRLA18---------263
BOHEMIA, Monarchs of	Europe	Glendinning=Logan desc.		CRLA18---------317
BOHUN (de)	Eng.			CFA25----------13
BOHUN (de)	Eng.		Arms:-*	CRLA1----------319
BOHUN (de)	Eng.		*(only)	CRLA2----------474
BOHUN (de), Earls of Northampton	Eng.	Jones=Paul=Knight desc. *(only)		CRLA2----------548
BOHUN (de)	Eng.		Arms:-*	CRLA5----------238
BOHUN (de)	Eng.	Olmsted descent		CRLA7----------115
BOHUN (de)	Eng.			CRLA7----------200
BOHUN (de)	Eng.	Haskell descent		CRLA8----------83
BOHUN (de)	Eng.	Hinton descent		CRLA8----------473
BOHUN (de)	Eng.			CRLA12---------279
BOHUN (de)	Eng.	Wales descent		CRLA13---------103
BOHUN (de)	Eng.		Arms:-*	CRLA17---------178
BOHUN (de)	Eng.	Cooley=Twining desc.		CRLA18---------131
BOHUN (de)	Eng.			CRLA18---------480
BOKER	———	Pa.		PPA------------587
BOLEBEC (de)	Eng.			CRLA5----------243

BOLEYN	Eng.			CRLA17----------161
BOLITHO	Eng.	Pa.	Arms:-*	AF*-------------11
BOLLES=BOWLES	———	Maine		MCS-------------67
BOLTWOOD	———	Conn.		CFA2------------115
BOLTWOOD	———	Conn.		CFA8------------346
BONAPARTE	France	Md.		PFU-------------434
BOND	Eng.	Mass.	Arms:-	CFA2------------144
BOND	———	Md.	Arms:-*	CRLA1-----------477
BOND	———	Md.		CRLA10----------227
BONHAM	Eng.	Pa./Del.		CRLA19----------224
BONNELL	Eng.?	Mass./Conn.	Arms:-*	CRLA13----------118
BONNELL	———	N.J.	Arms:-*	CRLA14-----------13
BONNELL	France/Eng.	Conn.	Arms:-*	AFA***----------303
BONNETT	France	Pa.	Arms:-*	CRLA11-----------16
BOOKER	Eng.	Va.	Arms:-*	CRLA11----------280
BOONE	———	Pa.		CRLA3-----------425
BOONE	Eng.	Md.	Arms:-*	CRLA8-------152,177
BOOTES	Eng.			CRLA2-----------435
BOOTH	Eng.			CRLA9-----------168
BOOTH	Eng.	Conn.	Arms:-*	AF****----------170
BORDEN	Eng.	R.I.		CFA6------------295
BORDEN	Eng.	R.I.	Arms:-*	CFA8------------166
BORDEN	Eng.	R.I.		CRLA9-----------405
BORDEN	Eng.	R.I.		CRLA11----------248
BORDEN	Eng.	N.J./Va.		CRLA13----------326
BORDEN	Eng.	R.I.		CRLA14-----------66
BORDEN	Eng.	R.I.	Arms:-*	CRLA20-----------53
BORDEN	Eng.?	R.I.	Arms:-	AF****-----------11
BORDEN	———	———	*(only)	TNEF-------btn.78-9
BORDEN, see: PILGRIMS				
BOREMAN=BOARMAN	Eng.	Mass.		CFA15----------144
BORIVIJ, see: BOHEMIA, Rulers of				
BORTON	Eng.	N.J.		CFA5------------340
BORTON	Eng.	N.J.	*(only)	CRLA17----------305
BORUM	———	Va.		CRLA4-----------305
BOSC (du)	France		Arms:-*	CRLA1------------45
BOSLER	Germany	Pa.		CRLA19----------292
BOSS	———	R.I.		CFA7------------217
BOSVILE	———	Mass.		MCS-------------79
BOSWORTH	———	Mass.	Arms:-	CRLA7-----------421
BOSWORTH	Eng.	Mass./R.I.	Arms:-*	CRLA18--------12,34
BOTELER=CLAIBORNE	———	Md.		MCS-------------51
BOTETOURT (de)	Eng.		Arms:-*	CRLA7-----------190
BOUCK	———	N.Y.		CFA7------------239
BOUDE	Eng.	N.J./Pa.	Arms:-*	CRLA14-----------22
BOUDINOT	France	Pa.		CFA12-----------142
BOUDINOT	France	N.Y.C.		CFA19-----------181
BOUDINOT	France	N.Y.C.		CFA25-----------148
BOULOGNE, Counts of	France		Arms:-*	CRLA5-----------244
BOULTON	———	Md.	Arms:-*	CRLA1-----------526
BOURCHIER	Eng.	———		CFA13-----------82
BOURCHIER=WHITAKER	———	Va.		MCS-------------59
BOURBON, House of	France		Gaither=Fownes desc.	CRLA11-----------67
BOURN	———	Mass./R.I.		PFU-------------474
BOURNE	Eng.	Mass.		CFA7-------------58
BOURNE	Eng.	Mass.		CRLA6-----------275
BOURNE	Eng.	Mass.	Arms:-*	CRLA18-----------26
BOURNE	Eng.		Arms:-*	CRLA20-----------29
BOUTON	Mass.			CFA7------------243
BOUTON	Eng.	Mass./Conn.	Arms:-*	CFA15-----------313
BOUTON	Eng.	Mass.		CFA16-----------216
BOUVET	France	La.	Arms:-	AF***-----------335
BOWATER	Eng.	Pa.		CFA7------------395
BOWATER	Eng.	Pa.	Arms:-*	CRLA17-----------77
BOWDEN	———	Mass.		CRLA18------------7
BOWDITCH	———	Mass.		CFA9------------355
BOWEN	Wales	Mass.		CFA12-----------121

BOWEN	Wales	Mass.		CFA13-----------104
BOWEN	Wales	Mass.		CFA19-----------292
BOWEN	Eng.	Mass.	Arms:-	ACF-------------80
BOWEN	Wales	Mass.	Arms:-*	CRLA2----,-------4
BOWEN	Wales	Mass.	Arms:-	CRLA6---------371-1
BOWEN	Wales	Mass.		CRLA9-----------178
BOWEN	Eng.	Mass./Conn.		CRLA13-----------26
BOWEN	Wales	Mass.		CRLA13----------169
BOWEN	Wales?	Mass.		CRLA13----------356
BOWEN	————	Mass.	Arms:-*	CRLA18-----------10
BOWEN	————	Mass.		ARSC------------141
BOWERS	Germany	Pa./Va.		TNEF------------177
BOWERS	————			CRLA11----------417
BOWIE	Scotland	Md.		CRLA17----------423
BOWKER	————	Mass.		CRLA12----------416
BOWLER	Eng.	Mass.		CFA11-----------91
BOWLES	Eng.	Mass.		CFA14-----------307
BOWLES, see: BOLLES				
BOWLEY	Eng.			CRLA2-----------431
BOWLING	————	Md.	Arms:-	AF***-----------430
BOWMAN	Eng.	Mass.	Arms:-*	AFA***----------383
BOWNE	Eng.	Mass.		CFA2------------274
BOWNE	Eng.	L.I.,N.Y.		CFA18-----------28
BOWNE	Eng.	N.Y.	Arms:-*	CRLA17----------315
BOWNE	————	Mass./N.Y./N.J.	Arms:-*	AF****----------20
BOWRON	Eng.	N.Y.		CFA14-----------209
BOYD	France	S.C.		CFA3------------359
BOYD	France	S.C.	Arms:-*	CFA13-----------228
BOYER	France		Arms:-*	CRLA1-----------46
BOYKIN	Wales?	Va.		CRLA17----------608
BOYLE	Ireland	Pa.	Arms:-*	CRLA1-----------468
BOYLE	————	Mass.		CRLA9-----------388
BOYLE	Ireland	Pa.		CRLA10----------222
BOYLE	————	N.Y./Tenn.	Arms:-*	CRLA16-----------2
BOYLSTON	Eng.	Mass.	Arms:-*	CFA4------------11
BOYLSTON	Eng.	Mass.		CFA17-----------134
BOYNTON	Eng.	Mass.		CFA11-----------340
BOYNTON	Eng.	Mass.		CFA21-----------238
BRABANT, Dukes of	Europe		Arms:-*	CRLA5-----------248
BRABANT, Dukes of	Europe	Giselbert	Arms:-*	CRLA17----------162
BRACKETT	Eng.?	Mass.	Arms:-	CFA1------------53
BRACKETT	————	N.H.	Arms:-*	CRLA3-----------382
BRACKETT	————	Mass.		CRLA6-----------273
BRADBURY	————	Mass.		MCS-------------102
BRADFIELD	Eng.	Pa.	Arms:-*	CRLA9-----------543
BRADFORD	Eng.	Mass.		CFA7------------326
BRADFORD	Eng.	Mass.		CFA9------------318
BRADFORD	Eng.	Mass.		CFA11-----------188
BRADFORD	Eng.	Mass.	Arms:-*	CFA12-----------15
BRADFORD	Eng.	Mass.	Arms:-	CFA15-----------103
BRADFORD	Eng.	Pa./N.Y.C.		CFA15-----------216
BRADFORD	Eng.	Mass.	Arms:-	CFA15-----------352
BRADFORD	Eng.	Mass.	Arms:-	CFA22-----------20
BRADFORD	Eng.	Mass.	Arms:-*	CRLA15-----------47
BRADFORD	Eng.	Mass.		CRLA15----------248
BRADFORD	Eng.	Mass.		CRLA15----------582
BRADFORD	Eng.	Mass.		CRLA19----------136
BRADFORD	Eng.?	Va./W. Va.		CRLA19----------185
BRADFORD	Eng.	Mass.	Arms:-	AF*-------------339
BRADFORD	Eng.	Mass.	Arms:-	AF**------------70
BRADFORD	Eng.	Mass.	Arms:-	AF**------------443
BRADFORD	————	Mass.	Arms:-*	AFA***----------329
BRADFORD	Eng.	N.Y.	Arms:-*	TNEF------------215
BRADFORTH	Eng.		Arms:-*	PBAF------------183
BRADISH	Eng.	N.Y.C.	Arms:-*	CFA27-----------35
BRADLEY	Eng.	Conn.		CFA2------------119
BRADLEY	Eng.	Mass.	Arms:-*	CFA5------------165

Surname	Origin	Location	Notes	Reference
BRADLEY	Eng.	Conn.	Arms:-*	CFA8------------308
BRADLEY	Eng.	Conn.		CFA15-----------380
BRADLEY	———	Conn.		CFA16-----------57
BRADLEY	Eng.	Pa./Ohio	Arms:-*	CRLA6-----------505
BRADLEY	———	Mass.	Arms:-*	AF****----------249
BRADLEY	———	Conn.;Pa.;etc.	Arms:-*	TNEF------------124
BRADSHAW	Eng.		Arms:-*	CRLA5-----------53
BRADSTREET	Eng.	Mass.		CRLA13------270,271
BRADY	Eng.	N.Y.C.		CFA4------------177
BRAFFORD	———	Va.		CRLA4-----------377
BRAILSFORD	Eng.		Arms:-*	CRLA1-----------71
BRAINARD	———	Conn.		PPA-------------237
BRAINERD	Eng.	Conn.		CFA1------------37
BRAINERD	Eng.	Conn.		CFA19-----------56
BRAINERD	———	Conn.		CFA19-----------60
BRAMLETTE	———	Va.		CRLA6-----------209
BRANCH	Eng.	Mass.		CRLA16----------140
BRANNAN	———	Pa.		CRLA15----------437
BRANSON	———	Va.		CRLA17----------51
BRANSTON	Eng.		Arms:-*	CRLA5-----------77
BRAOSE (de)	Eng.		Arms:-*	CRLA1-----------322
BRAOSE (de)	Eng.		*(only)	CRLA2-----------483
BRAOSE (de)	Eng.		Arms:-*	CRLA5-----------252
BRAOSE (de)	Eng.	Haskell descent		CRLA8-----------86
BRAOSE (de)	Eng.	Hinton descent		CRLA8-----------475
BRAOSE (de)	Eng.		Arms:-*	CRLA15----------109
BRATT	———	N.Y.?	Arms:-*	CRLA20----------51
BRATTLE	Eng.	Mass.	Arms:-*	CFA3------------44
BRAUN	Germany	N.Y./Ill.	Arms:-	AF***-----------172
BRAXTON, Carter	———	Va.		SDI---------201,216
BRAY	———	Conn.		CFA12-----------20
BRAY=SWART	Eng.	Mass.	Arms:-* (both)	CRLA7-----------118
BRAY	Eng.	Md./N.C.	Arms:-*	CRLA17----------30
BRAYTON	Eng.	R.I.		CFA8------------169
BRAYTON	Eng.	R.I./Mass.	Arms:-*	TNEF------------1
BRAZELTON	———	Md.		CRLA3-----------204
BRECK	Eng.	Mass.		CFA3------------80
BRECKINRIDGE	Scotland	Va.		PFU-------------189
BREED	Eng.	Mass.		CRLA7-----------437
BRINGLE	———	Md.		CFA22-----------54
BRENT	———	Md.		CRLA4-----------444
BRERETON	Eng.		Arms:-*	CRLA5-----------254
BRERETON	———	Va.	Arms:-*	CRLA14----------127
BREWER	———	Mass.	Arms:-*	CRLA12----------45
BREWER	———	Mass.	Arms:-*	CRLA17----------560
BREWER	Eng.	Mass.		CRLA19----------94
BREWER	———	N.C.		AF**------------316
BREWES	———	———	Cooley=Twining desc.	CRLA18----------111
BREWSTER	Eng.	Mass.		CFA5------------120
BREWSTER	Eng.	Mass.		CFA6------------361
BREWSTER	Eng.	Mass.	Arms:-*	CFA7------------316
BREWSTER	Eng.	Mass.	Arms:-*	CFA9------------210
BREWSTER	Eng.	Mass./L.I.,N.Y.		CFA14-----------275
BREWSTER	Eng.	Mass./Conn.	Arms:-	CFA16-----------58
BREWSTER	———	Conn.		CFA16-----------294
BREWSTER	Eng.	Mass.	Arms:-*	CFA23-----------41
BREWSTER	———	Mass./N.H.		CFA23-----------192
BREWSTER	Eng.	Conn.		CFA26-----------55
BREWSTER	Eng./Holland	Mass.	Arms:-*	CFA27---38,cht.opp.
BREWSTER, William	Mayflower passenger			CFA27-----------206
BREWSTER	Eng.	Mass./N.Y.		CRLA1-----------163
BREWSTER	———	Conn.		CRLA2-----------320
BREWSTER	Eng.	Mass.	Arms:-*	CRLA13----------247
BREWSTER	Eng.	Mass.		CRLA17----------211
BREWSTER	Eng.	Mass.		CRLA17----------452
BREWSTER, see: LUDLOW=BREWSTER				
BRIAN BOROIMHE (Boru)	Ireland		Gaither=Fownes desc.	CRLA11----------39

BRIAN BOROIMHE (Boru)	Ireland		Blackiston descent	CRLA11----------378
BRIAN BORU	Ireland		Bray descent	CRLA17----------123
BRIAN BORU	Ireland		Titus descent	CRLA18----------495
BRICK	——	N.J.		CFA13-----------41
BRICK	Ireland			CRLA13----------484
BRIDGE	——	Mass.		CFA12-----------278
BRIDGER	——	Va.		CRLA4------------84
BRIDGES	Eng.	Mass.		CFA14-----------119
BRIENNE, Counts of	France		Arms:-*	CRLA5-----------255
BRIENNE (de)	France			CRLA15----------111
BRIERE	France			CRLA1------------50
BRIGGS	——	R.I.		CFA9-------------86
BRIGGS	Eng.	R.I.		CFA18------------7.
BRIGGS	——	Mass.	Arms:-	CFA24-----------150
BRIGGS	Eng.		Arms:-	CRLA2-----------165
BRIGGS	——	Mass.	Arms:-*	CRLA12----------203
BRIGGS	Eng.	Mass./R.I.	Arms:-*	CRLA20-----------32
BRIGGS	——	R.I.	Arms:-*	**TNEF**------------130
BRIGHAM	Eng.	Mass.	Arms:-*	CFA2------------242
BRIGHAM	Eng.	Mass.		CFA10-----------273
BRIGHAM	Eng.	——	Arms:-*	CFA19-----------184
BRIGHAM	Eng.	Mass.	Arms:-*	CRLA16-----------16.
BRIGHT	Eng.	Mass.		CFA8------------246.
BRIGHT	——	Mass./Va./La.		PPA-------------315
BRINGHURST	Eng.	Pa.	Arms:-*	CRLA14-----------17
BRINGHURST	Eng./Holland	Pa.		CRLA17----------594
BRINGHURST	Eng.	Pa.	Arms:-*	AFA***----------219
BRINKER	Germany?	Pa.		CRLA3-----------356
BRINKERHOFF	Holland	N.Y.		CFA3------------338
BRINKERHOFF	Holland	N.Y.		CRLA18----------430.
BRINKLEY	——	N.C.		CFA12-----------353
BRINSMADE	——	Mass.		CFA7------------241
BRINSON	——	N.C.		CRLA4-----------426.
BRINTON	Eng.	Pa.		CRLA1-----------115
BRINTON	Eng.	Pa.		CRLA8-----------573
BRINTON	Eng.	Pa.	Arms:-*	CRLA17----------236
BRISCOE	Eng.	Md.		CFA16------------84
BRISTOL (City)		Conn.	Regional background	CRLA19----------251
BRISTOW	——	Ky./Va.		CFA3-------------25
BRITTANY, Dukes of			Conan I, ano. 987	CRLA20----------392
BRITTON	——	Pa.		CRLA11----------276
BROCK	——	Mass.	Arms:-*	CRLA3-----------380
BROCK	Eng.	Pa.		CRLA15----------554
BROCKHOLST	Eng.	N.Y.		CFA11------------29
BROCKMAN	Eng.	Md./Va.		CRLA11----------295
BRODIE	Scotland	——		CFA10-----------404
BROGAN	——	Pa.?/N.J.		CRLA4-----------328
BROKAW	——	N.Y.		CFA26------------59
BRONAUGH	——	Va.	Arms:-	CRLA3-----------114
BRONSON	——	Conn.		CFA13------------73
BRONSON	——	Conn.	Arms:-*	CRLA18----------611
BROOCKS	——	Tenn.?/Texas		CRLA12----------239
BROOKE	Eng.	Pa.	Arms:-*	CFA20------------78
BROOKE	Eng.	Md.	Arms:-*	CRLA2------------69
BROOKE	Eng.	Md.		CRLA8-----------177
BROOKE	Eng.	Md.	Arms:-*	CRLA17----------224
BROOKE	Eng.	Pa.	Arms:-*	AFA***-----------53
BROOKE	——	Md.		MCS--------------92
BROOKE	Eng.	Md.	Arms:-*	PFU--------------70.
BROOKS	Eng.	Mass.		CFA5------------105
BROOKS	Eng.	Mass.		CFA7------------133
BROOKS	Scotland	Mass.	Arms:-	CFA15-----------203
BROOKS	Eng.	Mass.		CFA17-----------133
BROOKS	——	Mass.		CRLA9-----------176
BROOKS	——	Mass.	Arms:-*	CRLA20----------122
BROOKS	——	Ky.		AF*-------------321
BROOKS	——	Mass.		PPA-------------495

BROOKS	-------	N.Y.		PPA-------------278
BROOME	-------	Del.	Arms:-	AF***-----------428
BROTTS	-------	N.Y.		CRLA3-----------347
BROUCARDEX	-------	L.I.,N.Y.		ACF-------------72
BROUWER	Germany	N.Y.		CRLA18----------215
BROUWER	-------	N.Y.		AFA***----------98
BROWN	Eng.	Va./Md.		CFA2-------------36
BROWN	-------	Pa.		CFA6-----------334
BROWN	-------	Mass.		CFA7-----------324
BROWN	-------	Mass.		CFA8-----------120
BROWN	Eng.	Mass./Conn.		CFA10----------313
BROWN	Eng.	Mass.		CFA10----------395
BROWN	Eng.	Mass.		CFA11----------313
BROWN	Eng.	Mass.		CFA12-----------97
BROWN	-------	R.I.		CFA12-----------99
BROWN	Eng.	Mass.		CFA13----------138
BROWN	Scotland	Md.		CFA17----------365
BROWN	Eng.	Mass.	Arms:-	CFA19--------65,71
BROWN	Eng.	Mass.	Arms:-*	CFA19----------221
BROWN	-------	Mass.		CFA19----------247
BROWN	-------	R.I.		CFA23-----------36
BROWN	-------	Mass.		ACF-------------86
BROWN	Eng.	Mass.		CRLA1----------203
BROWN	Scotland	Md.		CRLA1----------271
BROWN	-------	Va.		CRLA2----------117
BROWN	-------	Va.		CRLA4----------415
BROWN	-------	Mass./Conn.		CRLA8----------500
BROWN	Ireland	Pa./Md.		CRLA11---------359
BROWN	-------	Mass.		CRLA12---------307
BROWN	Eng.	N.H.;Mass.		CRLA14------148,160
BROWN	Eng.	R.I./N.J.	Arms:-*	CRLA15---------440
BROWN	Eng.	Pa.		CRLA16----------31
BROWN	-------	Pa.		CRLA17----------57
BROWN	Eng.?	Mass.	Arms:-*	CRLA18-------29,40
BROWN	-------	Mass.		CRLA18---------355
BROWN	-------	R.I./N.Y.		CRLA19----------11
BROWN	Eng.?	N.Y.		CRLA19---------171
BROWN	Eng.?	R.I.	Arms:-*	CRLA19---------285
BROWN	Ireland	N.Y.	Arms:-*	AF*------------150
BROWN	-------	N.Y.?		AF*------------319
BROWN	Eng.	Mass.	Arms:-*	AF**------------1
BROWNE	Eng.	Mass.		CFA7------------69
BROWNE	Eng.	Mass.		CRLA2----------146
BROWNE	No family data		Arms:-*	CRLA11-------opp.12
BROWNELL	Eng.	R.I.		CFA17----------335
BROWNELL	Eng.	R.I.		CRLA6----------548
BROWNELL	Eng.	R.I.	Arms:-*	CRLA12------344,368
BROWNELL	Eng.	R.I.	Arms:-*	CRLA20----------28
BROWNING	Eng.	Mass.	Arms:-*	CFA4-----------180
BROWNING	Eng.	Va.	Arms:-	CFA14----------187
BROWNING	-------	Va.		CRLA4----------379
BROWNING	Eng.	R.I.		CRLA7----------417
BROWNING	Holland	Pa.	Arms:-*	CRLA17---------494
BROWNING	Eng.	Mass./R.I.	Arms:-*	TNEF-----------222
BROWNLOW	Eng./Ireland	Pa.	Arms:-*	AFA***---------125
BRUCE	Scotland	N.Y.C.		CFA12----------128
BRUCE	-------	Mass.		CFA15----------205
BRUCE	Eng./Scotland			CRLA9----➤------348
BRUCE	-------		Cooley=Twining desc.	CRLA18---------115
BRUCE	Eng.			CRLA18---------288
BRUEN	-------	Mass./Conn.		ARSC------------48
BRUEN	-------	Conn.		MCS-------------81
BRUNDIGE	-------	Mass./Conn.		CRLA3----------169
BRYAN	Eng.	Conn.	Arms:-*	CFA5-----------137
BRYAN	Eng.	Pa.		CFA20----------189
BRYAN	Eng.	Conn.		CRLA2----------285
BRYAN	Ireland	Pa.		CRLA4----------431

BRYANT	——	Ky.		CRLA6----------528
BRYANT	Holland	N.Y.C.	Arms:-*	CRLA7------------1
BRYANT	Eng./Barbadoes	Mass.	Arms:-*	AFA***---------211
BRYANT, John	——	Mass.		PPA------------367
BRYANT, William	——	Mass.		PPA------------169
BUCHANAN	Ireland	N.Y.		CFA14----------346
BUCHANAN	——	Pa.	Arms:-*	PBAF------------21
BUCHER	Switzerland	Pa.	Arms:-*	AFA***----------33
BUCHER	Switzerland	Pa.	Arms:-*	AFA***---------179
BUCHER	Switzerland	Pa.	Arms:-*	AFA***---------363
BUCK	——	Conn.	Arms:-*	CRLA1-----------58
BUCK	——	Mass.		CRLA20---------111
BUCKELEY	——	Mass.		MCS------------82
BUCKINGHAM	Eng.	Mass.		CFA11----------198
BUCKINGHAM	Eng.	Mass./Conn.	Arms:-*	AFA***---------189
BUCKLAND	——	Mass.		CRLA18----------74
BUCKLIN	——	Mass.	*(only)	CRLA2------------6
BUCKLIN	——	Mass.		CRLA13---------358
BUCKMAN	——	Pa.		AFA***----------52
BUCKNAM	Eng.	Mass.	Arms:-*	CRLA17---------582
BUCKNAM	Eng.	Mass.	Arms:-*	CRLA18---------412
BUCKNELL	Eng.	Pa.	Arms:-*	CRLA11---------575
BUCKNER	Eng.	Va.		CRLA4----------141
BUDD	Eng.	Pa.		CRLA15---------241
BUDD	Eng.	N.J.		CRLA17---------294
BUDLONG=BURDILLON	France?	R.I.	Arms:-	AF*--------170,191
BUELL	Eng.	Mass./Conn.	Arms:-*	CFA18----------107
BUELL	Eng.	Conn.		CRLA19---------258
BUELL	Eng.	Mass.	Arms:-*	AFA1-----------45
BUFFUM	Eng.	Mass.		TNEF------------26
BUFORD	——	Va.		CRLA15---------416
BUGBEE	Eng.	Mass.		CRLA13---------167
BULKELEY	Eng.	Mass.	Arms:-	CFA20----------172
BULKELEY	Eng.	Mass.		CRLA10---------152
BULKELEY	Eng.	Mass.		CRLA11---------150
BULKELEY	Eng.	Mass.	Arms:-*	CRLA15----------22
BULKELEY	Eng.	Mass.		CRLA18---------460
BULKELEY	Eng.	Mass.		CRLA20---------135
BULKELEY	——	Mass.		ARSC-----------47
BULKELEY	Eng.	Mass.	Arms:-*	PFU------------429
BULKELEY, see: CHETWODE=BULKELEY				
BULL	Eng.	Conn.		CFA9------------29
BULL	Wales	Mass.		CFA11----------199
BULL	——	S.C.		PFU------------425
BULLARD	Eng.	Mass.		CFA10-----------86
BULLARD	Eng.	Mass.		CFA10----------106
BULLARD	Eng.	Mass.		CRLA15----------73
BULLARD	Eng.	Mass.	Arms:-	AF**-----------408
BULLEN	——	Mass.		CFA10----------106
BULLER	No family data		Arms:-*	CRLA11---------216
BULLINE	——	S.C.		CFA6-----------282
BULLOCH	Scotland	S.C.		CFA10----------149
BULLOCH	Scotland	S.C./Ga.	Arms:-*	AFA***---------165
BULLOCK	Ireland	Pa.		CRLA13---------288
BULLOCK	——	N.J.		CRLA14----------56
BULLOCK	Eng.	Mass.		CRLA16---------123
BULLOCK	Eng.	Mass.	Arms:-*	CRLA18----------62
BULLOCK	Eng.	Canada/Ill.	Arms:-*	AF*------------205
BULLOCK	——		*(only)	TNEF-------btn.78-9
BULLOCK, see: PILGRIMS				
BUMSTEAD	——	Mass.		CRLA13----------47
BUNCE	Eng.	Conn.		ACF-------------2
BUNCE	Eng.	Conn.	Arms:-	AF*------------428
BUNDY	——	Conn.		CFA16----------215
BUNDY	——	N.C.		AF**-----------134
BUNKER	France	Mass.		CRLA12---------266
BUNKER	——	Mass.	Arms:-*	CRLA15----------35

BUNKER	France/Eng.	Mass.	Arms:-*	CRLA18----------358
BUNNELL	———	Conn.	Arms:-*	CRLA12-----------46
BURBANK	———	Mass.	Arms:-*	CRLA19-----------40
BURBANK	———	Mass.	Arms:-*	AF****----------213
BURBANK	———	Mass.	Arms:-*	PBAF------------175
BURBECK	———	Mass.		CFA6------------188
BURBON, House of			Blackiston descent	CRLA11----------404
BURBON, House of	thru.John of Gaunt		Cooley=Twining desc.	CRLA18-----------96
BURCH	Eng.	Va./Md.		CRLA8-------507,524
BURCHAM	———	Mass.		CRLA14----------123
BURCHARD	Eng.	Mass.		CRLA3-----------78
BURCHE	———	Md.		CRLA16----------224
BURDICK	———	R.I.		CFA23----------113
BURDITT	———	Mass.	Arms:-*	CRLA17----------583
BURDITT	———	Mass.	Arms:-*	CRLA18----------415
BURDSALL	———	N.J.	Arms:-*	CRLA5------------5
BURFORD	———	Va.		CRLA4----------231
BURGER	———	N.Y.		CRLA18----------231
BURGESS	———	Va./Md.		CFA5------------88
BURGESS	Wales	Md.		CFA16-----------86
BURGESS	———	Va./Md.	Arms:-*	CRLA2----------125
BURGESS	———	Va./Md.	Arms:-*	CRLA11-----------24
BURGESS	———	Va./Md.		CRLA16-----------42
BURGESS	———	Mass.		CRLA18----------537
BURGH (de)	Eng./Scotland			CRLA9----------354
BURGUNDY, Dukes & Counts of	France		Arms:-	CRLA5------257,261
BURHOE	Eng.	Mass.		TNEF-----------155
BURKE	———	Pa.		CRLA11----------484
BURKE	———	Mass.		CRLA18----------620
BURKE	———	R.I.		AF***----------405
BURKET	Switzerland	Pa.		PFU------------402
BURLEIGH	Wales	Conn.		PPA------------486
BURLING	———	Pa.		CRLA8----------211
BURLINGAME	———	R.I.		CRLA19----------280
BURKNAP	Eng.	Mass.		CFA10-----------91
BURNET	———	Mass./L.I.,N.Y.		CFA16----------170
BURNETT	Eng.	Mass.		CRLA15-----------4
BURNHAM	Eng.	Mass.		CFA7------------84
BURNHAM	Eng.	Mass./N.H.	Arms:-	CFA22----------189
BURNHAM	Eng.	Conn.		CRLA1----------174
BURNHAM	Eng.	Mass.	Arms:-*	CRLA13----------446
BURNHAM	Eng.	Mass.	Arms:-*	CRLA15-----------52
BURNHAM	Eng.	Mass.	Arms:-*	CRLA15----------483
BURR	Eng.	N.J.		CFA5------------341
BURR	———	Conn.		CFA17----------157
BURR	———	N.J.		CRLA8----------150
BURR	Eng.	N.J.		CRLA11----------246
BURR	Eng.	N.J.	Arms:-*	CRLA17----------297
BURR	Eng.	Mass./Conn.	Arms:-*	CRLA18----------438
BURRILL	Eng.	Mass.		CRLA6----------445
BURRITT	———	Conn.		CFA2-----------294
BURRITT	———	N.Y.		CRLA18----------438
BURROUGHS	———	Mass.		CRLA7----------413
BURROUGHS	———	Mass./L.I.,N.Y.		CRLA11----------506
BURROUGHS	Eng.	Mass.	Arms:-*	AFA***------107,110
BURROUGHS	———	Maine		MCS-------------60
BURSLEY	Eng.	Mass.		CRLA19-----------38
BURT	———	Mass.		CFA8-----------265
BURT	Eng.	Mass.		CFA10----------242
BURTON	———	Mass.		CFA6-----------181
BURTON	Eng.	Pa.	*(only)	CRLA2----------396
BURTON	———	Va.		CRLA4----------407
BURTON	Eng.	Va./Pa./Del.		CRLA9-----------16
BURWELL	Eng.	Va.	Arms:-*	CFA24------------1
BURWELL	Eng.	Va.		CRLA4-----------70
BURWELL	Eng.	Va.	Arms:-*	CRLA4----------115
BURWELL	Eng.	Va.		CRLA18----------364

BURY	Ireland	Canada	Arms:-*	CRLA13----------484
BUSBY	Eng.	Mass.		CFA3------------123
BUSBY	Eng.	Mass.		ACF-------------96
BUSHNELL	———	Conn./Mass.		CFA7------------73
BUSHNELL	Eng.	Conn.		CFA8------------206
BUSHNELL	Eng.	Conn.	Arms:-*	CFA23-----------76
BUSHNELL	Eng.	Conn.	Arms:-*	CRLA7----------163
BUSHNELL	Eng.	Conn.	Arms:-*	CRLA7----------598
BUSHNELL	———	Conn.		CRLA10----------95
BUSHNELL	Eng.	Conn.	Arms:-*	AF**------------17
BUSSE	Eng.	Mass.		CFA7------------132
BUTCHER	Eng.	Pa.		CRLA2----------140
BUTCHER	Eng.	Pa.	Arms:-*	CRLA17----------335
BUTCHER	Eng.	N.J.	Arms:-*	CRLA18----------291
BUTLER	Eng.	Mass./Conn.		CFA1------------262
BUTLER	Eng.	Mass.		CFA5------------317
BUTLER	———	Conn.		CFA9------------209
BUTLER	Ireland	Pa.		CFA13----------270
BUTLER	Eng.	Mass.	Arms:-*	CFA21-----------43
BUTLER	———	Conn.		CRLA6----------440
BUTLER	Eng.	Mass.	Arms:-*	CRLA7----------429
BUTLER	Ireland	Pa.		CRLA7----------564
BUTLER	Ireland	Mass.		CRLA11----------584
BUTLER	———	Mass.		CRLA13----------17
BUTLER	———	———	Arms:-*	CRLA14-------opp.54
BUTLER	Eng./Ireland			CRLA17----------164
BUTLER	Ireland			CRLA18----------478
BUTLER	———	N.Y.		PPA-------------615
BUTMAN	———	Mass.		AF****----------241
BUTTERFIELD	———	Mass.		CFA19-------279,293
BUTTERFIELD	———	Mass.	Arms:-*	CRLA17----------546
BUTTERFIELD	Eng.	Mass.	Arms:-*	CRLA20----------97
BUTTOLPH	Eng.	Mass./Conn.		CFA17----------257
BUTTRILL	———	Ga.		CRLA4----------424
BUTTS	———	Va.		CRLA4-----------55
BUZBY	———	Pa.		CRLA2----------408
BUZBY	———	Pa.	Arms:-*	CRLA17----------331
BYE	Eng.	Pa.	Arms:-*	AFA***----------101
BYERS	Scotland	Pa.	Arms:-	CRLA3----------254
BYRAM	Eng.	Mass.		CFA10----------266
BYRD	Eng.	Va.	Arms:-	CFA17----------347
BYRD, see: HORSMANDEN=BYRD				

- C -

CABELL	Eng.	Va.		PFU-------------196
BABOT	Eng.	Mass.		CFA15---------19,26
CADMAN	———	R.I.	Arms:-*	CFA23-----------88
CADWALADER	Wales	Pa.		CRLA5----------517
CADWAKADER	Wales	Pa.		CRLA8----------185
CADY	———	Mass.		CFA17----------278
CADY	———	Mass.	Arms:-*	CRLA13----------452
CADY	———	Mass.	Arms:-*	CRLA15----------489
CAGE	———	Md.	Arms:-*	AF**------------318
CAKE	———	N.J.		CRLA5-----------66
CALDWELL	Eng.?	Mass.	Arms:-*	CFA4------------268
CALDWELL	———	N.H.		CFA17----------274
CALDWELL	———	Conn.		CRLA15----------509
CALHOUN=COLQUHOUN	Eng./Ireland	Pa.	Arms:-*	AF*-------------128
CALKIN=CALKINS	Wales	Mass.		CFA8------------313
CALKINS	Eng.	Conn.		CRLA10----------95
CALL	———	Va.		CRLA4----------292

CALLAWAY	———	Va.			CRLA4----------418
CALLENDER	Scotland	Pa.		Arms:-*	CFA6------------284
CALLENDER	———	Pa.			CRLA8-----------221
CALLENDER	———	Mass.		Arms:-	AF*-------------74
CALLERY	Eng.	N.J./Pa.			CRLA10------205,231
CALTHORPE	———		Cooley=Twining desc.		CRLA18----------118
CALVERT	———	Md.			MCS-------------53
CAMERON	Scotland	Va.		Arms:-*	CRLA4-----------465
CAMP	———	Conn.		Arms:-*	CRLA6-----------314
CAMPBELL	Scotland	Mass.			CFA13-----------211
CAMPBELL	———	N.Y.		Arms:-*	CRLA20----------182
CAMPBELL	Eng./Scotland			Arms:-*	AF*-------------159
CAMPBELL	Scotland	Mass./Ky.		Arms:-*	TNEF------------174
CAMPRON	Eng.?	Mass.			CFA9------------254
CAMVILLE (de)	Eng.			Arms:-	CRLA5-----------265
CAMVILLE (de)	Eng.				CRLA15----------112
CANBY	Eng.	Pa.	*(only)		CRLA13----------355
CANBY	Eng.	Del.			CRLA15----------588
CANDEE	———	Conn.			CRLA19----------80
CANDIANO	Italy	Bray descent	Arms:-*		CRLA17----------135
CANDIANO	Italy		Arms:-*		CRLA18----------441
CANDLER	Ireland?	S.C./Va.			PFU-------------379
CANFIELD	Eng.	Conn.		Arms:-	AF*-------------264
CANNON	Not given				CRLA11--------554
CANNON	———	Del.			CRLA18----------208
CANTERBURY	———	Mass.			TNEF------------159
CANTILUPE (de)	Eng.				CRLA1-----------364
CAPEN	Eng.	Mass.			CFA7------------177
CAPERTON	Eng.	N.Y./Va.			CRLA4-----------245
CAPET, House of	France				CRLA1------357,374
CAPET, Hugh	King of France, d. 996				CRLA1-----------463
CAPET Line	Robert I/Hugh the Great				CRLA2-----------40
CAPET, House of	France	Warren=Belknap desc. Arms:-*			CRLA2-----------173
CAPET, House of	France	Robert the Strong -867			CRLA2-----------356
CAPET, House of	France				CRLA2-----------458
CAPET, House of	France	Robert the Strong, ano. 853			CRLA5-----------266
CAPET, House of	France				CRLA7-----------211
CAPET, House of	France	Haskell descent			CRLA8-----------88
CAPET, House of	France				CRLA8-----------342
CAPET, House of	France	Hinton descent			CRLA8-----------476
CAPET, House of	France				CRLA9-----------372
CAPET, House of	France		Arms:-*		CRLA11----------78
CAPET, House of	France				CRLA11----------161
CAPET, House of	France				CRLA11----------420
CAPET, House of	France				CRLA12----------293
CAPET, House of	France		Arms:-*		CRLA15----------99
CAPET, House of	France		Arms:-*		CRLA17----------167
CAPET, House of	France	Schrack descent			CRLA17----------378
CAPET, House of	France	Cooley=Twining desc.			CRLA18----------119
CAPET, House of	France				CRLA20----------257
CAPRON	Eng.	Mass.		Arms:-*	CFA20----------283
CAPRON	———	Mass.		Arms:-*	CRLA7-----------338
CARDER	———	Mass./R.I.			CFA5------------44
CARDINALL	Eng.			Arms:-*	CRLA5-----------82
CARENT (de)	Eng.				CRLA7----------101
CAREY	Ireland	Pa.			CFA18-----------168
CAREY	Eng.	Mass.			CRLA4----------236
CAREY	Eng.	Mass.			CRLA16----------151
CARLETON	———	Mass.			ARSC------------22
CARLETON	———	Mass.			MCS-------------86
CARLILE	Eng.	Wisc.		Arms:-*	CFA6------------203
CARLILE	Eng.	———			CFA12-----------381
CARLISLE	Ireland	Pa./Ohio			PFU-------------219
CARLL	———	Maine			CFA8------------353
CARLOVINGIAN Kings of	France				CRLA2-----------522
CARLOVINGIAN Dynasty	France				CRLA5----------272
CARLOVINGIAN Kings	France				CRLA7----------219

CARLOVINGIAN	France		Haskell descent	CRLA8-----------89
CARLOVINGIAN	France		Hinton descent	CRLA8-----------478
CARLOVINGIAN Kings	France			CRLA9-----------378
CARLTON	Eng.	Mass.		CRLA3-----------216
CARLTON	Eng.	Mass.	Arms:-*	AF**-----------551
CARMAN	Eng.	Mass.		CFA2-----------85
CARMAN	Eng.	Mass./L.I.,N.Y.		CRLA2-----------243
CARNEY	———	Mass.		PFU-----------284
CARPENTER	Eng.	New Eng./L.I.,N.Y.		CFA1-----------196
CARPENTER	Eng.	Mass.		CFA5-----------361
CARPENTER	Eng.	R.I.		CFA7-----------387
CARPENTER	Eng.	Mass.	Arms:-*	CFA7-----------222
CARPENTER	Eng.	R.I.		CFA10-----------12
CARPENTER	Eng.	Mass.		CFA11-----------369
CARPENTER	Eng.	Mass.		CFA13-----------206
CARPENTER	Eng.	R.I.		CFA16-----------8
CARPENTER	Eng.	R.I./L.I.,N.Y.		CFA18-----------50
CARPENTER	Eng.	Mass.	Arms:-	ACF-----------78
CARPENTER	Eng.	Mass.	Arms:-*	CRLA3-----------1
CARPENTER	Eng.	Mass.	Arms:-*	CRLA7-----------333
CARPENTER	Eng.	Mass.		CRLA9-----------533
CARPENTER=STEWART	———	Pa.		CRLA9-----------540
CARPENTER	Eng.	Mass.		CRLA12-----------149
CARPENTER	Eng.	Mass.		CRLA15-----------430
CARPENTER	Eng.	Mass.	Arms:-*	CRLA15-----------562
CARPENTER	Eng.	Mass.		CRLA16-----------156
CARPENTER	———	Pa.	Arms:-*	CRLA17-----------322
CARPENTER	Eng.	Pa.	Arms:-*	CRLA18-----------276
CARPENTER	Eng.	R.I.	Arms:-*	CRLA18-----------424
CARPENTER	———	Pa.		CRLA19-----------232
CARPENTER	Eng.	Mass.	Arms:-*	CRLA20-----------57
CARR	Eng.	Mass.	Arms:-*	CFA1-----------108
CARR	Eng.	R.I.		CFA7-----------218
CARR	Eng.	Mass.		CFA8-----------244
CARR	———	Va.		CRLA4-----------32
CARR	———	Mass.		CRLA19-----------365
CARR	Eng.	R.I.	Arms:-*	CRLA20-----------376
CARR	Ireland	S.C.	Arms:-	AF**-----------294
CARR	Eng.	R.I.		AF****-----------128
CARR	Eng.		Arms:-*	PBAF-----------179
CARRINGTON	———	Conn.		CRLA7-----------284
CARRIQUE	Ireland		Arms:-*	CRLA13-----------489
CARROLL (or) O'CARROLL	Ireland	Md.	Arms:-*	AFA***-----------85
CARROLL	Ireland	Md.		HFA-----------82
CARROLL	Ireland	Md.	Arms:-*	PFU-----------411
CARROLL, Charles, of Carrollton	Ireland	Md.		SDI---------189,190
CARSTAIRS	Scotland	Pa.	Arms:-*	AFA***-----------99
CARTER	———	Mass.		CFA2-----------214
CARTER	Eng.	Mass.		CFA7-----------406
CARTER	Eng.	———		CFA9-----------198
CARTER	Eng.	Conn.	Arms:-*	CFA12-----------195
CARTER	Eng.	Mass.		CFA19-----------82
CARTER	Eng.	Va.		CRLA1-----------247
CARTER	Eng.	Va.		CRLA3-----------115
CARTER	———	Va.	Arms:-*	CRLA4-----------65
CARTER	———	Va.		CRLA4-----------279
CARTER	———	———	*(only)	CRLA2-------opp.88
CARTER	Eng.	Mass.	Arms:-*	CRLA15-----------1
CARTER	———	N.Y.	Arms:-*	CRLA19-----------57
CARTER	———	Va.		CRLA20-----------219
CARTER	———	Va.	Arms:-	AF**-----------218
CARTER	Eng.	Pa./N.Y.	Arms:-*	AFA***-----------11
CARTER, see: LUDLOW=CARTER=HARRISON				
CARTER	Eng.	Va.		PFU-----------54
CARVER	———	Mass.		CFA4-----------154
CARVER	———	Pa.		CRLA15-----------243
CARWITHEN	Eng.	Mass.		CRLA11-----------264

CHAMPLIN	——	R.I.		CFA23------------79
CHANDLEE	Ireland	Pa.		CRLA11----------480
CHANDLER	——	Mass.		CFA5------------49
CHANDLER	Eng.	Mass.		CFA6------------134
CHANDLER	Eng.	Mass.	Arms:-*	CFA8------------174
CHANDLER	Eng.	Mass.		CFA9------------214
CHANDLER	——	Mass./N.J.		CFA16----------174
CHANDLER=HEAD	——	Mass.		CFA22----------234
CHANDLER	Eng.	Pa.		CRLA1----------117
CHANDLER	Eng.	Mass.		CRLA10----------405
CHANDLER	——	——	*(only)	CRLA12-------opp.88
CHANDLER	Eng.	Mass.	Arms:-*	CRLA17----------549
CHANDLER	Eng.	Pa.	Arms:-*	AFA***-----------41
CHANDLER	Eng.	Pa.	Arms:-*	AFA***----------157
CHAPIN	Eng.	Mass.		CFA4-----------232
CHAPIN	Eng.	Mass.		CFA11----------327
CHAPIN	Eng.	Mass.		CFA15----------327
CHAPIN	Eng.	Mass.		CFA17----------321
CHAPIN	Eng.	Mass.		CRLA6----------550
CHAPIN	Eng.	Mass.		CRLA19----------88
CHAPIN	Eng.	Mass.		TNEF------------168
CHAPMAN	Eng.	Mass.	Arms:-*	CFA2-----------208
CHAPMAN=JOHNSON	——	Conn.		CRLA7-----------85
CHARLEMAGNE			Long descent	CFA23-----------28
CHARLEMAGNE				CFA27----------210
CHARLEMAGNE			Drake descent	CRLA1-------294,360
CHARLEMAGNE			Dudley=Tyng descent	CRLA1----------406
CHARLEMAGNE			Gaunt=French descent	CRLA1----------531
CHARLEMAGNE			Peck=Bowen descent	CRLA2-----------19
CHARLEMAGNE	Brooke (Md.) descent in error; see Md. Hist. Mag., vol. 19, p.	401, for correction.		CRLA2-----------79
CHARLEMAGNE			Warren=Belknap desc.	CRLA2----------167
CHARLEMAGNE			Ludlow=Brewster desc.	CRLA2----------366
CHARLEMAGNE			South=Grantham desc.	CRLA2----------436
CHARLEMAGNE			Washington=Lewis desc.	CRLA3----------122
CHARLEMAGNE			West descent	CRLA4----------129
CHARLEMAGNE			Schull descent	CRLA5-----------88
CHARLEMAGNE			Olmsted descent	CRLA7----------102
CHARLEMAGNE			Bray descent	CRLA7----------180
CHARLEMAGNE			Haskell descent	CRLA8-----------63
CHARLEMAGNE				CRLA8----------344
CHARLEMAGNE			Hinton descent	CRLA8----------457
CHARLEMAGNE			Baldwin descent	CRLA10----------79
CHARLEMAGNE			Gaither=Fownes desc.	CRLA11----------29
CHARLEMAGNE			Cornell descent	CRLA11----------252
CHARLEMAGNE			Earle descent	CRLA11----------314
CHARLEMAGNE			Blackiston descent	CRLA11----------374
CHARLEMAGNE			Wales descent	CRLA13----------64
CHARLEMAGNE			Carter=Boynton desc.	CRLA15----------153
CHARLEMAGNE			Smith descent	CRLA15----------295
CHARLEMAGNE			Ayres=Sheppard desc.	CRLA15----------343
CHARLEMAGNE			Steele descent	CRLA16----------129
CHARLEMAGNE			Bray descent	CRLA17-----------83
CHARLEMAGNE			Williams descent	CRLA17----------275
CHARLEMAGNE			Schrack descent	CRLA17----------371
CHARLEMAGNE			Washbourne=Willits desc.	CRLA17-------507
CHARLEMAGNE			Harwood descent	CRLA17----------669
CHARLEMAGNE			Cooley=Twining desc.	CRLA18-----------88
CHARLEMAGNE			Glendinning=Logan desc.	CRLA18--------298
CHARLEMAGNE			Titus descent	CRLA18----------449
CHARLEMAGNE			Hutchinson descent	CRLA19----------100
CHARLEMAGNE			Richardson descent	CRLA19------206,209
CHARLEMAGNE			Rhoads descent	CRLA19----------333
CHARLEMAGNE				CRLA20----------260
CHARLEMAGNE				CRLA20------384,386
CHARLEMAGNE			Wyatt=Clapp=Owen desc.	AF*-------------53
CHARLEMAGNE			Wilkinson descent	AF*------------100

CHARLEMAGNE			Warren descent	TNEF-------------93
CHARLES	———	Mass.	Arms:-*	CRLA12----------357
CHARLETON (de)	Eng.			CRLA2-----------555
CHARLTON	Eng.			CRLA11----------164
CHASE	———	N.H.		CFA6------------163
CHASE	———	N.H.		CFA7--------21,154
CHASE	———	N.H.		CFA7------------154
CHASE	———	N.H.	Arms:-	CFA16-----------340
CHASE	———	Mass.		CRLA13----------203
CHASE	———	Mass.		CRLA13----------277
CHASE	Eng.	N.H./Mass.		PFU-------------132
CHASE, Samuel	———	Md.		SDI---------189,196
CHASE	Eng.	Mass.	Arms:-*	TNEF-------------24
CHATFIELD	Eng.	Conn.	*(only)	CRLA12----------125
CHATTIN	———	La.		CFA2------------137
CHAUNCEY	Eng.	Mass.	Arms:-*	PFU-------------347
CHAUNCY	Eng.	Mass.	Arms:-*	AFA***-----------93
CHAUNCY	———	Mass.		ARSC-------------79
CHAUNCY	———	Mass.		MCS--------------8
CHAUNDERS	———	Pa.		CRLA14-----------38
CHAWORTH	Eng.			CRLA2-----------351
CHAWORTH (de)	Eng.		Arms:-*	CRLA5-----------286
CHAWORTH (de)	Eng.		Cooley=Twining desc.	CRLA18----------133
CHAWORTH (de), see: BEAUCHAMP (de)				
CHECKLEY	Eng.	Mass.		CRLA9------------20
CHEEVER	———	Mass.		CFA8------------265
CHENERY	Eng.	Mass.		CFA13-----------286
CHENEY	Eng.	Mass.		CFA7------------139
CHENEY	Eng.?	Mass.	Arms:-*	CRLA6------------79
CHENEY	Eng.?	Mass.		CRLA18----------625
CHENEY	Eng.	Mass.	Arms:-*	AF****----------211
CHENEY	———	Mass.		TNEF------------149
CHERRY	Eng.	Iowa		CRLA7-----------397
CHESEBROUGH	Eng.	Mass.	Arms:-	CFA6-------------88
CHESEBROUGH	Eng.	Mass.	Arms:-*	CFA19-----------230
CHESTER	Eng.	Mass.		CFA15-----------364
CHESTER, Earls of	Eng.			CRLA9-----------365
CHESTER, Earls of	Eng.		Arms:-*	CRLA11----------165
CHESTER, Earls of		early de Gernon	Arms:-	CRLA5-----------289
CHETWODE	Eng.			CRLA18----------467
CHETWODE	———	Mass.		ARSC-------------27
CHETWODE=BULKELEY	———	Mass.		MCS--------------93
CHEW	———	Va./Md.		CFA3------------305
CHEW	———	Va./Md.		CFA5-------------89
CHEW	Eng.	Va./Md.		CFA16------------92
CHEW	———	Va./Md.	Arms:-*	CRLA2-----------126
CHEW	Eng.	Va./Md.		CRLA4------------14
CHEW	———	Va./Md.	Arms:-*	CRLA11-----------27
CHEW	Eng.	Va./Md.		CRLA16-----------44
CHEW	Eng.	Va./Md.		HFA-------------185
CHICHESTER	Eng.			AF*--------------49
CHICKERING	Eng.	Mass.	Arms:-*	AFA***----------357
CHILD	Eng.	Mass.		CFA3-------------4
CHILD	Eng.	Mass.		CFA13-----------284
CHILD=CHILDS	Eng.	Mass.		CFA18-----------249
CHILD	Eng.?	Mass.		CFA19-----------293
CHILD	Eng.	Pa.	Arms:-	CFA22-----------228
CHILD	Eng.	Mass.		CRLA20----------212
CHILDS	———	Mass.		CFA25-----------131
CHILDS	Eng.	Mass.	*(only)	CRLA13----------163
CHILES	———	———		AF*-------------322
CHILTON	———	Mass.	Arms:-*	CFA1-------------56
CHILTON	———	Mass.		CFA7------------306
CHILTON	———	Mass.		CFA10-----------269
CHILTON	Eng.	Mass.		CRLA13------377,386
CHINN	Eng.	Va.	Arms:-*	AFA***------191,315
CHIPMAN	Eng.	Mass.		CRLA15----------257

CHIPMAN	Eng.	Mass.	Arms:-*	CRLA18---------599
CHIPMAN	Eng.	Mass.	Arms:-*	TNEF-----------51
CHISHOLM	-----	Va.		CFA14----------139
CHISMAN	-----	Va.		CRLA4----------346
CHISOLM	-----	S.C.	Arms:-*	CFA25----------51
CHITTENDEN	Eng.	Conn.		CFA1-----------67
CHITTENDEN	Eng.	Conn.		CFA8-----------315
CHITTENDEN	Eng..	Conn.	Arms:-*	CRLA7----------146
CHOATE	Eng.	Mass.		CFA1-----------86
CHOATE	Eng.	Mass.		CFA17----------202
CHOATE	Eng.	Mass.		CFA21----------134
CHORLEY	Eng.		Arms:-*	AFA***---------55
CHRISMAN	-----	Va./Pa.		CRLA6----------199
CHRISTIAN	-----	N.Y.		CRLA16---------87
CHRISTIE	Scotland	N.J.	Arms:-	CFA16----------63
CHRISTOPHER	-----	N.Y.		CRLA10---------384
CHRISTOPHERS	Eng.	Conn.		CFA16----------56
CHRYST	-----	Ohio		CRLA19---------362
CHURCH	Eng.	Mass.		CFA1-----------38
CHURCH	-----	Mass.		CRLA7----------355
CHURCH	-----	Mass.	Arms:-	CRLA3----------453
CHURCH	-----	Mass.		CRLA10---------328
CHURCH	-----	Mass.		CRLA10---------345
CHURCH	-----	Mass.		CRLA12---------121
CHURCH	-----	Mass.		CRLA15---------81
CHURCH=CHURCHE	Eng.	Mass.	Arms:-	AF*------------15
CHURCH	Eng.	Mass.	Arms:-*	AF**-----------345
CHURCH	Eng.	Mass.	Arms:-*	AF****---------54
CHURCHILL	Eng.	Mass.		CFA8-----------326
CHURCHILL	Eng.	Conn.		CFA20----------338
CHURCHILL	-----	Conn.	Arms:-	AF*------------27
CINCINNATI, Society of		Wales=Butler=Ellsworth descent		CRLA13------opp.62
CINCINNATI, Society of		Schrack descent		CRLA17---------370
CINCINNATI, Society of		Wright to Flagler		CRLA19---------57
CLAFLIN	-----	Mass.	Arms:-*	CFA10----------82
CLAFLIN	Scotland	Mass.	Arms:-	CFA14----------93
CLAIBORNE	Eng.	Va.		CFA5-----------296
CLAIBORNE	Eng.	Va.	Arms:-*	CRLA4----------59
CLAIBORNE	Eng.	Va.		CRLA12---------213
CLAIBORNE	Eng.	Va.	Arms:-*	CRLA14---------129
CLAIBORNE	Eng.	Va.	Arms:-*	AFA***------181,253
CLAIBORNE, see: BOTELER=CLAIBORNE				
CLAIBORNE	Eng.	Va.	Arms:-*	PFU------------231
CLAPP	Eng.	Mass.		CFA2-----------101
CLAPP	Eng.	Mass.		CFA8-----------349
CLAPP	Eng.	Mass.		CFA11----------360
CLAPP	Eng.	Mass.		CFA13----------197
CLAPP	Eng.	Mass.		CFA13----------221
CLAPP	Eng.	Mass.	Arms:-	CFA13----------329
CLAPP	Eng.	Mass.		CFA22----------166
CLAPP	Eng.	Mass.		CRLA4----------368
CLAPP	-----	Mass.		CRLA11---------236
CLAPP	Eng.	Mass.	Arms:-	AF*------------38
CLARE (de)	Eng.	Fitz Gilbert	Arms:-*	CRLA1----------325
CLARE (de)		Marshals of Eng.	Mareschall line	CRLA2----------343
CLARE (de)	Eng.		*(only)	CRLA2------476,487
CLARE (de)	Eng.		Arms:-*	CRLA5----------292
CLARE (de)	Eng.		Haskell descent	CRLA8----------96
CLARE (de)	Eng.		Hinton descent	CRLA8----------482
CLARE (de)	Eng.	Fitz Gilbert	Arms:-*	CRLA9----------356
CLARE (de)	Eng.		Gaither=Fownes desc.	CRLA11---------50
CLARE (de)	Eng.			CRLA11-----83,85,86
CLARE (de)	Eng.		Arms:-*	CRLA15------113,116
CLARE (de)	Eng.	Fitz Gilbert	Arms:-*	CRLA17---------181
CLARE (de)	Eng.	Clare descent	Arms:-*	CRLA17---------183
CLARE (de)	Eng.		Schrack descent	CRLA17---------386
CLARE (de)	Eng.		Cooley=Twining desc.	CRLA18---------134

CLARE (de)	Eng.	Glendinning=Logan desc.		CRLA18------324,326
CLARE (de)	Eng.	Titus descent		CRLA18----------502
CLARE (de)	Eng.	Fitz Gilbert -1090		CRLA20------264,266
CLARK	———	Conn.		CFA1-------------42
CLARK	———	Mass.		CFA5------------304
CLARK	———	Mass.		CFA10-----------221
CLARK	Eng.	Mass.	Arms:-*	CFA11-----------353
CLARK	Eng.	Mass.	Arms:-	CFA13-----------191
CLARK	———	S.C.		CFA14-----------128
CLARK	Eng.	Mass.		CFA15-----------315
CLARK	Eng.	Mass.		CFA15-----------342
CLARK	Eng.	Conn.	Arms:-	CFA17-----------154
CLARK	Eng.	Mass.		CFA19------------68
CLARK	Eng.	Mass.	Arms:-*	CFA22-----------157
CLARK	Eng.?	Conn.	Arms:-*	CFA27-----13cht.,41
CLARK	Eng.	Conn.		CRLA1-----------195
CLARK	Eng.	Mass.		CRLA2-----------388
CLARK	Eng.	Mass.	Arms:-*	CRLA3------------44
CLARK	———	N.J.		CRLA6-----------173
CLARK	———	Mass.		CRLA11----------224
CLARK	No family data		Arms:-*	CRLA15------opp.381
CLARK	Eng.	Mass.	Arms:-*	CRLA17----------431
CLARK	Eng.	Mass.		CRLA17----------649
CLARK	———	Mass./N.Y.		AF**------------283
CLARK	———	N.Y.		PPA-------------447
CLARK, Abraham	———	N.J.		SDI---------145,154
CLARKE	Eng.	Mass.		CFA2------------321
CLARKE	Eng.	Mass.	Arms:-	CFA3------------204
CLARKE	Eng.	Mass.		CFA8------------174
CLARKE	Eng.	Mass.		CFA12-----------277
CLARKE	Eng.	N.Y.	Arms:-*	CFA21-----------160
CLARKE	Eng.	R.I.	Arms:-*	CFA23-----------108
CLARKE	Eng.	Mass.	Arms:-*	CFA27-----38cht.,43
CLARKE	Eng.	N.J.		ACF-------------37
CLARKE	Eng.	R.I.		CRLA14-----------77
CLARKE	Eng.	R.I.		CRLA17----------492
CLARKE	Eng.	R.I.	Arms:-*	CRLA18-----------49
CLARKE	Eng.	R.I.		CRLA20------171,175
CLARKE	Eng.	Mass.	Arms:-	AF*-------------83
CLARKE	———	Pa.		AFA***-----------56
CLARKE	———	R.I.		ARSC-------------31
CLARKE	———	R.I.		MCS-------------84
CLARKE	Eng.	Mass.	Arms:-*	PBAF------------156
CLARKE	———	N.H./Mass.		PPA-------------460
CLARKE	———	———	*(only)	TNEF-------btn.78-9
CLARKE, see: PILGRIMS				
CLARKSON	Eng.	N.Y.	Arms:-*	CFA11-----------120
CLARKSON	Eng.	N.Y.		CRLA17----------635
CLARKSON	Eng.	N.Y.	Arms:-*	HFA-------------276
CLARKSON	Eng.	N.Y.	Arms:-*	CRLA14-----------19
CLASON	———	N.Y.		PPA-------------235
CLAVERING	Eng.	Fitz Roger, etc.		CRLA15----------104
CLAY	Eng.	Pa.		CRLA13----------223
CLAYES, CLOISE, CLOYES	———	Mass.		CFA26-----------118
CLAYPOOLE	Eng.	Pa.	Arms:-	CFA8------------195
CLAYPOOLE	Eng.	Pa.	Arms:-*	CFA10------------61
CLAYTON	Eng.	Pa./Del.		CRLA1------------63
CLAYTON	———	N.J.	Arms:-*	CRLA14-----------24
CLAYTON	———	Md.	Arms:-*	CRLA17----------218
CLAYTON	Eng.	Pa. & N.J.		CRLA17----------299
CLEAVES	———	Mass.	Arms:-*	CRLA15-----------61
CLEMENS	———	Pa.		CRLA9-----------449
CLEMENT	Eng.	N.Y./N.J.		CRLA8-----------219
CLEMENT	Eng.	Mass.	Arms:-*	CRLA13----------448
CLEMENT	Eng.	Mass.	Arms:-*	CRLA15----------485
CLEMENTS	Eng.	Mass.	Arms:-	CFA27------------46
CLEMENTS	———	N.C.	Arms:-*	CRLA9-----------260

CLEMENTS	Eng.	Mass.	Arms:-*	CRLA15----------80
CLEMMONS	———	Mass.	Arms:-	AF****----------244
CLEVELAND	Eng.	Mass.	Arms:-*	CFA12-----------41
CLEVELAND	Eng.	Mass.	Arms:-	CRLA10----------280
CLEVELAND	Eng.	Mass.		CRLA15----------599
CLEVELAND	Eng.	Mass.	Arms:-*	AFA***----------345
CLEWS	Eng.	N.Y.		CFA5-----------299
CLIFFORD (de)	Eng.			CRLA11----------86
CLIFFORD (de)	Eng.			CRLA11----------423
CLIFFORD (de)	Eng.			CRLA15----------116
CLIFFORD (de)	No family data		Arms:-*	CRLA15------opp.172
CLIFFORD (de)	Eng.		Cooley=Twining desc.	CRLA18----------136
CLIFFTON	———	Pa.		PPA--------------73
CLINTON	———	Mass./N.J.		CRLA6----------144
CLINTON	Eng.			CRLA9----------171
CLINTON	Eng.	Mass.		PFU-------------94
CLOPTON	———	Va.		CRLA4----------294
CLOPTON	———	Va.		MCS-------------10
CLOUD	Eng.	Pa.		CRLA11----------307
CLOUGH	Eng.	Mass.		CRLA15----------76
CLOVIS, King of Franks				CFA27----------218
CLOVIS, Frankish Monarchy	Carter=Boynton	Arms:-*		CRLA15----------197
CLOVIS, Frankish Monarchy		Bray descent		CRLA17-------97,103
CLOVIS, Frankish Monarchy		Cooley=Twining desc.		CRLA18--------79,86
CLOVIS, Charlemagne & Wm. I		Vou descent		CRLA18----------235
CLOVIS, Charlemagne & Wm. I	John of Gaunt; Vou descent			CRLA18----------252
CLOVIS, of Cologne		Andrews descent		CRLA19----------58
CLOVIS & Charlemagne		Richardson descent		CRLA19------206,209
CLOVIS, Frankish Monarchy	Merovech -427			CRLA20----------261
CLOVIS				CRLA20----------386
CLOWS	Eng.	Pa.		CRLA2----------433
CLOYES	———	Mass.		CRLA20----------82
CLYMER, George	———	Pa./N.J.		SDI--------159,175
COALE	———	Md.		CFA16----------82
COALE	———	Md.		PFU------------266
COATES	Ireland	Pa.		CRLA11----------244
COATES	Eng./Ireland	Pa.	Arms:-	AF**----------132
COBB	Eng.	Mass.		CFA7-----------343
COBB	Eng.	Mass.		CFA10----------219
COBB	———	Canada/Maine/Mass.		CFA16----------242
COBB	———	Mass.	Arms:-*	CFA17----------179
COBB	Eng.	Mass.		CRLA11----------230
COBB	Eng.	Mass.	Arms:-*	CRLA18----------601
COBBOLD	———	———	Arms:-*	CRLA20----------379
COBURN	———	Mass.		CFA1-----------247
COBURN	Eng.	Mass.	Arms:-*	CFA19-----------30
COCHRAN	Ireland	Mass.	Arms:-*	CFA12-----------59
COCK	Scotland	N.Y.		CFA9-------------4
COCK	Eng.	Conn.		CFA14----------212
COCK=COCKS	Eng.	Conn./L.I.,N.Y.		CFA16--------21,29
COCK=COCKS	Eng.	L.I.,N.Y.	Arms:-*	CFA18-----------29
COCKE	Eng.	Va.		CRLA4----------162
COCKE	Eng.	Va.		CRLA4----------207
COCKE	Eng.	Va.	Arms:-*	CRLA10-----------36
COCKE	Eng.	Va.		CRLA14----------113
CODDINGTON	Eng.	Mass./J.N.	Arms:-*	AFA***----------349
COE	Eng.	L.I.,N.Y.	Arms:-*	CFA7-----------258
COE	Eng.	———		CFA7-----------285
COE	Eng.	Mass./Conn.		CFA24----------100
COE	Eng.	Mass.		CRLA2----------382
COE	Eng.	Conn./Mass.	Arms:-*	CRLA20-----------36
COE	Eng.	L.I.,N.Y.		AF***-----------49
COE	———	Pa.		PPA------------608
COERTEN	Gelderland	N.Y.		CRLA20----------202
COFFIN=COFFYN	Eng.	Mass.	Arms:-*	CFA1-----------170
COFFIN	Eng.	Mass.	Arms:-	CFA4-----------298
COFFIN	Eng.	Mass.	Arms:-*	CRLA6----------88

COFFIN	Eng.	Mass.	Arms:-*	CRLA8------------26
COFFIN	Eng.	Mass.		CRLA10----------413
COFFIN	Eng.	Mass.		CRLA12------272,273
COFFIN	Eng.	Mass.		CRLA14----------152
COFFIN	Eng.	Mass.		CRLA15----------526
COFFIN	Eng.	Mass.	Arms:-*	CRLA18----------350
COFFIN	Eng.	Mass.	Arms:-*	AFA***----------333
COFFIN	Eng.	Mass.	Arms:-	TNEF-------------38
COGGESHALL	Eng.	Mass./R.I.	Arms:-	CFA3------------348
COGGESHALL	Eng.	R.I.	Arms:-*	CRLA7----------472
COGGESHALL	————	Mass./R.I.	Arms:-*	TNEF--------------7
COGGESHALL, see: PILGRIMS				
COGSWELL	Eng.	Mass.		CFA7------------158
COGSWELL	Eng.	Mass.	Arms:-*	CFA24-----------126
COGSWELL	Eng.	Mass.		CRLA12----------162
COGSWELL	————	Nova Scotia/Mass.		CRLA17----------601
COGSWELL	Eng.	Mass.		AFA***------14,18,20
COHR	————	Pa.		CRLA15----------536
COIT	Wales?	Mass./Conn.	Arms:-	AF*-------------124
COLBORNE	Eng.	Mass.		CRLA17----------446
COLBURN	————	Mass.?		CFA4------------166
COLBURN	Eng.	Mass.		CFA11-----------350
COLBURN	Eng.	Mass.		CFA13-----------282
COLBURN	————	Mass.		CRLA20----------207
COLBURN	Eng.	Mass.	Arms:-	AF***------------83
COLBY	Eng.	Mass.		CFA7------------161
COLBY	Eng.	Mass.		CFA8------------370
COLBY	————	Mass.	Arms:-*	CRLA7-----------245
COLBY	Eng.	Mass.		CRLA19----------307
COLE	————	Md.		CFA5-------------92
COLE	Eng.	Mass.		CFA8------------264
COLE	Eng.	Mass.	Arms:-	CFA17-----------120
COLE	Eng.	Maine/Mass.		CFA19-----------290
COLE	————	Del./Ind.		CRLA10----------366
COLE	Eng.	Mass./R.I.	Arms:-*	CRLA17----------314
COLE	Eng.	Mass./R.I.	Arms:-*	CRLA18--58,64,70,73
COLE	Eng.	Mass.	Arms:-*	CRLA19-----------55
COLEMAN	Ireland	Ky.	Arms:-*	CRLA1------------28
COLEMAN	————	Va.		CRLA4-----------239
COLEMAN	Ireland	Pa.		CRLA15----------559
COLEMAN	Ireland	Ky.		CRLA15----------586
COLEMAN	Eng.	Mass.	Arms:-*	CRLA18----------349
COLES	————	Mass.		CFA9-------------93
COLES	Eng.	Mass.	Arms:-*	CFA18------------22
COLES	Ireland	Va.		CRLA4-----------161
COLES	Ireland	Va.		CRLA13----------139
COLES	————	Mass.		CRLA13----------236
COLFLESH	Germany	Pa.		CRLA9-----------246
COLGATE	Eng.	N.Y.C.		CFA8------------381
COLHOUN	Ireland	Pa.		CRLA19----------357
COLLADAY	Germany?/Holland Pa.			CRLA2-----------130
COLLADAY	Holland	Pa.	Arms:-*	AFA***----------341
COLLES, see: COLONIAL DAMES				
COLLETT	Eng.	Pa.		CRLA2-----------227
COLLEY	————	Mass.	Arms:-*	CRLA18------------1
COLLIER	Eng.	Mass.		CFA3------------132
COLLIER	Eng.	Mass.		ACF-------------103
COLLIER	————	Mass./Conn.		CRLA19----------399
COLLINS	Eng.	Mass.		CFA12-----------118
COLLINS	Eng.	Mass.	Arms:-*	CRLA2-----------306
COLLINS	————	Pa.		CRLA11----------473
COLLINS	Eng.	Pa.		CRLA15----------238
COLLINS	————	Mass.		CRLA19----------263
COLLINS	Eng.	Mass.		PFU-------------418
COLMAN	————	Mass.		CFA2------------186
COLMAN	Eng.	Mass.	Arms:-*	CRLA10----------401
COLOMBIER (Du Colombier) France		Del.	Arms:-*	AF*---------------7

COLONIAL DAMES		N.Y.	Tienhoven to Colles	CRLA19----------145
COLONIAL POETS				PPA--------------15
COLSTON	Eng.	Va.		CRLA4-----------176
COLT	———	Conn./Mass.		CFA5-------------57
COLTON	Eng.?	Mass.		CRLA10----------301
COLTON	———	Conn.		PPA-------------541
COLTON	———	Vt.		PPA-------------245
COLWELL	Ireland	N.J.		CFA16-----------182
COMBS	No family data		Arms:-*	CRLA13----btn.124-5
COMMONS, House of	Eng.		Carter=Boynton desc.	CRLA15----------230
COMPTON	———	N.J./Ohio	Arms:-	AF***-----------237
COMSTOCK	Eng.	Conn.	Arms:-*	CFA9------------220
COMSTOCK	———	Conn.		CRLA6-----------404
COMSTOCK	Eng.	Conn.		CRLA17----------477
COMSTOCK	———	Conn.	Arms:-*	CRLA17----------666
COMSTOCK	Eng.	Conn.		PBAF------------73
COMYN, see: CUMMINGS				
CONAN I, see: BRITTANY, Dukes of				
CONANT	Eng.	Mass.		CFA8-------------90
CONANT	Eng.	Mass.		CFA19------------74
CONANT	Eng.	Mass.	Arms:-*	CRLA15-----------59
CONDIT	Wales?	N.J.	Arms:-*	CFA9------------145
CONDIT	———	N.J.	Arms:-	CFA15-----------302
CONDIT	———	N.J.		CFA16-----------177
CONFER	———	Pa.		CRLA3------------66
CONGER	France	N.J.		CFA22-----------244
CONNABLE	Eng.	Mass.	Arms:-*	CFA26-----------117
CONNECTICUT, Seal of			*(only)	CFA27-------148cht.
CONNECTICUT, Seal of			*(only)	CRLA12------opp.124
CONNECTICUT, Seal of			*(only)	CRLA19-------opp.10
CONNER	———	Md.		CRLA17----------418
CONNOR	Ireland	N.Y.	Arms:-*	AFA2------------189
CONNOWAY	Ireland	Del.		CRLA17----------357
CONOVER	Holland	N.Y.	Arms:-*	AFA3------------109
CONRAD	Germany	Pa.		CRLA17----------296
CONRAD	———	Pa.		PPA-------------465
CONROW	———	N.J.		CRLA15----------549
CONSTABLE	Eng.			CRLA15----------105
CONSTABLE	———	Md.	Arms:-*	CRLA17----------411
CONSTABLE	———	Conn.		MCS--------------63
CONVERSE	———	Mass.	Arms:-*	CFA9------------221
CONVERSE	Eng.	Mass.		CFA19-------------6
CONVERSE	———	———	*(only)	CRLA12-------opp.88
CONVERSE	———	Mass.		PFU-------------107
CONWAY	Eng.	Va.		CRLA1-----------263
CONWAY	Eng.	Va.		PFU-------------202
CONY	Eng.	Mass.		CFA6------------244
CONYERS	Eng.		Ayres=Sheppard desc.	CRLA15----------368
CONYNGHAM	Ireland	Pa.		CRLA2-----------112
COOCH	Eng.	Del.		CRLA9-----------326
COOK	Eng.	Conn.		CFA7------------266
COOK	Eng.	Mass.	Arms:-*	CFA8------------165
COOK	———	Mass.		CFA10-------------1
COOK	Eng.	Mass.		CFA11-----------356
COOK	———	Mass.		CFA12------------14
COOK	Eng.	Mass.		CFA13-----------194
COOK	Eng.	Mass.		CFA22-----------161
COOK	———	Mass.		CRLA2-----------300
COOK	Eng.	Pa.	Arms:-*	CRLA11----------214
COOKE	Holland	Mass.	Arms:-*	CFA1-------------54
COOKE	———	Va.	Arms:-*	CFA10------------47
COOKE	Eng./Holland	Mass.		CFA10-----------256
COOKE	Eng.	Mass.		CFA12------------73
COOKE	Eng.	Mass./Conn.		CFA15-----------360
COOKE	Eng.	Mass.	Arms:-*	CFA23------------48
COOKE	———	Mass.		CRLA7-----------480
COOKE	———	Mass.		CRLA8-----------442

COOKE	Eng./Holland	Mass.		CRLA12----------103
COOKE	Eng.	Mass.		CRLA17----------264
COOKE	——	Mass.		CRLA17----------524
COOKE	——	Mass.	Arms:-*	CRLA18----------272
COOKE	Eng.?	Mass.		CRLA18----------397
COOKE	Eng.	Mass.		CRLA19-----------47
COOKE	——	R.I.	Arms:-*	CRLA20-----------50
COOKE	Eng./Holland	Mass.		CRLA20----------190
COOKE (Cook)	Eng.?	Mass.	Arms:-	AF*------------187
COOKE	Eng./Ireland	Mass.	Arms:-*	AFA2------------27
COOKE	Eng.		Arms:-*	AFA***----------13
COOKE	——	Va.		PPA------------521
COOKE	——	Va.		PPA------------619
COOLEY	Eng.	Mass.	Arms:-	AF*------------247
COOLIDGE	No family data		Arms:-*	CRLA12-------opp.30
COOLIDGE	——	N.Y./Mass.	Arms:-	AF****----------239
COOMBS	France	Maine		CFA13----------146
COOMBS	——	Mass.		CRLA16----------142
COOPER	——	L.I.,N.Y./N.J.		CFA5------------52
COOPER	Eng.	N.J.		CFA7------------399
COOPER	Eng.	Conn.	Arms:-*	CFA8------------301
COOPER	——	Mass.		CFA18----------104
COOPER	Eng.	N.Y.		CFA19----------256
COOPER	Eng.	Mass.	Arms:-	CFA21-----------27
COOPER	Eng.	N.J.		ACF-------------34
COOPER	Ireland?	Pa.	Arms:-*	CRLA5----------489
COOPER	Eng.	Pa.		CRLA9----------158
COOPER	Scotland	N.C.	Arms:-*	CRLA18----------362
COOPER	Eng.	Mass.	Arms:-*	CRLA20-----------94
COOPER	——	Pa.	Arms:-*	AF*------------344
COOTS	Scotland	Del./Va./Ky.	Arms:-*	AF**-----------136
COPE	Eng.	Pa.		CFA18----------176
COPE	Eng.	Pa.	Arms:-*	PFU-------------49
COPLEY	Eng.	Mass.		CFA19----------159
COPPINGER	Ireland	D.C.	Arms:-*	PFU------------137
CORBET	Eng.	Pa.		CRLA17-----------80
CORBIN	Eng.	Va.		CRLA1----------254
CORDES	France	S.C.	Arms:-*	CRLA13----------496
CORE	Eng.	N.J.		CRLA17----------294
COREY	——	Mass.	Arms:-*	CRLA15-----------62
CORLIES	——	N.J.	Arms:-*	CRLA14-----------48
CORLISS	Eng.	Mass.		CFA22------------1
CORNELL	——	Mass./R.I.		CFA8------------48
CORNELL	Eng.	Mass.	Arms:-*	CFA8------------163
CORNELL	Eng.	Mass.	Arms:-*	CFA18-----------11
CORNELL	Eng.	Mass.		CRLA1----------455
CORNELL=CORNWELL	Eng.	Mass./R.I.	Arms:-	CRLA2----------154
CORNELL	——	Pa.		CRLA11----------241
CORNELL	Eng.	R.I.		CRLA14-----------76
CORNELL	——	Mass.?	Arms:-*	CRLA20-----------32
CORNELISSEN, see: LOUW				
CORNELIUS	Germany	Md./Ind.		CRLA7----------496
CORNWALL	Eng.	Conn.		CRLA19----------419
CORNWELL	——	N.Y.		CRLA19----------335
CORNWELL	——	Mass./N.Y./Md.		AF*------------388
CORSE	——	Md.		CFA2------------280
CORSE	——	Md./N.Y.C.		CFA9------------66
CORTELYOU	Netherlands	N.Y.C.		CFA1------------17
CORWIN	Eng.	Mass.		CFA8------------115
CORWIN	Eng.?	Conn./L.I.,N.Y.		CRLA6-----------16
CORWIN	Eng.	Mass./L.I.,N.Y.		PFU------------135
COSBY	Eng.	Va.	Arms:-*	CRLA4----------144
COSBY	Eng.	Va.		CRLA4----------287
COSBY	——	Ky.		PPA------------293
COSSART	France		Arms:-*	CRLA1-----------46
COSSITT	——	Conn.		CFA21----------121
COTTON	Eng.	Mass.		CFA13----------378

Surname	Origin	Location	Arms	Reference
COTTON	———	N.H.		CFA20------------68
COTTON (de Cotton)	No family data		Arms:-*	CRLA11------opp.160
COTTON	Eng.	Mass.		CRLA13----------269
COTTON	Eng.	Mass.	Arms:-*	CRLA14----------161
COTTON	Eng.	Va./Md.	Arms:-*	CRLA15----------322
COTTON	Eng.	Mass.	Arms:-*	CRLA20----------212
COULSTON	———	Pa.	Arms:-*	CRLA11----------466
COURSEY	———	Md.		CRLA3-----------235
COURTENAY	Eng.			CFA25------------12
COURTENAY (de)	France/Eng.			CRLA1-----------315
COURTENAY (de)	Eng.	Schull descent		CRLA5-----------191
COURTENAY (de)	Eng.	Athon	Arms:-	CRLA5-----------297
COURTENAY	Eng.	Haskell descent		CRLA8------------97
COURTS	———	Md.	Arms:-*	CRLA11-----------24
COVERT	———	L.I.,N.Y./S.C.		CFA13-----------233
COVILLANDEAU	France	S.C.		CFA3------------358
COWDEN	Scotland/Ireland	Mass.	Arms:-	CFA19------------48
COWLES	———	Mass./Conn.	Arms:-*	CFA4------------252
COWLES	———	Mass.		CFA9------------230
COWLES	Eng.	Conn.		AF***-------------65
COWPERTHWAIT	Eng.	N.Y./N.J.		CRLA17----------314
COWPLAND	Eng.	Pa.		CRLA17----------409
COX	———	Pa.		CFA17-----------364
COX	Eng.	S.C.	Arms:-*	CFA20-----------317
COX	———	Va.		CRLA4-----------284
COX	Br. West Indies	Pa.		CRLA17----------346
COX	———	Mass.		CRLA19----------147
COX	Scotland/Ireland		Arms:-*	AF*-------------158
COX	Eng.	Maine	Arms:-*	AF****------------8
COXE	———	N.J./N.Y.		PPA-------------544
COYL	———	Mich.	Arms:-*	AF****----------175
COYTHORE=TYNG	———	Mass.		MCS--------------87
COZZENS	Eng.	N.Y.		PPA-------------540
CRADOCK	Eng.	Pa./Md.		PFU-------------416
CRAFT	Eng.	Mass.		CFA13-----------357
CRAFT	———	Mass.		CRLA19----------378
CRAIG	———	N.J.	Arms:-	CRLA7------------26
CRAIG	Ireland	Mo.		CRLA7-----------374
CRAIG	Ireland		Arms:-*	CRLA5-----------485
CRAIG	Scotland	N.J.		CRLA13----------280
CRAM	———	Mass.		CFA17------------84
CRAM	No family data		Arms:-*	CRLA13------opp.130
CRAMER (Kramer)	Germany	N.Y.		CFA22------------48
CRANCH	———	Mass.		PPA-------------497
CRANE	Eng.	Mass.	Arms:-*	CFA9------------237
CRANE	Eng.	Conn./N.J.		CFA10-----------182
CRANE	Eng.	Conn.		CFA16-----------178
CRANE	Eng.	Conn.		CFA19-----------123
CRANE	———	Conn.		CRLA10----------202
CRANE	———	Conn./N.J.	Arms:-*	AFA***----------177
CRANSTON	Ireland	Md.		CRLA3-----------317
CRANSTON	———	R.I.		CRLA17----------488
CRANSTON	Scotland	R.I.	Arms:-*	CRLA18-----------19
CRANSTON	———	R.I.		MCS--------------35
CRARY	———	Conn.		CFA14------------39
CRARY	Scotland	Conn.	Arms:-*	CRLA12----------362
CRARY	Scotland	Mass.	Arms:-*	AFA***----------313
CRAWFORD	Ireland	Mass.	Arms:-*	CFA11-----------367
CRAWFORD	Scotland/Ireland	Mass.	Arms:-	CFA13-----------204
CRAWFORD	Scotland	R.I.		CFA22-----------175
CRAWFORD	Ireland	N.Y.		CFA23-------209,210
CRAWFORD	———	Pa.		CRLA18----------590
CRAWFORD (Crowfurd)	Eng.		Arms:-*	AF*-------------165
CRAWFORD	Mass./L.I.,N.Y.		Arms:-*	AF****-----------16
CRAWFORD	———	———	*(only)	TNEF--------opp.78
CRAWFORD, see: PILGRIMS				
CREASON	———	Ky.		CRLA10------------8

Surname	Origin	Location	Arms	Reference
CREHORNE	———	Mass.		CFA8-----------397
CRENSHAW	Eng.?	Va.		CRLA17----------219
CRESSEY	———	Mass.		CFA4-----------172
CRESSON	France?/Holland N.Y.			CFA16-----------69
CRESSON	Europe	N.Y./Pa.	Arms:-*	CRLA5----------499
CRICHTON	Eng.		Arms:-*	AF*-----------166
CRIGLER	———	Va.		CRLA6-----------299
CRIM	———	Pa.		CRLA12----------183
CRISPELL	———	N.Y.		CFA6------------3
CRISPELL	———	N.Y.?		CFA13----------248
CRISPIN	Eng.	Pa.	Arms:-	CFA14----------231
CRISPIN	Eng.	Pa.	Arms:-*	CFA19----------148
CRISPIN	Eng.	Pa.	Arms:-*	CRLA5----------27
CRISPIN		Pa.	Arms:-*	AFA***-----------5
CRISPIN, see: OWEN=CRISPIN				
CRISSEY	Eng.	Mass.		CFA20----------248
CRITTENDEN	———	Mass./N.Y.		CFA4-----------133
CROASDALE	Eng.?	Pa.		CRLA20----------298
CROCKER (Croker)	Eng.	Mass.	Arms:-*	TNEF-----------190
CROMMELIN	Holland?/France N.Y.			CFA26-----------93
CROMWELL	———	Md.	Arms:-*	AFA***-----------243
COOK	———	Tenn./Mo./Nebr.		CRLA12----------389
CROSBIE	Ireland		Arms:-*	CRLA13----------488
CROSBY	Eng.	Mass.		CFA24----------191
CROSBY	Eng.	Mass.	Arms:-*	CFA27----------49
CROSBY	Eng.	Pa.		CRLA8----------316
CROSBY	Eng.	Mass.		CRLA17----------455
CROSBY	Eng.	Pa.	Arms:-*	CRLA17----------630
CROSBY	———	Ohio?	Arms:-*	TNEF-----------122
CROSHAW	———	Va.		CFA24----------19
CROSHAW	———	Va.		CRLA4----------126
CROSS	Ireland	Pa.	Arms:-*	CRLA3----------299
CROSSMAN	Eng.	Mass./R.I.	Arms:-*	CFA6-----------197
CROSSMAN	Eng.	Mass.	Arms:-*	CFA12----------375
CROSWELL	———	N.Y./Conn.		PPA------------319
CROW	Eng.	Conn.		CFA16-----------54
CROW	———	Conn.		CFA17-----------157
CROWELL	———	Mass.		CRLA6----------123
CROWNE, see: MACKWORTH=CROWNE				
CRONINSHIELD	———	Mass.		CFA5-----------372
CROZER	———	Pa.		CRLA11----------527
CRUMLEY	Eng.	Va.		CRLA19----------173
CRUSADER ANCESTORS			Carter=Boynton desc.	CRLA15----------224
CULIN	———	Pa.		CRLA17----------231
CULLUM	———	N.C./Tenn.		CRLA10----------188
CULVER	———	Mass./Conn.		CRLA3----------271
CULVER	Eng.?	Mass.	Arms:-*	TNEF-----------97
CUMMIN	Ireland	Pa.	Arms:-*	CRLA16----------29
CUMMING	Scotland/Ireland N.J.			CRLA16----------173
CUMMINGS	———	Mass.		CFA4-----------243
CUMMINGS	———	Mass.		CFA6-----------184
CUMMINGS	Scotland	Mass.		CFA6-----------237
CUMMINGS (Comyn)	Scotland	N.Y.	Arms:-*	PBAF-----------36
CUNNINGHAM	———	Mass.	Arms:-*	CFA4------------9
CUNNINGHAM	Scotland	Va.		CRLA12----------331
CUNNINGHAM	Scotland/Ireland		Arms:-*	CRLA13----------135
CURLEE	———	N.C.		CRLA19----------389
CURRIER	———	Mass.	Arms:-	CFA16----------333
CURRIER	———	Mass.		CRLA7----------382
CURRIER	No family data		Arms:-*	CRLA14-------opp.18
CURRY		Va./Ohio		PPA------------317
CURTIN	Scotland/Ireland Pa.			CFA22-----------63
CURTIS	Eng.	Mass.		CFA6-----------245
CURTIS	Eng.	———		CFA8-----------246
CURTIS	Eng.?	Conn.		CFA8-----------332
CURTIS	———	Conn.	Arms:-*	CFA9----------112
CURTIS	Eng.	Mass.	Arms:-*	CFA13----------355

CURTIS	——	Mass.		CFA13----------359
CURTIS	Eng.	Conn.	Arms:-	CRLA7-----------137
CURTIS	——	N.J.	Arms:-*	CRLA18----------570
CURTIS	Eng.	Mass.		CRLA19----------157
CURTISS	Eng.	Conn.		PFU-------------155
CURTISS	Eng.	Conn.		CFA1-----------244
CURTISS	Eng.	Conn.		CFA14----------205
CURWEN	Scotland	——		CFA5-----------297
CURWEN	Eng.		Arms:-*	CRLA14------opp.129
CURWEN	——	Mass.		ARSC------------54
CUSHING	Eng.	Mass.		CRLA10----------241
CUSHING	Eng.	Mass.	Arms:-*	CRLA10----------409
CUSHING	Eng.	Mass.		CRLA11----------200
CUSHING	Eng.	Mass.		CRLA13----------265
CUSHING	Eng.	Mass.	Arms:-*	AF**-----------538
CUSHING	Eng.	Mass.		CFA7-----------142
CUSHMAN	Eng.	Mass.		CFA22----------205
CUSHMAN	Eng.	Mass.	Arms:-*	CRLA7-----------356
CUSHMAN	Eng.	Mass.		CRLA16----------137
CUSKER	Ireland	N.Y.C.		CFA16----------331
CUSTER	——	Pa.		AF*------------437
CURTIS	——	Mass.		CFA7-----------124
CUSTIS	Ireland?/Holland	Va.		CFA13----------226
CUSTIS	——	Va.		CRLA2-----------114
CUSTIS	Eng./Holland	Va.		CRLA9----------7,10
CUSTIS	——	Va.	Arms:-*	CRLA15----------333
CUTHBERT	——	N.C./Pa.	Arms:-*	AFA***----------91
CUTLER	Eng.	Mass.		CFA2-----------346
CUTLER	Eng.?	Mass.		CFA19-----------50
CUTLER	Eng.	Mass.		CFA20----------154
CUTLER	Eng.	Mass.	Arms:-*	CFA27----54,148cht.
CUTLER	Eng.	Mass.		TNEF------------99
CUTTER	——	Mass.		CRLA4-----------364
CUTTER	Eng.	Mass.	Arms:-*	CRLA20-----------85
CUTTER	——	Mass.		CRLA20----------245
CUTTER	——	Mass.	Arms:-	AF**-----------251
CUTTER	——	Ohio		PPA-------------463
CUTTING	Eng.	Mass.		CFA13------------1
CUYLER	Netherlands	N.Y.	Arms:-*	CFA8-------------1

- D -

DAAKE	Eng.	Va.	Arms:-*	CRLA15----------317
DABINOTT	Eng.			CRLA1-----------185
D'ABITOT	Eng.		Beauchamp line	CRLA2-----------355
D'ABITOT	Eng.		Arms:-*	CRLA5-----------300
D'ABITOT	Eng.		Cooley=Twining desc.	CRLA18----------128
DABNEY	Eng.[1] &	Mass.[2]	Arms:-	CFA17----------318
DADE	Eng.	Va.		CFA13-----------89
DAGGETT	Eng.	Mass.		CFA12----------335
DAHL	Norway	Ill.		CRLA6-----------25
DAKIN	——	Mass.		CFA7-----------132
DALBEY	——	Va.		CRLA12----------391
DALE	Eng.	Va.	Arms:-	CRLA3-----------117
DALLAS	Scotland	Jamaica/N.Y.	Arms:-*	PFU-------------311
DALLETT	Eng.	Pa.	Arms:-	AF*--------------1
DALMAS	France	Del.	Arms:-*	CRLA1-----------41
DALMAS	France	Del.		CRLA15----------251
DALMAS	France	Del.		CRLA15----------591
DALRYMPLE	——	Ky.		CRLA3-----------400
DALTON	——	Wash. state		CRLA16----------60
DAMON	Eng.	Mass.	Arms:-*	CRLA20------329,330

DAMPIERRE (de)	France		Arms:-	CRLA5-----------301
DANA	———	Mass.		CFA9-----------347
DANA	———	Mass.	Arms:-*	CFA14-----------121
DANA	France	Mass.		CRLA10-----------86
DANA	France	Mass.		CRLA15-----------378
DANA	France?/Eng. Conn.		Arms:-*	AF*-------------290
DANA		Mass.		HFA--------------47
DANA	Eng.	Mass.		PPA-------------111
DANDRIDGE	Eng.	Va.	Arms:-*	CFA24-----------15
DANDRIDGE	Eng.	Va.	Arms:-*	CRLA4-----------121
DANDRIDGE	———	Va.	Arms:-*	CRLA10-----------125
DANFORTH	Eng.	Mass.		CFA10-----------321
DANFORTH	Eng.	Mass.		CFA19-----------83
DANFORTH	Eng.	Mass.	Arms:-*	CFA22-----------69
DANFORTH	Eng.	Mass.		CRLA6-----------243
DANFORTH	Eng.	Mass.	Arms:-*	CRLA20-----------114
DANIEL	———	Va.		PFU-------------387
DANIELSON	Scotland	R.I.	Arms:-	AF****----------111
DANISH MONKS, see: LLYWELLYN ap IORWERTH				
DARBY	———	Md.	Arms:-	CRLA7----------503
DARBY	———	Mass.	Arms:-*	CRLA13-----------433
DARCE (de)	Eng.			CRLA11-----------428
DARLING	Scotland	N.Y.		CRLA16-----------81
DARLINGTON	Eng./Scotland N.Y.			CRLA11-----------569
DARLINGTON	Eng.	N.Y.		PFU-------------373
D'AUBIGNY	Eng.		Titus descent	CRLA18----------500
D'AUBIGNY (d'Aldini)	Eng.		ano. 1129	CRLA20----------393
D'AUBIGNY, see: ARUNDEL, Earls of				
DAVENPORT	Eng.	Conn./Mass.	Arms:-	CFA5-----------267
DAVENPORT	———	Mass./Conn.		CFA14-----------101
DAVENPORT	Eng.	Mass.	Arms:-	CFA20-----------252
DAVENPORT	Eng.	N.J.		CRLA9----------163
DAVENPORT	Eng.		Arms:-*	CRLA11----------166
DAVENPORT	Eng.	Mass.	Arms:-	AF*-------------423
DAVENPORT	Eng.	Conn./Md./W.Va.	Arms:-*	AFA***----------359
DAVENPORT	———	Conn.		MCS-------------101
DAVENPORT	Eng.	Conn./Mass.	Arms:-*	PFU-------------103
DAVID	France?	N.Y.		CRLA13----------148
DAVIDSON	Scotland	N.J.		CFA18-----------236
DAVIDSON	———	Pa./N.C./Ky.		CRLA4-----------300
DAVIDSON	Scotland	Ohio		CRLA7----------449
DAVIES	Eng.	N.Y.C.		CFA20-----------134
DAVIES	Wales	Conn.	Arms:-*	PFU-------------282
DAVIS	Eng./Wales	Md.		CFA2-------------30
DAVIS	———	Md.		CFA3-----------364
DAVIS (or) DAVIES	Eng.	Mass.		CFA5-----------186
DAVIS	Wales	Md.		CFA6-----------271
DAVIS	Eng.	Mass.		CFA6-----------321
DAVIS	Eng.	Mass.		CFA7----------298
DAVIS	———	Mass.		CFA7----------344
DAVIS	Eng.	Mass.		CFA8-----------292
DAVIS	Eng.	L.I.,N.Y.		CFA10-----------226
DAVIS	———	Conn.		CFA16-----------319
DAVIS	Wales	Mass.		CFA19----------264
DAVIS	Eng.	Mass.	Arms:-*	CRLA3-----------46
DAVIS	———	Va./W.Va./Tenn.		CRLA3-----------61
DAVIS	———	Va.		CRLA4-----------447
DAVIS	Wales	Pa.		CRLA9----------250
DAVIS	———	Va.		CRLA10-----------44
DAVIS	———	Va./Md.	Arms:-*	CRLA11----------20
DAVIS	———	N.Y.		CRLA12----------335
DAVIS	———	Mass.	Arms:-*	CRLA15-----------41
DAVIS	———	Pa.		CRLA15----------376
DAVIS	———	Md.		CRLA16-----------39
DAVIS	———	N.Y.		CRLA16----------94
DAVIS	Eng.	Mass.		PFU-------------114
DAVOL	———	Mass.		CFA12-----------101

DAVOL	———	Mass.		CFA20------------72
DAWES	Eng.	Mass.		CRLA13----------38
DAWES	———	Mass.		PPA------------308
DAWSON	———	Va.	Arms:-*	CRLA15----------320
DAWSON	———	Ohio		AF**------------112
DAY	Eng.	Mass./Conn.		CFA1------------261
DAY	———	L.I.,N.Y.		CFA16----------185
DAY	Wales	Mass.		CFA18----------102
DAY	Eng.	Conn.		CFA22-----------93
DAY	Eng.	Conn.		CRLA3----------225
DAY	———	N.J.		CRLA9----------163
DAY	———	Mass.	Arms:-*	CRLA19----------328
DAY	Eng.	Conn.		PFU------------209
DEAKE	———	R.I./N.Y.		CRLA6----------176
DEAN	Eng.	N.Y.		CFA2------------278
DEAN	Eng.	Mass.		CFA10----------263
DEAN	Eng.	Conn.		CFA13----------237
DEAN	———	N.J.		CRLA9----------475
DEAN	———	Va.		CRLA11----------287
DEAN	Eng.	Mass.		AF***----------375
DEARDEN	Eng.	Mass.	Arms:-*	AFA***----------147
DEAS	———	S.C.		CFA20----------243
DE BEAUBIEN	France	Canada	Arms:-	CFA22----------250
DE BLOIS	France	N.Y./R.I.	Arms:-	AF****----------188
DE CARENT	Eng.			CRLA1----------186
DE CLEVANT	France			CRLA1-----------89
DE COURSEY	Eng.	Md.	Arms:-	AFA***-----------26
DE ERGADIA	Eng./Scotland			CRLA9----------346
DE FOREST	Europe	N.Y.	Arms:-	CFA2------------72
DE FOREST	Holland	N.Y.		CFA10----------299
DE FOREST	France/Holland	N.Y.	Arms:-*	CFA16----------276
DE GARMO	———	Canada/N.Y.		CFA24-----------50
DE GRAAF	———	N.Y.	Arms:-*	CFA8------------27
DE GRAFF	———	N.Y.		CRLA6----------474
DE GRAFFENRIED	Switzerland	N.C.	Arms:-	AF*------------136
DE GROOT	Netherlands	N.Y.	Arms:-*	CFA15----------317
DE HAES	———	Del.	Arms:-*	AFA***----------325
DE HART	———	N.Y.		CRLA9----------477
DE HAVEN	Germany	Pa.		CRLA4----------329
DE HOOGES	Holland	N.Y.		CRLA20----------51
DEIGHTON	———	Mass.		ARSC------------87
DEIGHTON	———	Mass.		MCS------------25
DE JONGH	———	Mass.?	Arms:-*	CRLA18----------559
DE JONGH	———	———	Arms:-*	CRLA20----btn.10-11
DE KAY	Holland	N.Y.		CFA18----------286
DE KAY	France			CRLA14----------30
DE LA COUR	France	Pa.		CRLA8----------417
DELAFIELD	Eng.	N.Y.	Arms:-*	PFU------------269
DE LA FITE DE PELLEPORT	———		Arms:-*	CRLA1-----------87
DELAMATER	France	N.Y.		CFA8------------338
DELAMERE	Eng.			CRLA1----------187
DE LANCEY	Normandy	N.Y.	Arms:-	CFA20----------238
DELANO	Eng.	Mass.		CFA4------------134
DELANO	France/Eng.	Mass.		CFA5------------248
DELANO	France/Holland	Mass.		CRLA12----------416
DELANO	France/Holland	Mass.	Arms:-*	AF****-----------47
DE LA MONTAGNE	———	N.Y.C.		CFA7------------292
DELANY	Ireland	Pa.	Arms:-*	CRLA9----------305
DE LA PORTE, se: PORTE (de la)				
DELAUNAY	France	Pa.	Arms:-*	AFA***----------321
DELL	———	Mich.		CFA14----------354
DELL	Eng.	R.I.	Arms:-*	CRLA20---31,opp.379
DE LONG	France	Pa.	*(only)	CRLA8----------531
DEL PINO	Cuba	Fla.		ACF-------------92
DE MANDEVILLE	Holland	N.Y.		CFA16-----------68
DEMAREST	Europe/Germany	N.J.		CFA16--------64,69
DEMAREST	France	N.Y.		CRLA10----------379

DEMEREST	France	N.Y./N.J.		CRLA18------217,219
DEMING	———	Conn.		CFA8------------209
DEMING	Eng.	Conn.	Arms:-	AF****----------137
DEMMY	———	Pa.		CRLA15----------536
DE MOSS	———	W.Va./Ind.		CRLA11----------283
DE MOTT	———	N.Y.		CRLA20-----------57
DE MUN (Dumont)	France	N.J.	Arms:-*	AFA***----------187
DENBY	Eng.	Va.	Arms:-*	CRLA13------312,317
DE NEMOURS, see: DU PONT=de NEMOURS				
DENHAM	Scotland	Fla.	Arms:-	CRLA8-------------6
DENISE	Holland	L.I.,N.Y.		CFA1-------------15
DENISON	Eng.	Mass.		CFA11-----------317
DENISON	———	Mass.		CFA13-----------346
DENISON	Eng.	Mass.	Arms:-*	CFA19------------39
DENISON	Eng.	Conn.	Arms:-	CFA19-----------232
DENISON	Eng.	Mass.	Arms:-	CFA22-----------192
DENISON	Eng.	Conn.		ACF--------------89
DENISON	Eng.	Mass.		CRLA12----------313
DENISON	Eng.	Mass.	Arms:-*	CRLA18-----------42
DENISON	Eng.	Mass./Conn.	Arms:-*	AFA***----------305
DENMARK, Kings of		Gaither=Fownes desc.		CRLA11-----------58
DENMARK, Kings of		Blackiston descent		CRLA11----------395
DENNIS	———	R.I./N.J.		CFA10-----------198
DENNISON	Eng.	Mass.	Arms:-	CFA11-----------298
DENNISON	Ireland	Mass.		CRLA11----------146
DENSMORE	———	Conn.		CRLA18----------631
DENTON	Eng.	Mass.		CFA24-----------133
DEPEW	France	N.Y.	Arms:-	CRLA3-----------175
DE PEYSTER	———	N.Y.C.		CFA18-----------155
DE PEYSTER	Holland	N.Y.		CFA22-----------245
DE PEYSTER	France	N.Y.	Arms:-*	CRLA14-----------25
DE PEYSTER	Holland	N.Y.		AFA4-------------19
DERBY	Eng.	Mass.		CFA20-----------179
DERHAM	Eng.		Arms:-*	CFA25-------------6
DERHAM	Eng.			CRLA20----------395
DERRICKSON	———	Md.		CRLA9------------15
DE RUINE	France	N.Y.		CFA16------------65
DE RUSHALL	Eng.			CRLA9------------14
DESPENSER (Le)	Eng.			CRLA15----------139
DE SILLE	Belgium	N.Y.	Arms:-*	AFA***-----------79
DEUEL	———	Mass.		CRLA19-----------77
DE VAUX	France/Germany	N.Y.		CFA18-------------6.
DEVENISH	Eng.	N.J.	Arms:-*	AFA***----------293
DEVEREAUX	Eng.	Mass.	Arms:-*	CRLA20----------345
DEVOL	———	Mass.	Arms:-	CFA23-------------1
DEWEY	Eng.	Mass.	Arms:-*	CFA9------------186
DEWEY	Eng.	Mass./Conn.		CRLA4-----------258
DEWEY	No family data		Arms:-*	CRLA18------opp.352
DEWEY	Eng.	Mass./Conn.	*(only)	CRLA19-----29,31,34
DEWEY	———	Mass./Md./Pa.		PPA-------------549
DE WITT	Westphalia	N.Y.	Arms:-*	CFA8-------------31
DE WITT	No family data		Arms:-*	CRLA11------opp.192
DE WITT	Holland	N.Y.	Arms:-*	CRLA20-----------68
DE WITT	———	Conn.	Arms:-	AF*-------------301
DE WITT	Holland	N.Y.	Arms:-*	AFA***----------249
DE WOLF	———	Conn.		PFU-------------277
DEXTER	Ireland	Mass.		CFA4-------------41
DEXTER	Eng.	R.I.		CFA12-----------125
DEY	Holland	N.Y.		CFA18-----------160
DEY	———	N.Y./N.J.		CRLA8-----------234
DEYO	France/Germany	N.Y.		CRLA18----------234
DEYO	France	N.Y.		CRLA20-----------49
DICKERMAN	Eng.	Mass.		CFA8------------297
DICKERMAN	———	Mass.		CFA19------------67
DICKERSON	Eng.	L.I.,N.Y.		AF***------------48
DICKEY	———	Va.		CRLA19----------128
DICKINSON	Eng.	Conn.		CFA8------------352

DICKINSON	Eng.	Mass./Conn.		CFA9-----------223
DICKINSON	Eng.	Md.		CRLA8----------180
DICKINSON	Eng.	Mass.		CRLA8----------297
DICKINSON	Eng.	Mass.	Arms:-	AF**-----------164
DIGGES	Eng.	Va.	Arms:-*	MCS---42 PFU---296
DIGGS	————	Va.		CRLA4------204,205
DIGHTON	Eng.	Mass.		CRLA6----------365
DIGNAN	Ireland	N.Y.		CFA16----------330
DILLARD	————	Va.		CFA16----------162
DILLARD	————	Va.		CRLA4----------428
DILLINGHAM	————	Mass.		TNEF-----------114
DILWORTH	Eng.	Pa.		CRLA11---------459
DIMMICK	————	Mass.		CFA7-----------348
DIMOCK	Eng.	Mass.	Arms:-*	CFA5-----------276
DIMOCK	Eng.?	Mass.		CRLA12---------160
DIMOCK	Eng.?	Mass.		CRLA17---------653
DIMOCK	————	Mass.		CRLA19----------36
DINGLEY	Eng.	Mass.	Arms:-*	CRLA15----------46
DINAN (de)	France			CRLA5----------302
DINWIDDIE	Scotland	Pa.	Arms:-*	CRLA18---------588
DIRCKS	————	————	Arms:-*	CRLA20------opp.60
DITMARS	Europe	N.Y.	Arms:-*	CRLA13---------394
DIXON	Scotland	New Eng.	Arms:-*	CFA6-----------258
DIXON	————	Va.		CRLA9----------512
DIXON	Scotland/Ireland Pa.		Arms:-	AF*------------134
DIXSON	Ireland	Del.	Arms:-*	CRLA17-------55,65
DOANE	Eng.	Mass.	Arms:-	CFA3-----------74
DOANE	Eng.	Mass.		CFA8-----------144
DOANE	————	Mass.		CFA20----------118
DOANE	Eng.	Mass.		CRLA19----------39
DOANE	————	N.J./Mass.		PPA------------270
DOANE	————	Mass.		PPA------------621
DOD	————	Conn.		CFA9-----------150
DOD	Eng.	Conn.	Arms:-	ACF-------------67
DODD	————	Conn.	Arms:-*	CFA16----------127
DODD	————	Conn.	Arms:-	CFA16----------320
DODD	————	Mass.		CRLA18-----------9
DODGE	Scotland	N.Y.		CFA11----------261
DODGE	————	Mass.		CFA12----------130
DODGE	Eng.?	Mass./R.I.		CFA13----------140
DODGE	Eng.	Mass.	Arms:-	CFA17----------276
DODGE	————	N.Y.		CFA18----------221
DODGE	Eng.	Mass.	Arms:-	CFA21-----------49
DODGE	Eng.	Mass.	Arms:-*	CFA21----------102
DODGE	Eng.?	R.I./Mass./Conn. Arms:-		CFA22----------174
DODGE	Eng.	Mass.	Arms:-*	CRLA8------36,40,60
DODGE	Eng.	R.I.	Arms:-*	CRLA8----------362
DODGE	Eng.	Mass.		CRLA8----------494
DODGE	Eng.	Mass.		PFU------------193
DOBBINS	————	Pa.		AFA***---------294
DOGGETT	Eng.	Mass.		CRLA11---------233
DOGGETT	Eng.	Mass.		CRLA18---------627
DOLBY		Va.	Arms:-*	CRLA15---------319
DOLPH (de Wolf)	Belgium	Conn.		CFA22----------238
DOM	Germany	Pa.	Arms:-*	CRLA11----------11
DOMESDAY BOOK Ancestors Eng.		Carter=Boynton desc.		CRLA15---------225
DOMINICK	France	N.Y.C.		CFA9------------1
DOMVILLE	Eng.		Arms:-*	CRLA5----------303
DONALDSON	————	Pa.		CRLA20---------115
DOOLEY	Ireland/Newfoundland N.J.			CRLA19---------117
DOOLITTLE	Eng.	Mass.		CFA26----------148
DOOLITTLE	Eng.	Conn.		CRLA19---------270
DOOLITTLE	Eng.	Conn.		AF**-----------338
DORCHESTER (City)		Mass.	Regional background	CRLA19---------237
DORION	Canada			CRLA17---------707
DORMER	————	Md.	Arms:-*	CRLA11----------18
DORR	Eng.	Mass.		CFA13----------222

DORR	Eng.	Mass.		CFA21------------36
DORR	———	Mass.	Arms:-*	TNEF------77,opp.78
DORR, see: PILGRIMS				
DORRANCE	Ireland	Conn.	*(only)	CRLA2-------------1
DORRANCE	Ireland	Conn./R.I.	Arms:-*	CRLA13----------338
DORSEY	Eng.?	Md.	Arms:-	CFA3------------298
DORSEY	———	Md.		CFA5-------------85
DORSEY	Eng.	Va./Md.		CFA16------------92
DORSEY	Eng.?	Md.		CRLA1-----------282
DORSEY	———	Md.		CRLA8-----------170
DORSEY	———	Md.		CRLA9-----------520
DORSEY	———	Va./Md.		CRLA16-----------37
DOSWELL	———	Va.	Arms:-*	CRLA16-----------51
DOTTERER	———	Pa.		CRLA9-----------455
DOTY	Eng.	Mass.		CFA5------------251
DOTY	Eng.	Mass./N.J.		CFA20-----------227
DOTY.	———	Mass.		CRLA12----------102
DOUD=DOUDE	Eng.	Conn.		AF*-------------117
DOUGHTY	Eng.	N.Y.		CFA16------------16
DOUGHTY	Eng.	Mass.		CFA16-----------282
DOUGHTY	Eng.	Mass.		CFA18------------55
DOUGLAS	Scotland	N.Y.C.		CFA10-----------197
DOUGLAS	Scotland	Mass.	Arms:-	CFA12-----------311
DOUGLAS	Scotland	Mass./Conn.	Arms:-*	CRLA17-----------12
DOUGLAS	Scotland	Cooley=Twining desc.		CRLA18----------149
DOUGLAS	Eng.		Arms:-*	AF*-------------160
DOUGLAS	Scotland	Mass.		AF****----------115
DOUGLASS	———	N.J.		CFA9------------120
DOUGLASS	———	Del.		CRLA1------------62
DOUGLASS	Scotland?	Ohio		CRLA4-----------183
DOUGLASS	———	Pa.	Arms:-	AF*-------------410
DOW	Eng.	N.H.	Arms:-*	CRLA12------------1
DOWD=DOWDE	Eng.	Conn.	Arms:-	AF*--------------29
DOWLER	———	Md./Pa.		AF***-----------253
DOWNEY	———	Va.?		CRLA18----------367
DOWNEY	———	Pa.		CRLA18----------587
DOWNING	Eng.	Pa.	Arms:-*	CRLA13----------209
DOWSE	Eng.	Mass.		CFA9------------340
DOWSE	———	Mass.		CRLA9------------22
DOYNE	———	Md.	Arms:-*	CRLA15----------321
DOZIER	———	N.C./Conn.	Arms:-*	CRLA19----------269
DRAKE	Eng.	Conn.		CFA17-----------260
DRAKE	Eng.	N.Y.	Arms:-*	CFA18-----------211
DRAKE	Eng.	Mass.	Arms:-*	CFA20-----------224
DRAKE	Eng.	Mass. & Conn.		CRLA1-------171,193
DRAKE	Eng.	Mass.		CRLA17----------656
DRAKE	Eng.	N.H.	Arms:-*	AF***------------44
DRAKE	Eng.	Conn.	Arms:-*	AFA***-----------81
DRAKE	Eng.	Conn.	Arms:-*	AFA***----------155
DRAKE	———	Conn.		MCS--------------21
DRAKE	Eng.	Mass.	Arms:-*	PFU--------------57
DRAKE	———	N.Y.		PPA-------------203
DRAPER	Eng.	Mass.	Arms:-*	CFA1------------148
DRAPER	Eng.	Mass.	Arms:-*	CFA3--------------1
DRAPER	———	Mass.		CFA13-----------283
DRAPER	Eng.	Maine		CFA21-----------205
DRAPER	———	Pa.		CRLA5-----------471
DRAPER	Eng.	Mass.	Arms:-	AF**------------202
DRAPER	———	Mass.		PFU-------------127
DRESSER	———	Mass.		CFA4------------127
DRESSER	Eng.	Mass.		CFA7-------------78
DREW	Eng.	Mass.	Arms:-*	CFA5------------195
DREW	———	N.H.	Arms:-*	AF****-----------29
DREW	Eng.	Mass.	Arms:-*	AFA***----------209
DREXEL	Austria	Pa.		CRLA15----------514
DRINKWATER	———	Mass.	Arms:-	CFA13----------322
DRINKWATER	———	Mass./R.I.	Arms:-*	CRLA13----------241

DRUIT	No family data		Arms:-*	CRLA11------opp.448
DRUNHELLER	———	Pa.		AF****---------223
DU BOIS	France	N.Y.		CRLA12----------424
DU BOIS	France	N.Y.	Arms:-*	CRLA14----------177
DU BOIS	France	N.Y.		CRLA18----------233
DU BOIS	France	N.Y.	Arms:-*	CRLA18------553,560
DU BOIS	France/Germany	N.Y.		CRLA19-----376,382
DU BOIS	France	N.Y.	Arms:-*	CRLA20-----------64
DU BOIS	France/Germany	N.Y.		CRLA20----------184
DU BOIS	France	N.Y.	Arms:-*	AFA***---------289
DUBOSE	France	S.C.		CFA3-------357,359
DU COLOMBIER, see: COLOMBIER				
DUDLEY	———	Conn.		CFA1------------39
DUDLEY	Eng.	Mass.	Arms:-*	CFA21----------212
DUDLEY	Eng.	Mass.		CRLA1----------391
DUDLEY	Eng.	Mass.		CRLA8----------540
DUDLEY	Eng.	Mass.		CRLA13---------271
DUDLEY	Eng.	Mass.	Arms:-	AF***-----------78
DUDLEY	Eng.	Mass.		AFA***---------114
DUDLEY	———	Mass.		ARSC------------66
DUDLEY	———	Mass.		MCS-------------44
DUGAN	Ireland	R.I./Pa.	Arms:-*	AFA***----------51
DUGANNE	———	———		PPA------------536
DUMONT	France	N.Y.		CFA7-----------233
DUMONT, see: DE MUN				
DUN	Scotland	Va. & Ohio		CFA10-----------72
DUNBAR	Scotland	Mass.		CFA10----------260
DUNBAR	Eng./Scotland		Arms:-*	AFA1-----------217
DUNBAR	Scotland	Mass.		CRLA19---------272
DUNCAN	Scotland	Va.	Arms:-	CFA17----------372
DUNCAN	———	Mass.		CRLA17----------23
DUNCAN	Scotland	R.I.	Arms:-*	PFU-------------88
DUNDAS	Scotland	Pa.		CRLA8----------143
DUNDAS	Scotland	Pa.		CRLA9----------330
DUNDAS	Scotland/Eng.			CRLA18---------283
DUNGAN	Ireland	R.I.		CRLA15---------291
DUNGAN	Ireland	R.I.		CRLA19----------15
DUNHAM	Eng.	Mass.		CFA9-----------226
DUNHAM	Eng.?	Mass.	Arms:-*	CRLA10---------325
DUNLOP	———	Va.		CRLA4-----------56
DUNN	———	Pa./Ohio	Arms:-*	CRLA17---------535
DUNSTANVILLE (de)	Eng.			CRLA5----------304
DUPEE	———	Mass.	Arms:-*	AF**-----------485
DU PONT	France	Del/Pa.	Arms:-*	CRLA1---------1,65
DU PONT=EVERETT		Royal descents		CRLA9----------328
DU PONT	France	Del.		CRLA9----------391
DU PONT	France	Del.		CRLA11-----137,139
DU PONT		Hoyt	Royal descents	CRLA11---------157
DU PONT=de NEMOURS	France	Del.		CRLA15---------246
DU PONT	France	Del.		CRLA15---------577
DUPUY	France	Va.		CRLA4----------412
DURAND	France	Vt.	Arms:-*	AF**-----------377
DURAND	France	Vt.	Arms:-*	AF**-----------503
DURANT	———	Mass.	Arms:-*	CFA1-----------150
DURANT	———	Mass.		CRLA11---------583
DURDEN	———	Va.		CRLA4----------420
DURFEE	Eng.	R.I.		CFA12----------105
DUSTIN	Eng.	Maine		CRLA13---------204
DUTTON	Eng.	Pa.		CRLA2----------228
DUTTON	Eng.			CRLA9----------171
DUTTON	Eng.		Arms:-*	CRLA11---------167
DUTTON	———	Mass.		CRLA11---------586
DUTTON	———	———	*(only)	TNEF--------opp.44
DUVAL	France	Md.		CRLA16----------41
DUVAL	Normandy	Md.	Arms:-*	AF*------------105
DUVAL(L)	———	Md.	Arms:-*	AFA***---------283
DUVALL	———	Md.	Arms:-	CFA3-----------307

DUVOLL	France	Md.		CRLA2-----------191
DUYCKINCK	———	N.Y.		CFA17------------94
DUYCKINCK	Holland	N.Y.		CFA20-----------320
DWIGHT	———	Mass.		CFA10-----------105
DWIGHT	———	Mass.		CRLA6-----------135
DWIGHT	Eng.	Mass.	Arms:-*	CRLA15-----------92
DWIGHT	Eng.	Mass.		HFA--------------92
DWIGHT	———	Mass./Conn.		PPA--------------48
DYCKMAN	Westphalia	N.Y.	Arms:-	CFA21-------------1
DYON	Eng.	———		CFA9------------340
DYRENFORTH	———	Ill.	Arms:-*	AF****-----------95

- E -

EAGER	———	Mass.	Arms:-*	CFA7------------210
EAGLESFIELD	No family data		Arms:-*	CRLA13------opp.488
EAMES	Eng.	Mass.	Arms:-*	CRLA15-----------83
EAMES	Eng.	Mass.		CRLA20-----------91
EARLE	Eng.	R.I.		CFA21-----------209
EARLE	Eng.	Va./S.C.	Arms:-*	CRLA11--288,301,306
EARLE	———	N.J.		CRLA15----------398
EARLE	Eng.	Md./N.Y./N.J.	Arms:-*	CRLA20-----------13
EARLE	Eng.?	Va.		PFU-------------398
EARLY (or) ERLEIGH	Eng.			CRLA1-----------191
EARP	Eng.	Pa.		CRLA2------------50
EARP	———	Pa.		CRLA9-----------489
EASTBURN	———	N.Y.		PPA-------------248
EASTERN EMPERORS	Basil I, ano. 867		Schull desc.	CRLA5-----------137
EASTMAN	Eng.	Conn.		CFA2------------117
EASTMAN	Eng.	Mass.		CFA7-------------49
EASTMAN	Eng.	Mass.	Arms:-*	CFA14-----------175
EASTMAN	Wales	Mass.	Arms:-*	CRLA3------------13
EASTMAN	Wales	Mass.	Arms:-	CRLA3-----------333
EASTMAN	Eng.	Mass.		CRLA17----------470
EASTMAN	Eng.	Mass.	Arms:-*	CRLA17----------647
EASTMAN	———	Vt.		PPA-------------528
EASTMEAD	Eng.	N.Y.		CRLA3-----------311
EASTON	Eng.	Mass.		CFA11-----------201
EASTON	Eng.	Mass./R.I.	Arms:-*	CRLA18----------526
EASTON	Eng.	Mass.	Arms:-*	AF***-----------211
EASTON	———	———	*(only)	TNEF-------btn.78-9
EATON	Eng.	Mass.		CFA1------------240
EATON	Eng.	Mass.		CFA3--------------6
EATON	Eng.	Mass.		CFA14-----------248
EATON	Eng.	Mass.	Arms:-	CFA21-----------51
EATON	———	Mass.	Arms:-*	CRLA12-----------32
EATON	Eng.	Mass.		CRLA13-----------60
EATON	———	Mass.	Arms:-*	CRLA15-----------27
EATON	Eng.	Mass./Conn.		CRLA19----------113
EBERLEIN	———	Ill.		AF***-----------258
ECGBERT, see: SAXON KINGS of England				
ECKEL	———	N.Y.		CFA23------------20
ECKEL	Germany	Pa.		CFA24-----------122
ECKLEY	———	N.Y./N.J.		CRLA16-----------27
ECKSTEIN	Europe	Va.	Arms:-*	CFA16-----------192
EDDOWES, see: KENRICK=EDDOWES				
EDDY	Eng.	Mass.		CRLA9-----------416
EDES	Eng.	Mass.		CFA3------------211
EDES	Eng.	Mass.		AF****----------140
EDGAR	Scotland	N.J.		CRLA6-----------121
EDGE	Eng.	Pa.		CRLA17----------275
EDGERLY	Eng.	N.H.	Arms:-	CFA10-----------349

EDINGS	———	S.C.		CFA25------------57
EDINGTON	Eng.	Va.	Arms:-	AF***-----------157
EDMUNDS	———	Mass./N.J.	Arms:-*	CRLA11----------556
EDSON	Eng.	Mass./Conn.		CFA9------------225
EDWARD I, King of Eng.		Hyde descent		CFA21-----------156
EDWARD I, King of Eng.				CFA25------------25
EDWARD I, King of Eng.		Dudley descent		CRLA1-----------409
EDWARD III, King of Eng.		Jones=Paul=Knight desc. *(only)		CRLA2---------540
EDWARDS	———	Conn.		CFA7------------331
EDWARDS	Wales	Mass.		CFA15-----------347
EDWARDS	———	Ga.		CRLA7----------394
EDWARDS	———	Conn.		CRLA7----------529
EDWARDS	———	Mass.		CRLA8-----------11
EDWARDS	———	N.J.	Arms:-*	CRLA18----------574
EDWARDS	Eng.	N.Y./Va.		AF*------------107
EELLS	Eng.	Mass.		CRLA15----------541
EGBERT, see: ECGBERT				
EICHELBERGER	Holland	Pa./Md.		CFA16-----------110
ELDER	———	Md.		CFA5-------------92
ELDER	Eng.	Md.		CRLA19----------313
ELDER	Scotland/Ireland Pa.		Arms:-*	AFA***----------287
ELDRED	Eng.?	Mass.	Arms:-*	CFA17-----------282
ELFRETH	———	Pa.		CRLA15----------435
ELIOT	Eng.	Mass.		CFA13-----------355
ELIOT	Eng.	Mass.	Arms:-	CFA17-----------126
ELIOT	Eng.	Mass.		CRLA20-----------99
ELKINGTON	———	N.J.		MCS-------------14
ELKINS	Eng.	N.H./Mass.	Arms:-	CFA2-------------14
ELLEGOOD	Eng.	Del.		CRLA11----------553
ELLERY, William	———	R.I.		SDI---------121,124
ELLICOTT	Eng.	Mass.		CFA9------------121
ELLICOTT	Eng.	Pa.		CRLA15----------502
ELLINGWOOD	Eng.	Mass.	Arms:-*	CRLA8-----------59
ELLIOT=ELIOT	Eng.	Mass.	Arms:-*	CFA16-----------229
ELLIOT	———	Mass.	Arms:-*	CRLA20-----------81
ELLIOTT	———	Maine/N.H.		CFA3-------------87
ELLIOTT	Eng.	Pa.	Arms:-*	CRLA5-----------510
ELLIOTT	———	La./Ky.		CRLA6-----------533
ELLIOTT	———	Mass. from John Alden		CRLA6-----------558
ELLIS	———	Mass.		CFA15------------49
ELLIS	———	Mass.		CRLA1-----------229
ELLIS	———	Ohio/Md.		CRLA8-----------207
ELLIS	———	Va./Miss.		CRLA14----------112
ELLIS	Eng.	Pa.		CRLA17-----------41
ELLIS	———	Va.		CRLA11----------134
ELLSWORTH	Eng.	Conn.		CFA8------------122
ELLSWORTH	Holland	N.Y.		CFA10-----------243
ELLSWORTH	Eng.	Mass.	Arms:-*	CRLA13------------1
ELLSWORTH	———	N.Y./Conn.		PPA-------------579
ELMER	Eng.	Mass.		CFA7------------264
ELMER	Eng.	Mass.		CRLA17----------597
ELMER	Eng.	Mass.	Arms:-*	CRLA19----------319
ELMER	Eng.	Conn.	Arms:-*	AFA***----------257
ELSWORTH	Eng.	N.Y.	Arms:-*	CRLA20-----------14
ELTINGE	Holland	N.Y.		CRLA16-----------96
ELTONHEAD	Eng.			CRLA1-----------254
ELWELL	———	Mass.	Arms:-*	CRLA5-----------11
ELY	Eng.	Mass.	Arms:-*	CFA1-------------39
ELY	Eng.	Mass.		CFA26-----------146
ELY	Eng.	N.J.		CRLA8-----------299
ELY	Eng.	Mass./Conn.		CRLA15----------424
ELY	Eng.	Mass./Conn.	Arms:-*	AFA***----------261
ELY	Eng.	Conn.	Arms:-*	AFA***----------401
EMERSON	Eng.	Mass.	Arms:-	CFA4------------285
EMERSON	Eng.	Mass.	Arms:-*	CFA5------------180
EMERSON	Eng.	Mass.		CFA9------------273
EMERSON	Eng.	Mass.		CRLA11----------149

EMERSON	Eng.	Mass.	Arms:-*	CRLA15----------19
EMERSON	Eng.	Mass.		CRLA20----------130
EMERSON	Eng.	Mass.	Arms:-*	PBAF------------139
EMERSON	———	Mass.		PPA-------------298
EMERY	Eng.	Mass.		CFA3------------136
EMERY	Eng.	Mass.		CFA7------------155
EMERY	Eng.	Maine		CFA16-----------233
EMERY=EMORY	Eng.	Mass.		CFA19-----------52
EMERY	Eng.	Mass.		CFA19-----------267
EMERY	Eng.	Mass.	Arms:-*	CFA27-----13cht.,56
EMERY	Eng.	Mass./Maine		ACF-------------106
EMERY	Eng.	Mass.	Arms:-*	CRLA16----------11
EMLEN	Eng.	Pa.		CFA6------------255
EMLEN	Eng.	Pa.	Arms:-*	CRLA5-----------506
EMLEN	Eng.	Pa.		CRLA15----------461
EMLEN	Eng.	Pa.	Arms:-*	CRLA18----------282
EMMONS	———	———		CRLA18----------215
EMMONS	———	Mass./Vt.		CRLA20----------179
ENGLAND, Kings of		Cornell descent		CRLA11----------252
ENGLAND	———	Pa.	Arms:-*	CRLA13----------122
ENGLISH	———	Mass.		CFA26-----------123
ENGLISH	Eng.	Pa.	*(only)	CRLA2-----------424
ENGLISH	———	Pa.		CRLA19----------341
ENGLISH	———	Pa./Va.		PPA-------------576
ENNALS	———	Va./Md.		CRLA3-----------287
ENNALLS	———	Va./Md.		CFA16-----------91
ENNIS	———	Del./Pa.		CRLA19----------351
ENSIGN	———	Mass.		CFA20-----------263
ENO	Europe	Conn.		CRLA13----------35
ENO	Europe/Eng.	Conn.		PFU-------------299
EPES	———	Va.		CRLA4-----------401
EPPES	———	Va.		CRLA4-----------108
ERSKINE	———	Mass./Maine		CFA7------------341
ERSKINE	Eng./Ireland	Pa.	Arms:-*	AF*-------------150
ERSKINE	Scotland	Md.	Arms:-*	AFA***----------267
ERWIN	Ireland	Pa.		CRLA3-----------315
ESLEECK	———	N.Y./R.I.		CRLA10----------288
ESSICK (Essig)	Germany	Pa.		CRLA17----------714
ESTABROOK	———	Mass.		TNEF------------153
ESTE	Eng.	Mass.		CFA15-----------193
ESTE	Eng.	Mass.		CRLA15----------437
ESTE, House of		Bray descent		CRLA17----------142
ESTE, House of	Italy		Arms:-*	CRLA18----------445
ESTERBROOK	———	Mass.		CFA19-----------292
ESTES	Eng.	N.H.		CFA2------------177
ESTES	Eng.	Mass.		CRLA15----------266
ESTES	Eng.	Mass.		CRLA16----------64
EU, Counts of	France/Eng.		Arms:-*	CRLA5-----------305
EU, Counts of	Eng.			CRLA7-----------204
EVANS	Wales	Pa.		CRLA15----------500
EVANS	Eng.	S.C.	Arms:-*	CRLA16----------1
EVANS	———	Pa.		CRLA19----------340
EVANS	———	Mass.		CRLA20----------210
EVANS	———	Pa.		AFA***----------238
EVANS	Eng.	Mass./N.H.		PFU-------------65
EVERARD	Eng.	N.J.		CFA7------------237
EVERARD	———	N.C.		MCS-------------53
EVERETT	Eng.	Mass.		CFA8------------379
EVERETT	Eng.	Mass.		CRLA9-----------312
EVERETT	———	Mass.		PPA-------------143
EVERETT	———	Mass.		PPA-------------201
EVERITT	———	N.Y.?	Arms:-*	CRLA20--------18,24
EVERMAN	Germany	Pa.		PFU-------------156
EVERSLEY	———	Conn.		CRLA13----------172
EVERTSON	Holland	N.Y.	Arms:-*	CFA13-----------339
EVES	Eng.	N.J.		CFA15-----------223
EVES	Eng.?	N.J.	Arms:-*	CRLA5-----------19

EWERS	———	Mass.		CRLA12-----------34
EWING	Eng./Canada	Mich.		CFA10-----------186
EWING	Scotland/Ireland	Md.	Arms:-*	CFA23-----------134
EWING		Pa./N.Y.	Arms:-*	CRLA12-----------21
EWING	Ireland	N.Y./N.J.		HFA-------------308
EYRE	Eng.	Pa.	Arms:-*	CRLA9-----------293
EYRES, see: AYRES				

- F -

FAHNESTOCK	Prussia	N.Y.C.	Arms:-	CFA3------------286
FAIRBANKS	Eng.	Mass.	Arms:-*	CRLA1-----------220
FAIRBANKS	Eng.	Mass.		CFA11-----------218
FAIRBANKS	Eng.	Mass.	Arms:-	ACF-------------53
FAIRBANKS	Eng.	Mass.		CRLA9-----------424
FAIRBANKS	Eng.	Mass.	Arms:-*	CRLA15-----------90
FAIRFAX	Eng.	Va.		CRLA8-----------172
FAIRFAX	———	Md.	Arms:-	AF***-----------442
FAIRFAX	———	Va.		MCS-------------62
FAIRFIELD	———	Mass.		PPA-------------305
FANEUIL	France	Mass./N.Y.		CRLA20-----------214
FANNING	Ireland	Conn.		CFA26-----------144
FANNING	———	———	Arms:-*	CRLA20------opp.233
FANNING	Ireland	Conn.	Arms:-*	AF*-------------119
FANSHAWE	Eng.	———	Arms:-	CFA20-----------137
FARMINGTON (City)		Conn.	Regional background	CRLA19----------248
FARNAM	———	Mass.		CFA13-----------166
FARNHAM	———	Mass.		CFA26-----------145
FARNHAM	Eng.	Mass.	Arms:-*	CFA27------1,38cht.
FARNSWORTH	Eng.	Mass.		CFA8------------258
FARNSWORTH	Eng.	Mass.		CRLA11----------154
FARNUM	Wales	Mass.		CRLA17----------586
FARNUM	Eng.	Mass.	Arms:-*	AF***-----------23
FARRAR	———	Mass.		CFA19-----------75
FARRAR	Eng.?	Mass.		CRLA12-----------57
FARRINGTON	Eng.	Mass.		CFA7------------142
FARRINGTON	Eng.	Mass.	Arms:-*	TNEF------------60
FARROW	Eng.	Mass.	Arms:-*	CRLA20----------331
FARWELL	Eng.	Mass.	Arms:-*	CRLA15-----------32
FARWELL, see: WELBY=FARWELL				
FASSETT	———	Mass.		CRLA15----------476
FASTON, see: PILGRIMS				
FATIO	Switzerland	Fla.		CRLA16----------227
FATIO	Europe	Fla.	Arms:-*	AFA***----------353
FAUST	Germany?	Pa.		CRLA13----------423
FAY	Eng.	Mass.		CFA10-----------275
FAY	Eng.	Mass.		CFA12-----------53
FAY	———	N.Y.		PPA-------------381
FAYSSOUX	———	S.C.		CFA6------------280
FEAKE	Eng.	Mass.		CFA16-----------26
FEAKE	Eng.	Mass.	Arms:-*	CRLA17----------316
FEARING	Eng.	Mass.		CFA27-----------59
FEARING	Eng.	Mass.		CRLA17----------449
FEARNE	Eng.	Pa./N.J.		CRLA5-----------40
FELCH	Wales?	Mass.		CFA6------------193
FELCH	Wales	Mass.		CFA12-----------371
FELL	Eng.	Pa.	Arms:-*	CRLA15----------570
FELLOWES	Eng.	Mass.		CFA8------------295
FELLOWS	Eng.	Mass.	Arms:-*	AF**------------348
FELTON	Germany	Pa.	Arms:-*	CRLA11----------438
FELTON (de)	Eng.		Bray descent	CRLA17----------152
FELTON (de)	Eng.			CRLA17----------184

FELTUS	Ireland	N.Y.C.		CFA24-----------104
FENLEY (Finley)	Scotland	Md.	Arms:-*	CRLA15----------326
FENNER	Eng.	Conn.		CFA5------------47
FENNER	———	Conn.	Arms:-*	CFA5------------219
FENNER	———	———	*(only)	TNEF-------btn.78-9
FENNER, see: PILGRIMS				
FENTON	———	N.J.		CRLA9-----------156
FENTON	———	Conn./N.Y.		AF**------------85
FENWICK	———	D.C.		CRLA11----------205
FENWICK	———	N.J.		MCS-------------55
FERE	France			CRLA1-----------49
FERGUESON	———	N.C.		CRLA4-----------385
FERGUSON	———	S.C.		CRLA17----------609
FERNALD	Eng.	Maine		CFA10-----------367
FERNALD	———	Maine		AF**------------170
FERRAND	Eng.	Conn.	Arms:-*	CFA10-----------180
FERRERS (de)	Eng.		Arms:-*	CRLA5-----------307
FERRERS (de)	Eng.			CRLA11----------86
FERRERS	Eng.	Cooley=Twining desc.		CRLA18----------150
FERRERS	Eng.		Arms:-*	CRLA10-----btn.78-9
FERRIERES (de)	Eng.			CRLA5-----------311
FERRIN	Eng.?	Mass.		CFA19-----------271
FERRIS	Eng.	Mass.		CFA14-----------17
FERRIS	Eng.	Mass.		CFA14-----------203
FERRIS	———	Va.	Arms:-	CRLA3-----------371
FERRIS	Eng.	Conn.	Arms:-	CRLA7-----------42
FERRIS	Eng.	Va.	Arms:-*	CRLA10----------43
FESSENDEN	———	Mass.		CFA7------------360
FESSENDEN	Eng.	Mass.		CFA24-----------43
FFOULKE (Foulke)	———	Pa.		PFU-------------386
FFYSKE (Fiske)	Eng.	Mass.	Arms:-*	AFA***----------15
FFYSKE	Eng.		Arms:-*	AFA***----------103
FFYSKE, see: FISKE				
FIELD	Eng.	Mass.		CFA2------------322
FIELD	Eng.	R.I.	Arms:-	CFA12-----------147
FIELD	Eng.	R.I./L.I.,N.Y.	Arms:-*	CFA19-----------171
FIELD	Eng.	R.I./N.Y.	Arms:-	CFA25-----------152
FIELD	Eng.	R.I.		ACF-------------86
FIELD	Holland	Pa.		CRLA13----------281
FIELD	Eng.	N.Y.		PFU-------------239
FIELD	Eng.	La.		PPA-------------494
FIELDS	———	Mass.		CFA19-----------286
FIELDS	———	N.H./Mass.		PPA-------------573
FIENNES (de)	Eng.			CRLA2-----------482
FIENNES (de)	Eng.		Arms:-*	CRLA5-----------311
FIENNES (de)	Eng.			CRLA15----------119
FIENNES	———	Mass.		MCS-------------48
FILES	———	Va.		CFA3------------202
FILES	———	Va.	Arms:-*	CFA7------------209
FILLEY	Eng.	Mass.		CRLA20----------253
FILLEY	Eng.	Mass.	Arms:-	AF**------------261
FILSON	———	Pa.		CRLA20----------115
FILTER	———	N.J./Pa.		CRLA15----------541
FINCH	Eng.	Mass./Conn.		CRLA20----------186
FINCHAM (de)	Eng.		Arms:-*	CRLA20----------397
FINLEY	Scotland/Ireland Pa.		Arms:-*	CFA23-----------138
FINLEY, see: FENLEY				
FINNEY	Eng.	Mass.	Arms:-*	CRLA18----------37
FISH	Eng.	Mass.	Arms:-	CFA5------------261
FISH	Eng.	Mass.		CFA11-----------148
FISH	Eng.	Mass.		CFA15-----------47
FISH	Eng.	Mass.		CFA19-----------90
FISH	Eng.	N.Y.	Arms:-*	CFA25-----------111
FISH	———	Mass.	Arms:-*	CRLA7-----------427
FISH	Eng.	R.I.		CRLA16----------68
FISH	Eng.	Mass./N.Y.	Arms:-*	CRLA18----------550
FISH	———	Mass./L.I.,N.Y.		PFU-------------384

FISH	———	———	*(only)	TNEF--------opp.30
FISH	Eng.	Mass.	Arms:-*	AFA3-----------137
FISHER	Eng.	Mass.	Arms:-*	CFA1-----------145
FISHER	Eng.	Mass.		CFA10----------104
FISHER	Eng.	Mass.		CFA13----------324
FISHER	———	Conn./N.Y.		CFA18----------10
FISHER	Eng.	Mass.		CRLA1----------230
FISHER	Eng.?	Del.	Arms:-*	CRLA14----------61
FISHER	Eng.	Mass.	Arms:-*	CRLA15----------54
FISHER	Eng.?	Pa.	Arms:-*	CRLA18----------277
FISHER	Germany	N.J.	Arms:-*	AF***-----------138
FISHER	Eng.	Mass.		AFA***----------104
FISK	Eng.	Mass.	Arms:-*	CRLA20----------323
FISKE	Eng.	Mass.	Arms:-*	CRLA15----------70
FISKE, see: FFYSKE				
FITCH	———	Mass.		CFA14----------322
FITCH	Eng.	Conn.	Arms:-	CFA15----------101
FITCH	Eng.	Conn.	Arms:-*	CFA17----------267
FITCH	Eng.	Conn.	Arms:-*	CFA22---------17,19
FITCH	Eng.	Conn.		ACF-------------87
FITCH	Eng.	Conn.		CRLA13----------321
FITCH	Eng.	Conn.	Arms:-*	CRLA15----------389
FITCH	———	Conn.		AFA***----------330
FITLER	Germany	Pa.	Arms:-*	CRLA8-----------237
FITTON	Eng.			CRLA9-----------167
FITZ ALAN	Eng.		Earls of ARUNDEL(see:)	CRLA2-----------568
FITZ ALAN	Eng.		Bray desc. Arms:-*	CRLA17----------149
FITZGERALD	Ireland	N.Y.		CFA26----------102
FITZ GERALD	Eng./Ireland			CRLA17----------188
FITZGERALD	Ireland	Mass./N.Y.	Arms:-*	PFU-------------223
FITZ GILBERT, see: CLARE (de)				
FITZHUGH	Eng.	Va.		CRLA4-----------271
FITZHUGH	Eng.	Va.	Arms:-*	CRLA8-----------331
FITZHUGH	Eng.	Va.	Arms:-*	PFU-------------444
FITZ JOHN	Eng.			CRLA5-----------313
FITZ-JOHN	Eng.		Arms:-*	CRLA10-----btn.78-9
FITZ MAURICE	Eng.			CRLA2-----------478
FITZ MAURICE	Eng.		Arms:-*	CRLA5-----------314
FITZ MAURICE	Eng.			CRLA11----------89
FITZ MAURICE	Eng.			CRLA11----------430
FITZMAURICE	No family data		Arms:-*	CRLA15------opp.172
FITZ PIERS	Eng.		Arms:-*	CRLA5-----------316
FITZ-RANDOLPH	Eng.	Mass./N.J.		CRLA6-----------130
FITZ RANDOLPH	Eng.	Mass.	Arms:-*	AFA***-----------45
FITZRANDOLPH	———	N.J.		MCS-------------127
FITZ ROBERT	Eng.		Dudley descent	CRLA1-----------411
FITZ ROBERT	Eng.			CRLA2-----------481
FITZ ROBERT	Eng.		Arms:-*	CRLA5-----------317
FITZ ROBERT	———		Titus descent	CRLA18----------508
FITZ WALTER	Eng.		Titus descent	CRLA18----------509
FLAGG	Eng.	Mass.		CRLA20----------109
FLAGG	Eng.	Mass.		AF**--567 PFU--248
FLAGLER	Eng.	N.Y.		CFA5-----------153
FLAGLER	Germany?	N.Y.		CRLA19----------17
FLAHAVAN	Ireland	Pa.		CFA18----------171
FLANAGAN	Ireland	N.Y.	Arms:-	CFA4-----------176
FLANDERS, Ancient Counts of				CRLA1-----------354
FLANDERS, Counts of		Baldwin I -879 *(only)		CRLA2-----------37
FLANDERS, Counts of		Baldwin I	Arms:-*	CRLA2-----------175
FLANDERS, Counts of		Baldwin I		CRLA2-----------366
FLANDERS, Counts of		Baldwin I -879		CRLA2-----------519
FLANDERS, Counts of		Baldwin I	Arms:-*	CRLA5-----------318
FLANDERS, Ancient Counts of				CRLA8-----------101
FLANDERS, Ancient Counts of		Hinton descent	Arms:-*	CRLA8-----------484
FLANDERS, Ancient Counts of			Arms:-*	CRLA11----------168
FLANDERS, Ancient Counts of				CRLA11----------429
FLANDERS, Ancient Counts of		Baldwin I	Arms:-*	CRLA15----------137

FLANDERS, Ancient Counts of		Cooley=Twining desc.		CRLA18-----------154
FLANDERS, Ancient Counts of		Baldwin I -879		CRLA20-----------267
FLANDERS, Ancient Counts of		Baldwin I -879		CRLA20-----------399
FLEETE	Eng.	Md./Va.		CRLA1-----------266
FLEMING	Eng.	Va.		CRLA4-----------157
FLENNIKEN	———	Pa.		CRLA6-----------206
FLETCHER	Eng.	Mass.	Arms:-	CFA3-----------209
FLETCHER	Eng.	Mass.		CFA7-----------136
FLETCHER	Eng.	Mass.		CFA8-----------105
FLETCHER	Eng.	Mass.		CFA8-----------259
FLETCHER	Eng.	Mass.		CFA12-----------88
FLETCHER	Eng.	Mass.		CRLA1-----------146
FLETCHER	Eng.	Pa.		CRLA13-----------351
FLETCHER	Eng.	Mass.	Arms:-*	AF*-----------59
FLINN	Ireland/Canada Ill.			CRLA19-----------133
FLINN	Ireland	Pa.		CRLA19-----------361
FLINT	———	Mass.		CFA19-----------76
FLINT	Wales?	Mass.		PFU-----------439
FLINT	———	Mass.		PPA-----------354
FLINTHAM	———	———	Arms:-*	TNEF-----------216
FLOWER	Eng.	Conn.	Arms:-*	AFA2-----------129
FLOYD	Wales	N.Y.		CFA11-----------141
FLOYD	———	Mass.		PFU-----------423
FLOYD, William	Wales	N.Y.		SDI---------135,143
FOARD	———	Md.		CRLA10-----------332
FORBES	———	Mass.		CFA10-----------259
FOCKEN	———	———	Arms:-*	CRLA20-----btn.8-11
FOLGER	Eng.	Mass.		CRLA12-----------260
FOLGER	Eng.	Mass.	Arms:-*	CRLA18-----------345
FOLGER	Eng.	Mass.	Arms:-*	TNEF-----------35
FOLIOT	———	Va.		MCS-----------57
FOLLANSBEE	———	N.H./Mass.		CRLA14-----------170
FOLLETT	———	Mass.	Arms:-*	CFA9-----------182
FOLLETT	Eng.?	Mass.		CFA17-----------240
FOLLETT	Eng.?	Mass.	Arms:-	CFA24-----------57
FOLLETT	Eng.	Mass.		CRLA19-----------27
FOLSOM	Eng.	Mass.		CFA6-----------160
FOLSOM	Eng.	Mass.		CFA12-----------64
FONES	Eng.		Arms:-*	CFA18-----------35
FONES	No family data		Arms:-*	CRLA17------opp.344
FOOTE	Eng.	Conn.		CFA1-----------264
FOOTE	Eng.	Mass./Conn.	Arms:-*	CFA5-----------214
FOOTE	Eng.	Mass.		CFA12-----------347
FOOTE	———	N.H./Mass.		CFA16-----------336
FOOTE	Eng.	Mass./Conn.	Arms:-*	CRLA7-----------596
FOOTE	Eng.	Mass./Conn.		CRLA19-----------70
FOOTE	Eng.	Conn.	Arms:-	AF*-----------28
FOOTE	Eng.	Mass./Conn.	Arms:-*	AFA***-----------143
FOOTE	Eng.	Mass.	Arms:-*	TNEF-----------186
FORBES	———	Mass.	Arms:-*	CRLA15-----------84
FORCE	———	N.J./Ohio		CRLA6-----------213
FORD	———	Conn./Mass.		CFA15-----------346
FORD	Eng.	Mass.	Arms:-	CFA22-----------160
FORD	Eng.?	Mass./Conn.	Arms:-*	CRLA3-----------28
FORD	———	Ky./Pa.		CRLA6-----------42
FORD	———	Mass.	Arms:-*	CRLA15-----------44
FORD	Eng.	Mass.	Arms:-	AF*-----------42
FORDE	Ireland	Md./Pa.	Arms:-*	AFA***------127,130
FOREZ, Counts of	France			CRLA5-----------321
FORISTALL	———	Mass.	Arms:-	AF**-----------389
FORISTALL	———	Mass.	Arms:-	AF**-----------515
FORMAN	Eng.	L.I.,N.Y.	Arms:-*	CFA1-----------13
FORNEY	———	Pa.	Arms:-*	CRLA1-----------40
FOSDICK	———	Mass.		CFA9-----------117
FOSDICK	Eng.	Mass.		CRLA17-----------242
FOSS	———	Mass./N.H.	Arms:-	CFA11-----------269
FOSTER	Eng.	Mass.	Arms:-*	CFA2-----------196

FOSTER	Eng.	Mass.		CFA7------------81
FOSTER (Forster)	Eng.	Error, see: <u>A Pedigree of</u>		CFA8------------268

<u>the Forsters and Fosters of the North of</u>
<u>England</u> (1871), by Joseph Foster, pp. 9-11
& Chart, CS439.F6 1871 (DLC); <u>The Geneal-</u>
<u>ogist</u>, vol. 7, p. 181, foot-notes A - D,
CS410.G5 1890-1 ; and <u>An Historical and</u>
<u>Genealogical Chart of Robert Brooke of</u>
<u>England</u>, CS71.B87 1927a Folio & Rare Book
Div. DLC, as well as at the Maryland Hist-
orical Society, 1928 (Original).

FOSTER	Eng.	Mass.		CFA11-----------341
FOSTER	Eng.	Mass.		CFA12-----------85
FOSTER	———	Conn		CFA23-----------115
FOSTER	Eng.	Mass.		CRLA1----------205
FOSTER	———	R.I./N.J.		CRLA2-----------98
FOSTER	———	N.J.	Arms:-*	CRLA5----------497
FOSTER	Eng.	Mass.		CRLA7----------434
FOSTER	———	Mass.		CRLA7----------506
FOSTER	Eng.	Mass.	Arms:-*	CRLA10---------155
FOSTER	Eng.	Va.		CRLA10---------259
FOSTER	———	N.J.		CRLA11---------247
FOSTER	———	Mass.		CRLA11---------589
FOSTER	Eng.	Mass.	Arms:-*	CRLA12---------351
FOSTER	———	Maine		CRLA12---------411
FOSTER	Ireland	Pa.		CRLA19---------279
FOSTER	Eng.	Mass.	Arms:-*	AF**------------529
FOSTER (Forster)	Eng.	Mass.	Arms:-	AF***-----------344
FOSTER	Eng.	Mass.	Arms:-*	PBAF---------55,164
FOULKE	Eng.	Va./Md.	Arms:-	CFA20----------151
FOULKE	Eng.	N.J.	Arms:-*	CRLA18---------569
FOULKE, see: FFOULKE				
FOULKROD	Germany	Pa.		CRLA15---------272
FOUNTLEROY	Eng.	Va.		CRLA8----------549
FOWKE	Eng.	Va./Md.	Arms:-	CFA17----------366
FOWKE	Eng.	Va./Md.		CRLA1----------273
FOWKE	Eng.	Va.	Arms:-	CRLA3----------119
FOWLE	———	Mass.		CFA7------------404
FOWLE	———	Mass.		CRLA19---------385
FOWLE	———	N.Y.?	Arms:-*	CRLA20--------1,55
FOWLER	Eng.	Mass.		CFA7------------82
FOWLER	Eng.	Conn.	Arms:-*	CRLA6----------418
FOWLER	———	Mass./Conn.	Arms:-*	CRLA7----------576
FOWLER	———	Md.	Arms:-*	CRLA15---------569
FOWLER	Eng.	Mass.	Arms:-*	CRLA17---------483
FOWLKES	———	Va.	Arms:-	AF***-----------312
FOWNES	———	Pa.	Arms:-*	CRLA11----------10
FOX	———	Va.		CRLA4-----------71
FOX	———	Mass.		CRLA7----------400
FOX	———	N.J.		CRLA9----------156
FOX	———	Mass.		CRLA12----------35
FOX	———	Pa.		CRLA19---------219
FOX	———	Maine	Arms:-*	AF****----------246
FOX	Ireland	Wisc.		PFU------------287
FOX	Eng.	Mass./Conn.		PFU------------300
FOXWELL	———	Mass.		CFA19----------291
FRAILEY	Switzerland	Pa.		CRLA17---------229
FRANCIS	Eng.	Md.		CFA12-----------96
FRANCIS	No family data		Arms:-*	CRLA14-------opp.29
FRANCIS	Eng.?	Conn.		CRLA19---------415
FRANCIS	Eng.	Mass.	Arms:-	AF**------------199
FRANKISH MONARCHY		Wales descent		CRLA13----------83
FRANKLIN, Benjamin	———	Mass./Pa.		SDI--------159,160
FRANKLIN	———	———	*(only)	TNEF--------opp.35
FRARY	———	Mass.		CFA9------------195
FRAZIER	Scotland	Mass.	Arms:-*	CFA12----------225
FRAZIER	Scotland	Mass.	Arms:-*	CRLA9----1,22,45,80

FREAR	France	N.Y.	Arms:-*	CRLA12----------404
FREDERICK I (called Barbarossa)	Germany			CRLA2-----------465
FREDERICK I (called Barbarossa)	Germany	Blackiston descent		CRLA11----------408
FREEBORN	Eng.	Mass./R.I.		CRLA14----------73
FREEBORN	Eng.	R.I.		CRLA17----------439
FREELAND	Scotland/Ireland	Mass.		CFA2-----------215
FREELAND	Scotland	Mass.		CFA7------------22
FREEMAN	————	Mass.		CFA6------------360
FREEMAN	Eng.	Mass.		CFA7-----------343
FREEMAN	Eng.	N.Y./Mich.		CRLA6-----------493
FREEMAN	————	Va.	Arms:-*	AFA***----------254
FREEMAN	Eng.	Va.	Arms:-*	AFA***----------255
FREEMAN	————	————	*(only)	TNEF-------btn.70-1
FREEZE		Mass.		CRLA7-----------375
FREGE	Sweden/Ger.	————		CFA13-----------268
FRELINGHUYSEN	Holland	N.Y./N.J.		HFA-------------171
FRENCH	Eng.	Mass.		CFA10----------211
FRENCH	Eng.	N.Y.		CFA11-----------28
FRENCH	Eng.	Mass.		CFA19----------281
FRENCH	————	Mass.	Arms:-	CFA24-----------147
FRENCH	————	Mass.		ACF-------------82
FRENCH	————	Md.	Arms:-*	CRLA1-----------497
FRENCH	————	N.J.		CRLA3-----------211
FRENCH	Eng.	Mass.		CRLA6-----------219
FRENCH	Eng.	N.J.		CRLA8-----------349
FRENCH	Eng.	Mass.		CRLA11----------226
FRENCH	Eng.	N.J.		CRLA11----------531
FRENCH	Eng.	Mass.		CRLA11----------588
FRENCH	————	Mass.	Arms:-*	CRLA12-----------55
FRENCH	Eng.	Mass.		CRLA13-----------24
FRENCH	Eng.	Mass.	Arms:-*	CRLA14----------167
FRENCH	————	Mass.	Arms:-*	CRLA15-----------77
FRENCH	————	Pa.	Arms:-*	CRLA17----------321
FRENCH	Eng.	Mass.	Arms:-*	CRLA19------------9
FRENCH	————	Mass.		PFU-------------338
FRENEAU	————	N.Y.		PPA-------------31
FRINK	————	Mass./Conn.		CFA19----------235
FRISBIE	————	Mass.		PPA-------------96
FRISBY	————	Md.		CRLA17----------419
FRITZ	Germany	Pa.	Arms:-*	CRLA13----------296
FRIZELL		Ohio/Mo.		CRLA3-----------197
FRIZZELL	Eng.	Mass.	Arms:-	AF**------------559
FROST	Eng.	Maine		CFA7-----------148
FROST	————	Maine		CFA11----------175
FROST	————	L.I.,N.Y.		CFA16----------137
FROST	Eng.	Mass.		CRLA4-----------362
FROST	Eng.	Mass.		CRLA11----------586
FROST	————	Conn.		CRLA17-----------20
FROST	Eng.	Mass./Conn.	Arms:-*	CRLA20-----------33
FROST	Eng.	Mass.	Arms:-*	CRLA20-----------93
FROST	Eng.	Mass.	Arms:-*	AFA1-----------177
FROTHINGHAM	————	Mass.		PPA-------------165
FRYE	Eng.	Mass.		CFA14-----------39
FRYE	Eng.	Mass.	Arms:-*	CFA27-----13cht.,60
FRYE	————	Mass.	Arms:-*	CRLA15-----------71
FRYER	Eng.?	Mass.		CFA3------------88
FRYER	No family data		Arms:-*	CRLA18------opp.352
FULK I, see: ANJOU, Counts of				
FULLER	Eng.	Mass.		CFA7-----------144
FULLER	Eng.	Mass.		CFA7-----------407
FULLER	Wales?	Mass.	Arms:-*	CFA8------------80
FULLER	Eng.	Mass.		CFA9-----------272
FULLER	Eng.	Mass.		CFA18----------142
FULLER	Eng.	Mass.		CFA20----------264
FULLER	Eng.	Mass.		CFA23-----------58
FULLER	Eng.	Mass.		CFA23----------154
FULLER	Eng.	Mass.		CRLA11----------510

FULLER	Eng.	Mass.	Arms:-*	CRLA17----------513
FULLER	————	Mass.		CRLA19---------384
FULLER	Eng.	Mass.		AF****----------141
FULLER	————	Mass.		PFU------------458
FULLER	————	Mass.		TNEF------------116
FULTON	Ireland	Pa.	Arms:-*	CRLA8----------279
FULWOOD	Eng.		Arms:-*	CRLA7----------143
FUNK	————	Pa.		CRLA15---------399
FURMAN	————	L.I.,N.Y.		CRLA8----------374
FUST	Eng.		Arms:-	AF***----------333

- G -

GAEL (de)	Eng.			CRLA5----------323
GAEL (de)	Eng.			CRLA7----------238
GAGE	————	Mass.		CFA24----------130
GAGE	————	Mass.	Arms:-*	CRLA3-----------21
GAGE	Eng.	Mass.		CRLA6----------383
GAGE	Eng.	Mass.	Arms:-*	CRLA20---------343
GAGER	Eng.	Mass.		CFA19-----------90
GAGER	Eng.	Mass.		CRLA17---------519
GAILLARD	France	S.C.	Arms:-	CFA3-----------353
GAINER	————	N.C.	Arms:-*	CRLA9----------261
GAINES	Wales?	Va.	Arms:-	AF***-----------94
GAITHER	————	Va./Md.		CFA5------------87
GAITHER	Eng.	Va./Md.		CFA16-----------85
GAITHER	————	Va.		CRLA8----------308
GAITHER	————	Va./Md.	Arms:-*	CRLA11-----------1
GAITHER	Eng.	Va.		CRLA16----------33
GALE	Wales?	Mass.		CFA1-----------206
GALE	————	Mass.	Arms:-*	CRLA8-----------54
GALIHER	————	Pa.	Arms:-	AF***----------255
GALLAGHER	Ireland	Pa./Ohio		PPA------------409
GALLATIN	Switzerland	Mass./Va./Pa.		CFA12----------287
GALLOP	Eng.	Mass.		CFA7------------48
GALLOP	Eng.	Mass.		CFA14-----------39
GALLOWAY, Earls of	Eng.	Fergus		CRLA1----------370
GALLUP	Eng.	Mass.	Arms:-*	CRLA12---------365
GALLUP	Eng.	Mass.	Arms:-*	CRLA18----------47
GALPIN	Eng.	Pa.	Arms:-*	CRLA1----------138
GALPIN	Eng.	Pa.		CRLA8----------199
GALPIN	Eng.	Pa.	Arms:-*	CRLA11---------216
GALPIN	Eng.	Del./Pa.		CRLA15---------236
GAMAGE	————	Mass.		PFU------------305
GAMBRILL	Eng.?	Md.		CFA16-----------97
GANNETT	Eng.	Mass.		CFA3------------36
GARDINER	Scotland/Canada	N.Y.		CFA10----------403
GARDINER	Eng.	Mass./Conn.	Arms:-*	CFA4-----------213
GARDINER	————	Md.	Arms:-*	CRLA2-----------62
GARDNER	Eng.?	Mass.		CFA1-----------179
GARDNER	————	Mass.	Arms:-	CFA4------------11
GARDNER	Eng.	Mass.		CFA5------------96
GARDNER	Eng.	Mass.		CFA9------------32
GARDNER	Eng.	Mass.		CFA17----------135
GARDNER	Eng.?	Mass.		CFA20-----------20
GARDNER	————	Mass.		CFA24-----------43
GARDNER=DU PONT	————	Mass./R.I.		CRLA9----------514
GARDNER	Eng.	Mass.		CRLA12---------269
GARDNER	Eng.	Mass.	Arms:-*	CRLA18------356,359
GARDNER	Eng.	Mass.	Arms:-*	TNEF-------------9
GARLAND	————	Va.		CRLA4----------152
GARNER	————	Va./Ky./Mo.		CRLA7----------554

```
GARNETT              ————       Va.                        PFU-------------391
GARR                 Germany    Pa.            Arms:-*     CRLA6----------310
GARRABRANT           Holland    N.J.                       CFA4-----------194
GARRATT              Eng.       Pa./Calif.     Arms:-*     CRLA12---------194
GARRETSON            ————       N.J.                       CRLA4----------331
GARRETT              Eng.       Pa.            Arms:-*     CRLA5----------509
GARRETT              Eng.       Pa.                        CRLA15---------463
GARRISON             ————       N.Y.                       CFA4-----------227
GRATER, Order of the Eng.                 Schull descent  CRLA5----------165
GARTER, Knights of the Eng.           Gaither=Fownes desc. CRLA11----------53
GARTLEY              Ireland    N.J.                       CRLA20---------375
GARVER               ————       Md.            Arms:-*     CRLA11----------18
GASCOIGNE            Eng.                                  CRLA2-----------16
GASQUET              France/Cuba La.           Arms:-      CFA5-----------141
GASSAWAY             ————       Md.                        CFA2------------37
GASSNER              Switzerland N.Y.C.                    CFA24----------103
GASTON               France/Scotland/Ireland  S.C.        CRLA17---------611
GASTON               France/Ireland  Conn.    Arms:-*     AFA***---------281
GASTON               France     Conn.                      PFU------------208
GATES                Eng.       Mass.          Arms:-*     CFA19----------250
GATES                Eng.       Mass.          Arms:-      ACF-------------19
GATES                Eng.       Mass.                      CRLA16---------199
GAUL                 ————       Pa.                        CRLA8----------260
GAUNT                Eng.       Md.            Arms:-*     CRLA1----------503
GAUNT (Gant)         Flanders/Eng.             Arms:-*     CRLA20---------399
GAUSE                ————       Pa.                        CRLA17----------35
GAWTHORP             ————       Del.                       CRLA8----------548
GAWTON               Eng.                                  CRLA15---------318
GAY                  Eng.       Mass.          Arms:-      AF**------------67
GAY                  Eng.       Mass.          Arms:-      AF**-----------440
GAYER                Eng.       Mass.          Arms:-      CRLA8-----------44
GAYER                Eng.       N.Y./Mass.     *(only)     CRLA12-----252,275
GAYLORD              Eng.       Conn.                      CFA1-----------123
GAYLORD              Eng.       Conn.                      CFA14-----------18
GAYLORD              Eng.       Mass.          Arms:-*     CFA27----63,148cht.
GAYLORD=GAILLARD     Eng.       Mass./Conn.    Arms:-      AF*------------229
GAZZAM               Eng.       Pa.                        CRLA10----------60
GEARY                ————       Pa.                        CRLA15---------516
GEER                 Eng.       Mass./Conn.    Arms:-*     AFA***---------277
GEFFCKEN             Germany    ————                       CFA27-----------67
GENEVILLE (de)       France                    Arms:-*     QRLA5----------325
GEOFFREY V, see: ANJOU, Counts of
GEORGE               Eng.       Mass.          Arms:-*     CFA18----------131
GEORGE               Eng.                      Arms:-*     CRLA5-----------55
GEORGE               ————       Mass./R.I.                 CRLA8----------397
GEORGE               ————       Mass.          Arms:-*     AF****---------248
GERHARDT             Germany    Pa.            Arms:-*     CRLA11----------13
GERNAND              ————       Pa.                        AF*------------380
GERNON               Eng.       ————           Arms:-      CFA13-----------80
GERNON (de), see: CHESTER, Earls of
GERRISH              ————       Mass.                      CFA3------------87
GERRISH              Eng.       Mass.                      CRLA15---------274
GERRY                Eng.       Mass.                      CFA1-----------273
GERRY, Elbridge      ————       Mass.                      SDI--------105,118
GERULFE, see: HOLLAND, Counts of
GIBBES               Eng.       S.C.           Arms:-*     PFU------------475
GIBBINS, see: LEWIS=GIBBINS
GIBBONS              ————       Va.                        CFA14----------140
GIBBONS              No family data            Arms:-*     CRLA14-------opp.18
GIBBS                ————       Mass. & R.I.   Arms:-*     CFA5-----------220
GIBBS                Eng.       Mass.          Arms:-*     CRLA6----------338
GIBSON               ————       Va.                        CRLA4----------376
GIBSON               Ireland    Pa.                        CRLA9----------154
GIBSON, see: LEWIS=GIBSON
GIFFARD              Eng.       ————           Arms:-*     CFA25------------9
GIFFARD              Eng.                                  CRLA1----------327
GIFFARD              Eng.                                  CRLA2----------350
```

GIFFARD	Eng.			CRLA2-----------482
GIFFARD (Osborne de Bolebec)	France/Eng.		Arms:-*	CRLA5-----------328
GIFFORD	Normandy/Eng.		Arms:-*	TNEF------------48
GILBERT	------	L.I.,N.Y.	Arms:-*	CFA18-----------159
GILBERT	Eng.	Conn.		CRLA19----------108
GILCHRIST	------	N.C.		CRLA8-----------445
GILDERSLEEVE	Eng.	Mass./Conn./N.Y.		CRLA19----------412
GILES	------	Mass.		CFA16-----------214
GILES	Eng.	Mass.		CFA16-----------245
GILES	Eng.	Mass.	Arms:-*	CFA27-----------69
GILL	------	Va.		CFA14-----------139
GILL	Eng.			CRLA9-----------18
GILLET	------	Conn.		CFA17-----------152
GILLETT	Eng.?	Mass./Conn.		AF***-----------63
GILLETTE	------	Conn.		CRLA2-----------380
GILLINGHAM	------	Pa.	*(only)	CRLA13----------341
GILMAN	Eng.	N.H.	Arms:-*	CFA1------------28
GILMAN	Eng.	Mass.	Arms:-*	CFA4------------107
GILMAN	Eng.	Mass.	Arms:-	CFA6------------161
GILMAN	Eng.	Mass.	Arms:-	CFA22-----------29
GILMAN	Eng.	Mass.	Arms:-*	CRLA10----------411
GILMAN	------	Mass.		PPA-------------146
GILPIN	Eng.	Pa.	Arms:-*	AFA***----------59
GISELBERT, see: BRABANT, Dukes of				
GISH	Switzerland	Pa.		CRLA19----------296
GIST	------	Md.		CFA5------------92
GLASGOW	------	Del.	Arms:-	AF***-----------435
GLASS	------	Va.		AF***-----------117
GLEASON	Eng.	Mass.		CFA14-----------368
GLENDINNING	Scotland	Pa.	Arms:-*	CRLA18----------274
GLOVER	------	Md.		CFA3------------306
GLOVER	Eng.	Va./D.C.		CFA6------------69
GLOVER	Eng.	Mass.		CFA7------------20
GLOVER	Eng.	Mass.		CFA8------------396
GLOVER	------	Conn.		CRLA19----------33
GLOVER	Eng.	Mass.	Arms:-*	TNEF------------210
GODDARD	Eng.	Mass.		AFA***----------273
GODIVA, Lady	Eng.	Carter=Boynton desc.	Arms:-*	CRLA15----------216
GODWIN	------	Va.		CRLA4-----------83
GOELET	------	N.Y.C.		CFA1------------277
GOELET	France/Holland	N.Y.	Arms:-*	CFA27-----------244
GOFF	------	R.I.		CRLA16----------120
GOFF	------	Mass.		AF****----------191
GOLD	Eng.	Conn.	Arms:-	CFA20-----------254
GOLD	Eng.	Conn.	*(only)	CRLA13----------185
GOLD	Eng.	Conn.		CRLA19----------84
GOLDEN	------	N.Y./N.J.		CRLA10----------64
GOLDSBOROUGH	Eng.	Md.	Arms:-	CFA16-----------90
GOLDSBOROUGH	Eng.	Md.		CRLA1-----------106
GOLDSBOROUGH	Eng.	Md.		CRLA2-----------197
GOLDSBOROUGH	Eng.	Md.		CRLA15----------403
GOOD	------	Pa.		CRLA17----------271
GOODALE	Eng.	Mass.	Arms:-	CFA3------------350
GOODALE	Eng.	Mass.	Arms:-*	CRLA15----------17
GOODE	Eng.	Va.	Arms:-*	CFA5------------142
GOODMAN	Eng.?	Mass.		CFA13-----------200
GOODNER	Germany	Ill.		CRLA12----------222
GOODRICH	Eng.	Va.		CFA10-----------231
GOODRICH	Eng.	Conn.	Arms:-	CFA17-----------148
GOODRICH	Eng.	Conn.		CRLA19----------131
GOODRICH	Eng.	Conn.		CRLA19----------417
GOODRICH	Eng.	Conn.	Arms:-*	AF***-----------25
GOODRICH	Eng.	Conn.		PFU-------------261
GOODRICH	------	Conn.		PPA-------------232
GOODRIDGE	Eng.	Mass.	Arms:-	CFA18-----------152
GOODSPEED	Eng.	Mass.		CFA6------------337
GOODWIN	Eng.	Maine	Arms:-	CFA3------------82

GOODWIN	Eng.	Mass.	Arms:-	CFA6------------205
GOODWIN	Eng.	Conn.	Arms:-	CFA17-----------151
GOODWIN=RIDGELY	———	Md.		CFA20-----------191
GOODWIN	———	N.J.		CRLA11----------549
GOOKIN	Eng.	Va.		CRLA1-4----------412
GORDON	Scotland	Mass./N.H.	Arms:-	CFA3------------351
GORDON	Normandy/Ireland Mass.			CFA5------------259
GORDON	Eng.	N.Y.C.		CFA25-----------23
GORDON	Scotland		Arms:-*	CRLA8-----------391
GORDON	Ireland?	Pa.	Arms:-*	CRLA18----------581
GORDON	Scotland	N.H.	Arms:-*	AF****-----------1
GORDON	Ireland	Va.		PFU-------------96
GORDON	Ireland	Va.		PFU-------------178
GORE	———	Mass.		CRLA13----------46
GORGES	———	Maine		MCS-------------27
GORHAM	Eng.	Mass.		CFA1------------181
GORHAM	Eng.	Mass.		CFA6------------173
GORHAM	Eng.	Mass.		CFA6------------351
GORHAM	Eng.	Mass.		CFA7------------354
GORHAM	Eng.	Mass.		CFA8------------176
GORHAM	Eng.	Mass.		CFA9------------78
GORHAM	Eng.	Mass.		CFA13-----------348
GORHAM	Eng.	Mass.		CFA20-----------22
GORHAM	Eng.	Mass.	*(only)	CRLA6-----------257
GORHAM	Eng.	Mass.		CRLA11----------127
GORHAM	———	Mass.		AFA***----------150
GORHAM	———	N.Y./Mass.		TNEF------------170
GORMLEY	———	Pa.		CRLA6-----------193
GORSUCH, see: LOVELACE=GORSUCH				
GORTON	———	———	*(only)	TNEF-------btn.78-9
GORTON, see: PILGRIMS				
GOSSLER	Germany	Pa.	Arms:-*	CRLA13----------226
GOTT	Eng.	Mass.		CRLA7-----------447
GOULD	Eng.	Mass.	Arms:-*	CFA3------------233
GOULD	Eng.?	Mass./Maine		CFA5------------253
GOULD	Eng.	Mass.		CFA7------------14
GOULD	———	Conn.		CRLA1-----------154
GOULD	Eng.	Mass.	Arms:-*	CRLA15----------74
GOURNAY (de)	Eng.			CRLA1-----------365
GOURNAY (de)	Normandy		Gaunt=French desc.	CRLA1-----------547
GOURNAY (de)	Eng.			CRLA20----------393
GOUSHILL	Eng.			CRLA5-----------329
GOVERTSZ	Holland		Arms:-*	CRLA20----------152
GRACE	Eng./Ireland N.Y.		Arms:-*	AFA1------------259
GRAFTON	Eng.	R.I.	Arms:-	TNEF------------132
GRAHAM	Scotland	———	Arms:-*	CFA10-----------75
GRAHAM	Scotland	N.Y.		CFA12-----------237
GRAHAM	Scotland	N.Y.	Arms:-*	CFA25-----------79
GRAHAM	Ireland	Pa./S.C./N.C.	Arms:-*	CRLA4-----------478
GRAHAM	———	N.Y.	Arms:-*	CRLA18----------437
GRAHAM	Scotland	Pa.	Arms:-*	AFA***----------245
GRANGER	———	Mass./Conn.	Arms:-*	CFA18-----------73
GRANGER	Eng.	Mass.		CRLA7-----------290
GRANGER	———	Mass./Conn.		CRLA19----------43
GRANT	Scotland?	Mass.		CFA17-----------374
GRANT	Scotland	Pa.	Arms:-*	CRLA17----------540
GRANT	———	Mass.	Arms:-	AF**------------193
GRANT	Eng.	Mass.	Arms:-*	AF***-----------51
GRANT	Eng.	Mass.	Arms:-	AF***-----------240
GRANT	Eng.	Mass./Conn.	Arms:-*	PBAF------------115
GRANT	Eng.	Mass./Conn.		PFU-------------172
GRANTHAM	Eng.	Pa.		CRLA2-----------434
GRANVILLE	Eng.			CRLA1-----------313
GRASSETT	France/Eng. N.Y.		Arms:-*	CRLA20----------62
GRAVES	Eng.	Mass.		CFA8------------112
GRAVES (or) GREAVES	Eng.	Conn./Mass.	Arms:-	ACF-------------3
GRAY	Ireland	Mass.		CFA1------------228

GRAY	———	Mass.		CFA8-----------172
GRAY	Eng.	Mass.		CFA8-----------257
GRAY	———	Md.		CFA10----------113
GRAY	———	Pa.	Arms:-*	CRLA9----------287
GRAY	———	Mass.		CRLA15---------255
GRAY	Eng.	Maine		CRLA16---------205
GRAY	Ireland	Mass.	Arms:-*	CRLA19---------26
GRAY	———	Indiana	Arms:-*	AF***----------230
GRAY	Eng.	Mass.		AF****---------64
GRAZEBROOK	Eng.	Two generations	Arms:-*	CFA7-----------164

GRAZEBROOK ... missing between XI & XII, see:
Miscellanea Genealogica et Heraldica,
3rd ser. no. 3, pp. 117-161, CS410.M3
(DLC); also, origin as 'Busli' subject
to question, see: Family Origins and
Other Studies, by J. Horace Round, pp.
13-21, CS438.R6 (DLC).

GREELE	Eng.	Mass.		CFA16----------234
GREELE=GREELEY	———	Mass.		CFA16----------269
GREELE=GREELEY	———	Mass./N.H.		CFA18----------129
GREELE=GREELEY	Eng.?	N.H./Mass.		CFA19-------275,282
GREELEY	———	Mass.		CFA19----------135
GREELEY	———	Mass.		CRLA14---------169
GREEN	———	Mass.		CFA13----------300
GREEN	———	Conn.?/Mass.		CFA19----------54
GREEN	———	Mass.		CFA21----------221
GREEN=MOORE	Eng.	Va.		CFA22----------150
GREEN	Eng.	Mass./R.I.	*(only)	CRLA6-------266,270
GREEN	Eng.	N.J.		CRLA8----------291
GREEN	Eng.	R.I.	Arms:-*	CRLA13------470,472
GREEN	———	Mass.	Arms:-*	CRLA15---------490
GREEN	———	Mass.		CRLA15---------594
GREEN	———	Mass.	Arms:-*	CRLA17---------544
GREEN	Eng.	Mass.	Arms:-*	CRLA20---------112
GREEN	———	N.J.		CRLA20---------198
GREEN (Greene)	Eng.	Mass.	Arms:-	AF*------------399
GREEN	———	———	*(only)	TNEF-------opp.82
GREENBERRY	———	Md.		CFA2-----------45
GREENBERRY	Eng.	Md.		CFA16----------93
GREENBERRY	Eng.	Md.		CFA17----------369
GREENE	Eng.	Mass.	Arms:-*	CFA1-----------151
GREENE=GREEN	———	Mass.		CFA6-----------347
GREENE	Eng.	Mass.		CFA7-----------221
GREENE	Eng.	Mass.		CFA8-----------150
GREENE	———	Mass.		CFA8-----------158
GREENE	Eng.	Mass.		CFA12----------185
GREENE	Eng.	Mass./R.I.	Arms:-*	CFA14----------32
GREENE	———	Ill./Ohio		CRLA6----------59
GREENE	Eng.	Mass./R.I.		CRLA6----------442
GREENE	———	R.I.		CRLA7----------323
GREENE	Eng.	Mass./R.I.		CRLA15---------288
GREENE	Eng.	Mass./R.I.		CRLA17---------680
GREENE	Eng.	Mass./R.I.	Arms:-	AF**-----------93
GREENE (de Boketon)	Eng.	Mass.	Arms:-	AF****---------130
GREENE	Eng.	Mass./R.I.		PFU------41,141,323
GREENE	———	R.I.		PPA------------295
GREENE	———	———	*(only)	TNEF-------btn.78-9
GREENE, see: PILGRIMS				
GREENLEAF	Eng.	Mass.		CFA1-----------274
GREENLEAF	Eng.	Mass.		CRLA6----------84
GREENLEAF	Eng.	Mass.		CRLA14---------155
GREENLEAF	Eng.	Mass.		AF*------------251
GREENMAN	———	R.I.		CRLA20---------174
GREENOUGH	Eng.	Mass.	Arms:-	CFA3-----------69
GREENOUGH	Eng.	Mass.	Arms:-	CFA6-----------118
GREENOUGH	———	Mass.		AFA***---------110
GREENOUGH	Eng.	Mass.	Arms:-*	AFA***---------269

GREER	Scotland/Ireland	Pa.	Arms:-*	CFA14-----------342
GREER	————	Ky.		CFA17-----------376
GREER	Ireland	Tenn.		CRLA12----------224
GREER	————	N.C.		CRLA12----------325
GREGG	Scotland	Pa.	Arms:-	CFA22-----------89
GREGG	Scotland/Ireland	N.H.	Arms:-*	CRLA11----------144
GREGG	Scotland/Ireland	Del.	Arms:-*	CRLA17----------69
GREGG	Scotland	N.H.		CRLA19----------363
GREGORY	Eng.	Conn.	Arms:-	CFA2------------164
GREGORY	Eng.	Mass.	Arms:-*	CFA27-----------72
GREGORY	Eng.	Mass./Conn.		CRLA7-----------534
GREGORY	Eng.	Mass./Conn.	Arms:-*	AFA***----------221
GREINER	————	Pa.		CRLA2-----------153
GREVENRAEDT	Holland		Arms:-*	CRLA20----------16
GRENVILLE	Eng.			CRLA17----------659
GREY	Eng.			CRLA2-----------454
GREY	Eng.		Arms:-*	PBAF------------204
GREYSTOKE (de)	Eng.			CRLA11----------91
GRICE	Ireland		Arms:-*	CRLA13----------490
GRIDLEY	Eng.	Mass.		CFA7------------125
GRIDLEY	Eng.	Mass./Conn.		CRLA10----------314
GRIFFETH, Prince of Wales				CRLA1-----------463
GRIFFIN	Wales	Mass.	Arms:-*	CFA21-----------33
GRIFFIN	————	Pa./N.Y.		PPA-------------313
GRIFFITH	————	Md.		CFA5------------86
GRIFFITH	————	Mass./Vt.	Arms:-	CRLA7-----------298
GRIFFITH	————	Del.	Arms:-*	CRLA11----------213
GRIGGS	————	Mass.	Arms:-*	AF****----------107
GRIMSTONE	No family data		Arms:-*	CRLA14-------opp.18
GRINDALL	Eng.	————	Arms:-	CFA4------------23
GRINDALL	Eng.	————		CFA7------------24
GRINDLE	————	N.H.	Arms:-*	CRLA15----------8
GRINNELL	————	R.I.		CRLA20----------175
GRISWOLD	Eng.	Conn.		CFA1------------9
GRISWOLD	Eng./Nova Scotia		Arms:-*	CFA17----------259
GRISWOLD	Eng.	Mass.	Arms:-*	CFA18----------113
GRISWOLD	Eng.	Conn.	Arms:-	CFA21-----------37
GRISWOLD	Eng.	Conn.	Arms:-*	CFA23-----------69
GRISWOLD	Eng.	Conn.	Arms:-*	CRLA1-----------158
GRISWOLD	Eng.	Conn.		CRLA10----------91
GRISWOLD	Eng.	Conn.		CRLA12----------158
GRISWOLD	Eng.	Conn.		CRLA12----------420
GRISWOLD	————	Conn.		PFU-------------408
GRITH	Eng.			CRLA5-----------84
GROOME	Eng.?	Md.	Arms:-*	CRLA17----------415
GROSS	Eng.	Mass.		CFA3------------71
GROSS	Eng.	Mass.	Arms:-*	CRLA16----------105
GROSVENOR	Eng.	Mass.		CFA20----------255
GROSVENOR	Eng.			CRLA11----------152
GROVE	Eng.	Mass.		CRLA14----------149
GROVER	————	Mass.		CFA1------------7
GROVER	————	N.Y./N.J.		CRLA8-----------223
GROVES	————	Pa.	*(only)	CRLA2-----------48
GROVESNOR	Eng.		Arms:-*	CRLA15----------24
GROVESNOR	Eng.			CRLA18----------463
GROW	Eng.	Mass.		CFA7------------303
GROWDON	Eng.	Pa.		CFA7------------396
GRUBB	Eng.	Pa.		CRLA2-----------223
GRUBB	————	Pa.		CRLA3-----------147
GRUBB	Eng.	Pa.		CRLA8-----------404
GRUBB	Eng.	Pa.		CRLA15----------237
GUERRY	France			CRLA1-----------51
GUILD	Eng.	Mass.		CFA7------------371
GUILD	————	R.I.		TNEF------------125
GUILFORD (City)	————	Conn.	Regional background	CRLA19----------246
GUION			Arms:-	CFA10----------225
GUION	France?/Eng.	N.Y.	Arms:-*	CFA18-----------5

GUION	———	N.Y.	Arms:-	CFA18----------220
GUISCARD, Robert, The Norman				CFA27----------208
GULLIVER	———	Mass.		CFA21----------215
GUMMERE	———	Pa.		CRLA8----------286
GUNDRED, dau. to William the Conqueror		Warren desc.		TNEF---------92,93
GUNN	———	Va.		CRLA19----------233
GUNNE	Eng.			CRLA7----------143
GURDON	———	Mass.		ARSC-------------24
GURDON=SALTONSTALL	———	Mass.		MCS--------------18
GURNEE	———	N.Y.		CFA7----------281
GUY	———	Mass./Conn.		CRLA7----------593
GUY	Eng.	Mass.	Arms:-*	CRLA15----------89
GWINN	———	N.C./Va.		CRLA19----------127
GWINNETT, Button	Wales/Eng.	Ga.		SDI---------239,242
GWYNN	———	Md.	Arms:-*	CRLA2----------65
GWYNNE	———	Pa.		CFA2----------69
GWYNNE	———	Va./Texas		CRLA12----------233
GWYNEDD, North Wales, Kings of		Schull descent		CRLA5----------120
GWYNEDD, North Wales, Kings of		Blackiston descent		CRLA11----------390
GWYNEDD, North Wales, Kings of		Ayres=Sheppard desc.		CRLA15----------365
GWYNEDD, see: WALES, Kings of				
GYLES	———	Maine/Mass.		CFA8----------263

- H -

HACK	Germany	Va.	Arms:-*	CRLA15----------327
HACKER	———	Pa.		CRLA8----------349
HACKER	———	Mass.		CRLA19----------214
HACKETT	———	N.H./Mass.		CFA8----------114
HACKLEY	———	Va.		CRLA12----------166
HADLEY	———	Mass.		CRLA7----------469
HADLEY	Ireland	Del.	Arms:-*	CRLA17----------61
HAFF	———	N.Y.	Arms:-	ACF-------------72
HAGEN	No family data		Arms:-*	CRLA13------opp.130
HAIGHT	Eng.	Mass./Conn.		CFA2----------275
HAIGHT	———	N.Y.		CRLA18----------427
HAIGHT	Eng.	Conn./N.Y.		CRLA20----------183
HAIN	Holland	Pa.		AF*-----------385
HAINAULT, Counts of	France	Rainier or Raginar I		CRLA5----------331
HAINAULT, Counts of	France			CRLA7----------241
HAINAULT, Counts of, see: HOLLAND & HAINAULT				
HAINES	Eng.	N.J.		CFA5----------338
HAINES	Eng.	N.J.		CFA7----------398
HAINES	———	Pa.	Arms:-*	CRLA15----------268
HAINES	Eng.	Pa.	Arms:-*	AFA***----------223
HALE	Wales/Eng.		Arms:-	CFA6----------125
HALE	Eng.	Conn.	Arms:-*	CFA9----------191
HALE	———	Conn.		CFA9----------199
HALE	Eng.	Mass.	Arms:-*	CFA14----------124
HALE	Eng.	Mass.		CFA16----------292
HALE	Eng.	Mass.		CFA23----------214
HALE	———	Mass.		ACF-------------56
HALE	Eng.	Mass.		CRLA13----------273
HALE	Eng.	Mass.	*(only)	CRLA13----------367
HALL	Eng.	Mass.		CFA1----------114
HALL	———	Mass.		CFA2----------234
HALL	Eng.	Mass.	Arms:-*	CFA4----------261
HALL	Eng.	Mass.		CFA20----------168
HALL	———	Va.		CRLA4----------232
HALL	Eng.	Conn.	Arms:-*	CRLA7----------263
HALL	Eng.	Pa.	Arms:-*	CRLA8----------252
HALL	———	Mass.	Arms:-*	CRLA9----------483

HARDY	———	Mass.		CFA27-----13cht.,77
HARDY	———	Mass.	Arms:-*	CRLA15-----------15
HARDY	———	———	Arms:-*	CRLA16------------9
HARDY	———	Mass.		CRLA17----------463
HARE	Eng.	Pa.		CRLA15----------460
HARE=POWELL	Eng.	Pa.	Arms:-*	PFU-------------303
HARGROVE	———	Md.	Arms:-	CRLA3-----------403
HARING	Holland	N.Y.		CFA16-----------65
HARINGTON	Eng.		Arms:-*	CRLA5----------339
HARKNESS	Scotland	Mass.	Arms:-*	CFA9--------177,181
HARKNESS	Ireland	Mass./R.I.		CRLA16----------159
HARKNESS	Scotland	Mass.	Arms:-*	CRLA19-----------24
HARLAKENDEN	———	Mass.		MCS-------------73
HARLAN	Ireland	Pa.		CRLA17----------273
HARMAN	Germany	Md.	Arms:-*	CRLA15----------328
HARMAR	———	Pa.		CRLA8-----------134
HARMENSEN	Holland	L.I.,N.Y.		CFA5------------12
HARMENSEN	———	N.Y.		CFA9-----------302
HARMON	Eng.	Mass.		CRLA16----------143
HARNEY	———	Del./Ky./Tenn.		PPA-------------140
HARPER	Eng.	Pa.	Arms:-*	CRLA2-----------138
HARPER	Ireland	Pa.		CRLA2-----------407
HARPER	Ireland	Mass.		CRLA15----------505
HARPER	Eng.	Pa.	Arms:-*	CRLA17------323,327
HARRIMAN	Eng.	N.Y.C.		CFA1------------216
HARRIMAN	———	Mass.		CFA7------------160
HARRIMAN	Eng.	N.Y.C.		CRLA9-----------263
HARRINGTON	Eng.	Mass.		CFA11-----------235
HARRINGTON	———	Mass.	Arms:-*	CRLA15-----------86
HARRINGTON	———	Mass.	Arms:-*	CRLA20-----------87
HARRINGTON	———	R.I.	Arms:-*	AF****----------103
HARRIS	Eng.?	R.I.		CFA10-----------16
HARRIS	Eng.	Conn.		CFA23-----------101
HARRIS	———	Va.		CRLA4-----------229
HARRIS	———	Va.		CRLA4------397,404
HARRIS	Eng.	Mass.		CRLA16----------178
HARRIS	Eng.	R.I.		CRLA17----------444
HARRIS	———	Mass./Conn.		CRLA18----------519
HARRIS	———	N.J.		CRLA19------------1
HARRIS	———	———	*(only)	TNEF-------btn.78-9
HARRIS, see: PILGRIMS				
HARRISON	———	Md.	Arms:-	CFA6------------384
HARRISON	Eng.	Conn.		CFA9------------146
HARRISON	———	Conn.?/N.J.		CFA16-----------177
HARRISON	———	Md.	Arms:-*	CRLA1-----------481
HARRISON	Eng.?	N.Y.		CRLA3-----------414
HARRISON	———	Va.		CRLA4------------57
HARRISON	———	Va./N.C.		CRLA4-----------106
HARRISON	Eng.	L.I.,N.Y.		CRLA4-----------211
HARRISON	Eng.	Pa.		CRLA9------------4
HARRISON	Eng.	Conn./N.J.		CRLA9-----------470
HARRISON	Eng.	Pa.		CRLA15----------520
HARRISON	Eng.	Conn.		CRLA18----------227
HARRISON, Benjamin		Va.		SDI---------201,210
HARRISON, see: LUDLOW=CARTER=HARRISON				
HARROD of Harrodsburg	Eng.	Va./Pa.		CFA8------------316
HART	———	Mass.		CFA6------------242
HART	Eng.	Mass.		CFA7------------11
HART	Eng.	Mass.		CFA11-----------196
HART	———	Mass.	Arms:-*	CRLA8-----------62
HART	Ireland	Pa.		CRLA11----------563
HART	Ireland	Pa.	Arms:-*	CRLA16-----------30
HART	———	R.I.		CRLA17----------490
HART	———	Mass./R.I.		CRLA18----------387
HART	Ireland	Pa.	Arms:-*	CRLA19----------314
HART	———	Mass.	Arms:-*	CRLA20-----------44
HART	———	Mass.	Arms:-	AF***-----------194

HART	———	Va.?/N.C.		AF***-----------318
HART	———	N.J.		AFA***----------50
HART	———	N.J.		AFA***----------386
HART, John	———	Conn./N.J.		SDI---------145,146
HARTER	———	Pa./Ind.	Arms:-*	TNEF------------172
HARTFORD (City)		Conn. Regional background		CRLA19----------243
HARTMAN	———	Pa.?	Arms:-*	CRLA19----------217
HARTWELL	———	Mass.		CFA21-----------232
HARTWELL	———	Mass.		CRLA3-----------328
HARTZELL	———	Pa.		CRLA9-----------459
HARVEY	Eng.	Mass.	Arms:-*	CFA19------------35
HARVEY	Eng.	Pa./Del.	Arms:-*	CRLA1-----------111
HARVEY	———	N.C.		CRLA4-----------254
HARVEY	Eng.			CRLA13----------135
HARVEY	Eng.	Pa.		CRLA13----------353
HARVY	Eng.			CRLA17----------531
HARWOOD	———	Pa.	Arms:-*	CRLA17----------641
HARWOOD	Eng.	Mass.		CRLA20----------168
HASBROUCK	France	N.Y.		CFA8------------384
HASBROUCK	France	N.Y.	Arms:-*	CRLA20-----------26
HASELTINE	Eng.	Mass.	Arms:-*	CRLA16-----------14
HASKELL	———	Mass.		CFA13-----------322
HASKELL	Eng.	Mass.	Arms:-*	CFA19------------27
HASKELL	Eng.	Mass.		CFA27-----38cht.,79
HASKELL	Eng.	Mass.	Arms:-*	CRLA8----------1,18
HASKELL	Eng.	Mass.		CRLA17----------461
HASSELL	———	Mass.		CFA19-----------286
HASTINGS	Eng.	Mass.		CFA8------------361
HASTINGS	———	Mass.	Arms:-*	CRLA15----------480
HASTINGS	Eng.	Mass.		CRLA18----------624
HASTINGS	———	Mass.	Arms:-*	CRLA20-----------95
HATCH	———	Mass.	Arms:-*	CRLA3------------42
HATCH	———	Mass.		CRLA6------------73
HATCH	No family data		Arms:-*	CRLA18-------opp.24
HATFIELD	———	N.Y.		CRLA17----------487
HATHAWAY	Eng.	Mass.	Arms:-*	CFA7------------101
HATHAWAY	———	Mass.	Arms:-*	CFA23------------90
HATHAWAY	———	Mass.		CRLA7-----------477
HATHAWAY	Eng.	Mass.	Arms:-*	CRLA12----------114
HATHORN	Not given			CRLA13----------283
HATTON	Eng.	Md.		CRLA2------------75
HAVENS	Wales	Mass./R.I.		CFA19-----------116
HAWES	Eng.	Mass.		CFA6------------350
HAWES	Eng.	Mass.	Arms:-*	CRLA19-----------34
HAWKE	Eng.	Mass.	Arms:-*	CRLA20----------101
HAWKES	Eng.	Mass.		CFA7------------141
HAWKINS	———	———		ACF--------------87
HAWKINS	Eng.	Md.	Arms:-*	CRLA1-----------481
HAWKINS	Eng.?	Md.		CRLA10----------230
HAWKINS	———	Va./Ky.		CRLA12----------172
HAWKINS	Eng.	Va.		CRLA13----------333
HAWLEY	Eng.	Conn.	Arms:-*	CRLA7------134,153
HAWLEY	———	Mass.		CRLA13----------187
HAWLEY	Eng.	Mass./Conn.		CRLA17----------664
HAWTHORNE	Eng.	Mass.		PFU-------------355
HAWXHURST	Eng.	Mass.		CFA18------------21
HAY	———	———		CRLA18----------156
HAYDEN	———	Mass.?/Conn.		CFA6------------346
HAYDEN	———	Mass.		CFA8------------107
HAYDEN	———	N.C.	Arms:-*	CRLA20----------138
HAYNE (de la)	Eng.			CRLA5-----------341
HAYES	———	Conn.		CFA24------------35
HAYES	———	Conn.		CRLA19----------308
HAYNE	———	S.C.		PFU--------------67
HAYMAN	Eng.	Pa.	Arms:-*	CFA20-----------101
HAYNES	———	N.C.		CRLA10----------196
HAYNES	Eng.	Mass.	Arms:-*	CFA16-----------261

HAYWARD	——	Mass.		CFA4------------167
HAYWARD	Eng.	Mass.		CFA6------------195
HAYWARD	——	Mass.		CFA12-----------373
HAZARD	——	Mass.	Arms:-*	CFA15-----------331
HAZARD	——	Mass.	Arms:-	CFA23-----------225
HAZARD	——	Mass./R.I.		CRLA18----------528
HAZARD	——	Mass./R.I.		CRLA20----------371
HAZARD	——	——	*(only)	TNEF--------opp.30
HAZARD	Eng.?	R.I.	Arms:-	TNEF------------225
HAZELTINE (Hazelton)	Eng.	Mass.	Arms:-*	CRLA3------------23
HAZELTON	——	Mass.	Arms:-*	AF****----------193
HAZEN	Eng.	Mass.		CFA1-------------59
HAZZARD	——	Va./Del.		CRLA4-----------251
HAZZARD	——	Va./Del.		CRLA4-----------326
HAZZARD	——	Del.		CRLA19----------355
HEAD	Eng.	Pa.		CRLA9-----------159
HEAD	No family data		Arms:-*	CRLA5-------opp.496
HEAD	Eng.	Md.		CRLA20----------304
HEADLEY	——	Pa.	Arms:-	AF***------------91
HEARD	——	N.H.		CRLA4-----------343
HEARST	——	Va./N.C.		CFA14-----------131
HEARTT	Eng.	Conn./Pa.		CRLA4-----------256
HEATH	Eng.	Mass.	Arms:-*	CFA8------------153
HEATH	Eng.	Mass.		CFA8------------376
HEATH	Eng.	Mass.		CFA21-----------222
HEATH	Eng.	Pa.	Arms:-*	CRLA5-----------507
HEATH	Eng.	Pa.		CRLA15----------462
HEATH	Eng.	Pa.	Arms:-*	CRLA17----------338
HEATHCOTE	Eng.	N.Y.		CRLA15----------452
HEATON	Eng.	Conn.	Arms:-	CRLA6-----------342
HEBBERD	Eng.	Mass.		CFA9-------------82
HEDDEN	Eng.	Mass.	Arms:-*	ACF--------------64
HEDGE	Eng.	Mass.		CFA8------------175
HEDGE	Eng.	N.J.	Arms:-*	CRLA5------------73
HEDGE	Eng.	Schull descent		CRLA5-----------198
HEFFELINGER	Germany	Pa./Va.		CRLA2-----------390
HEFFRON	——	N.H.		CRLA11----------580
HEGEMAN	Holland	N.Y.		CFA11------------47
HEISSENBUTTEL	Germany	N.Y.		CRLA3-----------304
HEISTER (Hiester)	Germany	Pa.	Arms:-*	AF*-------------384
HELM	Eng.	Va.		CRLA4-----------394
HELME	——	L.I.,N.Y.		CFA16-----------293
HEMENWAY	Eng.	Mass.		CFA14-----------318
HEMINGWAY	Eng.	Mass.		CFA15-----------243
HENDERSON	Scotland	Va.	Arms:-*	CFA5------------205
HENDERSON	——	N.J.		CRLA8-----------293
HENDRICKSON	Holland	N.Y.	Arms:-*	CRLA20------------1
HENDRY	——	N.J.		CRLA11----------258
HENNEN	Ireland	Md.	Arms:-	CFA15-----------129
HENRY	Eng.	Va.		CFA17-----------311
HENRY	Ireland	Pa.		CRLA14----------663
HENRY	——	Pa.		AFA***-----------40
HENRY	——	Pa.		AFA***----------168
HENRY	Scotland	Va.		PFU-------------449
HENSHAW	Eng.	Mass.	*(only)	CRLA6-----------253
HENTZ	Germany		Arms:-*	CRLA11-----------13
HENVIS	Eng.	Pa.		CRLA9-----------295
HEPBURN	Scotland	Conn.	Arms:-*	CFA1------------222
HEPBURN	Scotland	Pa.	Arms:-*	CRLA9-----------491
HERBERT	Wales	——		CFA20------------98
HERBERT	——	Md.	Arms:-*	CRLA1-----------525
HERBERT	Ireland	Va.		CRLA8-----------157
HERBERT	——	Pa./Md.		CRLA18----------586
HEREFORD	——	Va.	Arms:-	CRLA3------------97
HERMAN	Bohemia	N.Y./Md.		CFA7------------392
HERNDON	——	Va.	Arms:-*	CRLA3-----------366
HERNDON	——	Va.		CRLA16----------222

HERR	Switzerland	Pa.		CRLA10----------284
HERRICK	Eng.	Mass.	Arms:-	AF***-----------180
HERRMAN	————	Md.	Arms:-*	CRLA17----------420
HERSEY	————	Mass.		CFA14-----------290
HESSELIUS	Sweden	Pa./Md.		CRLA9-----------339
HETON	Eng.		Arms:-*	PBAF------------207
HEUISLER	Germany	Md.		CRLA2------------77
HEWES	————	Mass.		CFA13-----------295
HEWES, Joseph	————	N.J./N.C.		SDI---------221,222
HEWETT	Eng.			CRLA9------------12
HEWETT	Eng.		Arms:-*	CRLA15----------340
HEWLINGS	Eng.	N.J.	Arms:-	CRLA5------------31
HEYWARD, Thomas, Jr.	————	S.C.		SDI---------227,232
HEYWOOD	Eng.	Mass.	Arms:-*	CFA9-------------69
HEYWOOD	Eng.	Mass.		CFA19---------80,81
HIBBARD=HIBBERD	Eng.	Mass.	Arms:-	AF*-------------33
HIBNER	————	Pa./Del.		CRLA18----------400
HICKCOX	————	Conn.	Arms:-	AF*------------364
HICKEY	————	Md./D.C.		CRLA4-----------438
HICKLEY	Eng.	Mass.	Arms:-	TNEF------------216
HICKMAN	Eng.	Pa.		CRLA13----------291
HICKMAN	————	Pa.		CRLA17----------355
HICKOK=HICKKOX=HICKCOX	Eng.	Conn.	Arms:-*	CFA27-----38cht.,82
HICKS	Eng.	Mass.		CFA7------------386
HICKS	Eng.	Mass.		CFA8------------329
HICKS	Eng.	Mass.	Arms:-	CFA16-------------1
HICKS	Eng.	Mass./R.I./L.I.,N.Y.	Arms:-*	CFA18------------45
HICKS	Eng.	Mass.	Arms:-*	CRLA2-----------312
HICKS	Eng.	Mass.	Arms:-*	CRLA12----------399
HICKS	Eng.	Mass.	Arms:-*	AF****-----------58
HIELS	————	————	*(only)	TNEF---------opp.31
HIETT	Ireland	Pa.	Arms:-*	CRLA17-----------64
HIGGINS	Eng.	Mass.		CFA2------------158
HIGGINSON	Ireland	Pa./etc.		CFA8------------404
HIGGINSON	Eng.	Va.		CFA24-------------2
HIGGINSON	Eng.	Mass.		CRLA1-----------417
HIGGINSON	Eng.	Va.		CRLA4-----------128
HIGGINSON	Ireland	N.Y.	Arms:-*	PFU-------------375
HIGH=HOCH	————	Pa.	Arms:-*	AF*------------379
HIGHAM	————	Pa.		CRLA4-----------451
HILDRETH	————	N.Y.		CFA3------------340
HILDRETH	Eng.	Mass.		CFA17-----------123
HILDRETH	————	Mass.		CFA19-----------295
HILDRETH	————	Mass.		CRLA13----------451
HILDRETH	Eng.	Mass.		CRLA15----------488
HILL	————	Mass.		CFA2------------175
HILL	————	Mass.		CFA2------------325
HILL	Eng.	Maine		CFA3-------------86
HILL	Eng.	Maine	Arms:-*	CFA7------------146
HILL	————	Mass.		CFA11-----------217
HILL	————	Md.		CFA14-----------134
HILL	Eng.	Mass.		CFA19------------83
HILL	Ireland	N.Y.		CFA22------------51
HILL	Ireland	N.Y.		CFA23-----------204
HILL	————	Mass.		ACF--------------52
HILL	————	Va.		CRLA4------------43
HILL	Ireland?	Va.?		CRLA4-----------473
HILL	————	Mass.		CRLA6-----------512
HILL	————	Pa.		CRLA8-----------403
HILL	————	Conn.		CRLA10-----------75
HILL	————	Pa.		CRLA12----------340
HILL	————	Va.		CRLA15----------317
HILL	————	Conn.		CRLA18----------229
HILL	Eng.	Mass.	Arms:-*	CRLA20-----------75
HILL	————	N.H.		AF**------------15
HILL	————	Mich.	Arms:-	AF****----------144
HILL	Eng.?	Mass.	Arms:-*	PFU-------------308

HILL	————	Conn.		PPA------------275
HILLHOUSE	Scotland/Ireland	N.H./Conn.	Arms:-*	HFA------------246
HILLHOUSE	Ireland	Conn.		PPA------------129
HILLIARD	Eng.	Mass./R.I.	Arms:-*	CFA3-----------228
HILLIARD	Eng.	Md.		CRLA4-----------34
HILLIARD	Eng.	Md.		CRLA4-----------73
HILLIARD	————	Md.		CRLA11---------126
HILLMAN	Eng.	Mass.	Arms:-*	CFA8-----------183
HILLS	Eng.	Mass.		CRLA1----------217
HILLS	Eng.	Mass.	Arms:-*	CRLA16-----------3
HILLS	Eng.	Mass.		CRLA18---------413
HILTON	Eng.		Arms:-	PBAF-----------194
HILYARD	Eng.	N.J.		AFA***---------294
HIMPEL	Holland			CRLA20---------153
HINCKLEY	Eng.	Mass.		CFA3-----------252
HINCKLEY	Eng.	Mass.		CFA22-----------42
HINCKLEY	Eng.	Mass.	Arms:-*	CFA27-----13cht.,88
HINCKLEY	Eng.	Mass.	Arms:-*	CRLA17---------457
HINDS	————	Mass.	Arms:-*	CRLA17----------19
HINE	————	Conn.		CFA19-----------66
HINE	————	Conn.		CRLA3----------220
HINE	————	————	*(only)	TNEF--------opp.82
HINMAN	————	Conn.		CRLA6-----------33
HINSDALE	————	Mass.	Arms:-*	CRLA7----------277
HINTON	Eng.	N.C.	Arms:-*	CRLA4-----------27
HINTON	Eng.	N.C.		CRLA8----------449
HINSDALE	Eng.	Mass.	Arms:-*	CFA18-----------83
HIRST	Eng.	Pa.		CRLA13---------252
HIRST	————	Pa.		PPA------------533
HISKEY	————	Pa.		CRLA6----------508
HITCH	————	Mass.	Arms:-*	AF****----------52
HITCHCOCK	Eng.	Mass.		CFA10----------398
HITCHCOCK	Eng.	Conn.		CFA11----------326
HITCHCOCK	Eng.	Conn./Mass.		CFA20----------267
HITCHCOCK	————	Conn.		CRLA3----------221
HITCHINGS	————	Mass.		TNEF-----------161
HITE	Germany	N.Y.		CRLA6----------211
HITT	Germany	Va.		CRLA3-----------84
HITT	————	Ky.		CRLA6----------542
HIX	————	Va.		CRLA10----------17
HIXON	————	Mass.	Arms:-	AF*------------243
HOALEY	Eng.	Conn.		CFA12-----------20
HOAGLAND	Holland	N.Y.	Arms:-*	CRLA13---------397
HOBART	Eng.	Mass.		CFA1-----------40
HOBART	Eng.	Mass.	Arms:-*	CFA6-----------191
HOBART	Eng.	Mass.	Arms:-*	CFA12----------369
HOBART	Eng.	Mass.		CFA19-----------61
HOBART	Eng.	Mass.		CFA26----------142
HOBART	Eng.	Mass.	Arms:-*	CRLA18---------360
HOBART	Eng.	Mass.		CRLA20---------334
HOCHE	France	Conn.		CFA9-----------300
HODGE	Ireland	Pa.		CRLA9-----------19
HODGES	————	Mass.		CFA4-----------173
HODGES	————	Mass.	Arms:-*	CRLA7----------342
HOE	Eng.	N.Y.	Arms:-*	CFA12----------207
HOFFMAN	————	N.Y.	Arms:-*	CFA6------------1
HOFFMAN	Sweden	N.Y.	Arms:-	CFA11----------158
HOFFMAN	Sweden/Holland	N.Y.	Arms:-	CFA13----------246
HOFFMAN	————	N.Y.		PPA------------329
HOGAN	————	N.Y.		CRLA16----------89
HOGEBOOM	Holland	N.Y.		CFA17-----------36
HOLBROOK	————	Mass.		CFA4-----------48
HOLBROOK	Eng.	Mass.	Arms:-	AF*------------37
HOLBROOK	————	Mass.	Arms:-*	AF**-----------400
HOLBROOKE	Eng.	Mass.	Arms:-*	CFA1-----------146
HOLCOMB	Eng.	Conn.	Arms:-*	CFA8-----------124
HOLCOMBE	Eng.	Conn.	Arms:-*	CFA17----------255

HOLCOMBE	Eng.?	Va.		CRLA10---------268
HOLDEN	———	R.I.		CFA17----------291
HOLDEN	Eng.	Mass.		CRLA10---------211
HOLDEN	Eng.	Mass.	Arms:-*	CRLA17---------560
HOLGATE	Eng.	Pa.		CRLA9----------238
HOLLAND	———	Md.	Arms:-*	CRLA1----------484
HOLLAND & HAINAULT, Counts of				CRLA2----------494
HOLLAND, Earls of Kent Eng. Jones=Paul=Knight desc. *(only)				CRLA2----------545
HOLLAND (de)	Eng.			CRLA2----------558
HOLLAND	Eng.		Arms:-	CRLA5----------342
HOLLAND, Counts of	Europe		Arms:-*	CRLA5----------346
HOLLAND, Counts of		Gerulfe	Arms:-*	CRLA17---------191
HOLLAND, John		Easton "Mayflower" descent		CRLA18---------533
HOLLANDER	———	Mass.		CFA11----------263
HOLLIDAY	———	N.Y.		CRLA7----------581
HOLLINGSHEAD	Eng.	N.J.		CFA7-----------400
HOLLINGSWORTH	———	Md.	Arms:-*	CRLA1----------518
HOLLINGSWORTH	Ireland	Del.	Arms:-*	CRLA17----------75
HOLLINGSWORTH	Ireland	Del.	Arms:-*	CRLA17---------358
HOLLISTER	Eng.	Mass.		CFA9-------203,204
HOLLOWAY	———	Va./Ky.		CRLA6----------456
HOLLOWAY	———	N.J.	Arms:-*	CRLA17----------60
HOLLEY	———	Mass.		CRLA13---------361
HOLLY	Eng.	Conn.	Arms:-	AF*------------421
HOLLYDAY	Eng.	Md.	Arms:-	AF*-------------80
HOLMAN	Eng.	Mass.	Arms:-*	CFA1-----------141
HOLMAN	———	Mass.		CFA19-----------52
HOLMES	Eng.	Mass.		CFA8-----------331
HOLMES	———	Mass.		CFA19----------194
HOLMES	———	Mass.?/Conn.		CFA20------------1
HOLMES	Eng.	Va./Conn.	Arms:-	CFA27-----------94
HOLMES	Eng.	Conn.	Arms:-*	CRLA2----------268
HOLMES	———	Mass./S.C.		CRLA8-----------30
HOLMES	Eng.	Mass.		CRLA18---------629
HOLMES	———	Conn.		CRLA19---------133
HOLMES	Eng.	Mass.	Arms:-*	CRLA19---------286
HOLMES	Eng.	Mass./R.I.	Arms:-	AF****----------25
HOLMES	Ireland	Pa.		AFA***----------26
HOLMES	———	Mass.		PPA------------415
HOLMES	Eng.	Mass.	Arms:-*	TNEF------------24
HOLSTEIN	———	Pa.		CFA20-----------99
HOLT	———	Mass.		CFA4-----------167
HOLT	Eng.	Mass.		CFA11----------380
HOLT	———	———		CFA20----------340
HOLT	Eng.	Mass.	Arms:-*	CFA27----97,148cht.
HOLT	Eng.	Mass.		CRLA9----------271
HOLT	———	———	*(only)	CRLA12-------opp.88
HOLT	Eng.	Mass.	Arms:-*	AF*------------195
HOLT	Eng.	Mass.	Arms:-*	AF***------------1
HOLYOKE	Eng.	Mass.		CFA8------------88
HOLYOKE	Eng.	Mass.	Arms:-*	CFA9-----------203
HOLYOKE	Eng.	Mass.		CFA15----------366
HOMAN	Germany	Pa.		CRLA20---------367
HOMER	Eng.	Mass.	Arms:-*	CRLA20----------69
HONEYWOOD	———	Mass.		PPA-------------65
HOO (de)	Eng.			CRLA17---------185
HOOD	Ireland	Pa.		CRLA17---------678
HOOE	Eng.	Va.		CFA13-----------88
HOOGLAND	Netherlands	N.Y.		CFA7-----------235
HOOGLAND	Holland?	N.Y.	Arms:-*	AF**-----------475
HOOGLANDT	———	———		CFA17-----------95
HOOKE	———	———	Arms:-*	CRLA14-------opp.54
HOOKE	Eng.	Mass.	Arms:-*	CRLA14---------141
HOOKE	———	Pa.		CRLA15---------515
HOOKER	Eng.	Mass.	Arms:-*	CFA4------------24
HOOKER	Eng.	Mass.		CFA14----------266
HOOKER	Eng.	Mass./Conn.		CFA15----------240

HOOKER	Eng.	Mass.	Arms:-*	CFA25------------32
HOOKER	Eng.	Conn.	Arms:-*	CRLA18----------45
HOOPER	Eng.	Mass.		CFA8-----------277
HOOPER=HOPPE	Holland?	N.Y./N.J.		CFA20------126,133
HOOPER	Eng.	Mass.	Arms:-*	CRLA8-----------34
HOOPER	Eng.?	Mass.		CRLA10---------254
HOOPER	Eng.	N.J./Pa.	Arms:-*	CRLA13---------331
HOOPER, William	———	Mass./N.C.		SDI--------221,225
HOOPES	Eng.?	Pa.	Arms:-*	AF*------------342
HOOVER	———	Md.	Arms:-	CRLA3----------427
HOOVER	Germany	N.C.	Arms:-*	CRLA20---------141
HOUGH	Eng.	Pa.		CRLA2----------431
HOPEWELL	Eng.	Mass.		CFA6-----------166
HOPEWELL	Eng.	N.J.		CRLA9----------493
HOPKINS	———	Md.		CFA3-----------307
HOPKINS	Eng.	R.I.		CFA7-----------385
HOPKINS	———	Va.		CFA10----------123
HOPKINS	Eng.	Mass.		CFA27----------100
HOPKINS, Stephen	Mayflower passenger			CFA27----------207
HOPKINS	Eng.	Mass.	Arms:-*	CRLA2----------303
HOPKINS	Eng.	Mass.	Arms:-*	CRLA7----------355
HOPKINS	———	Mass.		CRLA7----------446
HOPKINS	Eng.	Mass.		CRLA10---------357
HOPKINS	———	Mass.	Arms:-*	CRLA12---------399
HOPKINS	———	Mass. Gross descent		CRLA16---------111
HOPKINS	Eng.	Mass.		CRLA17---------446
HOPKINS	Eng.	Mass.		CRLA17---------563
HOPKINS	Eng.	Mass.	Arms:-*	CRLA18----------76
HOPKINS	Eng.	Mass./Conn.	Arms:-*	CRLA18---------610
HOPKINS	———	Mass.		CRLA20---------329
HOPKINS	———	R.I.	Arms:-*	AF*------------224
HOPKINS	———	Ky.		AF*------------320
HOPKINS	Eng.	Mass.	Arms:-	AF*------------323
HOPKINS	———	———	*(only)	TNEF-------btn.78-9
HOPKINS, Stephen	———	R.I.		SDI--------121,122
HOPKINS, see: PILGRIMS				
HOPKINSON	———	Pa.		PPA-------------72
HOPKINSON, Francis	———	Pa./N.J.		SDI--------145,156
HOPPE	Germany	———		CFA27----------105
HOPPIN	———	Mass.		CFA7-----------307
HORNBECK	———	N.Y.	Arms:-*	CRLA20----------41
HORSEY	Eng.	Md.		CFA17----------376
HORSEY	———	Md.		CRLA15---------576
HORSFORD	Eng.?	Conn.	Arms:-*	CFA4-----------196
HORSMANDEN	Eng.	Va.		CFA17----------348
HORSMANDEN=BYRD	———	Va.		MCS-------------42
HORTON	Eng.	Conn.	Arms:-*	CFA14------------1
HORTON	Eng.	N.Y.	Arms:-	CRLA16----------76
HORTON	Eng.	Conn.		CRLA17---------479
HORTON	Eng.	Mass.	Arms:-	AF***----------188
HOSKINS	Eng.	Pa.		CFA7-----------397
HOSMER	Eng.	Mass.		CFA2------------97
HOSMER	Eng.	Mass.		CFA10----------388
HOSMER	Eng.	Mass.		CFA11----------200
HOSMER	Eng.	Mass.		CRLA15----------56
HOSMER	Eng.	Mass.		PFU------------389
HOSMER	———	Conn./N.Y.		PPA------------507
HOTCHKISS	Eng.	Conn.		CFA18----------193
HOUCK	———	Pa.		AF****---------224
HOUGH	———	Md.		CFA15----------168
HOUGH	Eng.	Mass.		CRLA6----------102
HOUGH	Eng.	Conn./Mass.	Arms:-*	CRLA17----------23
HOUGHTELING	———	N.Y.		CRLA12---------428
HOUGHTON	Eng.	Mass.	Arms:-	CFA4------------92
HOUGHTON	Eng.	Mass.	Arms:-*	CFA10----------175
HOUGHTON	———	Mass.		CFA13----------153
HOUGHTON	Eng.	Mass.	Arms:-*	CFA15-----------72

HOUGHTON	Eng.	Mass.		CFA21-----------243
HOUGHTON	————	Mass.		CRLA20----------209
HOUNSFIELD	Eng.	N.Y.	Arms:-*	CRLA1------------70
HOVEY	Eng.	Mass.	Arms:-	CFA6-------------98
HOVEY	Eng.	Mass.	Crest & Motto only	CFA18-----------139
HOVEY	Eng.	Mass.		CFA20------------70
HOVEY	Eng.	Mass.		CRLA19----------46
HOVEY	Eng.	Mass.		CRLA20----------77
HOW (or) HOWE	Eng.	Mass.		CFA7-------------79
HOWARD	Eng.	Md.	Arms:-	CFA2-------------44
HOWARD	————	Va./Md.		CFA5-------------91
HOWARD	Eng.	Mass.		CFA10-----------265
HOWARD	Eng.	Md.	Arms:-	CFA16------------89
HOWARD	————	Va./Md.		CFA16------------95
HOWARD	————	Va.		CRLA6-----------168
HOWARD=SMITH	Eng.	Pa./Tenn.		CRLA8-----------534
HOWARD	————	Conn.?/N.Y./Pa.		CRLA10----------272
HOWARD	Eng.	Mass.	*(only)	CRLA13----------371
HOWARD	————	Mass.	Arms:-*	CRLA15-----------34
HOWARD	————	Mass.		PFU-------------205
HOWE	Eng.	Mass.		CFA3------------208
HOWE	————	Mass.	Arms:-*	CFA18-----------145
HOWE, Abraham	————	Mass.		CRLA18------385,389
HOWE, John	————	Mass.		CRLA18------394,396
HOWEL	Wales			CRLA2-----------452
HOWELL	Eng.	L.I.,N.Y.		CFA5-------------53
HOWELL	————	N.J.		CRLA6------------1
HOWELL	————	Md./S.C.		CRLA8------------41
HOWELL	Wales	Pa.		CRLA11----------520
HOWELL	Eng.	Mass./N.Y.	Arms:-*	CRLA18----------564
HOWELL	Eng.	Mass./L.I.,N.Y.	Arms:-*	AFA***-----------49
HOWELL	Eng.	Del./N.J.	Arms:-*	AFA***----------121
HOWELL	Eng.	N.J./Pa.	Arms:-*	AFA***----------153
HOWELL	Eng.	Mass./L.I.,N.Y.	Arms:-*	AFA***----------183
HOWLAND	Eng.	Mass.		CFA1------------182
HOWLAND	Eng.	Mass.		CFA6------------352
HOWLAND	Eng.	Mass.		CFA7------------357
HOWLAND	Eng.	Mass.	Arms:-*	CFA8------------178
HOWLAND	————	Mass.		CFA8------------263
HOWLAND	————	Mass.		CFA9------------79
HOWLAND	Eng.	Mass.		CFA11-----------316
HOWLAND	Eng./Holland	Mass.	Arms:-	CFA13----------348
HOWLAND	Eng.	Mass.		CFA20-----------24
HOWLAND	Eng.	Mass.	Arms:-	ACF-------------88
HOWLAND	————	Mass.		CRLA12----------316
HOWLAND	————	Mass.	Arms:-*	CRLA18-----------49
HOWLAND	————	Mass.		CRLA18----------573
HOWLAND	————	Mass.	Arms:-*	CRLA18----------602
HOWLAND	————	Mass.	Arms:-*	AFA***----------149
HOWLAND	————	Mass.	Arms:-*	AFA***----------171
HOWLAND	Eng.	Mass.	Arms:-*	TNEF------------54
HOWLAND	————	————	*(only)	TNEF---------opp.78
HOWLAND	————	Mass.	Arms:-*	TNEF-----------191
HOWLAND, see: PILGRIMS				
HOWLEY	Eng.	Conn.		CFA7-----------262
HOY	Scotland	N.Y.	Arms:-*	PBAF------------31
HOYT	Eng.	Mass.		CFA9---------42,56
HOYT	Eng.	Mass.		CFA9-----------217
HOYT=HAIT	Eng.	Mass.		CFA20----------250
HOYT=HAIGHT	Eng.	Mass.		CFA21-----------51
HOYT	Eng.	Mass.	Arms:-	CFA21----------175
HOYT	————	Mass.		CFA22------------7
HOYT	————	Mass.		CRLA11----------137
HOYT	Eng.	Mass.		PFU------------359
HOYT	————	N.Y.		PPA------------442
HUBBARD	Eng.	Mass.		CFA7-----------176
HUBBARD	Eng.	Conn.		CFA11----------208

HUBBARD	Eng.	Mass.		CFA12----------324
HUBBARD	Eng.?	Mass.		CFA14-----------28
HUBBARD	Eng.	Conn.		CFA8-----------256
HUBBARD	Eng.	Conn.	Arms:-*	CFA23----------111
HUBBARD	Eng.	Mass.	Arms:-*	CFA27----13cht.,106
HUBBARD	Eng.	Mass./Conn.	Arms:-*	CRLA7----------599
HUBBARD	Eng.	Mass./Conn.		CRLA10---------150
HUBBARD	Eng.	Conn.		CRLA18---------230
HUBBARD	Eng.	Mass./N.Y.	Arms:-*	CRLA20----------22
HUBBARD	———	N.Y.		AF*------------123
HUBBARD	Eng.	Mass.	Arms:-*	AF***---------8,16
HUCKINS	———	Mass.		CFA7-----------358
HUDE	Eng.	N.J.		CFA9------------91
HUDSON	———	N.Y.		CRLA19---------182
HUESTIS	———	Mass.		CRLA20---------177
HUFF	———	N.J.		AF***----------162
HUFFMAN	———	N.J.		CFA6-----------331
HUGER	France	S.C.	Arms:-*	CRLA13---------493
HUGER	France	S.C.	Arms:-*	PFU------------451
HUGGINS	Eng.	N.H.		CFA18-----------63
HUGGINS	Eng.	N.H.		CFA18----------128
HUGGINS	———	Mass./N.H.	Arms:-*	CRLA19----------45
HUGH THE GREAT, see: ISABEL, daughter of				
HUGH I thru X, see: LE BRUN				
HUGHES	Ireland	Pa.		CRLA6----------195
HUGHES	———	Pa.		CRLA13---------425
HUGHES	———	Md./Del.		CRLA13---------463
HUGUS	France	Pa.	Arms:-*	CRLA11----------14
HUIDEKOPER	Holland	Pa.		PFU-------------74
HULBERT	Eng.	Conn.	Arms:-*	CRLA18---------435
HULETT	———	R.I.		CRLA16---------202
HULL	Eng.	Mass.	Arms:-*	CFA4-----------187
HULL	Eng.	Mass.		CFA24-----------36
HULL	Eng.	Mass.		CRLA4----------344
HULL	Eng.	Conn.		CRLA6-----------54
HULL	Eng.	Mass.		CRLA19----------38
HULL	Eng.	Conn.	Arms:-*	PBAF-----------119
HULL	Eng.	Mass.	Arms:-*	TNEF-----------227
HULME	Eng.?	Pa.		CRLA13---------347
HULSE (de)	Eng.		Arms:-*	CRLA5----------350
HUMISTON	Eng.	Conn.	Arms:-*	CRLA6----------350
HUMPHREY	Eng.	Mass.		CFA8-----------116
HUMPHREY	Eng.	Mass.	Arms:-*	CFA17----------258
HUMPHREY	Eng.	Mass.	Arms:-*	CRLA15----------72
HUMPHREY	Eng.	Mass.	Arms:-*	CRLA18----------23
HUMPHREY	Eng.	Mass.		CRLA18---------631
HUMPHREY	———	N.Y.		CRLA19---------235
HUMPHREYS	Eng.	———		CFA27----------109
HUMPHREYS	———	Conn.		PPA-------------55
HUNDLEY	———	Va.		CRLA4----------405
HUNGARY, Kings of		Arpad, d. 907		CRLA5----------351
HUNGARY, Kings of		Arpad	Arms:-*	CRLA17---------192
HUNGARY, Kings of				CRLA18---------158
HUNGARY=BOHEMIA=POLAND, Royal descent		Vou descent		CRLA18---------263
HUNGARY=POLAND=BOHEMIA, Monarchs of		Glendinning=Logan desc.		CRLA18---------317
HUNGERFORD	Eng.?	Conn.	Arms:-*	CRLA2----------264
HUNGINGTON	Eng.	Mass.	Arms:-*	CRLA20---------126
HUNNEMAN	———	Va.?/Mass.		CFA13----------293
HUNT	Eng.	Mass.		CFA3-----------207
HUNT	Eng.	Pa.	Arms:-*	CFA3-----------186
HUNT	Eng.	———	Arms:-*	CFA7-----------192
HUNT	———	N.Y.		CFA9------------88
HUNT	Eng.	Mass.		CFA11----------210
HUNT	———	N.Y.		CFA11----------259
HUNT	———	Conn./N.Y.		CFA18-----------10
HUNT	———	Mass.		CFA19-----------80
HUNT	Eng.	Mass.		CFA22----------164

HUNT	Eng.	Mass.		ACF-------------85
HUNT	Eng.	Mass.	Arms:-*	CRLA3-----------277
HUNT	———	Mass.		CRLA7-----------64
HUNTER	Scotland/Ireland	Pa./N.Y.		CFA13-----------40
HUNTER	———	Pa.		CFA20-----------86
HUNTER	Scotland/Ireland	Pa.	Arms:-	CFA23-----------201
HUNTINGTON	Eng.	Conn.		CFA4------------129
HUNTINGTON	Eng.	Conn.		CFA19---------63,90
HUNTINGTON	Eng.	Mass.		CRLA10-----------89
HUNTINGTON	Eng.	Mass.	Arms:-*	AFA***----------227
HUNTINGTON	———	Conn./N.Y.		PPA-------------511
HUNTINGTON, Samuel	———	Conn.		SDI--------125,132
HUNTLEY	———	Oregon		CFA11-----------247
HUNTON	Eng.	Va.	Arms:-*	AFA***----------131
HUNTTING	Eng.	Mass.		CFA24-----------78
HURLBUT	———	Conn.		CRLA6-----------21
HURLBUT	———	Conn.		CFA2------------289
HURLEY	———	Conn./Minn.	Arms:-	CRLA3-----------69
HURST	———	Pa.		CFA15-----------162
HURTZIG	Sweden/Germany			CFA27-----------110
HUSBAND	Eng.	Md.		CFA7------------391
HUSSEY	Eng.	Mass.		CFA1------------185
HUSSEY	Eng.	Mass.		CFA8------------169
HUSSEY	Eng.	Mass./N.H.		CFA20-----------26
HUSSEY	Eng.	Mass.		CRLA12----------263
HUSSEY	Eng.	Mass.	Arms:-*	CRLA18----------352
HUSSEY	———	N.Y.	Arms:-*	CRLA20-----------25
HUSSEY	———	———	*(only)	TNEF--------opp.35
HUSTON	———	Va./Pa.		CFA5------------319
HUSTON	———	Pa.		CRLA6-----------504
HUSTON	Ireland	Pa.	Arms:-*	CRLA14--------1,344
HUSTON	Royal descents from Charlemagne			CRLA14------180-342
HUTCHINS	———	N.H.		CFA10-----------332
HUTCHINSON	Eng.	Mass.		CFA6------------180
HUTCHINSON	———	Mass.		CFA12-----------358
HUTCHINSON	Eng.	Mass.		CFA27----13cht.,111
HUTCHINSON	———	Va.		CRLA4-----------150
HUTCHINSON	Eng.	Mass.		CRLA9-----------21
HUTCHINSON	Eng.	Mass.		CRLA13----------275
HUTCHINSON	Eng.	Mass.		CRLA13----------380
HUTCHINSON	Eng.	Mass.	Arms:-*	CRLA17----------578
HUTCHINSON	Eng.	Mass./R.I.		CRLA19-----------98
HUTCHINSON, see: MARBURY=HUTCHINSON				
HUTTON	Eng./Ireland	Md./R.I.		CFA18-----------290
HUTTON	Ireland	Pa.	Arms:-*	CRLA17-----------53
HUTTON	Eng.		Arms:-*	CRLA20----------402
HYATT	———	Conn.		CRLA13----------175
HYDE	Eng.?	Mass.		CFA19-----------280
HYDE	———	Conn.		CFA21-----------40
HYDE	Eng.	N.C.	Arms:-*	CFA21-----------150
HYDE	———	Conn.	Arms:-*	CFA26-------------1
HYDE	———	N.Y.		CRLA7-----------260
HYDE	Eng.?	Conn.	Arms:-*	CRLA10-----------82
HYMAN	———	Mass.		CFA3------------48

- I -

IDDENDEN	Eng.	———		CFA27-----------114
IESTYN ap GWRGAN	Wales		Arms:-*	AFA***----------167
ILSLEY, see: INSLEE				
INGALLS	Eng.	Mass.		CFA8------------281
INGALLS	Eng.	Mass.	Arms:-*	CFA27----13cht.,116

INGERSOLL	———	Mass./L.I.,N.Y.		CFA9------------326
INGERSOLL	Eng.	Mass.		CFA11-----------331
INGERSOLL	Eng.	L.I.,N.Y.	Arms:-	CFA14-----------13
INGERSOLL	Eng.	Mass.	Arms:-*	CRLA3-----------386
INGERSOLL	Eng.	Mass.		CRLA13----------194
INGERSOLL	Eng.	Mass.	Arms:-*	CRLA17----------26
INGERSON	———	Mass.		CFA4------------172
INGRAHAM	Eng.	Maine		CFA6------------243
INGRAHAM	Scotland?	Mass.		CRLA9-----------19
INGRAM	Eng.	Mass.		CFA8------------348
INGRAM	———	Va.		CRLA7-----------53
INMAN	———	R.I.		ACF-------------91
INMAN	Eng.	R.I.	Arms:-*	PBAF------------98
INMAN	———	———	*(only)	TNEF-------btn.70-1
INMAN, see: PILGRIMS				
INSLEE (Ilsley)	Eng.	Mass.	Arms:-*	CRLA20----------340
IREDALE	Eng.	Tenn.		CRLA10----------99
IRELAND	Eng.?	Conn./L.I.,N.Y.	Arms:-*	CFA5------------280
IRELAND	Eng./Ireland	N.Y.	Arms:-	CFA19-----------32
IRELAND, Kings of		Brian Boroimhe (Boru)		CRLA15----------167
		Carter=Boynton descent		
IRELAND	———	Pa.		CRLA15----------376
IRELAND, Monarchs of		Bray descent		CRLA17------118,122
IRELAND, Ancient Monarchs of	Mor	Schrack descent		CRLA17----------383
IRELAND, Ancient Monarchs of		Vou descent		CRLA18----------248
IRELAND, Ancient Monarchs of		Glendinning=Logan desc.		CRLA18----------314
IRELAND, Ancient Monarchs of		Richardson descent		CRLA19----------211
IRELAND, Danish Monarchs of, see: LLEWELYN ap IORWERTH				
IRISH Kings		Drake descent		CRLA1-----------308
IRISH Kings	MacMorough	Peck=Bowen desc. *(only)		CRLA2-----------42
IRISH Kings	Warren=FitzAlan	Ludlow=Brewster desc.		CRLA2-----------345
			Arms:-*	
IRISH Kings	MacMorough	de Clare=Mareschall *(only)		CRLA2-----------526
IRISH Kings		Schull descent		CRLA5-----------123
IRISH Kings		Haskell descent		CRLA8-----------70
IRISH Kings		Gaither=Fownes desc.		CRLA11----------34
IRISH Kings		Wales descent		CRLA13----------70
IRISH Kings	de Clare line	Smith descent		CRLA15----------311
IRISH Kings	MacMorough	Ayres=Sheppard desc.		CRLA15----------349
IRISH Kings	MacMorough		Arms:-*	CRLA15--opp.144,172
IRISH Kings				CRLA18----------161
IRISH Kings	Ugaine Mor			CRLA20----------268
IRVINE	Scotland	Pa.	Arms:-*	CFA6------------282
IRVINE	———	Ga.		MCS-------------77
IRVING	Scotland	N.Y./Pa.	Arms:-*	CRLA8-----------400
ISAACS	———	Conn.		CFA18-----------204
ISABEL, daughter of Hugh the Great		Warren descent		TNEF------------92
ISLE OF MAN, see: MAN, Isle of, Kings of				
ISTYN ap GWRGAN	Wales		Arms:-*	AFA***----------39
IVES	Eng.	Conn.		CFA15-----------382
IVES	———	Mass.		CFA16-----------244
IVES	———	Mass./Conn.		CRLA19----------111
IVES	Eng.?	Conn.	Arms:-	AF***-----------67
IVINS	———	N.J.		CRLA2-----------375
IVINS	———	N.J.	Arms:-*	CRLA18----------546
IZARD	Eng.	S.C.	Arms:-	CFA20-----------242
IZARD	Eng.	S.C.		PFU----------45,167

- J -

JACKSON	Eng.	N.Y.		CFA5------------19
JACKSON	Eng.	Mass.		CFA7------------383

JACKSON	Eng.	Mass.		CFA18------------56
JACKSON	————	Md.	Arms:-*	CRLA1----------530
JACKSON	————	Mass.	Arms:-*	CRLA8-----------40
JACKSON	————	N.H./Maine		CRLA15---------395
JACKSON	————	L.I.,N.Y.		CRLA18---------428
JACKSON	————	Georgia		PPA------------468
JACOBSEN	————	N.Y.	Arms:-*	CRLA20-------35,56
JAMES	————	Md.		CFA10-----------35
JAMES	————	R.I./Vt.		CFA12----------210
JAMES	————	Pa.	Arms:-*	CRLA17---------541
JAMES	————	N.Y.		PFU------------193
JAMESON	Scotland	Mass.		CFA7-----------338
JAMESON	Scotland/Ireland Pa.		Arms:-*	CRLA17----------51
JAMIESON	Scotland	Wisc.		CRLA13---------154
JENKINS	Wales	Pa.	Arms:-*	AFA***---------217
JANNEY	Eng.	Pa.		ACF-------------31
JANNEY	Eng.	Pa.	Arms:-*	AFA***----------69
JANS	Maesterlandt N.Y.			ACF-------------72
JANS	Netherlands		Arms:-*	CRLA20-------15,48
JANS	Holland	N.Y.		AF**------------64
JANSEN	————	Pa.		CFA5-----------345
JANSEN	————	Pa.		CFA6-----------382
JAQUES	————	N.J.	Arms:-*	CRLA13---------475
JAQUET	Switzerland	N.Y./Del.	Arms:-*	AFA***---------387
JAQUITH	————	Mass.		CRLA11---------585
JARBOE	France	Md.		CRLA2-----------74
JARRETT	————	Va.		CRLA19---------126
JARVIS	————	L.I.,N.Y.		CFA11----------193
JARVIS	————	L.I.,N.Y.		CRLA10---------210
JARVIS	Eng.	N.Y.		CRLA19---------409
JAUDON	France	Pa.		CFA18----------174
JAY	France	N.Y.		CFA11----------132
JAY	France	N.Y.		CFA15----------250
JAY	France	S.C.		CFA25----------100
JAY	France	N.Y.	Arms:-*	HFA------------145
JAY	France	N.Y.		PFU-------------82
JAYNE	Eng.	L.I.,N.Y.	Arms:-*	CRLA11---------190
JEFFERSON	Wales?	Va.		CFA5-----------143
JEFFERSON, Thomas	————	Va.		SDI--------201,205
JEFFERY	————	Pa./Md.	Arms:-*	CRLA1----------489
JEFFERYS	Eng.	Pa.	Arms:-*	AFA***----------61
JEFFORDS	————	S.C.		AF***----------155
JEFFRAY	Scotland	N.Y.C.		CFA21-----------57
JEFFREYS	————	Pa.		MCS-------------28
JEFTS (Jeffs)	Eng.	Mass.	Arms:-*	AF*------------215
JENCKES (Jenks)	Eng.	Mass.	Arms:-*	CRLA6----------409
JENISON	————	Mass.		CRLA1----------213
JENKIN	Eng.		Arms:-*	CRLA15----------28
JENKINS	————	Mass.		CFA20-----------28
JENKINS	————	S.C./Ohio		CRLA3-----------57
JENKINS	————	Md.		CRLA8----------174
JENKINS	Eng.	N.C.	Arms:-*	CRLA9----------255
JENKINS	No family data		Arms:-*	CRLA15------opp.485
JENKINSON	Eng.	Pa.	Arms:-*	AF*------------13
JENKS	Eng.	Mass.	Arms:-*	CFA7------------65
JENKS	Eng.	Mass.	Arms:-*	CRLA18---------530
JENKS	Eng.	Mass.	Arms:-*	AFA***---------241
JENNER	Eng.	N.Y., etc.	Arms:-*	AF***----------328
JENNEY	Holland	Mass.		CFA27----------120
JENNEY	Eng.	Mass.	Arms:-*	CRLA10---------293
JENNEY	Eng.	Mass.		CRLA17---------460
JENNINGS	Eng.	Va.		CRLA1----------252
JENNINGS	Eng.	Va.	Arms:-*	CRLA4----------474
JENNINGS	Eng.	N.J.	Arms:-*	CRLA12---------400
JENNINGS	————	Va.		CRLA16---------220
JENNINGS	Eng.	Mass.		CRLA19----------86
JENNINGS	————	Va.		AF***----------316

JEPHSON	Ireland	N.Y.C.		CFA20-----------150
JESSOP	Eng.	Md.	Arms:-*	CFA3------------196
JESSOP	Eng.	Md.	Arms:-*	CFA7------------202
JESSUP	———	Mass./Conn.		CFA24------------75
JESUP	———	N.Y.		PFU-------------473
JEWELL	Eng.	Mass.		CFA6------------217
JEWETT	Eng.	Mass.		CFA7------------393
JEWETT	Eng.	Mass.		CFA8------------373
JEWETT	Eng.	Mass.	Arms:-*	AFA***---------320
JOB	———	N.H./Pa./Md.		CRLA11----------487
JOHANSEN	———	Mo.		AF*-------------442
JOHN	Wales	Pa.		CRLA13----------210
JOHNS	Wales	Md.		CRLA4-------------5
JOHNSON	Eng.	Mass.		CFA11-----------372
JOHNSON	Eng.	Conn.		CFA12-----------200
JOHNSON	———	N.C.		CFA14-----------138
JOHNSON	Eng.	Mass.		CFA13-----------209
JOHNSON	———	Conn.		CFA13-----------237
JOHNSON	———	Mass.		CFA18------------86
JOHNSON	Eng.	Mass.		CFA22-----------217
JOHNSON	———	Mass.		CRLA4-----------357
JOHNSON	No family data		Arms:-*	CRLA5-------opp.496
JOHNSON	———	Conn.		CRLA7-----------162
JOHNSON	———	R.I.		CRLA7-----------318
JOHNSON	———	Mass./Conn.	Arms:-*	CRLA7-------569,598
JOHNSON	———	———	*(only)	CRLA12-------opp.88
JOHNSON	Eng.	Mass.		CRLA13-----------27
JOHNSON	———	Pa.		CRLA13----------437
JOHNSON	———	Va.		CRLA15----------319
JOHNSON	———	Va.		CRLA15----------589
JOHNSON	———	Pa.		CRLA17----------410
JOHNSON	Eng.?	Conn.		CRLA18----------221
JOHNSON	———	Conn.		CRLA19----------106
JOHNSON	———	Pa./Va./W.Va.		CRLA19----------125
JOHNSON	Eng.	Mass.		CRLA19----------393
JOHNSON	———	Mass.		CRLA20----------208
JOHNSTON	———	N.J.	*(only)	CRLA2-----------316
JOHNSTON	———	———		CRLA19----------151
JOHNSTONE	Scotland	N.J.		CRLA15----------451
JOLLIFFE	Eng.	Va.	Arms:-*	CRLA17----------221
JOLLS	———	———		ACF--------------77
JONES	———	Conn.		CFA1-------------44
JONES	Wales	R.I.		CFA7------------312
JONES	Eng.	Mass.	Arms:-*	CFA8------------310
JONES	———	Va.		CFA13-----------225
JONES	———	R.I.?/Mass.		CFA19-----------289
JONES	Wales	Pa.		CFA20------------86
JONES	Eng.	Va.		CRLA1------------99
JONES	Wales	Pa.		CRLA2-----------414
JONES	———	Tenn./Ill.		CRLA3------------92
JONES	Wales	Va.		CRLA8-----------448
JONES	Wales	Pa.		CRLA9------------17
JONES	———	Pa./N.J.		CRLA9-------154,176
JONES	Wales	Pa./Ala.		CRLA10-----------59
JONES	———	N.J./Ohio		CRLA12----------393
JONES	———	Mass.		CRLA15-----------11
JONES	———	Pa.		CRLA15----------243
JONES	———	Mich./Calif.		CRLA16-----------33
JONES	———	Mass.		CRLA17----------251
JONES	Wales	Pa.		CRLA17----------274
JONES	Eng.	Conn.		CRLA19----------112
JONES	Eng.	Mass./Conn.		CRLA19------301,303
JONES	Eng.	Mass.		CRLA20----------203
JONES	———	Pa.		CRLA20----------296
JORDAN	———	Maine		CRLA5-----------194
JORDAN	Eng.	Conn.		CRLA7-----------164
JORDAN	———	Mass.		CRLA15-----------14

JORDAN	———	Maine	Arms:-*	AF**-------------28
JORISSE	———	N.Y.?	Arms:-*	CRLA20----------67
JOSLIN	———	Mass.		CFA10-----------178
JOSSELYN	———	Maine		MCS-------------110
JOY	Eng.	Mass.		CFA7-------------46
JOY	Eng.?	Mass.	Arms:-*	CRLA18----------24
JOY	Eng.	Mass.	Arms:-*	AFA***----------323
JUDD	Eng.	Mass.		CRLA13----------56
JUDD	Eng.	Mass./Conn.		CRLA18---------607
JUDD	Eng.	Mass.		CRLA19---------259
JUDSON	Eng.	Mass.	Arms:-*	CFA5------------138
JUDSON	Eng.	Mass.		CRLA6------------29

- K -

KAAPP	Eng.	Mass.	Arms:-*	CRLA15---------491
KATZENBACH	Germany	N.J.		CRLA12---------199
KAY	Eng.	N.J.	Arms:-	CRLA5------------36
KEARNY	Eng./Ireland	N.J.	Arms:-*	AFA***----------137
KEEN	Sweden	Pa.		CRLA9-----------303
KEENE	———	Va./Md.		CRLA8-----------139
KEENE	———	———		CRLA13---------463
KEENAN	———	Va./W.Va.		CRLA19---------129
KEENEY	———	Mass./Conn.		CFA23-----------118
KEENEY	———	Conn.		AF***-----------288
KEEP	Eng.	Mass.	Arms:-*	CFA26-----------105
KEEP	Eng.	Mass./Conn.	Arms:-	AF***-----------411
KEIM	Germany	Pa.	Arms:-*	AFA***----------173
KEITH	Scotland	Mass.		CFA12------------79
KEITH	———	Md.		CRLA1-----------495
KEITH	Scotland	Va.		CRLA4-----------180
KEITH	Scotland		Arms:-*	AF*-------------167
KELLAM	———	Va.		CRLA15---------320
KELLOGG	Eng.	Conn./Mass.		CFA2------------110
KELLOGG	Eng.?	Mass.		CFA6------------342
KELLOGG	Eng.	Conn.		CFA7------------242
KELLOGG	Eng.	Conn.		CFA7------------253
KELLOGG	Eng.	Conn./Mass.		CFA8------------342
KELLOGG	Eng.	Conn.	Arms:-*	CFA15-----------311
KELLOGG	Eng.	Conn.		CFA18-----------194
KELLOGG	Eng.	Conn./Mass.		ACF---------------7
KELLOGG	Eng.	Mass.		CRLA13----------49
KELLOGG	Eng.	Mass.		CRLA19---------263
KELLOGG	Eng.	Mass.	Arms:-	AF***-------361,378
KELLY	———	R.I.		AF*-------------270
KELSEY	Eng.?	Conn.		CRLA6------------60
KELSEY	Eng.	Mass./Conn.		CRLA10---------219
KEMPE	———	Va.		MCS-------------61
KENDALL	Eng.	Va.		CFA13-----------227
KENDALL	Eng.	Mass.	Arms:-	CFA17-----------116
KENDALL	———	Mass.	Arms:-*	CRLA15----------28
KENDALL	———	Va.	Arms:-*	CRLA15---------331
KENDALL	Eng.	Mass.	Arms:-*	AFA2------------113
KENDALL	———	———	*(only)	TNEF--------opp.35
KENDIG	Switzerland	Pa.		CRLA19---------234
KENNARD	Eng.	N.H.	Arms:-*	CFA7------------168
KENNEDY	Scotland	N.C.	Arms:-	CFA3------------341
KENNEDY	Scotland/Eng./Ireland Pa.			CRLA2-----------220
KENNEDY	———	Pa.		CRLA15---------237
KENNEDY	Canada		Arms:-	AF**------------180
KENNEN	———	Mass.	Arms:-	TNEF------------244
KENNER	———	Va.		CRLA14-----------92

KENNETH I	Scotland		MacAlpin descent	CRLA2-----------362
KENNETT	Eng.	Va.	Arms:-*	AF**-----------367
KENNETT	Eng.	Va.	Arms:-	AF**-----------492
KENNON	------	Va.		CRLA4-----------110
KENRIC	Eng.	Mass.		CFA15-----------351
KENRICK=EDDOWES	------	Pa.		MCS-------------88
KENT	------	Mass.		CFA7-----------224
KENT	------	Mass.		CFA7-----------356
KENT	Eng.	Mass.		CFA18-----------202
KENT	Eng.	Mass.		CFA24-----------154
KENT	Eng.	Mass.		CRLA1-----------415
KENT	Eng.	Mass.	Arms:-*	CRLA18--------33,35
KERDESTON	Eng.		Arms:-*	CRLA20-----------403
KERN	Bavaria	Ind./Ill.		CRLA8-----------367
KERN	------	Pa.		CRLA9-----------458
KERNOCHAN	Scotland	La./N.Y.C.		CFA5-----------144
KERR	Scotland	Pa.		CRLA9-----------286
KETCHAM	Eng.	Mass.		CFA12-----------113
KETCHUM	------	Mass.?/Conn./N.Y.		CFA2-----------287
KETCHUM	------	Conn.		CRLA18-----------434
KETELTAS	------	N.Y.		CFA11-----------45
KEY	Eng.	Md.		CFA9-----------135
KEY	------	N.C.		CRLA17-----------610
KEY	------	Md.		PPA-------------128
KEYES	------	Va.		CRLA6-----------207
KEYES	------	Mass.		TNEF-----------150
KEYSER	Holland	Pa.		CRLA3-----------248
KEYSER	Holland	Pa.	Arms:-*	CRLA20-----------150
KEYTE	Eng.	Pa.	Arms:-*	AFA***-----------185
KIBBE	Eng.?	Mass.	Arms:-*	CRLA17-----------516
KIDDER	Eng.	Mass.		CFA19-----------79
KIDDER	Eng.	Mass.		CFA19-----------282
KIDDER	Eng.	Mass.		CRLA15-----------377
KIDDER	Eng.?	Mass.		CRLA17-----------684
KIDDER	------	Vt.		TNEF-----------204
KIERSTEDE	Europe	Ft. George, ?		ACF-------------71
KIERSTEDE	Germany	N.Y.		CRLA20-----------48
KIERSTEDE	Prussian Saxony N.Y.		Arms:-	AF**-----------63
KIEV, Grand Dukes of	Russia		Gaither=Fownes desc.	CRLA11-----------56
KIEV, Grand Dukes of	Russia		Blackiston descent	CRLA11-----------392
KIEV, Dukes of	Russia	Rurik	Schrack descent	CRLA17-----------388
KILBOURNE	Eng.	Conn.		CFA9-----------115
KILBOURNE	Eng.	Conn.		CFA9-----------194
KILBOURNE	Eng.	Conn.		CFA18-----------93
KILBOURNE	Eng.	Conn.		CRLA17-----------525
KILBOURNE	Eng.	Conn.	Arms:-*	PBAF-----------160
KILHAM	Eng.	Mass.	Arms:-*	CRLA8-----------37
KIMBALL	Eng.	Mass.	Arms:-*	CFA7-----------88
KIMBALL	Eng.	Mass.	Arms:-	CFA9-----------330
KIMBALL	Eng.	Mass.	Arms:-*	CFA14-----------5
KIMBALL	Eng.	Mass.	Arms:-*	CFA16-----------122
KIMBALL	------	Maine		CFA18-----------131
KIMBALL	Eng.	Mass.	Arms:-*	CRLA3-----------18
KIMBALL	Eng.	Mass.	Arms:-*	CRLA8-----------58
KIMBALL	------	Mass.	Arms:-*	CRLA15-----------12
KIMBALL	Eng.	Mass.		CRLA15-----------426
KIMBALL	No family data		Arms:-*	CRLA18-----------358
KIMBALL	Eng.	Mass.	Arms:-*	CRLA20-----------73
KING	------	New Eng.	Arms:-*	CFA4-----------3
KING	------	Mass.		CFA4-----------48
KING	Eng.	Mass.	Arms:-	CFA5-----------255
KING	Eng.	Mass.	Arms:-*	CFA6-----------37
KING	Eng.	Mass.	Arms:-*	CFA6-----------200
KING	Eng.	Mass.		CFA7-----------121
KING	Eng.	Mass.		CFA12-----------81
KING	------	Mass.	Arms:-*	CFA12-----------378
KING	------	Mass.		CRLA13----------195

KING	————	Pa.		CRLA17---------699
KING	————	Maine		HFA--------------60
KING	Eng.	Mass.	Arms:-	TNEF------------131
KING	————	Mass.		TNEF------------236
KINGSBURY	Eng.	Mass.		CFA4------------171
KINGSBURY	Eng.	Mass.		CFA7------------351
KINGSBURY	————	Mass.		CRLA20---------205
KINGSBURY	————	Mass.		PFU-------------447
KINGSLEY	Eng.	Mass.	Arms:-*	CFA1-------------50
KINGSLEY	Eng.	Mass.		CFA9------------238
KINGSLEY	————	Mass.		CFA19----------289
KINERT, see: KYNETT				
KINNE	Eng.	Mass.		CRLA8----------502
KINSMAN	————	Mass.	Arms:-*	CRLA20---------372
KINNEY	————	Mass.		CFA7------------330
KINNEY	Scotland	N.J.	Arms:-*	CFA16----------166
KIP	Holland	————		CFA8------------42
KIP	Holland	N.Y.		CFA20----------179
KIP (de Kype)	France/Holland	N.Y.	Arms:-*	AFA2------------17
KIP	————	N.Y.	Arms:-*	AFA***---------231
KIRBY	Eng.	Mass./L.I.,N.Y.		CFA7------------385
KIRBY	————	Mass.	Arms:-*	AFA***---------193
KIRK	Scotland	N.Y.C.		CFA26----------113
KIRK	Eng./Ireland		Arms:-*	CRLA13---------136
KIRK	————	Pa.	Arms:-*	CRLA13---------391
KIRKBRIDGE	Eng.	Pa.		CRLA13---------349
KIRKBRIDGE	Eng.		Arms:-*	CRLA14------opp.129
KIRKBY	Eng.		Arms:-*	PBAF-----------199
KIRKPATRICK	Scotland	N.J.	Arms:-	CFA15----------289
KIRKPATRICK	No family data		Arms:-*	CRLA13------opp.132
KIRKWOOD	Ireland	Del.		CRLA6----------427
KITCHELL	Eng.	Conn.		CFA14----------202
KITCHELL	Eng.	Conn.		CFA16----------317
KITE	————	Pa.	Arms:-*	CRLA9----------297
KITTELL	————	Pa.		CRLA19---------309
KIRTLAND	Eng.	Mass.		CFA10----------248
KLAEBOE	Norway			CRLA6-----------26
KLAPP	Eng.	N.Y.		CRLA15---------444
KLEIN	————	Pa.		CRLA15---------539
KLINE	Germany	N.Y./Pa.		CRLA19---------337
KLIPSTEIN	————	Va.		CRLA4----------307
KLOSTERMANN	Germany	Ohio/Mo.		AF*------------431
KNAPP	Eng.	Mass.		CFA10----------314
KNAPP	Eng.	Mass.		CFA14-----------15
KNAPP	Eng.	Mass.	Arms:-*	CRLA13---------454
KNEELAND	Scotland	Mass.	Arms:-*	CFA8-----------126
KNEELAND	Eng.	Mass.		CRLA20---------111
KNICKERBOCKER	Holland	N.Y.		AF*------------233
KNIGHT	————	R.I.		CFA4-----------168
KNIGHT	Eng.	Mass.	Arms:-*	CFA6-----------183
KNIGHT	Eng.	Mass.		CFA7-----------331
KNIGHT	Eng.	Mass.	Arms:-*	CFA11----------243
KNIGHT	————	Mass.		CFA19----------295
KNIGHT	Eng.	Mass.		CFA21-----------49
KNIGHT	Eng.	Pa.	*(only)	CRLA2----------399
KNIGHT	Eng.?	Mass.	Arms:-*	CRLA3----------374
KNIGHT	Eng.	Pa.		CRLA13---------125
KNIGHT	Eng.?	Mich.	Arms:-*	CRLA13---------483
KNIGHT	————	Pa.		CRLA17---------211
KNIGHT	————	Mass.		CRLA20---------215
KNOWLES	————	Mass.	Arms:-*	CFA8-----------137
KNOWLES	————	Mass.	Arms:-*	CRLA2----------308
KNOWLES	————	Mass.		CRLA7----------440
KNOWLES	————	R.I.		CRLA19---------291
KNOWLTON	Eng.	Mass.		CFA7------------13
KNOWLTON	Eng.	Mass.	Arms:-*	CRLA12----------31
KOHRS	Germany	Iowa		CRLA19---------123

KOLB	Germany	Pa.		CRLA9-----------450
KOMECKI	Poland	Pa.	Arms:-*	AFA***---------139
KONANTZ	Germany	Ill.		CRLA13----------409
KOONS	——	Pa.	Arms:-	AF**-----------289
KORNHAUS	——	Pa.		CRLA11----------476
KORNHOFF	Germany	N.J.		CRLA19----------164
KOUNSE	——	Pa./W.Va.		CRLA19----------127
KRAUSS	Germany	Pa.	Arms:-*	CRLA20----------150
KRETSINGER	——	N.Y.		AF*------------362
KROM	Holland	N.Y.		CRLA16----------91
KRUMBHAAR	Germany/Eng.	Pa.		CFA13-----------265
KRUMBHAAR	Germany	Pa.	Arms:-*	AFA***---------117
KUNHARDT	Germany	N.Y.C.	Arms:-*	CFA27------------9
KUNST	Holland	N.Y.	Arms:-*	CRLA18----------559
KURTZ	——	Pa.	Arms:-*	CRLA8-----------249
KURTZ	Europe	Md./Pa.		CRLA19----------220
KYME (de)	Eng.			CRLA15----------120
KYNASTON	Wales			CRLA2-----------452
KYNETT (Kinert)	Germany?	Pa.	Arms:-*	CRLA18----------339

- L -

LACKEY	——	Va.	Arms:-	AF***----------266
LACY (de)	Eng.			CRLA2-----------479
LACY (de)	Eng.		Arms:-*	CRLA5-----------355
LACY (de)	Eng.		Gaither=Fownes desc.	CRLA11----------51
LACY (de)	Eng.			CRLA15----------122
LACY (de)	Eng.		Bray descent	CRLA17----------146
LACY (de)	Eng.		Cooley=Twining desc.	CRLA18----------141
LACY (de)	Eng.		Titus descent	CRLA18----------511
LADD	——	Mass.	Arms:-*	CRLA3-----------38
LADD	——	Mass.		CRLA3-----------223
LA DUE	——	N.Y.		CFA1------------61
LAFFERTY	——	Del./Ohio		CRLA16----------46
LAFITTE	France	S.C.	Arms:-*	CRLA13----------490
LAING	Scotland	N.J.	Arms:-	ACF------------84
LAIRD	Ireland	Pa./Md./Del.	Arms:-*	CRLA1-----------90
LAKE	Eng.	N.Y.C.		CFA23----------123
LAKE	——	Conn.	Arms:-	CRLA6-----------151
LAMAR	——	——		CFA17----------376
LAMB	——	Mass.		CFA2-----------320
LAMB	——	N.J.		CRLA17----------290
LAMBERT	Eng.	Mass.	Arms:-	CFA3-----------310
LAMBERT	Eng.	Mass.	Arms:-*	CFA24----------131
LAMBORN	Eng.	Pa.	Arms:-*	CRLA8-----------188
LAMMOT	France	S.C./Md./Pa.	Arms:-*	CRLA1-----------32
LAMONT	Scotland	N.Y.	Arms:-*	CFA5-----------150
LAMONT	Scotland	N.Y.	Arms:-*	CRLA19----------49
LANCASTER	No family data		**Arms:-***	CRLA13------opp.132
LANCASTER	Eng.		Arms:-*	CRLA14------opp.129
LAND	Eng.	Del.	Arms:-*	CRLA1-----------80
LANDIS	Germany	Pa.		CRLA9-----------453
LANDON	Eng.	Mass./L.I.,N.Y.		CFA2-----------290
LANDON	——	N.Y.	Arms:-*	CRLA18----------436
LANE	Eng.	Mass.	Arms:-*	CFA6-----------199
LANE	Eng.	Mass.	Arms:-*	CFA12----------377
LANE	Eng.	Mass.	Arms:-*	CFA17----------129
LANE	——	Va./N.C.		CRLA8-----------446
LANE	——	Pa.		CRLA19----------185
LANGDON	——	Mass.		CFA9------------77
LANGDON	——	Mass.		CFA13----------163
LANGDON	Eng.	Mass.		CRLA20----------199

LANGDON	——	N.H.	Arms:-*	HFA-------------238
LANGHORNE	Wales	Va.	Arms:-	CFA19-------211,217
LANGWORTHY	——	R.I.?/N.Y.		CFA20-----------269
LANGWORTHY	Eng.?	Mass.		CRLA7-----------309
LANPHIER	Ireland	Va.		CRLA3-----------297
LANSDALE	Eng.	Md.		CRLA17----------557
LANSDALE	Eng.	Md.		CFA20-----------322
LANSING	NETHERLANDS	N.Y.	Arms:-*	CFA22------------26
LANVALLEI (de)		Titus descent		CRLA18----------504
LARCUM	——	Mass.		CRLA8------------53
LARKIN	Eng.	Mass.	Arms:-*	CFA4-------------16
LARKIN	Eng.	Mass.		CFA8------------102
LARKIN	Eng.	Mass.		CFA21-----------222
LARKIN	Eng.?	Md.	Arms:-*	CRLA1-----------487
LARNED	Eng.	Mass.		CFA2------------250
LARNED=LEARNED	Eng.	Mass.		CFA15-----------354
LARRABEE	——	Mass./Maine		CFA5------------189
LARRABEE	——	Wisc./Pa.		CRLA6-----------157
LARZELERE	——	L.I.,N.Y.		CRLA11----------269
LASHAR	——	Conn.		CRLA20----------338
LASHER	——	N.Y.		CRLA7-----------269
LASSITER	——	Va.		AF***-----------295
LATHAM	Eng.	Conn.	Arms:-*	CFA1-------------10
LATHAM	——	Mass.		CFA7------------305
LATHAM	Eng.	Mass.		CFA10-----------266
LATHAM	——	Mass.		CFA13-----------323
LATHAM (de)	Eng.		Arms:-*	CRLA5-----------357
LATHAM	Eng.	R.I.		CRLA17----------492
LATHAM	——	R.I.?	Arms:-*	CRLA18-------opp.24
LATHAM	Eng.	R.I.	Arms:-*	AFA***----------309
LATHROP	Eng.	Mass.		CFA7------------348
LATHROP	Eng.	Mass.	Arms:-*	CFA11-----------240
LATHROP	Eng.	Mass.		CFA19------------87
LATHROP	Eng.	Mass.		CRLA11----------515
LATHROP	Eng.	Mass.		CRLA17----------516
LATHROP	Eng.	Mass.		PFU-------------356
LATIMER	Ireland	Pa.		CRLA2-----------110
LAUGHLIN	——	Ky.		AF*-------------315
LAUNCE	——	Mass.		ARSC------------33
LAUNCE=SHERMAN	——	Mass.		MCS-------------29
LAW	Eng.	Pa.		CRLA15----------255
LAWRENCE	Eng.	Mass.		CFA6------------151
LAWRENCE	Eng.	Mass.		CFA8------------255
LAWRENCE	——	Mass.		CFA9------------257
LAWRENCE	——	L.I.,N.Y.		CFA10-----------194
LAWRENCE	Eng.	Mass.	Arms:-*	CFA13-----------166
LAWRENCE	Eng.	N.Y.		CFA13-----------241
LAWRENCE	Eng.	L.I.,N.Y.	Arms:-	CFA14------------56
LAWRENCE	Eng.	Mass.		CFA14-----------214
LAWRENCE	Eng.	Mass.		CFA14-----------336
LAWRENCE	Eng.	Mass.	Arms:-*	CFA21-----------217
LAWRENCE	Eng.	N.H.		CRLA15----------275
LAWRENCE	Eng.	Mass.	Arms:-*	CRLA17----------554
LAWRENCE	Eng.	Mass.		CRLA19----------332
LAWRENCE	Eng.	Mass.	Arms:-*	AF*-------------217
LAWRENCE	——	N.Y.		PPA-------------349
LAWTON	Eng.	Mass.		CFA2------------319
LAWTON	——	R.I.		CFA6------------290
LAWTON	——	R.I.		CFA9-------------15
LAWTON	Eng.	R.I.		CFA10-----------278
LAWTON	——	R.I.	Arms:-	CRLA3-----------447
LAWTON	Eng.	R.I.		CRLA20----------370
LAWTON	Eng.	Mass./Conn.	Arms:-	TNEF-------------44
LAYTON	Eng.		Arms:-*	CRLA14------opp.129
LEA	Eng.	Pa.	Arms:-*	CFA18-----------162
LEA	Eng.	Pa.		CRLA15----------602
LEACH	——	Mass.	Arms:-*	CRLA8------------14

LEACH	———	Mass.	Arms:-*	CRLA13---------243
LEAKE	———	Va.	Arms:-	AF***----------263
LEARNED	———	Mass.		CFA10----------107
LEARNED	Eng.	Mass.	Arms:-*	CRLA15----------38
LEAS	———	Pa.		CRLA19---------229
LEAVENWORTH	———	Conn.	Arms:-	CRLA7-------525,537
LE BAILEY (de)	France	N.Y.		AF***----------159
LE BRUN	France	Hugh I - X Warren descent		CRLA2----------338
LE DEE DE RENCOURT	France			CRLA15---------252
LE DEE DE RENCOURT	France			CRLA15---------593
LE DEE DE ROCCOURT	France			CRLA1-----------41
LEDERACH	———	Pa.		CRLA9----------448
LEDYARD	Eng.	Conn.	Arms:-*	CFA1-------------1
LEDYARD	Eng.	L.I.,N.Y.		CFA12----------284
LEDYARD	Eng.	N.Y.	Arms:-	CFA16----------124
LEE	Eng.	Conn.		CFA1------------43
LEE	Eng.	Md.		CFA3----------303
LEE	Eng.	Mass.		CFA15---------349
LEE	Eng.	Conn.		CFA19---------183
LEE	Eng.	Md.		CFA20---------219
LEE	Eng.	Va.		CRLA1-------103,105
LEE	Eng.		Arms:-*	CRLA15---------318
LEE	———	Mass.		CRLA16---------122
LEE	Eng.	L.I.,N.Y.		CRLA17---------532
LEE	Eng.	Va.		HFA------------336
LEE	———	Va.		MCS------------103
LEE, Francis Lightfoot	———	Va.	Brother to Richard	SDI---------201,214
LEE, Richard Henry	———	Va.	Brother to Francis	SDI---------201,203
LEECH	Eng.	Pa.		CRLA19---------349
LEETE	Eng.	Conn.		CRLA19---------267
LEETE	———	Conn.		MCS------------106
LEETES (Leete)	———	———	*(only)	TNEF---------opp.44
LEFFERTS	Holland	N.Y.		CFA22----------142
LEFFINGWELL	Eng.	Conn.		CFA23-----------92
LEFFINGWELL	Eng.?	Conn.		CRLA10----------93
LEFFINGWELL	———	Conn.		PFU------------258
LEGARE	———	S.C.		PPA------------577
LEGGETT	Eng.	N.Y.		CFA20-----------29
LEGGETT	———	N.Y.		PPA------------285
LEGH	Eng.			CRLA9----------167
LEIB	———	Pa.		CRLA9-----------16
LEIGHTON	———	Maine		CFA2-----------180
LELAND	———	Mass.		CFA2-----------250
LELAND	Eng.	Mass./Pa.		PPA------------595
LEMON	Ireland	Pa.		ACF-------------62
LEOFRIC, Earl of Mercia	Eng.		Nelson descent	CRLA2----------117
LEOFRIC, Earl of Mercia	Eng.		Bray descent	CRLA17---------128
LEONARD	Eng.	Mass.		CRLA20---------216
LEONARD, see: NORTON=LEONARD				
LE PELLETIER	France		Arms:-*	CRLA1-----------49
LEQUIER	———	N.Y.		CFA4-----------175
LE ROY	France	N.Y.		CFA5-----------260
LE ROY	———			CFA20---------333
LE VAN	France/Holland	Pa.		CRLA12---------341
LE VAN	Europe	Pa.		CRLA20---------370
LEVERING	Germany	Pa.		CRLA8----------204
LEVESON	Eng.			CRLA9-----------13
LEVESON	Eng.		Arms:-*	CRLA15------340,341
LEWESTON (Lewistown)	———	———	*(only)	TNEF---------opp.44
LEWIS	———	Mass.		CFA2-----------372
LEWIS	Ireland	Va.		CFA5-----------291
LEWIS	———	Mass.		CFA7-----------368
LEWIS	Wales	Pa.		CFA7-----------395
LEWIS	———	N.Y.C./Conn.		CFA14----------280
LEWIS	Eng.	Mass.		CFA15---------359
LEWIS	Wales	Va.	Arms:-*	CFA23----------168
LEWIS	———	Va.	Arms:-	CRLA3----------100

LEWIS	Wales	Va.		CRLA4------------36
LEWIS	Wales	Va.		CRLA4-----------111
LEWIS	France/Eng./Wales	Va.		CRLA4-----------199
LEWIS	Wales	Va.		CRLA4-----------216
LEWIS	------	Mass./R.I.		CRLA7-----------314
LEWIS	------	Calif.	Arms:-*	CRLA10-----------97
LEWIS	Wales/Eng.?	Va.		CRLA10----------115
LEWIS	------	Mass.		CRLA13-----------57
LEWIS	------	N.J./Pa.		CRLA15----------493
LEWIS	------	Mass.		CRLA18----------609
LEWIS	------	Mass.	Arms:-*	CRLA20----------336
LEWIS	Wales	Va.	Arms:-	AF**------------151
LEWIS	Eng.	Mass.	Arms:-*	AFA***----------195
LEWIS	Wales	Pa.	Arms:-*	AFA***------299,301
LEWIS	------	Mass./Maine		ARSC------------37
LEWIS=GIBBINS	------	Maine		MCS-------------99
LEWIS=GIBSON	------	N.H.		MCS-------------99
LEWIS, Francis	Wales	N.Y.		SDI---------135,136
LEWIS, see: LUDLOW=LEWIS				
LEYCESTER	Eng.		Arms:-*	CRLA11----------170
L'HOMMEDIEU	------	N.Y.		CFA4------------222
LIEVENS	------	N.Y.	Arms:-*	CRLA14-----------33
LIGHTFOOT	Eng.	Va.	Arms:-*	CFA10-----------299
LIGON, see: LYGON=LIGON				
LILLIE	------	Mass.		CFA4------------167
LILLY	------	Pa.		CRLA19----------312
LIMBOURG, Ancient Counts & Dukes of	Europe	Arms:-*	CRLA5----------360
LINCOLN	Eng.	Mass.	Arms:-*	CFA27----38cht.,122
LINCOLN	------	Mass.		CRLA10----------407
LINCOLN	Eng.	Mass.		CRLA13----------378
LINCOLN	------	Mass.		CRLA17----------448
LINCOLN, Abraham	16th U. S. President	Arms:-* opp.25	TNEF-------------24
LINDALL	------	Conn.		CFA2------------287
LINDSAY	Scotland?	Mass.		ACF--------------77
LINDSAY	------	Va.		MCS-------------38
LINDSLEY	Eng.	Conn.		CFA9------------149
LINES	------	Conn.		CRLA19----------104
LINGEN	Eng.			CRLA5-----------361
LINTON	------	Mass.	Arms:-*	CRLA13----------258
LINTON	Eng.	Pa.	Arms:-*	CRLA17----------298
LIPPINCOTT	Eng.	Mass.	Arms:-*	CFA15-----------220
LIPPINCOTT	------	Pa.		CRLA8-----------137
LIPPINCOTT	Eng.	N.J.		CRLA8-----------357
LIPPINCOTT	Eng.	N.J.		CRLA11----------539
LIPPINCOTT	Eng.	Mass.	Arms:-*	CRLA13----------142
LIPPINCOTT	Eng.	Mass./N.J.		CRLA13----------250
LIPPINCOTT	Eng.	Mass./N.J.		CRLA14-----------82
LIPPITT	------	R.I.		CRLA19----------290
LIPSCOMBE	------	Va.		CRLA12----------212
LISPENARD	France	N.Y.		CFA16-----------305
LISPENARD	------	N.Y.		CFA17-----------82
LISTER=LISETER	No family data		Arms:-*	CRLA13------opp.130
LITTLE	------	Mass.		CFA6------------186
LITTLEFIELD	------	Mass.		CFA10------------29
LITTLEFIELD	Eng.	N.H./Maine		CFA10-----------214
LITTLEFIELD	Eng.	N.H./Maine		CRLA11----------239
LITTLEFIELD	Eng.	Mass./N.H.	Arms:-*	CRLA20-----------83
LITTLETON	Eng.	Va.	Arms:-*	CFA10------------57
LIVERMORE	Eng.	Mass.		CFA12------------90
LIVERMORE	Eng.	Conn./Mass.		CFA15------------58
LIVERMORE	------	Mass.		CFA7-------------80
LIVERSIDGE	Eng.	Pa.		CRLA13----------211
LIVESEY	Eng.	Pa.	Arms:-*	AFA***----------151
LIVESEY	Eng.	Pa.	Arms:-*	AFA***----------279
LIVEZEY	------	Pa.		CRLA4-----------357
LIVEZEY	Eng.	Pa.	Arms:-*	CRLA17----------332
LIVINGSTON	Scotland	N.Y.	Arms:-*	CFA11-------------1

```
LIVINGSTON              Scotland    N.Y.              Arms:-*        CFA13------------42
LIVINGSTON              Eng./Scotland  Mass.          Arms:-         CFA20----------193
LIVINGSTON              Scotland    Mass./N.Y.                       CFA20----------325
LIVINGSTON              Scotland    N.Y.              Arms:-*        CFA25-----------42
LIVINGSTON              ------      N.Y.                             MCS-------------37
LIVINGSTON              Scotland/Ireland  Mass./N.Y.  Arms:-*        PFU-------------33
LIVINGSTON, Philip      ------      N.Y.                             SDI---------135,138
LIVINGSTON(E)           Scotland    N.Y.              Arms:-*        PBAF------------43
LLYWELLYN ap IORWERTH   Wales                         Arms:-*        CRLA15---------176
                        His descent from Niall, d. 405,
                        and monarchs of Ireland   -845
LLOYD                   ------      Pa.                              CFA5-----------332
LLOYD                   Wales       Pa.               Arms:-         CFA6-----------385
LLOYD                   Wales       Md.                              CFA9-----------139
LLOYD=PRESTON           Wales       Pa./Md.                          CFA15----------152
LLOYD                   Wales       Pa.                              CRLA11---------490
LLOYD                   ------      Pa.                              CRLA15---------239
LLOYD                   Wales       Pa.               Arms:-*        AFA***---------73
LLOYD                   Wales       Pa.               Arms:-*        AFA***--------197
LLOYD                   Wales       Pa.               Arms:-*        AFA***--------259
LLOYD                   ------      Pa.                              MCS-------------28
LOBDELL                 ------      Mass.                            CFA1-----------226
LOCKE                   Eng.        Mass.             Arms:-*        CRLA20---------89
LOCKRIDGE               ------      Va./S.C.                         CRLA19--------129
LOCKWOOD                Eng.        Mass./Conn.       Arms:-*        CFA27---125,127,148
LOCKWOOD                Eng.        N.Y./Mich         Arms:-         CRLA3---------313
LOCKWOOD                Eng.        Mass.             *(only)        CRLA13--------182
LOCKWOOD                Eng.        Mass./Conn.       Arms:-         AF****--------117
LOCKWOOD                Eng.        Mass.                            PFU-----------229
LODGE                   ------      N.J.                             AF***---------322
LOGAN                   Scotland    Pa.          Tartan & Arms:-*    CRLA18--------279
LOGAN                   ------      N.J.                             CRLA19--------163
LOGUE                   ------      Md.                              CRLA10--------340
LOKER                   Eng.        Mass.                            CRLA17--------252
LOMBARD                 Eng.?       Maine                            CFA5----------254
LOMBARD                 ------      Mass.                            CFA8-----------58
LONG                    ------      N.Y.C.                           CFA10----------68
LONG                    Ireland     Pa.                              CFA23----------12
LONG                    Ireland     N.Y./Va./N.C.                    CRLA4---------105
LONG                    Germany?    Pa.                              CRLA6---------230
LONG                    ------      Pa./Ohio/Ind.                    CRLA10---------49
LONG                    ------      ------            *(only)        CRLA12-------opp.88
LONG                    ------      Mass.             Arms:-*        CRLA15---------77
LONG                    ------      N.C.                             CRLA19--------390
LONG                    Eng.        Mass.             Arms:-*        CRLA20---------75
LONGAN                  ------      Va.                              CRLA4---------192
LONGESPEE (de)          Eng.                          Arms:-         CRLA5---------363
LONGESPEE (de)          Eng.                                         CRLA15--------123
LONGFELLOW              Eng.        Mass.                            CFA2------------1
LONGFELLOW              Eng.        Mass.                            CFA7----------161
LONGFELLOW              Eng.        Mass.                            CRLA13--------478
LONGFELLOW              Eng.        Mass.                            PFU-----------339
LONGFELLOW              ------      Maine                            PPA-----------355
LONGHORNE               ------      Mass.                            CRLA16---------16
LOOK                    Eng.        Mass.                            CRLA18--------538
LOOMIS                  Eng.        Mass.                            CFA8----------121
LOOMIS (or) LOMAS       Eng.        Conn./Mass.       Arms:-         ACF-------------4
LOOMIS                  Eng.        Mass./Conn.                      CRLA1---------168
LOOMIS                  Eng.        Conn.             Arms:-         CRLA7----------40
LOOMIS                  Eng.        Mass./Conn.                      CRLA13---------32
LOOMIS                  Eng.        Conn.                            CRLA19--------266
LOOMIS                  Eng.?       Mass.             Arms:-*        AF**----------330
LOOMIS                  Eng.        Mass.             Arms:-         AF****---------33
LOOMIS                  ------      Conn.                            AFA***--------336
LORD                    ------      Mass.             Arms:-*        AF****--------110
LORD                    ------      New Eng./N.Y.                    PPA-----------547
LORDS, House of         Eng.                    Carter=Boynton desc. CRLA15--------229
```

LORING	Eng.	Mass.		CRLA12----------383
LORING	Eng.	Mass.		CRLA17----------255
LORING	Eng.	Mass.	Arms:-*	CRLA20----------100
LOTHROP	Eng.	Mass.	Arms:-*	CFA6------------46
LOTSPEICH	Germany	Pa./Va./Tenn.		AF***-----------149
LOTT	———	N.Y./N.J.	Arms:-*	CRLA13----------402
LOTTS	Eng.	N.J.		CFA16------------68
LOUW (Cornelissen)	Denmark	N.Y.	Arms:-*	CRLA20----------62
LOVEJOY	Eng.	Mass.		CFA12------------87
LOVEL	———	———	Bray descent	CRLA17----------153
LOVEL	Eng.			CRLA17----------193
LOVELACE=GORSUCH	———	Va.		MCS-------------94
LOVELAND	———	Conn.		CRLA18----------631
LOVELL	Eng.	Mass.		CRLA20----------206
LOVETT	———	Mass.	Arms:-*	CRLA8------------32
LOVETT	———	Mass.		CRLA9----------434
LOVEWELL	———	Mass.		CFA19----------284
LOW	———	Mass.		CFA6------------172
LOW	Eng.	Mass.		CFA9------------75
LOW	———	Mass.		CFA15----------255
LOW	———	Mass.	Arms:-*	CRLA18----------30
LOW (Lowe)	———	Mass.		CRLA19----------152
LOW	———	N.J.	Arms:-* Book plate	AFA***----------265
LOW	———	Mass.		PFU-------------98
LOWELL	Eng.	Mass.	Arms:-	CFA3------------107
LOWELL	Eng.	Mass.	Arms:-*	CFA15------------31
LOWELL	Eng.	Mass.	Arms:-*	CRLA15------------9
LOWELL	———	Mass.		PPA------------565
LOWNDES	Eng.	Md.	Arms:-*	PFU-------------381
LOWNES	———	Pa.		CRLA17----------632
LOWRIE	Scotland	N.Y.	Arms:-*	CFA26-----22cht.,33
LOWTHER	Eng.		Arms:-*	CRLA14------opp.129
LOZIER	France/Holland	N.Y.		CFA16------------70
LUCADO	———	Va.	Arms:-	AF***-----------111
LUCAS	Eng.	Pa.	Arms:-*	CRLA3------------269
LUCE	———	Mass.		CRLA17----------561
LUCY (de)	Eng.		Arms:-*	CRLA5------------365
LUDDEN	Eng.	Mass.	Arms:-	AF*-------------35
LUDDOLF, see: SAXONY, Dukes of				
LUDLAM	Eng.	L.I.,N.Y.		CFA18------------36
LUDLAM	Eng.	Mass./N.Y.		CRLA20--------17,39
LUDLOW	Eng.	Mass.		CFA14----------275
LUDLOW	Eng.	N.J.		CFA16----------187
LUDLOW	Eng.	Mass.		CFA16----------294
LUDLOW	Eng.	Mass./Conn.	Arms:-*	CRLA1----------165
LUDLOW	Eng.	Mass./Conn.	*(only)	CRLA2----------322
LUDLOW	Eng.			CRLA5----------366
LUDLOW	———	Mass./Conn.		ARSC------------32
LUDLOW=BREWSTER	———	Conn.		MCS-------------72
LUDLOW=CARTER=HARRISON	———	Va.		MCS-------------72
LUDWIG=LEWIS	Germany	Pa.	Arms:-*	AFA***----------57
LUKENS	———	Pa.		CFA5------------329
LUMLEY (de)	Eng.			CRLA15----------124
LUMSDEN	———	Va.		AF*------------439
LUNT	Eng.	Mass.		AF****----------61
LUNT	———	Mass.		PPA------------363
LURMAN	———	Md.		CRLA2----------113
LUSIGNAN (de)	France		Arms:-*	CRLA5----------368
LUSIGNAN (de)	France			CRLA7----------203
LUSIGNAN (de)	France			CRLA15----------126
LUSIGNAN	France		Arms:-*	CRLA17----------186
LUTHER	———	Mass.	Arms:-*	CRLA18--------65,68
LUTHER	Eng.	Mass.	Arms:-*	TNEF-------------8
LUTKINS	———	N.J.		CRLA19----------167
LYCETT	Eng.	Md./Pa.		CRLA19----------217
LYGON=LIGON	———	Va.		MCS-------------56
LYMAN	Eng.	Mass.		CFA7----------250

```
LYMAN                         Eng.          Mass.                        CFA7------------328
LYMAN                         Eng.          Mass.                        CFA8------------362
LYMAN                         Eng.          Mass.         Arms:-*        CFA15------------1
LYMAN                         Eng.          Mass.                        CFA15-----------384
LYMAN                         Eng.          Conn.         Arms:-         AF**-----------207
LYNCH                         Ireland       Va./Ill.                     CRLA12----------207
LYNCH, Thomas, Jr.           ------         S.C.                         SDI--------227,236
LYNDE                         Belgium/Eng.  Mass.                        CFA13-----------377
LYNDE                         Eng.          Mass.         Arms:-         ACF-------------20
LYNDE                         Eng.          Mass.         Arms:-*        CRLA17----------581
IYNDE                         Eng.          Mass.         Arms:-*        CRLA18----------410
LYNDE                         ------        Mass.                        ARSC------------98
LYNDE                         ------        Mass.                        MCS-------------47
LYNDE                         ------        ------        *(only)        TNEF--------opp.48
LYON                          Eng.          Conn./N.J.    Arms:-*        CFA11-----------284
LYON                          ------        R.I.                         CRLA12----------79
LYON                          Scotland      Conn.                        AF***-----------368
LYON                          Ireland       Pa.           Arms:-         AF***-----------417
LYON                          France/Eng.   Mass.         Arms:-*        AFA2------------89
LYSLE                         ------        Del./Pa.                     CRLA6-----------40
```

- M -

```
MAC ALPIN, see: SCOTLAND, Kings of
MAC CALLUM                    Canada        Wash.                        CRLA11----------199
MACCUBBIN                     Scotland      Md.           Arms:-*        CRLA2-----------123
MACCUBBIN=CARROLL            ------         Md.                          AFA***----------86
MACDONALD                    ------         ------                       CFA16-----------302
MACDONALD                     Canada                                     CRLA8-----------313
MAC DONOUGH                   Scotland/Ireland  Del.                     CRLA10----------338
MACFARLAND                   ------         Mass.                        CRLA9-----------20
MACK                          Scotland?     Mass./Conn.                  CRLA19----------305
MACKAY                        Scotland      N.Y.          Arms:-*        CRLA18----------211
MACKELLAR                     Eng.          N.Y.                         PPA-------------493
MACKIE                        Scotland      Mass.         Arms:-         AF****----------250
MACKINLAY (McKinlay)          Scotland      La./Ill.      Arms:-*        AFA***----------271
MAC KNIGHT                    Nova Scotia   Mass./Pa.     Arms:-*        CRLA17----------431
MACKWORTH=CROWNE             ------         Mass.                        MCS-------------34
MAC LAREN                     No family data              Arms:-*        CRLA13------opp.440
MAC MOROUGH                   Ireland       Schrack desc. Arms:-*        CRLA17----------386
MAC MOROUGH, see: IRISH Kings
MACOMBER, see: Mc OMBER
MAC VEAGH                     Ireland       Pa.           Arms:-*        AFA***----------296
MAC WORTER                    Ireland       Del.                         CRLA16----------172
MACY                          Eng.          Mass.                        CFA1------------177
MACY                          Eng.          Mass.                        CFA20-----------18
MACY                         ------         Mass.                        CRLA12------254,275
MADEIRA                       Spain         Pa.                          CFA2------------227
MADISON                      ------         Va.                          CFA5------------289
MADOC                        ------        ------         *(only)        TNEF--------opp.44
MAGNA CHARTA Barons, Arms of                              *(only)        CFA18-----btn.14-15
MAGNA CHARTA Dames, The National Society                 *(only)        CFA18-----btn.14-15
MAGNA CHARTA Barons          Carter=Boynton desc.         Arms:-*        CRLA15----------218
MAGRUDER (MacGregor)          Scotland/Eng. Md.                          CRLA16----------74
MAINE, Counts of              France              Haskell descent        CRLA8-----------104
MAINWARING                    Eng.                        Arms:-*        CRLA5-----------370
MAINWARING                    Eng.                        Arms:-*        CRLA11----------171
MAINWARING                    Eng.                                       CRLA15----------141
MAINWARING                    Eng.                                       CRLA18----------465
MAJOR                        ------         Va.           Arms:-*        CRLA15----------331
MAKEPEACE                     Eng.          Mass.                        CFA19-----------73
MALCOLM                      ------         Conn.                        CFA14-----------38
```

```
MALCOLM I, see: SCOTLAND, Kings of
MALET                  Eng.                        Arms:-*        CRLA5----------373
MALET                  Eng.              Titus descent           CRLA18---------506
MALI                   Europe      N.Y.                          CRLA19---------144
MALLET=PREVOST         France/Switzerland  N.J.  Arms:-*         PFU------------180
MALLORY                Eng.        Conn.                         CFA11----------329
MALLORY                Eng.        Va.               Arms:-*     PFU------------419
MALTBIE                Eng.        Conn.             Arms:-*     AF*------------416
MALTBY                 Eng.        Conn.             Arms:-*     AFA***---------311
MAN, Isle of, Kings of Eng.              Gaither=Fownes desc.    CRLA11----------62
MAN, Isle of, Kings of Eng.              Blackiston descent      CRLA11---------399
MANCHESTER             ------      R.I.                          CFA8-----------260
MANCHESTER             ------      R.I.                          CRLA3----------456
MANCILL                Wales       Pa.               Arms:-*     AFA***---------285
MANDEVILLE             ------      N.Y.              Arms:-      CRLA3----------189
MANDEVILLE (de)        Eng.                          Arms:-      CRLA5------375,377
MANDEVILLE (de)        Eng.                                     CRLA7----------224
MANDEVILLE (de)        Eng.                                     CRLA15---------128
MANLOVE                Eng.        Va./Del.          Arms:-*     CRLA1-----------86
MANLOVE                ------      Md.               Arms:-      AF****---------153
MANN                   Eng.        Conn./N.Y.                    CFA19-----------19
MANNING                Eng.        Mass.             Arms:-*     CFA1-----------134
MANNING                Eng.        Mass.                         CFA10----------327
MANNING                Eng.        Mass.                         CFA13----------153
MANNING                ------      Mass.                         CRLA15---------401
MANORIAL ANCESTORS     Eng.              Gaither=Fownes desc.    CRLA11----------54
MANORIAL ANCESTORS     Eng.              Carter=Boynton desc.    CRLA15---------226
MANSER                 ------      Mass.                         AFA***---------346
MANSFIELD              Eng.        ------            Arms:-*     CFA4------------24
MANSFIELD              Eng.        Mass.                         CFA19-----------75
MANSFIELD              Eng.        Mass.             Arms:-*     CRLA15----------63
MANTON                 ------      R.I.                          CRLA9----------401
MAPES                  Eng.        L.I.,N.Y.                     CRLA8----------368
MARBURY                Eng.        Md.               Arms:-*     CRLA15---------323
MARBURY                ------      Mass./R.I.                    ARSC------------34
MARBURY=HUTCHINSON     ------      Mass.                         MCS-------------30
MARBURY=SCOTT          ------      R.I.                          MCS-------------30
MARCH                  ------      Maine                         CFA7-----------170
MARCH                  Switzerland Pa.               Arms:-      AF***----------308
MARESCHALL (or) MARSHALL Eng.                        Arms:-*     CRLA1----------323
MARESCHALL             Eng.        Warren desc. *(only)          CRLA2----------341
MARESCHALL             Eng.                  *(only)             CRLA2----------484
MARESCHALL             Eng.                        Arms:-*       CRLA5----------378
MARESCHALL             Eng.        Haskell; Hinton desc.         CRLA8------105;485
MARESCHALL             Eng.                                     CRLA11----------95
MARESCHALL             Eng.                        Arms:-*       CRLA15---------143
MARESCHALL             Eng.        Glendinning=Logan desc.       CRLA18---------328
MARESCHALL             Eng.                                     CRLA20---------272
MARESCHALLE (de)       France                                   CRLA1-----------44
MARESHALL              ------      ------                        CRLA18---------164
MARGERUM               ------      Pa.                           CRLA11---------485
MARIS                  Eng.        Pa.               Arms:-*     AFA***---------175
MARIS                  Eng.        Pa.               Arms:-*     AFA***---------233
MARK                   Eng.        Pa.                           CRLA2----------429
MARKHAM                ------      Mass.             Arms:-      AF*------------285
MARKLEY                ------      Pa.                           CRLA9----------454
MARLE                  ------      Pa.               Arms:-*     CRLA11---------467
MARMADUKE              Eng.        Va.               Arms:-      AF*------------304
MARRIOTT               Eng.        Md.                           CFA16----------100
MARSALL                ------      Pa.                           CRLA20---------115
MARSH                  Eng.        Mass./Conn.                   CFA15----------357
MARSH                  Eng.        Mass.                         CFA19-----------51
MARSH                  ------      Mass.             Arms:-*     CRLA15----------78
MARSH                  Eng.        Mass./Conn.                   CRLA19---------401
MARSH                  Eng.        Mass./Conn.                   CRLA20---------180
MARSHALL               Eng.        Pa.                           CFA3-----------182
MARSHALL               Barbadoes, W.I.  N.Y.         Arms:-*     CFA5-----------133
```

MARSHALL	Eng.	Mass.		CFA6------------349
MARSHALL	Eng.	Pa.	Arms:-*	CFA7------------188
MARSHALL	Ireland	Va.		CRLA4-----------178
MARSHALL	Eng.	Va.		CRLA4-----------393
MARSHALL	Eng.			CRLA13----------431
MARSHALL	———	Mass.	Arms:-*	AF****----------156
MARSHALL	Eng.	Mass./Conn.	Arms:-*	AFA***--------82,83
MARSHALS of England, see: CLARE (de)				
MARSHAM	Eng.?	Md.		CRLA2------------74
MARSTERS	———	Mass.		CRLA8------------13
MARSTERS	———	Mass.		TNEF-----------232
MARTIAU	France	Va.		CRLA3-----------112
MARTIAU	———	Va.		CRLA4-----------354
MARTIN	———	Maine		CFA5------------244
MARTIN	Eng.	Mass.		CFA6------------324
MARTIN	———	Mass.		CFA7------------300
MARTIN	Eng.	Mass.	Arms:-*	CFA27---129,148cht.
MARTIN	Scotland	Md.		CRLA3-----------293
MARTIN	Eng.		Arms:-*	CRLA5-----------381
MARTIN	———	Mass.		CRLA6-----------522
MARTIN	Eng.	Mass.	Arms:-	CRLA18-----------52
MARTIN	Canada		Arms:-*	AF**------------465
MARTIN	Eng.	Mass.	Arms:-	AFA3------------61
MARTINDALE	———	Md.		CFA10-----------319
MARTN	———	N.Y./Mich.		CRLA6-----------171
MARTYN	———	Mass./N.H.		CFA7------------168
MARVIN	Eng.	Conn.	Arms:-	CFA1-------------40
MARVIN	Eng.	Conn.	Arms:-	CFA17-----------149
MARVIN	Eng.	Conn.	Arms:-*	CFA23-----------120
MARVIN	Eng.	Conn.	Arms:-*	CFA27----38cht.,131
MARYLAND, Seal of			*(only)	CRLA19-------opp.10
MASON	Eng.	Mass.		CFA5------------302
MASON	———	Mass.		CFA19-----------292
MASON	Scotland	N.Y./N.J.		CFA22-----------139
MASON	Eng.	Mass.	Arms:-*	CFA26-----------134
MASON	Eng.	Va.	Arms:-	CRLA3-----------118
MASON	———	Mass.	Arms:-*	CRLA7-----------328
MASON	———	Mass.	Arms:-*	CRLA10----------291
MASON	———	Mass.		CRLA12-----------33
MASON	———	Va.		CRLA15----------332
MASON	Eng.	Mass.	Arms:-*	AF*-------------63
MASON	Eng.	Mass.	Arms:-	AF**------------216
MASSACHUSETTS BAY COLONY, Seal of			*(only)	CFA27-------148cht.
MASSACHUSETTS BAY COLONY, Seal of			*(only)	CRLA15------opp.478
MASSACHUSETTS, Seal of			*(only)	CRLA19-------opp.10
MASSEY	———	Mass.		CRLA9-----------431
MASTEN	———	N.Y.		CRLA18----------232
MATERN	Germany/Eng.			CRLA17----------715
MATHER	Eng.	Mass.		CFA13-----------310
MATHER	Eng.	Mass.		CFA13-----------374
MATHER	Eng.	Mass.		CRLA20----------212
MATHER	Eng.	Mass.	Arms:-*	PBAF------------107
MATHER	Eng.	Mass.		PFU-------------441
MATHESON	———	Wisc.	Arms:-*	CRLA4-----------301
MATHEWSON	Scotland	R.I.		CFA26------------34
MATHIAS	Wales		Arms:-*	CRLA8-----------273
MATLACK	Eng.	N.J.		CFA20-----------190
MATLACK	Eng.	N.J.		CRLA1-----------116
MATTESON	———	Conn./N.Y.		CFA19------------84
MATTESON	———	R.I.		CRLA17----------437
MATTHEWS	———	Va.		CRLA4-----------227
MATTHEWS	———	Ky./Mo.	Arms:-*	CRLA12----------319
MATTLEWS	France?	Mass.	Arms:-*	CRLA15----------418
MATTHEWS	———	N.Y.		PPA-------------513
MATTHIES	———	N.Y.		CRLA12----------105
MAUDUIT	Eng.		Beauchamp line	CRLA2-----------353
MAUDUIT	Eng.		Arms:-*	CRLA5-----------385

MAUDUIT	Eng.		Arms:-*	CRLA10-----btn.78-9
MAUDUIT	Eng.			CRLA18----------166
MAUDUIT, see: HAMESLAPE				
MAUDUIT, see: NEWBURGH				
MAULEVERER	Eng.			CRLA11----------250
MAULEVERER	Eng.			CRLA15----------240
MAULEVERER	Eng.	Pa.	Arms:-*	AFA***----------237
MAULL	Eng.?	Pa.		CRLA17----------565
MAULL	————	Pa.		AFA***----------366
MAURAN	Europe	R.I.	Arms:-*	CRLA18-----------61
MAVERICK	Eng.	Mass.	Arms:-*	CFA18----------153
MAVERICK	Eng.	Mass.		CRLA17-----------27
MAXFIELD	Eng.	N.Y.	Arms:-*	CRLA16-----------58
MAXSON	————	R.I.		CRLA20----------171
MAXWELL	Ireland	Pa.		CFA6------------334
MAXWELL	Scotland	N.Y.		CFA10----------270
MAXWELL	Scotland	N.Y.		CFA14----------356
MAXWELL	————	Mass./Nova Scotia		CFA26----------127
MAXWELL	————	Del.		CRLA9----------321
MAXWELL	————	Pa.		CRLA11----------273
MAXWELL	————	Pa.		CRLA17----------326
MAY	Eng.	Md.		CRLA8----------567
MAY	Eng.	Mass.		CRLA13-----------44
MAY	Eng.	Mass.	Arms:-*	AFA***----------229
MAYFIELD	————	Va./Ky.		CRLA3----------419
MAYFLOWER Descent from Thomas Rogers			Higgins descent	CRLA18-----------77
MAYFLOWER Descent, see: HOLLAND, John				
MAYFLOWER Descent, see: WARREN				
MAYHEW	Eng.	Mass.	Arms:-*	AFA***----------275
MAYNARD	————	Mass.		TNEF------------147
MAYO	Eng.	Mass.		CFA3------------127
MAYO	Eng.	Mass.		CFA8------------143
MAYO	Eng.	Mass.	Arms:-*	CFA27----38cht.,139
MAYO	Eng.	Mass.		ACF-------------99
MAYO	Eng.	Mass.	Arms:-*	CRLA2----------311
MAYO	Eng.	Va.		CRLA3----------236
MAYO	Eng.	Mass.		CRLA17----------450
MAYO	Eng.	Mass.		CRLA19-----------76
MAYS	Eng.	Va.		CRLA6----------371
MAZYCK	France/Holland	S.C.		PFU------------432
Mc ADAMS	————	————	*(only)	CRLA12-------opp.88
Mc CAHAN	Ireland	Pa.	Arms:-*	CRLA5----------474
Mc CAIN	Scotland	N.C.		CRLA11----------279
Mc CAIN	Scotland	N.C.		CRLA11----------299
Mc CALL	————	N.Y.		CFA1------------68
Mc CAMPBELL	Ireland	Va.		CRLA11----------547
Mc CAWLEY	Ireland	Pa.		PFU------------179
Mc CARTHY and PATRICK	————	Ind./Colo.		CFA14----------356
Mc CLEERY		Pa.		CRLA9----------469
Mc CLELLAN	Ireland	Pa.	Arms:-*	CRLA17----------574
Mc CLELLAND	Scotland	Pa.	Arms:-*	AFA***----------317
Mc CLENACHAN	Ireland	Pa.	Arms:-	CFA6------------383
Mc CLUNG	Eng.	Pa./Va.		CFA12-----------46
Mc CORMICK	Ireland	Pa.	Arms:-	CRLA3-----------70
Mc CORMICK	Ireland	Va.		CRLA10----------247
Mc CORMICK	Ireland	Va.		CRLA12----------370
Mc COY	Scotland	Pa.		CFA6------------335
Mc COY	————	Pa.		CRLA6----------457
Mc COY	Scotland	Pa.		AF*------------103
Mc CRACKEN	————	Pa.	Arms:-*	CRLA17----------573
Mc CREA	Ireland	Pa.		CRLA2-----------89
Mc CREERY	Ireland	N.Y.	Arms:-*	CRLA2----------121
Mc CUEN	Ireland/Canada	N.Y.		CFA19----------243
Mc CURDY	Scotland/Ireland		Arms:-*	CRLA8----------565
Mc DONALD	————	Del.		CRLA7-----------68
Mc DOWELL	————	Pa.		CFA20----------114
Mc DUFFEE	Scotland/Ireland	Pa.		CFA26-----------33

Mc ELROY	———	Pa.		CRLA17---------216
Mc EVERS	———	N.Y.C.		CFA13---------35,38
Mc FADDEN=CASS	Ireland	Pa./S.C.	Arms:-*	CRLA15----------407
Mc FARLAND	———	N.J.		ACF-------------84
Mc GAW	Eng.	Calif.		CRLA10--------75,79
Mc GILL	———	Md.		CRLA8----------548
Mc GREW	Ireland	Pa.	Arms:-*	CRLA13----------390
Mc ILHENNY	———	Pa.		CRLA7----------568
Mc ILWAIN, see: BEALE=Mc ILWAIN				
Mc KEAN	Scotland	N.Y.C.		CFA4------------177
Mc KEAN, Thomas	———	Pa./Del.		SDI---------181,186
Mc KEE (McKay)	Ireland	Pa.	Arms:-*	AF*------------153
Mc KEEVER	———	Pa.		CRLA8----------402
Mc LINLEY=OLSEN	Ireland	Pa.		CRLA15----------433
Mc KINNEY	———	N.C./Pa.		CRLA8----------537
Mc KITTRICK	Ireland	N.Y.C./Mo.		CRLA20----------244
Mc KITTRICK	Ireland	N.Y.		AF**-----------249
Mc LANAHAN	Scotland/Ireland	Pa./Md.		CFA22------------88
Mc LAREN	———	N.Y.?	Arms:-*	CRLA15----------476
Mc LAURINE	Scotland	Va.	Arms:-*	CRLA15----------412
Mc LEAN	———	Pa.		CRLA17----------274
Mc LELLAN	———	Maine/Mass.		PPA------------455
Mc LEMORE	———	Newberry, _____		CFA3------------201
Mc LEMORE	———	Newberry, _____		CFA7----------207
Mc MILLAN (MacMillan)	———	Md./Pa.		CRLA6----------184
Mc MILLAN	Scotland	Md./Pa.		CRLA6----------438
Mc MORRIES	Ireland	S.C.	Arms:-	CFA3------------201
Mc MORRIES	Ireland	S.C.	Arms:-*	CFA7----------208
Mc NEIR	Eng.	Md.		CRLA2----------122
Mc OMBER (Macomber)	Eng.?	Mass.		CRLA18----------376
Mc SHERRY	Ireland	Va.		CRLA19----------312
Mc WILLIAMS	———	N.Y.		CFA15----------390
Mc WILLIAMS	Ireland	Pa.	Arms:-	AF****----------219
MEACHAM	Eng.	Mass.		CRLA19----------306
MEACHAM	Eng.?	Mass.	Arms:-	AF*---------178,192
MEAD	Eng.	Mass./Conn.	Arms:-*	CFA26-----10,22cht.
MEAD	———	Conn.	Arms:-	CRLA3----------149
MEADE	———	Va.		CRLA6----------463
MEANS	Scotland/Ireland	Mass.	Arms:-	CFA3------------369
MEANS	Scotland	Mass.	Arms:-	CFA6------------276
MAIGS	Eng.?	Mass./Conn.		CRLA10----------221
MEIGS	Eng.?	Conn. & Ohio	Arms:-*	CRLA7----------155
MEIGS	———	———	*(only)	TNEF--------opp.82
MELLEN	———	Mass.		CFA7-------------7
MELLEN	———	Mass.		CFA10-----------89
MELLEN	———	Maine		PPA------------267
MELVILL (Melvin)	———	Md.		CRLA4----------243
MELVIN	———	Md.		CRLA4----------324
MENDENHALL	———	Pa.		CFA7------------399
MENDENHALL	Eng.	Pa.		CRLA8----------575
MENDENHALL	Eng.	Pa.		CRLA17----------351
MENDENHALL	Eng.	Pa.		CRLA18----------418
MEPHAM	Eng.	Mo.	Arms:-	AF***----------320
MERCER	———	Mass.		CFA21----------207
MEREDITH	Wales	Pa.		CRLA8----------184
MERIWETHER	Eng.	Va.	Arms:-	CFA5------------31
MERIWETHER	Wales/Eng.?	Va.	Arms:-	AF*------------143
MERRICK	———	Mass.		CFA7----------348
MERRICK	Wales	Maine	Arms:-*	CFA18----------179
MERRICK	Wales?	Mass.		CFA18----------100
MERRICK	Wales	Mass.	Arms:-	CFA27----------142
MERRICK	Eng.	Pa.		CRLA13----------344
MERRICK	Eng.	Maine/Pa.		CRLA17----------267
MERRICK	Wales	Mass.	Arms:-*	CRLA17----------453
MERRELL	Eng.	Mass.	Arms:-	CRLA3----------340
MERRILL	———	Mass.		CFA11----------388
MERRILL	Eng.	Mass.		CRLA7-----------44

MERRILL	Eng.	Mass.		CRLA13----------263
MERRILL	Eng.	Mass.	Arms:-*	CRLA19-----------42
MERRILL	Eng.	Mass.		CRLA19----------256
MERRILL	Eng.	Mass.		CRLA19----------397
MESIER	———	N.Y.		CFA8-------------38
MESSENGER	———	Mass.		PPA-------------366
MESSERVY	Eng.	N.H.	Arms:-*	AFA***-----------63
MESTA	Germany	Pa.		CRLA7----------557
METCALF	Eng.	Mass.	Arms:-	CFA6------------147
METCALF	Eng.	Mass.		CFA8------------253
METCALF	Eng.	Mass.		CFA15----------350
METCALF	Eng.	Mass.	Arms:-*	CRLA1-----------141
METCALF	Eng.	Mass.		CRLA19-----------89
METCALF	Eng.	Mass.	Arms:-	AF**-------------39
METCALF	Eng.	Mass.	Arms:-	AF**------------425
MEYER	Holland?	N.Y.	Arms:-*	CRLA20-----------16
M'HOON	———	N.C.		CFA12-----------355
MICHAEL	Eng.	Va.		CRLA2-----------115
MICHAEL	———	Va.		CRLA9-----------10
MICHAEL	———	Va.	Arms:-*	CRLA15----------337
MICHEL	———	———	Arms:-*	CRLA20----btn.10-11
MICHENER	Eng.	Pa.		CRLA9----------546
MICHENER	———	Pa.		AF**------------131
MICKLEY.	France	Pa.		CRLA6----------491
MIDDLETON	Eng.	S.C.	Arms:-	CFA23-----------202
MIDDLETON	Eng.			CRLA2-----------12
MIDDLETON	Eng.	S.C.		PFU-------------318
MIDDLETON	———	S.C.		SDI--------227,229
MILDEBERGER	———	N.Y.	Arms:-*	AF*-------------406
MILES	———	Md.		CFA23-----------150
MILK	———	Mass.		CFA6------------188
MILLAR	———	N.J./Va.		CRLA19------367,368
MILLER	———	L.I.,N.Y.		CFA2------------293
MILLER	Germany	Md.		CFA24-----------87
MILLER	———	Md.	Arms:-*	CRLA1-----------527.
MILLER	———	Pa.		CRLA6----------488
MILLER	———	Va.		CRLA10----------273
MILLER	No family data		Arms:-*	CRLA13------opp.298
MILLER	Ireland	Mich.	Arms:-*	CRLA13----------482
MILLER	Eng.	Mass.	Arms:-*	CRLA15-----------51
MILLER	Ireland	Pa.		CRLA17-----------70
MILLER	Eng.	Pa.		CRLA17----------528
MILLER	———	N.Y.		CRLA19-----------87
MILLER	Switzerland	Pa.		CRLA19----------230
MILLER	Ireland?	Va.	Arms:-	AF***-----------391
MILLER	———	———		PFU-------------416
MILLER	———	N.J.		PPA-------------537.
MILLER	———	Mass./West Indies		PPA-------------294
MILLER, see: RULON=MILLER				
MILLETT	Eng.	Mass.	Arms:-*	CFA15----------258
MILLING	Scotland/Ireland S.C.			CFA3------------371
MILLING	Scotland	S.C.		CFA6------------277
MILLS	———	N.Y.C.		CFA9------------94
MILLS	Eng.?	Conn.		CRLA19----------252
MILLS	Eng.	Mass./N.Y.	Arms:-*	CRLA20--------7,112
MILLSPAUGH	Germany	N.Y.		CRLA16-----------72
MILNOR	———	Pa.		CRLA13----------343
MINER	Eng.	Mass.	Arms:-	CFA6------------93
MINER	Eng.	Mass.		CFA14-----------19.
MINER	Eng.	Mass.	Arms:-	CFA15----------140
MINER	Eng.	Mass.		CFA19-----------65
MINER	Eng.	Mass./Conn.	Arms:-*	CFA19----------225
MINER=MINERS	Eng.	Mass.	Arms:-*	AF*-------------67.
MINER	Eng.	Mass./Conn.	Arms:-	AF***-----------247
MINGE	———	Va.		CRLA4----------196.
MINNS	Eng.	Mass.	Arms:-*	CFA4-------------1
MINOR	———	Va.		CRLA4----------170

MINOR	Eng.	Mass./Conn.	Arms:-*	CRLA14----------107
MINOT	Eng.	Mass.	Arms:-	CFA4------------275
MINOT	Eng.	Mass.		CFA7------------136
MINOT	Eng.	Mass.		CFA11-----------206
MINOT	Eng.	Mass.		PFU-------------467
MINSHALL	No family data		Arms:-*	CRLA13------opp.206
MIRRIAM	Eng.	Mass.		CRLA12-----------40
MITCHELL	Eng.	Mass.	Arms:-*	CFA1-------------54
MITCHELL	-------	Vt.	Arms:-	CFA1-------------67
MITCHELL	Eng./Holland	Mass.		CFA10-----------255
MITCHELL	Eng.	Mass.		CFA12------------73
MITCHELL	Eng.	Conn.		CRLA11----------509
MITCHELL	-------	Mass.	Arms:-	CRLA12----------396
MITCHELL	Scotland/Ireland	Va.		CRLA10----------126
MITCHELL	-------	Mass.		CRLA17----------246
MITCHELL	-------	Va.	Arms:-	AF***----------437
MITCHELL	Scotland	Va.	Arms:-*	AFA***-----------65
MITCHELL	R.I.;Va.;Pa.;Md.;N.Y.;Mass.;etc.		Arms:-*	TNEF----------32-3
MITTON	Eng.	Mass.		CFA20------------75
MIX	-------	Conn.	Arms:-*	CRLA19----------254
MOEHRING	Germany	N.Y.		CRLA16-----------80
MONCURE	Eng.	Va.		CRLA1-----------262
MONNET(T)	France	Md.	Arms:-*	AFA***-----------27
MONROE	Scotland	Md./Va.	Arms:-	CFA10-----------169
MONROW (Munro)	Scotland/Eng.	Mass.		CRLA2-----------385
MONTAGUE	Eng.	Mass.		CFA5------------364
MONTAGUE	Eng.	Va.	Arms:-*	AFA***----------391
MONTCHANIN (de)	France		Arms:-*	CRLA1------------42
MONTFERRAT, Marquises of	France		Arms:-*	CRLA5-----------386
MONTFORT (de)	Eng.		Arms:-*	CRLA5-----------388
MONTFORT (de)	Eng.		Haskell descent	CRLA8-----------107
MONTGOMERY	Ireland	Pa./N.H.	Arms:-*	CFA8------------231
MONTGOMERY	Ireland	Pa.		CRLA2------------97
MONTGOMERY (de)	No family data		Arms:-*	CRLA15------opp.172
MONTGOMERY	Eng.	N.J./Pa.	Arms:-*	HFA-------------244
MONTLHERY (de)	France		Arms:-	CRLA5-----------389
MOODY	Eng.	Mass.		CRLA19-----------99
MOODY	Eng.	Mass.		CRLA19----------381
MOORE	-------	Mass.		CFA14----------370
MOORE	Ireland	Md.	Arms:-	CFA15----------150
MOORE	-------	L.I.,N.Y./Mass.		CFA16------------12
MOORE	-------	Mass./Conn.		CRLA1-----------173
MOORE	-------	N.Y.		CRLA3-----------172
MOORE	Ireland	Va./N.C.	Arms:-	CRLA3-----------201
MOORE	-------	Va.		CRLA4------------56
MOORE	Eng.	Pa./N.J.		CRLA5--------17,67
MOORE	Eng.			CRLA5-----------199
MOORE	-------	Pa.		CRLA7-----------458
MOORE	-------	L.I.,N.Y.		CRLA8-------182,184
MOORE	Eng.	Va./Md.		CRLA8------505,519
MOORE	Ireland	Pa.	Arms:-*	CRLA13----------206
MOORE	-------	Pa.		CRLA17----------355
MOORE	Eng.	Mass./N.Y.	Arms:-*	CRLA18----------560
MOORE	Eng./Ireland	Va./Md./Pa.		CRLA20--236,242,250
MOORE	-------	Pa.	Arms:-	AF*-------------81
MOORE	Ireland	Pa.	Arms:-*	AF*------------352
MOORE	-------	Va.	Arms:-	AF*------------433
MOORE	Eng./Ireland	Va./Md./Pa.	Arms:-	AF**----240,247,257
MOORE	-------	Tenn.		AF***----------153
MOORE	-------	N.Y.		PPA-------------81
MOORE, see: GREEN=MOORE				
MOORHEAD	Ireland	Pa.		CRLA15----------235
MOR, see: IRELAND, Ancient Monarchs of				
MORE	-------	-------	*(only)	TNEF---------opp.44
MOREHEAD	-------	N.C.	Arms:-*	AFA***-----------31
MORGAN	Wales	Conn.	Arms:-*	CFA1-------------10
MORGAN	Wales	Va.	Arms:-	CFA3------------202

MORGAN	Wales	Va.	Arms:-*	CFA7------------208
MORGAN	Wales	Mass.		CFA8------------104
MORGAN	Wales?	Mass.		CFA8------------205
MORGAN	Wales	Mass./Conn.		CFA9------------114
MORGAN	———	N.Y.	Arms:-*	CFA18------------5
MORGAN	———	Pa.		CFA20-----------86
MORGAN	Wales	Mass.	Arms:-*	CFA23-----------65
MORGAN	Wales	Ky.	Arms:-*	CRLA1-----------31
MORGAN	———	Md.		CRLA1----------501
MORGAN	———	N.Y.		CRLA6----------155
MORGAN	———	Md.		CRLA15---------568
MORGAN	———	Va./N.C.	Arms:-*	AF***----------133
MORGAN	Eng.	Mass.		PFU-------------85
MORLEY	———	Md.	Arms:-*	CRLA11----------28
MORLEY	———	Md.		CRLA16----------45
MORLEY	Eng.			CRLA17---------196
MORRILL	Eng.	Mass.	Arms:-	CFA16----------339
MORRILL	———	Mass.	Arms:-*	CRLA15----------80
MORRILL	———	———	*(only)	TNEF--------opp.31
MORRIS	Eng.	Pa.	Arms:-	CFA6-----------377
MORRIS	Wales	N.Y.	Arms:-	CFA12----------229
MORRIS	———	Ky./Ind.		CFA14----------352
MORRIS	Eng.	N.J.	Arms:-	CFA15----------114
MORRIS	Eng.	N.Y.	Arms:-	CFA16----------308
MORRIS	Wales	N.Y.	Arms:-	CFA24----------186
MORRIS	Wales	N.Y.	Arms:-*	CFA25-----------68
MORRIS	Eng.	Pa.	Arms:-*	CRLA5----------512
MORRIS	Eng.	Pa.		CRLA11---------494
MORRIS	———	Mass./Conn.		CRLA13----------19
MORRIS	Wales	Va.	Arms:-*	CRLA16----------55
MORRIS	———	Mass./Conn.	Arms:-*	CRLA17---------644
MORRIS	Eng.	N.Y.		CRLA18---------439
MORRIS	———	N.Y.	Arms:-*	CRLA18---------449
MORRIS	Eng.	Pa.		CRLA19---------222
MORRIS	———	N.Y.C.	Arms:-*	CRLA20----------14
MORRIS	Wales	Pa.	Arms:-*	AF*------------355
MORRIS	Eng.	Pa.	Arms:-*	AFA***----------47
MORRIS	———	Del.		AFA***---------326
MORRIS	Wales	N.Y.	Arms:-*	HFA------------196
MORRIS	———	Pa.		PPA------------281
MORRIS, Lewis	———	N.Y.		SDI---------135,141
MORRIS, Robert	Eng.	Pa.		SDI---------159;168
MORRISON	———	N.Y.		CRLA12---------154
MORRISON	———	N.Y.C.		CRLA20---------202
MORSE	Eng.	Mass.		CFA3-----------205
MORSE	Eng.	Mass.		CFA7-----------126
MORSE	Eng.	Mass.		CFA9-----------153
MORSE (or) MORSS	Eng.	Mass.		CFA9-----------174
MORSE	Eng.	Mass.		CFA10-----------99
MORSE	———	Mass.		CFA10----------105
MORSE	Eng.	Mass.	Arms:-*	CFA10----------383
MORSE	Eng.?	Mass.		CFA19-----------53
MORSE	Eng.	Mass.		CRLA10---------185
MORSE	Eng.?	Mass.		CRLA12----------97
MORSE	Eng.	Mass.		CRLA17---------439
MORSE	Eng.	Mass.		CRLA19---------375
MORSE	———	Mass.?	Arms:-*	CRLA20----------76
MORTAIN, Counts of	Eng.			CRLA5----------390
MORTIMER (de)	Eng.		Arms:-*	CRLA5----------392
MORTIMER (de)	Eng.			CRLA7----------192
MORTIMER (de)	Eng.		Arms:-*	CRLA10-----btn.78-9
MORTIMER (de)	Eng.			CRLA11---------432
MORTIMER (de)	Eng.		Arms:-*	CRLA15---------129
MORTIMER (de)	Eng.		Arms:-*	AFA2-----------237
MORTON	Eng.	Mass.	Arms:-	CFA5------------73
MORTON	Eng.	Mass.		CFA6-----------355
MORTON	———	Pa.		CRLA3----------317

MORTON	Eng.	Mass.		CRLA6----------234
MORTON	Eng.	Mass.	Arms:-*	CRLA7----------352
MORTON	———	Pa.		CRLA8----------313
MORTON	———	Va.		CRLA8----------437
MORTON	———	Va.		CRLA10----------23
MORTON	Sweden	Pa.		CRLA17---------233
MORTON	Sewden	Pa.		CRLA17---------628
MORTON	Eng.	Mass.		PFU------------118
MORTON. John	———	Pa./Del.		SDI--------159,165
MOSELEY	———	Mass.		PFU------------182
MOSHER	———	R.I.		CRLA20---------188
MOSS	———	Va.		CRLA4----------282
MOTT	Eng.	N.Y.	Arms:-	CFA1------------61
MOTT	Eng.	Mass.		CFA9------------22
MOTT	Eng.	Mass.		CFA10----------285
MOTT	———	N.Y.		CRLA15---------524
MOTT	———	R.I.	Arms:-*	CRLA20----------46
MOTTROM	———	Va.	Arms:-*	CRLA15---------330
MOULTON	Eng.	N.H.		CFA7-----------159
MOULTON	Eng.	Mass.		CRLA7----------409
MOULTON	Eng.	Mass.	Arms:-*	CRLA12----------68
MOUSALL	———	Mass.		CFA15----------205
MOWBRAY	Eng.			CRLA2----------455
MOWBRAY (de)	Eng.		Titus descent	CRLA18---------505
MOWRY	Eng.	Mass.		CFA19----------290
MOWRY	———	R.I.		ACF-------------90
MOWRY	———	R.I.		CRLA20---------208
MOXHAM	Eng.	Va.		CRLA15---------580
MOYCE	———	Mass.		CRLA14---------169
MUCEGROS (de) (Muscegros) Eng.			Arms:-*	CRLA5----------398
MUDGE	Eng.	Mass.	Arms:-*	CRLA17---------566
MUDGE	Eng.	Mass.		CRLA17---------584
MUDGE	Eng.	Mass.	Arms:-*	CRLA18---------404
MUDGE	Eng.	Mass.	Arms:-*	CRLA20----------81
MUGRIDGE	Eng.	Maine	Arms:-	AF**-----------169
MUHLENBERG	Germany	Pa.		CFA25-----------60
MULLINS	Eng.	Mass.		CFA7-----------180
MULLINS	Eng.	Mass.	Arms:-*	CFA9-----------215
MULLINS	Eng.	Mass.		CFA10----------375
MULLINS	Eng.	Mass.		CFA11----------179
MULLINS	Eng.	Mass.		CFA12-----------77
MULLINS	Eng.	Mass.		CFA12----------227
MULLINS	Eng.	Mass.		CFA13----------361
MULLINS	Eng.	Mass.	Arms:-*	CRLA20----------50
MULLINS	———	———	*(only)	TNEF-------btn.70-1
MULLINS, see: PILGRIMS				
MULTON (de)	Eng.		Arms:-*	CRLA5----------400
MUNDAY	———	Va./Ohio		CRLA6----------227
MUNFORD	———	Va.		PFU------------176
MUNFORD	———	Va.		PPA-------------78
MUNRO	Scotland	Va.	Arms:-*	CRLA10----------12
MUNRO, see: MONROW				
MUNSELL	———	Conn.		CRLA1----------167
MUNSON	———	Maine		CRLA10---------184
MURDOCK	Scotland	Mass.		CRLA19---------377
MURPHY	Ireland	Conn.	Arms:-*	CFA16----------181
MURPHY	———	Pa.		CRLA9----------160
MURPHY	———	Del./Pa.	Arms:-*	CRLA19---------226
MURRAY	———	Md.		CFA5------------93
MURRAY	Eng.	Mass./Conn.	Arms:-*	CFA13-----------62
MUSCHE	Germany	Pa.	Arms:-*	CRLA8----------276
MYERS	Germany	N.C.		AF***----------261
MYGATT	Eng.	Mass.		CFA20-----------56
MYRTLE	———	Va.	Arms:-	AF**-----------159
MYTINGER	———	Pa.		AFA***----------34
MYTTON	Eng.		Arms:-*	CRLA7----------145

- N -

NACK	———	N.Y.		PPA-----,--------342
NAMES in England, Some Account of		(Origins)		AF*-------------243
NAMUR, Counts of	Europe		Arms:-*	CRLA5-----------401
NAMUR, Counts of	France	Berenger	Arms:-*	CRLA17----------198
NANNA	Wales?	Pa.	Arms:-*	CRLA11----------464
NASH	Eng.	Mass./N.H.		CFA7------------252
NASH	Eng.	Conn./Mass.		CRLA4-----------366
NASH	Eng.	Mass./Conn.	Arms:-*	CRLA14----------165
NAVARRE, Kings of	Spain/France			CFA27-----------233
NAVARRE, Kings of	Carter=Boynton desc.		Arms:-*	CRLA15----------213
NAVARRE, Kings of	Sapin/France			CRLA18----------167
NEAL	———	Maine/Md.		PPA-------------194
NEEDHAM	Eng.			CRLA18----------471
NEERGAARD	Denmark	N.Y.		CRLA18----------376
NEFF	Switzerland	Pa.	Arms:-*	CRLA2-----------137
NEGEREL	France			CRLA1------------52
NEILSON	Ireland	N.Y.C.	Arms:-*	CFA9-------------89
NEILSON	———	Pa.		CRLA8-----------136
NEILSON	Ireland	N.J.		CRLA9-----------274
NELSON	No family data		Arms:-*	CRLA19--------opp.1
NELSON	Eng.	Va.		CRLA20----------234
NELSON	Eng.	Va.		PFU-------------121
NELSON, Thomas, Jr.	———	Va.		SDI---------201,218
NESBIT	Scotland/Ireland	Pa.	Arms:-*	AF*-------------156
NESMITH	Scotland	N.H.		CRLA6-----------380
NESMITH	Scotland/Ireland	N.H.		CRLA10----------369
NEVENS	Ireland	Mass.		CRLA3-----------321
NEVERS, Counts of	France		Arms:-	CRLA5-----------402
NEVIL	Eng.	Md.	Arms:-*	AFA***----------368
NEVILL (de)	Eng.			CRLA11--------96,98
NEVILLE (de)	Eng.		Arms:-*	CRLA15----------131
NEVINS	Ireland/Nova Scotia	Mass./N.H.		CFA4------------294
NEVIUS	———	N.J.		CFA10-----------342
NEW	Eng.	Del./Va.		CFA8------------321
NEWBERRY	Eng.	Mass./Conn.		CFA7-------------31
NEWBERRY	Eng.	Mass.		CFA17-----------154
NEWBERRY	Europe/Eng.	Mass.		CRLA1-----------175
NEWBERRY	Eng.	Mass.		CRLA7------------90
NEWBERRY=NEWBURGH	———	———	Arms:-	AF*-------------43
NEWBOLD	Eng.	N.J.	Arms:-*	CFA6------------251
NEWBOLD	Eng.	N.Y./N.J.	Arms:-*	CRLA5-----------495
NEWBOLD	Eng.	N.J.		CRLA14-----------23
NEWBOLD	Eng.	N.J.		CRLA17----------285
NEWBOLD	Eng.	N.J.	Arms:-*	AFA***----------111
NEWBURGH	Eng.	Mauduit line		CRLA2-----------354
NEWBURGH (de)	France/Eng.		Arms:-*	CRLA5-----------404
NEWBURGH (de)		Cooley=Teining desc.		CRLA18----------140
NEWCOMB	Eng.	Va.		CFA6------------357
NEWCOMB	Eng.	Mass.		CFA7------------324
NEWCOMB	———	Va.		CRLA4-----------234
NEWCOMB	Eng.	Mass.	Arms:-	AF*-------------334
NEWELL	———	Mass.		CRLA6-----------519
NEWHALL	Eng.	Mass.		CFA19-----------223
NEWHALL	Eng.	Mass.	Arms:-	CFA22-----------202
NEW HAMPSHIRE, Seal of		*(only)		CRLA15-------opp.70
NEW HAVEN (City)	Conn.	Regional background		CRLA19----------244
NEWLAND	No family data		Arms:-*	CRLA18------opp.574
NEWLIN	Eng.	Pa.		CFA7------------398
NEWLIN	Eng.	Pa.		CFA26-----------99
NEWMAN	Germany	N.Y.		CFA7------------249
NEWMAN	Eng.	Pa.		CRLA8-----------219
NEWTON	———	Mass.	Arms:-*	CFA5------------222
NEWTON	———	Mass.		CFA8------------146

NEWTON	Eng.	Mass.	Arms:-	ACF--------------10
NEWTON	Eng.			CRLA9-----------166
NEWTON	———	Mass.	Arms:-*	CRLA15-----------46
NEWTON	———	Mass.		TNEF------------162
NICE	Europe	Pa.	Arms:-*	CRLA8-----------249
NICE	France	N.Y./Pa.	Arms:-*	CRLA20----------147
NICHOLAS	Eng.	Va.		CRLA1-----------244
NICHOLL	Eng.	N.Y.	Arms:-*	PFU-------------395
NICHOLS	———	Mass.		CFA2------------323
NICHOLS	———	Maine		CFA4------------157
NICHOLS	Eng.	Mass./Conn.		CFA11-----------190
NICHOLS	———	Mass.		CFA17-----------123
NICHOLS	———	N.Y.	Arms:-*	CFA19-----------247
NICHOLSON	Eng.	Md.		CFA12-----------289
NICHOLSON	———	N.C.	Arms:-*	CRLA12----------250
NICKERSON	Eng.	Mass.		CFA3------------120
NICKERSON	Eng.	Mass.		ACF--------------94
NICKERSON	Eng.	Mass.	Arms:-*	CRLA2-----------295
NICOLL	Eng.	N.Y.		CFA20-----------236
NIELL, see: LLYWELYN ap IORWERTH				
NIEUKIRK	———	N.Y.	Arms:-*	CRLA18----------555
NIGHTINGALE	Eng.	Mass.		CRLA6-----------250
NILES	Eng.	Mass.		CFA1------------123
NIVIN	Ireland	Del.		CRLA8-----------422
NIXON	———	Del.	Arms:-*	CRLA1------------83
NIXON	———	Del.		CRLA4------------11
NOBLE	Eng.?	Mass.		CFA11-----------275
NOBLE	———	N.Y.		PPA-------------491
NOEL	Eng.	N.Y.		CFA16-----------306
NORMANDIE (de)	France		Arms:-*	CRLA9-----------494
NORMANDY, Dukes of		Ivar, ano. 790-Richard I, d. 1034		CRLA20----------404
NORRIS	———	Md.		CFA5-------------82
NORRIS	Ireland	N.H.	Arms:-*	CFA6------------158
NORRIS	Eng./Ireland	N.H.	Arms:-	CFA24------------61
NORRIS	Eng.	Pa.		CRLA17----------369
NORTH	Ireland	Pa.	Arms:-*	CRLA18----------296
NORTH	Eng.	Pa.	Arms:-*	AFA***----------105
NORTHEND	Eng.	Mass.		CFA24-----------127
NORTHROP	Eng.	Pa.		CFA2------------139
NORTHROP	———	Pa.		CRLA17----------407
NORTHRUP	Eng.	R.I.		CFA17-----------147
NORTON	Eng.	S.C.	Arms:-*	CFA1------------164
NORTON	Eng.	Conn.		CFA11-----------387
NORTON=LEONARD	———	Pa.		CFA22-----------148
NORTON	Eng.	Mass.	Arms:-*	CFA27----13cht.,144
NORTON	———	Conn.	Arms:-*	CRLA1-----------160
NORTON	Eng.	Mass.	Arms:-*	CRLA3------------34
NORTON	Eng.	Conn.	Arms:-*	CRLA10----------316
NORTON	Eng.?	Mass.		CRLA15----------497
NORTON	———	Mass.	Arms:-*	CRLA20-----------75
NORTON	Eng.	Conn.	Arms:-*	AF*-------------109
NORTON	Eng.	Mass.		AFA***----------336
NORTON	———	Mass.		PPA-------------106
NORWAY, Kings of			Gaither=Fownes desc.	CRLA11-----------65
NORWAY, Kings of			Blackiston descent	CRLA11----------402
NORWOOD	Eng./Bermuda	N.Y.	Arms:-*	CFA24-----------170
NORWOOD	———	N.C.		MCS--------------56
NORWOOD	———	Va.		MCS--------------57
NOTT	Eng.	Conn.		CFA21------------15
NOURSE	Eng.	Va.	Arms:-*	AFA***----------339
NOYES	Eng.	Mass.		CFA16-----------265
NOYES	Eng.	Mass.		CRLA1-----------202
NOYES	Eng.	Mass.	Arms:-*	CRLA6------------75
NOYES	Eng.	Mass.		CRLA19----------140
NUGENT	Canada	Mo.		CRLA6-----------140
NURSE	Eng.	Mass.	Arms:-*	CFA27----13cht.,146
NUTTING	———	Mass.		CFA8------------402

NYCE	———	Pa.		AFA***----------156
NYE	Denmark/Eng.	Mass.	*(only)	CRLA6-----------282

- O -

OAKES	Eng.	Pa.	Arms:-*	CRLA16----------47
OBER	Eng.	Mass.		CFA8-----------103
OBER	Eng.	Mass.		CFA14----------370
OBLENIS	Holland?	N.Y.		CRLA18---------209
O'BRIEN	No family data		Arms:-*	CRLA15---------172
O'CARROLL, see: CARROLL				
O'CONNELL	Ireland	Mass.		TNEF-----------158
ODDING	———	———	*(only)	TNEF--------opp.48
ODDELL	Eng.	Mass.	Arms:-*	CFA12----------127
ODIORNE	———	N.H.		CRLA8-----------43
OFFLEY	Eng.	Va.		CRLA9-----------11
OFFLEY	Eng.		Arms:-*	CRLA15---------338
OGDEN	Eng.	N.Y./N.J.	Arms:-*	CFA15----------306
OGDEN	Eng.	N.J.		CRLA18---------222
OGDEN	Eng.	Pa.	Arms:-*	AFA***---------123
OGILVIE	———	N.Y.C.		CFA24----------177
OGILVIE	———	N.Y.		CRLA16---------169
OGLE	———	Del.		CRLA7-----------71
OGLE	Eng.		Arms:-*	PBAF-----------189
O'KEEFE	Ireland	Mass.		TNEF-----------157
OLCOTT	———	Conn.		CFA13-----------74
OLD	Eng.	Conn.	Arms:-*	CFA18-----------69
OLDSIELD	———	N.Y.	Arms:-*	CRLA20----------61
OLDHAM	Eng.	Va.		CFA5------------36
OLDHAM	———	Md.		CRLA11---------488
OLDMAN	Eng.	Pa.		CRLA13---------216
OLIN	Wales?	Mass./R.I.		CRLA16----------62
OLIPHANT	Scotland	N.J.	Arms:-*	CFA23----------127
OLMSTEAD	Eng.	Mass.		CFA10----------240
OLMSTEAD	Eng.	Mass.		CFA19----------168
OLMSTEAD	Eng.	Mass./Conn.		CFA25----------164
OLMSTED	Eng.	Conn.		CRLA7-----------87
OLNEY	Eng.	R.I.	Arms:-*	CFA4--------142,146
OLNEY	Eng.	Mass./R.I.		CRLA6----------106
OLNEY	Eng.	R.I.		CRLA9----------421
OLNEY	Eng.	R.I.	Arms:-*	PBAF------------85
OLNEY	———	———	*(only)	TNEF-------btn.70-1
OP DE GRAEFF	Holland/Germany	Del./Pa.	Arms:-*	CRLA17---------303
OPDYCK	———	L.I.,N.Y.		CRLA11---------262
ORCUTT	———	Mass.		CFA8-----------354
ORDWAY	Wales?	Mass.		CFA19----------267
ORIGIN of Eng. Names, see: NAMES in England, Some Account of				
ORKNEY, Earls of	Scotland		Gaither=Fownes desc.	CRLA11----------63
ORKNEY, Earls of	Scotland		Blackiston descent	CRLA11---------400
ORMSBY	Eng.	Mass.	Arms:-*	CFA4-----------163
ORSEOLO	Italy	Bray desc.	Arms:-*	CRLA17---------137
ORSEOLO	Italy		Arms:-*	CRLA18---------443
ORTON	Eng.	Conn.		CFA9-----------188
ORTON	———	Conn.	Arms:-*	CRLA6----------332
ORTON	———	Conn.	*(only)	CRLA19----------31
OSBORN	Eng.	Mass./R.I.	Arms:-	AF**-----------188
OSBORNE	———	Conn.		CFA14----------274
OSBORNE	Eng.			CRLA1----------260
OSBORNE	———	Va.		CRLA6----------540
OSBORNE	Eng.			CRLA9-----------12
OSBORNE	Eng.		Arms:-*	CRLA15---------339
OSGOOD	Eng.	Mass.	Arms:-	CFA16----------335

OSGOOD	Eng.	Mass.		CFA19-----------287
OSGOOD	Eng.	N.H./Mass.	Arms:-*	CFA27-----------148
OSGOOD	------	Mass.		CRLA15-----------15
OSGOOD	Eng.	Mass.	Arms:-*	AFA***---------355
OSMUND		N.J.		CRLA17-----------68
O'SULLIVAN, see: SULLIVAN				
OSTROGOTHIC Kings		Wales descent		CRLA13-----------74
OTIS	Eng.	Mass.	Arms:-	CFA12-----------295
OTIS	Eng.	Mass.		CFA17-----------339
OTIS	Eng.?	Mass.	Arms:-	CFA24-----------152
OTIS	Eng.	Mass.		CRLA18-----------521
OTT	------	N.J.	Arms:-*	CRLA18----------577
OTT	Holland	N.Y.		CRLA20-----------184
OVERTON	Eng.	Va.		CRLA4-----------151
OWEN	------	Mass.		CFA9-----------240
OWEN		Mass./Maine		CFA20-----------67
OWEN	Wales	Pa./N.J.		CRLA5--------48,50
OWEN		Va.		CRLA6----------530
OWEN	------	Conn./N.Y.	Arms:-	AF*-------------31
OWEN=CRISPIN	------	N.J.		MCS-------------89
OXENBRIDGE	------	Mass.		MCS-------------78

- P -

PABODIE	------	R.I.		PPA------------515
PACA, William	------	Md.		SDI---------189,194
PACKARD	Eng.	Mass.	Arms:-*	CFA1-------------55
PACKARD	Eng.	Mass.		CFA10-----------257
PACKARD	Eng.	Mass.	Arms:-	CFA19-----------126
PACKARD	Eng.	Mass.		CFA20-----------41
PACKARD	Eng.	Mass.		CRLA1-----------95
PACKARD	Eng.	Mass.		CRLA13-----------374
PADDOCK	Eng.	Mass.		CFA9-----------265
PAERRE, see: PILGRIMS				
PAGAN	------	S.C.		CFA6-----------279
PAGE	Eng.	Mass.		CFA7-----------161
PAGE	------	N.J.		CRLA8----------346
PAGE	------	N.J.		CRLA11----------523
PAGE	------	N.J.		CRLA13----------199
PAGE	Eng.	Mass.	Arms:-*	CRLA15-----------78
PAGE	Eng.	Ohio		CRLA15-----------394
PAGE	Eng.	Conn.	Arms:-	AF*-------------275
PAGE	Eng.	Va.	Arms:-*	AFA1-----------125
PAGE	Eng.	Va.		PFU------------376
PAINE	------	Mass.		CFA2-----------308
PAINE	------	Mass.		CFA8-----------140
PAINE	Eng.	Mass.		CRLA15----------604
PAINE	Eng.?	Mass.	Arms:-*	CRLA18-----------71
PAINE	------	R.I.		CRLA19----------290
PAINE	------	Mass.		PPA-------------75
PAINE	------	R.I.	Arms:-*	TNEF------------30
PAINE, Robert Treat	------	Mass.		SDI---------105,116
PAINTER	Germany	Pa.		CRLA7----------455
PAISTED	Eng.	Maine		CFA3-----------83
PALFREY	Eng.	Mass.		CFA16-----------247
PALGRAVE	Eng.	Mass.	Arms:-*	CRLA20----------105
PALGRAVE	------	Mass.		ARSC------------35
PALGRAVE	------	Mass.		MCS-------------19
PALM	Germany	Pa.	Arms:-*	CRLA6----------498
PALMER	------	Mass./Conn.		CFA5-----------364
PALMER	Eng.	Mass.		ACF-------------85
PALMER	Eng.	Pa.	Arms:-*	CRLA8----------574

PALMER	Eng.	Pa.		CRLA13----------348
PALMER	————	Mass.	Arms:-*	CRLA14----------123
PALMER	Eng.	Conn.		CRLA19-----------79
PALMER	Eng.	Mass.	Arms:-*	AF*-------------70
PALMER	————	Mass.		PPA-------------325
PALMES	Eng.	Conn.	Arms:-*	CRLA2-----------258
PANTZ	Germany	N.J.		CFA5------------151
PARDEE	Eng.	Conn.	Arms:-*	CFA12-------------1
PARDEE	Eng.	Conn.		CFA14-----------204
PARGITER	Eng.		Arms:-*	TNEF-------------48
PARHAM	————	Pa.	Arms:-*	CRLA1------------36
PARK	Eng.	Mass.		CFA19------------92
PARKE	Eng.	Mass.	Arms:-	CFA17-----------126
PARKE	Ireland	Pa.		CRLA17----------272
PARKE	Eng.	Conn.		CRLA17----------472
PARKER	————	Mass.		CFA1------------253
PARKER	Ireland	Pa.		CFA2------------123
PARKER	————	Mass.	Arms:-*	CFA4-------------14
PARKER	————	N.H.		CFA6-------------63
PARKER	————	Mass.		CFA7------------342
PARKER	————	Mass.		CFA23-----------116
PARKER	Eng.?	Conn.	Arms:-*	CFA27---148cht.,150
PARKER	Eng.?	Pa.	Arms:-*	CRLA1------------35
PARKER	Eng.	Mass.	Arms:-*	CRLA8------------55
PARKER	Eng.	Mass.		CRLA10----------309
PARKER	Eng.	Mass.	Arms:-*	CRLA15-----------21
PARKER	————	Pa.		CRLA15----------540
PARKER	————	N.Y.C.	Arms:-*	CRLA20-----------11
PARKER	————	N.H.		AF***-----------32
PARKER	————	Va.		PFU-------------143
PARKER	Eng.?	Mass.		PFU-------------406
PARKER	————	N.Y.		PPA-------------617
PARKHURST	————	Conn.		CFA1------------268
PARKHURST	Eng.	Mass.	Arms:-*	CFA7------------108
PARKHURST (or) PARKIS	Eng.	Mass.		CFA19----------279
PARKHURST	Eng.	Mass.	Arms:-	CRLA6-----------417
PARKHURST	Eng.	Mass.	Arms:-*	PBAF------------81
PARKMAN	Eng.	Mass.		CFA3-------------79
PARKS	Eng.	Mass./Conn.		CFA7------------335
PARKS	Eng.	Mass.	Arms:-*	CRLA15----------477
PARKS	Ireland	Pa.	Arms:-	AF**------------145
PARLIN=PARLING	————	Mass.		CFA21-----------232
PARMELEE	Eng.	Conn.		CFA7------------263
PARMELEE	Eng.	Conn.	Arms:-*	CFA22------------13
PARMELEE	Eng.?	Conn.		CRLA10-----------77
PARMELEE	Eng.?	Conn.	Arms:-*	AF**--------------8
PARMENTIER	————	N.Y.		CRLA12----------437
PARRIS	Eng.	Mass.		CRLA1-----------201
PARRISH	————	Mass.		CRLA10----------279
PARRY	————	Maine		CFA7------------172
PARRY	Wales	Pa.	Arms:-*	CRLA8-----------256
PARSHALL	————	N.Y.	Arms:-*	CRLA8-----------398
PARSONS	Eng.	Mass.		CFA8-------------61
PARSONS	————	N.Y.		CFA6-------------43
PARSONS	————	Mass.	Arms:-*	CFA15-----------325
PARSONS	Eng.	Mass.		CFA15-----------343
PARSONS	Eng.	Mass.	Arms:-*	CFA24------------34
PARSONS	————	Mass.		CRLA4-----------371
PARSONS	————	R.I.		CRLA17----------438
PARSONS	Eng.	Pa.	Arms:-*	AFA***-----------87
PARSONS	Eng.?	Mass.		PFU-------------464
PARSONS	————	Mass.		PPA-------------559
PARTRIDGE	Eng.	Mass.		CFA7------------320
PARTRIDGE	Eng.	Mass.		CFA8------------129
PARTRIDGE	Eng.	Conn./Mass.		CFA18------------90
PARTRIDGE	Eng.?	Mass.	Arms:-	CFA20-----------164
PARTRIDGE	————	Mass.		CRLA14----------159

PARVIN	———	N.J.		CRLA11----------240
PASCAL	———	———		AFA***----------386
PASCALL	Eng.	N.Y.	Arms:-*	CRLA7----------267
PASSAGE	France	N.Y.		CRLA16----------70
PATCH	———	Mass.		CFA8------------101
PATCH	Eng.	Mass.	Arms:-*	CRLA8-----------17
PATTEN	———	Mass.		CFA10----------215
PATTEN	———	Mass.		CFA13----------303
PATTEN	———	Mass.		CRLA11----------237
PATTEN	———	Mass.	Arms:-*	CRLA15----------42
PATTEN	Scotland	N.Y.	Arms:-*	PBAF-------------8
PATTEN	———	R.I.		PPA-------------407
PATRICK, see: Mc CARTHY and PATRICK				
PATTERSON	Scotland/Eng. Mass.			CFA8------------259
PATTERSON	Scotland	Mass.		CFA19----------294
PATTERSON	———	Pa.	Arms:-*	CRLA14----------106
PATTERSON	———	Ohio	Arms:-	AF*------------78
PATTERSON	Scotland/Ireland Pa.		Arms:-*	AFA***----------26
PATTERSON	Scotland/Ireland Pa.		Arms:-*	AFA***----------95
PAUL	Eng.	Pa.	*(only)	CRLA2-----------410
PAULDING	———	N.Y.		PPA-------------83
PAULI	Germany	Pa.	Arms:-*	AF****----------98
PAXSON	Eng.?	Pa.		CFA24----------37
PAXSON	Eng.	Pa.	Arms:-*	AF*------------349
PAXTON	Eng.	Pa.	Arms:-*	CRLA11----------559
PAYNE	Eng.			CRLA2-----------425
PAYNE	———	Va.		CRLA6----------161
PAYNE	Eng.	Mass.	Arms:-*	CRLA15----------43
PAYNE	———	N.Y./Ind.		CRLA17----------6
PAYNE	Eng.	Mass.		AFA***----------16
PAYNE	Eng.	Va.	Arms:-*	AFA***----------133
PAYNE	Eng.?	Mass.		PFU-------------236
PAYNE	———	N.Y.		PPA-------------128
PAYSON	Eng.	Mass.		CFA24----------128
PAYSON	Eng.	Mass.		CRLA13----------410
PAYSON	Eng.	Mass.		CRLA20----------208
PEABODY	Eng.	Mass.		CFA7------------80
PEABODY	Eng.	Mass.		CFA7------------331
PEABODY	Eng.	Mass.	Arms:-*	CFA8------------267
PEABODY	Eng.	Mass.		CRLA17----------260
PEABODY	Eng.	Mass.	Arms:-*	CRLA20----------43
PEABODY	Eng.	Mass.	Arms:-*	AF**------------35
PEABODY	Eng.?	Mass.	Arms:-	AF**------------79
PEABODY	Eng.	Mass.	Arms:-	AF**------------452
PEABODY	———	N.H./Mass.		PPA-------------264
PEABODY	———	N.H./Mass.		PPA-------------387
PEAKE	Eng.	Mass./Conn.		CFA18----------34
PEAKE	———	Mass.		CRLA13----------23
PEARCE=PIERCE	Eng.	Mass.		CFA7------------219
PEARCE	Eng.?	R.I.	*(only)	CRLA6----------247
PEARCE	Eng.	R.I.		CRLA16----------69
PEARCE	Eng.	R.I.		CRLA18----------32
PEARCE	Eng.	R.I.	Arms:-*	CRLA20----------31
PEARCE	Eng.	R.I.	Arms:-*	CRLA20----------378
PEARCE	———	Md.		PFU-------------394
PEARCE	———	———	*(only)	TNEF-------btn.78-9
PEARSALL	———	N.Y.	Arms:-*	CRLA18----------570
PEARSE	Eng.	Mass.	Arms:-	ACF-------------73
PEARSON	Eng.	Mass.	Arms:-*	CFA3------------141
PEARSON	Eng.	Pa.		CRLA9----------157
PEARSON	———	Mass.		CRLA17----------254
PEASLEY	Eng.	Mass.		CFA19----------283
PEASLEY	———	Mass.		CRLA3-----------23
PEATERS (Peters)	Eng.		Arms:-*	CRLA18----btn.546-7
PECHIN	France	Pa.	Arms:-*	AFA***----------343
PECK	Eng.	Conn.		CFA1------------41
PECK	Eng.	Conn.	Arms:-*	CFA3------------213

PECK	Eng.	Mass.		CFA14-----------200
PECK	Eng.	Conn.		CFA15-----------379
PECK	Eng.	Mass./Conn.		CFA21-----------34
PECK	Eng.	Conn.		CFA26-----------140
PECK	Eng.	Mass.	*(only)	CRLA24-----------7
PECK	Eng.	Mass./Conn.	Arms:-*	CRLA7-----------13
PECK	Eng.	Mass.		CRLA7-----------346
PECK	———	Mass.		CRLA13-----------364
PECK	Eng.	Mass.		CRLA17-----------485
PECK	———	Conn.		PFU-------------139
PECK	Eng.	Mass.		PFU-------------190
PECKHAM		———	*(only)	TNEF-------btn.78-9
PECKHAM, see: PILGRIMS				
PEDDLE	Eng.	Pa.	Arms:-*	CRLA5-----------466
PEIRCE	Eng.	Pa.		CRLA8-----------196
PEIRCE	———	Pa.		CRLA8-----------319
PEIRCE	Eng.	Pa.	Arms:-*	CRLA8-----------557
PEIRCE	———	Mass.	Arms:-*	CRLA15-----------74
PELHAM	———	Mass.		ARSC-------------21
PELHAM	———	Mass.		MCS-------------65
PELL	Eng.	N.Y.		CFA14-----------193
PELL	Eng.	N.Y.	Arms:-*	PFU-------------461
PELS	———	N.Y.	Arms:-*	CRLA20--------35,36
PEMBERTON	Eng.		Arms:-*	CRLA20-----------383
PEMBERTON	Eng.	Mass.	Arms:-	AF*-------------374
PENDLETON	———	Mass.		CFA4-----------158
PENDLETON	———	Mass.		CFA6-----------90
PENDLETON	Eng.	Va.	Arms:-	CFA9-----------125
PENDLETON	Eng.	Va.		CFA10-----------124
PENDLETON	Eng.	Va.	Arms:-	CFA14-----------188
PENDLETON	———	Mass./N.H.	Arms:-*	CFA13-----------130
PENDLETON	Eng.	Mass.		CFA18-----------190
PENDLETON	———	Mass.		CRLA20-----------172
PENDLETON	Eng.	N.H./N.Y.		AF***-----------32
PENDLETON	Eng.	Va.	Arms:-	AF***-----------99
PENDLETON	Eng.	Va.	Arms:-*	PFU-------------243
PENGILLY	Wales	Mass./Conn.		CRLA15-----------438
PENHALLOW	———	N.H.		MCS-------------22
PENHALLOW	Eng.	N.H.	Arms:-*	PFU-------------216
PENLLYN, Lords of	Wales			CRLA2-----------448
PENN	Eng.	Pa.		CFA16-----------142
PENN	Eng.	Pa.	Arms:-*	CRLA5-----------53
PENN	———	Va.		CRLA6-----------50
PENN, John	———	Va./N.C.		SDI--------221,224
PENNELL	Eng.	Pa.	Arms:-*	CRLA17-----------356
PENNELL	———	Mass.	Arms:-	AF*-------------250
PENNINGTON	Eng.	Pa.		CRLA9-----------545
PENNOCK	Eng.	Pa.	Arms:-*	CFA3-----------189
PENNOCK	Eng.?	Pa.		CFA5-----------334
PENNOCK	Ireland	Pa.	Arms:-*	CFA7-----------195
PENNOCK	Eng./Ireland	Pa.	Arms:-	AF*-------------347
PENNOCK	Eng.	Vt./Ind.	Arms:-	AF*-------------436
PENNY	———	Va.		CRLA12-----------168
PENOYER	Eng.	Conn.		CFA16-----------220
PENROSE	Eng.	Pa.		CRLA15-----------511
PENROSE	Eng.	Pa.	Arms:-*	AFA***-----------35
PENROSE	Eng.	Pa.		PFU-------------144
PENTZ	Germany	N.J./N.Y.	Arms:-*	CRLA19-----------56
PEPIN I, Royal Descent				CFA21-----------212
PEPPER	———	Mass.		CRLA9-----------391
PEPPERRELL	Eng.	Maine	Arms:-	CFA10-----------368
PERCIVAL	———	Conn.		PPA-------------219
PERCY, Earl of Northumberland	Eng.		*(only)	CRLA2-----------541
		Jones=Paul=Kinght descent		
PERCY (de Perci)	France/Eng.			CRLA2-----------550
PERCY (de)	Eng.		Arms:-*	CRLA15--------133
PERCY (de)	Eng.			CRLA15------372,374

PERHAM	Eng.	Mass.	CFA19----------279
PERKINS	Eng.	Mass.	CFA8------------202
PERKINS	Eng.	Mass.	CFA15------------60
PERKINS	Eng.	Mass.	CFA17-----------214
PERKINS	Eng.	Mass.	CFA20-----------342
PERKINS	Eng.	Mass.	Arms:-	CFA21------------48
PERKINS	Eng.	Mass.	CFA21------------59
PERKINS	Eng.	Mass.	CFA21-----------239
PERKINS	------	Va./Mo.	CRLA3-----------370
PERKINS	------	Mass.	Arms:-*	CRLA7-----------426
PERKINS	Eng.	N.H.	Arms:-*	AFA***----------75
PERLEY	Eng.	Mass.	CFA7-------------77
PERLEY	Eng.	Mass.	Arms:-	CRLA16---------210
PERLEY	Wales	Mass.	CRLA19---------380
PERNE	Eng.	------	CFA7-------------19
PERRY	Eng.	Mass.	CFA9-----------102
PERRY	------	Mass.	CFA9-----------350
PERRY	Eng.	Mass.	CFA11----------201
PERRY	Eng.	Mass.	CFA15------------54
PERRY	Eng.	Mass.	CFA23----------223
PERRY	------	Mass.	CRLA6----------289
PERRY	------	N.C.	Arms:-*	CRLA9----------257
PERRY	------	Mass.	AFA***---------104
PERRY	------	Mass.?	Arms:-*	TNEF-------------2
PESHALL (de)	Eng.		Arms:-*	CRLA7----------145
PETERS	Eng.	Mass.	CFA14-----------38
PETERS, see: PEATERS			
PETERSON	------	N.Y.	CRLA7----------259
PETERSON	Sweden	Del./N.J.	PFU------------238
PETSCH	No family data		Arms:-*	CRLA11------opp.456
PETTIBONE	------	Conn.	CFA17----------264
PETTIGREW	------	Va.	AF***----------126
PETTIT	Eng.	Mass.	Arms:-*	CRLA15---------381
PETTY	------	N.Y.	Arms:-*	AFA***---------328
PEVEREL	Eng.		Arms:-*	CRLA5----------406
PEW	------	N.J.	CFA18----------238
PEYTON	Eng.	Va.	Arms:-*	CFA13-----------79
PEYTON	Europe/Eng.	Va.	Arms:-*	CFA22----------151
PEYTON	Eng.	Va.	CRLA1----------258
PFEIFFER	Germany	Pa.	Arms:-*	CRLA8----------265
PHARO	Eng.	N.J.	Arms:-*	CRLA17----------81
PHARO	Eng.	N.J.	CRLA17---------496
PHELPS	Eng.	Conn.	CFA1-----------123
PHELPS	Eng.	Mass.	CFA7-----------330
PHELPS	Eng.	Mass.	CFA7-----------410
PHELPS	Eng.	Mass.	CFA11----------320
PHELPS	Eng.	Mass./Conn.	CFA12----------210
PHELPS	Eng.	Mass.	Arms:-*	CFA18-----------96
PHELPS	Eng.	Mass.	CFA19-----------82
PHELPS	Eng.	Mass.	CFA21----------112
PHELPS	Eng.	Conn.	CRLA10---------131
PHELPS	------	Mass.	Arms:-*	CRLA17---------551
PHELPS	Eng.	Conn.	Arms:-	AF*------------329
PHELPS	Eng.	Mass.	Arms:-*	AF***-----------57
PHELPS	Eng.	Mass.	Arms:-	AF***----------382
PHELPS	Eng.	Mass./Conn.	Arms:-*	AFA***---------361
PHILIPSE	Bohemia	N.Y.	CFA11-----------29
PHILLIPS	Eng.	Maine	CFA10----------358
PHILLIPS	Eng.	Mass.	CFA24----------128
PHILLIPS	------	Va.	CRLA4----------407
PHILLIPS	------	N.Y.?/Ohio	CRLA7----------502
PHILLIPS	Wales	Pa.	CRLA9----------248
PHIPPS	Eng.	Maine	CFA10----------102
PHIPPS	------	Pa.	Arms:-*	CRLA3----------301
PHIPPS	------	------	AFA***---------186
PHYSICK, see: SYNG=PHYSICK			
PIAST, see: POLAND, Rulers of			

PICKERING	Eng.	N.H.		CFA7------------52
PICKERING	Eng.	N.H.		CFA7------------150
PICKERING	Eng.	Conn.	Arms:-*	CRLA7-----------276
PICKWORTH	------	Mass.	Arms:-*	CRLA8------------39
PIERCE	Eng.	Mass.	Arms:-*	CFA8-----------180
PIERCE	Eng.	Mass.	Arms:-	CFA17----------119
PIERCE	------	Mass.	Arms:-*	CRLA12----------346
PIERCE	------	Del.	Arms:-*	CRLA13----------285
PIERCE	Eng.	Mass.	Arms:-*	CRLA20-----------80
PIERPONT	Eng.	Md.	Arms:-*	CRLA11-----------21
PIERPONT	Eng.	Mass.		CFA14----------266
PIERPONT	Eng.	Md.		CRLA16-----------40
PIERPONT	------	Conn.		PPA-------------97
PIERREPONT	Eng.	Mass.	Arms:-*	CFA15----------236
PIERREPONT (Errors)	Eng.	Mass.	Arms:-*	AFA***----------29
PIERSON	Eng.	L.I.,N.Y.	Arms:-	CFA5------------51
PIERSON	Eng.	N.Y./N.J.		CRLA15----------600
PIET	------	Md./Va.		CRLA19----------311
PIETERSEN	Holland	N.J.		CFA16-----------68
PIKE	Eng.	Mass.	Arms:-*	CFA1-----------110
PIKE	------	Mass.		CRLA2-----------249
PIKE	------	------	Arms:-*	CRLA14-------opp.54
PIKE	Eng.	Mass.	Arms:-*	CRLA14----------145
PIKE	------	R.I.	Arms:-*	PBAF-----------103
PIKE	------	Mass.		PPA-------------425

PILGRIMS, Coats of Arms of   *(only)   CFA4--------opp.143
           MULLINS   STEERE   INMAN   RHODES

           DORR   BERNON   FENNER   PECKHAM   CFA4--------opp.145
           CRAWFORD   HOWLAND   WATERMAN   WEEDEN
           ALLEN   ALDEN   TEW   GREENE

           BULLOCK   GORTON   ARNOLD   FASTON   CFA4-------after146
           TOWNSEND   HARRIS   COGGESHALL TILLEY
           RICHMOND   WILKINSON   CLARKE   BORDEN
           WINTHROP   HOPKINS   ALMY   PAERRE

PINDER	Eng.	Mass.	Arms:-	CFA27-----------152
PINGREE	------	Mass.		CRLA13----------447
PINGREE	------	Mass.		CRLA15----------484
PINKHAM	------	Mass.		CFA1-----------183
PINKHAM	------	Mass.		CFA20-----------24
PINKHAM	Eng.?	Mass.	Arms:-*	CRLA15----------262
PINKNEY	------	Md.		PPA------------287
PINNEY	Eng.	Mass./Conn.		CRLA19----------264
PINSON	------	Mass.	Arms:-*	CRLA15-----------18
PINTARD	France	N.Y.		CFA13------------6
PITKIN	Eng.	Conn.		CFA9-----------205
PITMAN	------	Maine/Mass./Hawaii Arms:-*		CFA11----------264
PITNEY	------	Mass.		CRLA15-----------52
PITT	Eng.	Va.		CRLA4-----------87
PLAISTED	Eng.	Maine		CFA7-----------150
PLANT	------	Conn.	Arms:-*	CFA20----------289
PLANT	Eng.	Mass.	Arms:-*	AF***----------204
PLANTAGENET	Geoffrey V, Count of Anjou & Maine			CRLA5----------141
		Schull descent		
PLANTAGENET		Wales descent		CRLA13-----------90
PLATT	Eng.	Conn.	Arms:-*	CFA12-----------22
PLATT	------	Conn.		CFA15----------314
PLATT	------	L.I.,N.Y.		CFA16----------290
PLATT	------	Conn.	Arms:-*	CFA27---148cht.,154
PLATT	Eng.	Conn.	Arms:-*	CRLA6----------322
PLATT	------	N.Y.		CRLA18----------434
PLEASANTS	Eng.	Va.		CRLA4----------224
PLEDGER	No family data		Arms:-*	CRLA18----btn.546-7
PLEDGER	Eng.	N.J.		CRLA20----------199
PLIMPTON	Eng.	Mass.		CRLA7----------511
PLOWDEN	Eng.	Md.	Arms:-*	CRLA4----------441
PLUM	Eng.	Conn.	Arms:-*	CFA10----------181

PLUMB	Eng.	Conn.	Arms:-	CFA27----------157
PLUMB	Eng.	Conn.	Arms:-*	CRLA12--------50,51
PLUMB	Eng.	Conn.	Arms:-*	PFU------------147
PLUMBE	Eng.	Conn.		CFA7------------329
PLUMBE (or) PLUMB	Eng.	Conn.		CFA16----------226
PLUMER	———	Mass.		CRLA17---------257
PLUMME	Eng.		Arms:-*	AFA***----------17
PLUMMER	Wales?/Eng.	Maine		CFA5------------193
PLUMMER	———	Md.		CFA23----------146
PLUMPTON	Eng.		*(only)	CRLA2----------17
PLYMOUTH COLONY, First Seal of			*(only)	CFA27-------148cht.
PLYMPTON	Eng.	Mass.		PFU------------422
POAT, see: POTE				
POE	———	Md.		PPA------------469
POIGNAND	France/Eng.	Mass.	Arms:-	AF***----------209
POINTZ	Eng.			CRLA1---------189
POIRIER	France	Canada/Pa.		CRLA17---------701
POLAND, Rulers of		Piast	Arms:-*	CRLA17---------199
POLAND, Rulers of		Piast Shrack descent		CRLA17---------389
POLAND, Rulers of				CRLA18---------170
POLAND, see: HUNGARY=BOHEMIA=POLAND, Royal Descents from				
POLHEMUS	———	N.J.		AFA***----------386
POLK	———	Md.		CRLA8----------176
POLK	———	Pa.		CRLA8----------199
POLK	Ireland	Md./N.C.		CRLA12---------240
POLLY	———	Mass.	Arms:-*	CRLA15----------21
POLSON	Scotland	Canada		CRLA12---------300
POMEROY	Eng.	Mass./Conn.		CFA15----------387
POMEROY	Eng.	Mass./Conn.		CRLA6----------478
POMEROY	———	Mass./Conn.		ARSC-----------109
POMEROY	Eng.	Mass.		PFU------------274
POND	———	Mass.		CFA9-----------338
PONSONBY	Eng./Ireland		Arms:-*	CRLA13---------485
PONTHIEU, Counts of	France			CRLA5----------408
PONTUS	———	Mass.		CFA8-----------328
POOLE	Ireland	Md.		CFA5------------93
POOLE	Eng.?	Mass.	Arms:-	CFA6------------149
POOLE	———	Mass.		CFA8-----------254
POOLE	Eng.	Pa.		ACF-------------31
POOLE	———	Mass.		CRLA20---------207
POOLE (Pole)	———	Mass.		MCS-------------24
POOLE	Eng.	Mass.		PFU------------453
POOR	Eng.	Mass.		CFA6------------82
POOR	Eng.	Mass.	Arms:-	CFA27----------161
POOR	Eng.	Mass.	Arms:-*	PBAF-----------168
POORE	———	Mass.		TNEF-----------218
POPE	Eng.	Mass.	Arms:-*	CFA15----------192
POPE	———	Mass.	Arms:-	CFA27----------163
POPE	———	Mass.		CRLA17---------459
POPE	Eng.	Md./Va.	Arms:-*	AFA***---------331
POPE	———	Mass.	*(only)	TNEF--------opp.48
POPE	———	Mass.		TNEF-----------214
POPHAM	Ireland	N.Y.		CFA16----------306
PORCHER	France	S.C.		CFA3-----------356
PORTE (de la)	France		Arms:-*	CRLA1-----------44
PORTER	Eng.	R.I.		CFA1------------16
PORTER	Eng.	Conn.	Arms:-*	CFA1-----------122
PORTER	———	Conn.		CFA2-----------194
PORTER	Eng.?	Conn.		CFA9-----------229
PORTER	Eng.	Conn.		CFA15----------359
PORTER	Eng.	Conn.	Arms:-	CFA17----------153
PORTER	———	Conn.		CRLA6----------335
PORTER	———	Del.	Arms:-*	CRLA9-------481,497
PORTER	———	Pa./Ky.		AF**-----------398
PORTER	———	Pa.		AF**-----------517
PORTER	Eng.	Conn.		AF****---------205
PORTER	———	Conn.		AF****---------232

PORTER	Ireland	N.H./Pa.	Arms:-*	AFA***----------135
PORTER	------	Conn.	Arms:-*	AFA***----------251
PORTER	------	Conn.	Arms:-*	TNEF------------80
PORTUGAL, Royal Line of	Robert, King of Franks	*(only)		CRLA2-----------38
PORTUGAL, Royal Line of				CRLA2-----------500
PORTUGAL, Royal Line of			Arms:-*	CRLA5-----------410
PORTUGAL, Royal Line of		Haskell descent		CRLA8-----------108
PORTUGAL, Royal Line of		Hinton desc.	Arms:-	CRLA8-----------486
PORTUGAL, House of			Arms:-*	CRLA11----------99
PORTUGAL, Royal House of			Arms:-*	CRLA15----------144
PORTUGAL, Royal House of				CRLA18----------173
POST	Eng.	Mass.		CFA3------------333
POST	Holland/Eng.	Mass./L.I.,N.Y.		CRLA11----------363
POTE (Poat)	------	Mass./Maine	Arms:-	CRLA3-----------337
POTTENGER	Eng.	Md.	Arms:-	CFA15-----------170
POTTENGER	Eng.	Md.	Arms:-	CFA16-----------83
POTTENGER	------	Md.	Arms:-*	AFA***----------297
POTTER	Ireland	S.C.		CFA12-----------155
POTTER	Eng.	R.I.		CFA18-----------33
POTTER	Ireland	Pa.		CFA22-----------90
POTTER	Eng.	Mass.		CFA24-----------124
POTTER	Ireland	N.J.		CFA25-----------160
POTTER	------	Conn./Ohio		CRLA6-----------305
POTTER	------	R.I.	Arms:-*	CRLA12----------366
POTTER	------	R.I.	Arms:-*	CRLA20----------45
POTTS	Wales	Pa.		CFA8------------194
POTTS	------	Pa.		CRLA5-----------470
POTTS	Eng.	Pa.	Arms:-*	CRLA8-----------569
POTTS	------	Pa.		CRLA9-----------463
POTTS	Eng.	N.J.		CRLA9-----------517
POTTS	------	Pa.		CRLA13----------115
POTTS	Wales?	Pa.		CRLA20----------297
POTTS	------	Pa.	Arms:-*	AFA***----------89
POTTS	Eng.	Pa.	Arms:-*	AFA***----------389
POUCHOT	France		Arms:-*	CRLA1-----------48
POULTER	------	Mass.?	Arms:-*	CRLA20----------99
POULTNEY	Eng.	Pa.		CRLA17----------271
POWELL	------	L.I.,N.Y.		CFA7------------278
POWELL	Wales	L.I.,N.Y.		CFA7------------382
POWELL	------	Pa./Ind.		CRLA3-----------210
POWELL	------	Va./N.C.		CRLA4-----------92
POWELL	------	Va.		CRLA4-----------275
POWELL	------	Va.		CRLA4-----------304
POWELL	Eng.	Pa.		CRLA11----------519
POWELL	Eng.	Pa.		CRLA14----------35
POWELL	------	Pa.		CRLA17----------73
POWELL, see: HARE=POWELL				
POWERS	Eng.	Mass.		CFA2------------247
POWLES	------	N.J.		CRLA10----------392
POWIS, Kings of, see: WALES, Kings of				
PRACHEN (Prache)	Eng.	Pa.		CRLA17----------715
PRATT	Eng.	Mass.		CFA1------------42
PRATT	------	Mass.		CFA7------------8
PRATT	------	Mass.		CFA10-----------90
PRATT	Eng.	Mass.		CRLA6-----------240
PRATT	------	Mass.	Arms:-*	CRLA15----------68
PRATT	------	Mass.	Arms:-*	CRLA20----------77
PRATT	Eng.	Mass.	Arms:-*	AF**------------533
PRENCE=PRINCE	Eng.	Mass.		CFA7------------346
PRENCE	Eng.	Mass.		CFA27----38cht.,165
PRENCE	Eng.	Mass.		CRLA17----------451
PRENTICE	------	Mass.	Arms:-	CFA4------------19
PRENTICE	Eng.	Mass.		CFA7------------9
PRENTICE	------	Mass.		CFA16-----------213
PRENTICE	Eng.	Mass.	Arms:-*	CFA16-----------251
PRENTICE	Eng.?	Mass.	Arms:-*	CFA23-----------83
PRENTICE	Eng.	Mass.	Arms:-*	CRLA20----------79

PRENTICE	———	Conn.		PPA------------322
PRENTIS	Eng.	Va.	Arms:-*	CRLA4-----------17
PRENTISS	Eng.	Mass.		CFA6------------240
PRENTISS	Eng.	Mass.	Arms:-*	CFA7-------------1
PRENTISS	———	Mass.	*(only)	CRLA6-----------261
PRESCOT	———	———	*(only)	CRLA12-------opp.88
PRESCOTT	Eng.	Mass.		CFA8------------261
PRESCOTT	Eng.	Mass.	Arms:-	CFA20-----------169
PRESCOTT	Eng.	Mass.	Arms:-*	CRLA1-----------224
PRESCOTT	Eng.	N.H.	Arms:-	CRLA7-----------370
PRESCOTT	———	N.H.		ARSC------------42
PRESCOTT	———	Mass.		ARSC------------52
PRESCOTT	———	N.H.		MCS-------------7
PRESCOTT	———	Mass.		MCS-------------96
PRESTON	Eng.	Mass.		CFA13-----------259
PRESTON	———	Mass.		CFA19-----------78
PRESTON	Eng.	Mass.		CFA22-----------111
PRESTON	———	Md.		CRLA1-----------231
PRESTON	———	Ill./Iowa		CRLA3-----------219
PRESTON	Ireland	Va.		CRLA6-----------170
PRESTON	Eng.	Pa.		CRLA13----------213
PRESTON	Eng.			CRLA13----------429
PRESTON, see: LLOYD=PRESTON				
PRESTWOOD	Eng.			CRLA9-----------14
PRESTWOOD	Eng.		Arms:-*	CRLA15----------341
PREVENCE	France		Berenger	CRLA2-----------359
PREVENCE, see: PROVENCE, Counts of				
PREVOST, see: MALLET				
PRICE	———	L.I.,N.Y.		CRLA9-----------155
PRICE	———	Pa.		CRLA9-----------309
PRICE	Wales	Md.		CRLA15----------592
PRICE	Eng.	Md.	Arms:-*	AF**------------126
PRIDE	———	Mass.		CRLA8-----------48
PRIEST	———	Mass.	Arms:-	CFA10-----------373
PRIEST	———	Mass.		CRLA6-----------243
PRIEST	———	Mass.		CRLA17----------444
PRINCE	Eng.	Mass.		CFA1------------46
PRINCE	Eng.	Mass.		CFA3------------130
PRINCE	Eng.	Mass.	Arms:-	CFA26-----------65
PRINCE	Eng.	Mass.		ACF-------------101
PRINCE	———	Mass.	Arms:-*	CRLA13----------239
PRINCE	Eng.	Mass.	Arms:-*	CRLA18----------38
PRIME	Eng.	Conn.		CFA6------------307
PRIME	Eng.	Mass.		CFA11-----------152
PRIOLEAU	———	S.C.	Arms:-*	CFA25-----------55
PRIOR	———	Mass./N.Y.	Arms:-*	CFA18-----------26
PRIOR	———	Mass.		CRLA17----------21
PROCTOR	———	Mass.		CFA10-----------331
PROCTOR	———	Mass.		CFA17-----------122
PROCTOR	———	Mass.		CFA21-----------224
PROCTOR	———	Pa.		CRLA18----------524
PROCTOR	———	Mass.		CRLA20----------167
PROUSE	———	Mass.	Arms:-*	CRLA15----------12
PROUT	———	Conn.		CFA16-----------57
PROVENCE, Counts of	France			CRLA1-----------332
PROVENCE Line	France		Peck=Bowen desc.	CRLA2-----------33
PROVENCE, Counts of	France		Berenger	CRLA2-----------502
PROVENCE, Counts of	France		Arms:-	CRLA5-----------412
PROVENCE, Counts of	France		Haskell descent	CRLA8-----------109
PROVENCE, Counts of	France	Hinton descent	Arms:-*	CRLA8-----------487
PROVENCE, Counts of	France			CRLA17----------201
PROVENCE, Counts of	France			CRLA18----------174
PUGH	Wales	Pa.	Arms:-*	CRLA8-----------273
PULESTON	Eng.		Arms:-*	CRLA5-----------415
PURCHASE	No family data		Arms:-*	CRLA19------opp.274
PURDY	Eng.	Mass.		CFA10-----------310
PURDY	———	Conn.		CRLA7-----------553

PUREFOY	Eng.	Va.		CRLA3-----------246
PURMORT	Eng.	Mass.	Arms:-	AF*------------439
PUSLEY	------	Pa.		CFA7------------392
PUTNAM	Eng.	Mass.	Arms:-*	CFA3--,--------91
PUTNAM	Eng.	Mass.		CFA6-----------176
PUTNAM	------	Mass.		CFA8------------72
PUTNAM	Eng.	Mass.	Arms:-*	CFA8------------85
PUTNAM	Eng.	Mass.	Arms:-	CFA15-----------40
PUTNAM	Eng.	Mass.	Arms:-*	CFA27--148cht.,167,
				210cht.
PUTNAM (Puttenham)	Eng.	Mass.		CRLA6-----------92
PUTNAM	Eng.	Mass.	Arms:-	CRLA7----------492
PUTNAM	Eng.	Mass.	Arms:-*	CRLA12---------109
PUTNAM	Eng.	Mass.	Arms:-	CRLA16---------187
PUTNAM	Eng.	Mass.?	Arms:-*	CRLA20----btn.134-5
PUTNAM	Eng.	Mass.	Arms:-*	AF*------------294
PYLE	Eng.	Pa.		CRLA17---------268
PYNCHON	Wales	Mass.		CFA9-----------204
PYNCHON	Eng.	Mass.		CFA15----------366
PYNE	Eng.	N.Y.C.	Arms:-	CFA12----------159

- Q -

QUACKENBUSH	Germany	N.Y.		CRLA13---------162
QUINCEY (de)	Eng.			CRLA2----------480
QUINCY (de)	Eng.			CRLA1----------368
QUINCY (de)	Eng.	Earls of Winchester		CRLA2----------337
QUINCY (de)	Eng.	Arms:-*		CRLA5----------417
QUINCY (de), Seyer	Eng.	Gaither=Fownes desc.		CRLA11----------48
QUINCY (de)	Eng.			CRLA11---------173
QUINCY (de)	Eng.	Wales descent		CRLA13---------104
QUINCY (de)	Eng.			CRLA15---------134
QUINCY (de)	Eng.	Bray desc.	Arms:-*	CRLA17---------146
QUINCY (de)	Eng.			CRLA17---------187
QUINCY (de)	Eng.	Titus descent		CRLA18---------511
QUINCY	Eng.	Arms:-*		AFA***---------335

- R -

RAINSFORD	Eng.	S.C.		PFU-------------241
RAISCH	------	Calif.		CRLA10----------98
RALYEA	------	N.Y.		CRLA16---------150
RAMBO	Sweden	N.Y./Pa.		CRLA2----------201
RAMBO	Sweden	Pa.		CRLA17---------410
RAMBO	Sweden	Pa.	Arms:-*	CRLA18---------297
RAMIREZ I, see: ARAGON, Kings of				
RAND	------	Mass.		CFA7-------------4
RAND	------	Mass.		CRLA8----------543
RANDALL	Eng.	R.I.		CFA6-----------164
RANDALL	------	Mass.		CFA26-----------37
RANDALL	Eng.		Arms:-*	CRLA9----------490
RANDOLPH	Eng.	Mass.		CFA17----------101
RANDOLPH	Eng.	Va.		CRLA1----------241
RANDOLPH	Eng.	Va.		CRLA3----------240
RANDOLPH	Eng.	Va.		CRLA4----------166
RANDOLPH	Eng.	Va.		CRLA4----------180
RANDOLPH	Eng.	Va.		CRLA8----------553

RANDOLPH	Scotland			CRLA18----------287
RANDOLPH	————	Va.		MCS------------57
RAPALJE	France	N.Y.		CFA7------------228
RAPALJE	Holland	N.Y.	Arms:-*	CRLA13----------400
RAPER	————	Pa.		CFA7------------398
RASTALL	Eng.			CRLA5------------54
RAVENELL	France	S.C.		PFU------------333
RAVLIN=WHITE	————	Vt.		CRLA7------------399
RAWSON	Eng.	Mass.		CFA2------------178
RAWSON	Eng.	Mass.	Arms:-*	CFA7------------17
RAWSON	Eng.	Mass.		CFA7------------310
RAWSON	Eng.	Mass.	Arms:-*	AF**------------356
RAY	Eng.	Mass.	Arms:-*	CFA14------------29
RAY	Eng.	Md.		CRLA4----------411
RAYMOND	Eng.	Mass.		CFA2------------321
RAYMOND	Eng.	Mass.		CFA9------------321
RAYMOND	————	Mass.		CFA21------------239
RAYMOND	————	Conn.		CRLA13----------178
RAYMOND	————	Mass./Conn.		CRLA20----------216
RAYMORE	————	Mass.		CFA13----------155
REA	————	Va./Ohio	Arms:-	AF****----------148
READ	————	R.I.		CFA6------------291
READ	————	Mass.		CFA16----------235
READ	Eng.	R.I.		CFA16------------55
READ	————	Pa.		PPA------------581
READ, George	————	Md./Del.		SDI--------181,184
READ=REED	Eng.	Mass.	Arms:-	CFA17------115,120
READE	Eng.	N.Y.C.		CFA25------------41
READE	Eng.	Va.	Arms:-	CRLA3----------111
READE	Eng.	Va.		CRLA4------------40
READE	Eng.	Va.		CRLA4------------113
READE	Eng.	Va.		CRLA4------------223
READE	Eng.	Va.	Arms:-*	CRLA4----------352
READE	Eng.	Va.	Arms:-*	CRLA4----------470
READE=WASHINGTON	————	Va.		MCS------------70
REASONER	————	N.Y.		CRLA12----------387
RECKEFUS	Germany	Md./Pa.		CRLA13----------134
REDAWAY	————	Mass.		CRLA12----------152
REDD	————	Va.		CFA16----------163
REDIAT	————	Mass.		CRLA15------------89
REDINGTON	Eng.?	Mass.		CFA11----------223
REDWOOD	Eng.	Mass./R.I.		CRLA18----------529
REED	Eng.	Mass.		CFA7------------56
REED	————	Mass.		CFA8------------282
REED	Eng.?	Mass.		CFA9------------358
REED	Ireland	Maine		CFA13----------363
REED	Scotland	Md./Pa.		CRLA6----------182
REED	Eng.	Mass.		CRLA11----------593
REED	————	————	*(only)	CRLA12-------opp.88
REED	Ireland	N.J.		CRLA15----------450
REED	No family data		Arms:-*	CRLA17-------opp.74
REED	————	Pa.		CRLA19----------183
REED	————	Mass.	Arms:-*	TNEF------------59
REEDER	————	N.Y.		CFA15------------70
REES	Wales?	Pa.		CRLA13----------426
REESE	————	Pa.		CFA8------------36
REEVE	Wales	L.I.,N.Y.		CFA10----------335
REEVES	————	N.J.		CRLA10----------129
REID	————	Md./Ohio		CRLA7----------562
REINHARDT	Germany	N.J.		CFA24----------104
REMINGTON	————	Mass.		CRLA2----------384
REMINGTON	————	Pa.		CRLA15----------231
REMINGTON	————	Mass.		CRLA19----------257
REMINGTON	Eng.	Mass.	Arms:-*	CRLA20----------380
REMINGTON	Eng.	Mass./Conn.	Arms:-	AF**--------267,285
REMY	————	Va.		CRLA10----------368
REVEL	————	Va./Md.		CFA17----------377

REYNER	Eng.	N.H.		CRLA7-----------414
REYNER	Eng.	Mass./N.H.		CFA17-------131,132
REYNOLDS	------	Pa.	Arms:-*	CFA6------------332
REYNOLDS	Eng.	Pa.		CRLA11----------487,
REYNOLDS	Eng.?	Mass./R.I.	Arms:-*	AF***-----------128
RHINELANDER	Germany	N.Y.	Arms:-	CFA5------------264
RHINELANDER	Germany	N.Y.		CFA25------------59
RHINELANDER	Germany	N.Y.		PFU-------------211
RHOADES	Eng.	Pa.	Arms:-*	CRLA19----------322
RHOADES	------	N.Y.	Arms:-*	CRLA20-----------59
RHOADES	------	Mass.	Arms:-*	CRLA20----------342
RHODE ISLAND, Seal of			Arms:-*	CRLA19-------opp.10
RHODES	Eng.	Mass.		CFA5-------------40
RHODES	Eng.	Pa.	Arms:-*	AFA***----------337
RHODES	------		*(only)	TNEF-------btn.70-1
RHODES, see: PILGRIMS				
RHODRI MAWR (Roderick)	Wales		The Welsh Princes	CRLA2-----------450
RHODRI MAWR	Wales		The Welsh Princes	CRLA2-----------493
RHODRI MAWR, see: WALES, Kings of				
RICE	Wales	Mass.		CFA7------------345
RICE	Eng.	Mass.		CFA13-----------238
RICE	Wales	Mass.	Arms:-	CFA21-----------230.
RICE	Wales	Maine	Arms:-*	CFA23-----------189
RICE	Eng.	Mass.	Arms:-*	ACF--------------15
RICE, see: ROYCE				
RICH	------	N.H./Mass.		CRLA18-----------56
RICHARDS	Eng.	Mass.		CFA3--------------8
RICHARDS	Eng.	Mass.		CFA15-----------353
RICHARDS	Eng.	Mass.	Arms:-*	CFA13-----------278
RICHARDS	Eng.	Mass.	Arms:-	CFA27-----------172
RICHARDS	Eng.	Mass.		CRLA6-----------526
RICHARDS	------	Pa.		CRLA9------------17
RICHARDS	Eng.	Mass.	Arms:-*	CRLA15-----------48
RICHARDS	Eng.	Va.	Arms:-*	CRLA17------------1
RICHARDS	Eng.	Mass.		CRLA17----------460
RICHARDS	Wales?	Pa.	Arms:-*	CRLA18----------515
RICHARDSON	Eng.	Va.		CFA3------------360
RICHARDSON	Eng.	N.Y.		CFA7------------394
RICHARDSON	------	Mass.		CFA7------------402
RICHARDSON	Eng.	Mass.		CFA8-------------83,
RICHARDSON	Eng.	Mass.		CFA8------------247,
RICHARDSON	------	Va./S.C.		CFA13-----------231
RICHARDSON	------	Mass.		CFA15-----------206
RICHARDSON	Eng.?	Conn.		CFA19-----------229
RICHARDSON	Eng.	Mass.		CFA20------------60
RICHARDSON	Eng.	Mass.		CFA21-----------203
RICHARDSON	Eng.	Del.		ACF--------------42
RICHARDSON	Eng.	Mass.		CRLA11----------581
RICHARDSON	------	------	*(only)	CRLA12-------opp.88
RICHARDSON	Eng.	Mass.	Arms:-*	CRLA15-----------37
RICHARDSON	Eng.	Mass.		CRLA19----------190
RICHARDSON	Eng.	Mass.		CRLA19----------204
RICHARDSON	Ireland	Pa.		AF*--------------26
RICHARDSON	------	Mass.		PFU-------------371
RICHARDSON	Eng.	Mass.	Arms:-*	TNEF-------------57
RICHMOND	Eng.	Mass.		CRLA17----------256
RICHMOND	------	------	*(only)	TNEF-------btn.78-9
RICHMOND, see: PILGRIMS				
RIDDLE	Eng.	Md./Pa.		CFA15-----------212
RICK	------	Pa.		CRLA20----------367
RIDDLE	Ireland	Mass.		CRLA7-----------404
RIDER	------	Mass.		CFA10-----------101
RIDGELY	------	Md.	Arms:-	CFA2-------------44
RIDGELY	Eng.	Md.	Arms:-	CFA3------------297
RIDGELY	------	Md.		CFA5-------------89
RIDGELY	Eng.	Md.		CFA14-----------134
RIDGELY	------	Md.		CFA16------------88

RIDGELY	Eng.	Md.		CFA17-----------368
RIDGELY	Eng.	Md.		CRLA1-----------290
RIDGELY	------	Md.		CRLA8-----------168
RIDGELY	Eng.	Md.		CRLA16-----------39
RIDGELY, see: GOODWIN=RIDGELY				
RIDGWAY	Eng.	N.J.		CRLA11----------242
RIDGWAY	Eng.	Pa./N.J.		CRLA17---------503
RIDPATH	Eng.	N.C./Va.		CRLA10---------363
RIGBY	------	Maine		MCS--------------89
RIGGS	Ireland	Pa.		CFA7------------400
RIGGS	------	Md.	Arms:-*	CRLA11-----------20
RIGGS	Eng.	Md.	Arms:-	CRLA16-----------36
RIKER	Eng.	N.Y.	Arms:-*	CFA5-------------11
RIKER	------	N.Y.	Arms:-	CFA9------------301
RILEY	------	Pa.		CRLA9-------------6
RILEY	------	N.J.	Arms:-*	CRLA18---------575
RINDGE	------	Mass.	Arms:-*	CRLA11----------229
RING	Eng.	Mass.	Arms:-*	CFA27----38cht.,174
RING	Eng.	Mass.	Arms:-*	CRLA7----------354
RING	------	Mass.	Arms:-*	CRLA12---------394
RING	------	Mass.		CRLA17---------465
RING	Eng.	Mass.	Arms:-*	CRLA20---------326
RIPLEY	Eng.	Mass.		CFA8------------284
RIPLEY	Eng.	Mass.	Arms:-*	CFA12------------14
RIPLEY	Eng.	Mass.	Arms:-	CFA22------------19
RIPLEY	------	Mass.	Arms:-*	CRLA13---------404
RISKE	Ireland	Ohio		CRLA14-----------97
RISLEY	Eng.	Mass.		CRLA18---------604
RITTER	------	Conn.		CRLA16---------124
RIVINGTON	Eng.	------	Arms:-	CFA12----------166
ROBBINS	Eng.	Mass.	Arms:-	CFA15----------138
ROBERT I, King of France				CFA27-----------216
ROBERT "The Strong," see: CAPET, House of				
ROBERTS	Wales	Pa.	Arms:-*	CFA3------------193
ROBERTS	Wales	N.J.		CFA4------------173
ROBERTS	Wales	Pa.	Arms:-*	CFA7------------200
ROBERTS	Wales	Pa.	Arms:-	CFA22----------230
ROBERTS	Eng.	N.J.	Arms:-*	CRLA5-----------21
ROBERTS	------	Pa.		CRLA9----------247
ROBERTS	------	Pa.		CRLA15---------507
ROBERTS	Wales	Pa.		CRLA15---------595
ROBERTS	Eng.	N.J.		CRLA17---------300
ROBERTS	------	Pa.	Arms:-*	CRLA17---------328
ROBERTS	------	Pa.	Arms:-*	AFA***----------43
ROBERTSON	------	Md.		CRLA1----------496
ROBERTSON	Scotland	Va.		CRLA4----------298
ROBERTSON	------	Pa.		CRLA10---------139
ROBERTSON	Scotland	N.Y.	Arms:-*	PBAF------------38
ROBERTSON	Scotland	Va.		PFU------------456
ROBESON	Scotland	N.J.		CFA5------------64
ROBESON	Scotland?	N.J./Pa.		CFA8------------192
ROBINS	Eng.	Va.		CFA10-----------56
ROBINS (Robyns)	Eng.	Va.	Arms:-*	CRLA2----------128
ROBINS	------	Mass.	Arms:-*	CRLA10---------304
ROBINS	------	Va.	Arms:-*	CRLA11----------28
ROBINS	------	Va.		CRLA16----------45
ROBINSON	Ireland	Del.		ACF-------------47
ROBINSON	Eng.	Mass.		ACF-------------82
ROBINSON	Eng.	R.I.		CFA8-----------368
ROBINSON=ROBERTSON	Scotland	N.Y.	Arms:-	CFA10----------166
ROBINSON	Eng.	Mass.[1] & R.I.[2]		CFA11-161 CFA24-98
ROBINSON	Eng.	Va.		CRLA1----------235
ROBINSON	------	Va.		CRLA9------------8
ROBINSON	------	Pa./Ohio		CRLA10----------55
ROBINSON	------	Mass.		CRLA13----------46
ROBINSON	Ireland	N.J.		CRLA13---------284
ROBINSON	------	Mass.		CRLA13---------412

ROBINSON	———	Va.	Arms:-*	CRLA15----------335
ROBINSON	———	Conn.	Arms:-	AF*------------371
ROBINSON	———	Mass.	Arms:-*	PBAF------------172
ROBINSON	———	Va.		PFU------------344
ROBISON	No family data		Arms:-*	CRLA13------opp.298
ROCKEFELLER	Germany	N.J.		CFA2------------253
ROCKHILL	Eng.	N.J.		CFA8------------185
ROCKHILL=ROCKKELL	Eng.	N.J.	Arms:-	AF*------------22
ROCKWELL	Eng.	Mass./Conn.	Arms:-*	CRLA19----------268
ROCKWELL	———	Conn.		PPA------------351
ROCKWOOD	Eng.	Mass.		CRLA1----------226
RODGERS	Scotland	Md.		CFA9------------97
RODHAM	Eng.	Va.	Arms:-*	CRLA14----------136
RODMAN	———	N.Y.		CFA24------------38
RODMAN	Eng.	R.I.	Arms:-*	CRLA14----------64
RODNEY	———	Del.		MCS------------34
RODNEY, Caesar	———	Del.		SDI--------181,182
ROEBLING	Germany	N.Y.	Arms:-*	CRLA1----------126
ROEBLING	Germany	Pa.		CRLA8------------529
ROGERS	Eng.	Mass.		CFA5------------306
ROGERS	Eng.	Mass.		CFA6------------171
ROGERS	Eng.	Mass.		CFA9------------76
ROGERS	Ireland	N.Y.		CFA10------------273
ROGERS	Eng./Ireland	N.Y.		CFA14----------358
ROGERS	Eng.	Va.	Arms:-	CFA17----------346
ROGERS	———	Conn.		CFA21----------126
ROGERS	Eng.	R.I.	Arms:-*	CFA23----------96
ROGERS	———	Mass.		CFA25------------58
ROGERS	———	Mass.		CRLA6------------27
ROGERS	———	Md.	Arms:-*	CRLA11----------23
ROGERS	———	Pa.	Arms:-*	CRLA13----------132
ROGERS	———	N.Y.		CRLA15----------508
ROGERS	Scotland	Va.		CRLA17----------18
ROGERS	Eng.	Mass.		CRLA17----------258
ROGERS, Thomas		Higgins Mayflower desc.		CRLA18----------77
ROGERS	———	Conn.		CRLA18----------523
ROGERS	———	Conn.	Arms:-*	CRLA20----------191
ROGERS	———	———	Arms:-*	AF*------------358
ROGERS	Eng.	Mass.	Arms:-	AF**------------74
ROGERS	Eng.	Mass.	Arms:-	AF**------------447
ROGERS	———	Mass.		AF**------------566
ROGERSON	Eng.	Va.		ACF------------78
ROLFE (or) ROLPH	Eng.	Mass.		CFA16----------291
ROLFE	Eng.?	Mass.	Arms:-*	CRLA20----------86
ROLLINS	Eng.	Mass./N.H.	Arms:-*	CFA8------------212
ROLLO, First Duke of Normandy				CFA27----------228
ROOME	———	N.Y.		CRLA10----------96
ROOS	———	———		CFA6------------5
ROORBACH	———	N.Y.		CRLA16----------168
ROOSA	Netherlands	N.Y.		CRLA12----------428
ROOSA	Netherlands	N.Y.	Arms:-*	CRLA18----------558
ROOSA	Netherlands	N.Y.	Arms:-*	CRLA20----------52
ROOSEVELT	Holland	N.Y.C.	Arms:-	CFA10----------127
ROOSEVELT	Holland	N.Y.C.	Arms:-	CFA25----------103
ROOSEVELT	Netherlands	N.Y.		CRLA12----------429
ROOSEVELT	Holland	N.Y.		PFU--------92,116
ROOT	Eng.	Conn.		CFA18----------91
ROOT	Eng.	Conn./Mass.		CRLA13----------120
ROOT	Eng.	Conn.		CRLA17----------521
ROOT	———	Conn./Pa.		CRLA18----------518
ROOTS	———	Mass.	Arms:-*	CRLA8------------50
ROPER	Eng.	Mass.	Arms:-	CFA16----------344
ROS (de)	Eng.			CRLA15----------135
ROS (de)	Eng.	Bray descent	Arms:-*	CRLA17----------144
ROS (de)	Eng.	Titus descent		CRLA18----------510
ROSE	Eng.	Va.	Arms:-*	CRLA8------------326
ROSE	———	Conn.		CRLA17----------475

ROSE	Eng.	Pa.	Arms:-*	AF*-------------13
ROSEBOROUGH	Ireland	S.C.		CRLA17---------607
ROSECRANS	Holland	N.Y.	Arms:-	ACF-------------69
ROSENKRANS	Norway	N.Y.	Arms:-*	CRLA20----------41
ROSS	————	Md.	Arms:-	CFA3-----------367
ROSS	Scotland	Md.	Arms:-	CFA6-----------274
ROSS	Eng.	Md.		CFA9-----------137
ROSS	————	Pa./Ohio		CFA23----------142
ROSS, George	————	Del./Pa.		SDI--------159,173
ROSSITER	Eng.	Conn.	Arms:-*	CFA3-----------268
ROSSITER	————	Mass./Conn.	Arms:-*	CRLA14---------164
ROSSITER	————	————	Arms:-*	CRLA20----------44
ROUSSET (du)	France		Arms:-*	CRLA1-----------44
ROWAN	Eng.	Pa.		CRLA4----------248
ROWE	Germany	N.Y.	Arms:-	AF**---------52,57
ROWELL	————	Mass.		CFA19----------273
ROWELL	————	Mass.		CRLA15----------79
ROWLAND	————	Mass./Conn.		CFA23----------119
ROWLAND	Wales	Pa.		CRLA17---------319
ROWLAND	————	————	Arms:-*	CRLA18---------278
ROWLEY	Eng.	Mass.		CRLA11---------514
ROYALL	Eng.?	Mass.		CRLA1----------451
ROYALL	————	Mass.	Arms:-*	CRLA4-----------94
ROYALL	————	Mass.	Arms:-*	CRLA7----------165
ROYCE (Rice)	————	Conn.		CRLA20---------170
RUARK	————	Md.		CRLA13---------154
RUDD	No family data		Arms:-*	CRLA11---------444
RUDDEROW	————	Pa./N.J.		CRLA9----------161
RUFFIN	————	Va.		CRLA4-----------77
RUFFIN	————	Va.		CRLA4----------467
RUFFNER	Germany	Pa./Va.		CRLA4----------313
RUGAN	————	Pa.		CRLA5----------470
RUGGLES	Eng.	Mass.		CFA8----------245
RUGGLES	Eng.	Mass.	Arms:-*	AFA***---------347
RULON	————	N.J.	Arms:-*	CRLA9----------290
RULON=MILLER (Rulon by decree)		Pa.		PFU------------415
RUMRILL	————	Conn.	Arms:-*	CFA14-----------75
RUMSEY	Wales	Md.		CRLA6----------556
RURIC, Prince of Russia				CRLA1----------463
RURIK, Royal Line of				CFA21----------215
RURIK, see: KIEV, Dukes of				
RUSH	Eng.	Pa.		PFU------------213
RUSH, Benjamin	————	Pa.		SDI--------159,177
RUSHALL (de)	Eng.		Arms:-*	CRLA15---------340
RUSSELL	————	Mass.	Arms:-	CFA4------------20
RUSSELL	————	Mass.		CFA5-----------128
RUSSELL	————	Maine		CFA8-----------241
RUSSELL	————	Mass.		CFA12----------321
RUSSELL	Eng.	Conn.	Arms:-*	CFA14----------258
RUSSELL	————	Va./Tenn.		CFA15----------371
RUSSELL	————	Mass.		CFA18-----------13
RUSSELL	————	Mass.		CFA19----------296
RUSSELL	Eng.	Mass.		CRLA1----------196
RUSSELL	Eng.	Mass.		CRLA1----------427
RUSSELL	————	Mass.		CRLA9----------181
RUSSELL	————	N.Y./N.J.		CRLA19---------391
RUSSELL	Eng.	Mass.	Arms:-*	AF**----------115
RUSSELL	————	Mass.	Arms:-	AF****--------162
RUSSIA, Royal House of	Carter=Boynton desc.		Arms:-*	CRLA15---------195
RUST	Eng.	Mass.		CFA7------------12
RUST	Eng.	Mass.		CFA15----------341
RUST	Eng.	Mass.	Arms:-*	CRLA3-----------39
RUTGERS	————	N.Y.	Arms:-*	CFA5-----------135
RUTGERS	Holland	N.Y.		CFA16----------304
RUTHERFURD	————	Conn.		CFA16-----------61
RUTHRAUFF	Germany	Pa.	Arms:-	CRLA3----------437
RUTLEDGE, Edward	————	S.C.		SDI--------227,234

RUTTER	Eng.	Pa.	Arms:-*	CRLA8----------258
RUXTON	------	N.Y.		PFU------------304
RYAN	------	Pa.	Arms:-	CRLA3------------53
RYCKMAN	------	N.Y.		CFA9-----------328
RYDER	Eng.	Mass.		CFA15-----------51
RYDER	------	N.Y.	Arms:-*	CRLA20-----------60
RYERSON	Holland	L.I.,N.Y.	Arms:-*	AF**-----------478

- S -

SABIN	------	Mass.		CRLA13----------361
SABIN	------	Mass.	Arms:-*	TNEF------------192
SACKETT	Eng.	Mass.	Arms:-*	CRLA1-----------180
SACKETT	Eng.	Mass.	Arms:-*	CRLA18----------562
SACKETT	------	Mass.	Arms:-*	AFA***----------203
SADLEIR	Eng.	------	Arms:-*	CFA3------------266
SAGE	Wales	Conn.	Arms:-*	CFA16------------49
ST. CLAIR	Ireland	Va.		CRLA15----------415
ST. JOHN	Eng.	------		CFA19------------62
ST. JOHN	Eng.	Mass./Conn.	Arms:-	CFA27-----------190
ST. JOHN	Eng.	Mass.	*(only)	CRLA13----------173
ST. JOHN	Eng.			CRLA17----------203
ST. JOHN	------	Mass.		ARSC-------------88
ST. JOHN	Eng.	Mass.	Arms:-*	TNEF-------------88
ST. VALERIE	Normandy/Eng.			CRLA2-----------491
SALISBURY	------	Mass.		CFA8------------399
SALISBURY	Wales	Mass.	Arms:-*	CRLA6-----------366
SALISBURY	Wales?	Mass./R.I.	Arms:-*	CRLA18--------56,70
SALISBURY, Earls of	Eng.			CRLA5-----------419
SALISBURY, Earls of	Eng.			CRLA15----------145
SALISBURY, Earls of	Eng.			CRLA18----------176
SALKELD	Eng.	Pa.	Arms:-*	CRLA20----------348
SALLADA	Switzerland	Pa.		CRLA8-----------435
SALLIS	------	Mass.	Arms:-*	CRLA8------------33
SALTMARSH	------	Mass.		CRLA19----------130
SALTER	------	N.J.		CFA1-------------48
SALTER	Eng.	Md.	Arms:-	CFA15-----------180
SALTONSTALL	Eng.	Mass.	Arms:-*	CFA3-------------50
SALTONSTALL	Eng.	Mass.		CRLA15----------259
SALTONSTALL	------	Mass.		ARSC-------------23
SALTONSTALL	------	Mass.		MCS-------------39
SALTONSTALL	Eng.	Mass./Conn.	Arms:-*	PFU---------123,275
SALTONSTALL, see: GURDON=SALTONSTALL				
SALTUS	Bermuda	N.Y.		CFA13----------335
SALUZZO, Marquises of	France	FitzAlan	Arms:-*	CRLA5-----------420
SAMBORNE (or) SANBORN	Eng.	N.H.		CFA11-----------337
SAMLER	------	N.Y.		CFA14-----------349
SAMPSON	Eng.	Mass.		CFA10----------261
SAMPSON	------	Mass.		CRLA13------414,416
SAMSON	------	N.H./Vt.		CFA9-----------234
SAMWELL	Eng.		Arms:-*	TNEF-------------48
SANBORN	------	------	*(only)	CRLA12-------opp.88
SANBORN	Eng.	Mass.		CRLA14----------150
SANDERLANDS	Scotland	Pa.	Arms:-*	CRLA9-----------300
SANDERS	------	Mass.		CFA17----------320
SANDERS	------	Mass.		CRLA6-----------543
SANDERSON	Scotland	Pa.	Arms:-*	CRLA12----------188
SANDS	Eng.	Pa.		CRLA2-----------150
SANDS	Eng.	Mass.	Arms:-*	CRLA20----------217
SANDS	------	Md.		AFA***----------284
SANDS	------	Mass./R.I.		PFU------------414
SANDS	------	N.Y.		PPA------------249

SANDYS	Eng.	Mass.		CFA20------------50
SANDYS	No family data		Arms:-*	CRLA13----------488
SANDYS (or) SANDS	———	Mass./R.I.	Arms:-*	AFA***----------155
SANFORD	Eng.	Mass.		CFA13----------179
SANFORD	Eng.	Mass./R.I.	Arms:-*	CRLA18----------347
SANFORD	———	R.I.		CRLA20----------176
SANFORD	Eng.	Pa./N.C.	Arms:-	AF***----------119
SANFORD		N.Y.		PPA------------383
SANGER	Germany	Mass.		CFA6------------228
SANGER	Germany?/Eng.Mass.			CFA10------------97
SANGER	Eng.	Mass.		AF**------------406
SANSOM	Eng.	Pa.	Arms:-*	CRLA5----------503
SANXAY	France/Eng.	Ohio		PFU------------220
SAPPINGTON	———	Md.		CFA16----------105
SAPPINGTON	———	Md.	Arms:-	AF*------------311
SARD	———	N.Y.		CFA11----------366
SARGENT	Eng.	Mass.	Arms:-*	CFA6------------193
SARGENT	Eng.	Mass.		CFA7------------162
SARGENT	Eng.	Mass.	Arms:-*	CFA12----------371
SARGENT	———	Mass.		ARSC------------59
SARGENT	———	Mass.		PFU------------158
SARGENT	———	Mass./N.Y.		PPA------------517
SARGENT	Eng.	Mass.	Arms:-*	TNEF------------45
SATTERLEE	Eng.	Conn.	Arms:-*	CFA26-----22cht.,35
SATTERTHWAITE	Eng.	Pa.	Arms:-	AF***----------106
SAUNDERS	Eng.	Mass.		CFA17----------129
SAUNDERS	Holland?	Pa.	Arms:-*	CRLA10------------1
SAUNDERS	———	Conn.	*(only)	CRLA12----------92
SAUNDERS	———	Va./N.C./Ga.		CRLA17----------602
SAUVE	France	La.		CRLA19----------348
SAVAGE	Eng.	Va.	Arms:-*	CFA10------------51
SAVAGE	Eng.	Mass.	Arms:-*	CFA14----------294
SAVAGE	Eng.?	Mass./Conn.	Arms:-*	CRLA10----------317
SAVAGE	———	———	Arms:-*	CRLA15----btn.342-3
SAVIL	———	Mass.		CFA9------------241
SAVOY, House of	France	Odo -1060		CRLA2------------38
SAVOY, House of	France	Odo -1060		CRLA2----------360
SAVOY, House of	France			CRLA2----------505
SAVOY, House of	France		Arms:-*	CRLA5----------422
SAVOY, House of	France	Haskell descent		CRLA8----------112
SAVOY, House of	France	Hinton desc. Arms:-*		CRLA8----------488
SAVOY, House of	France		Arms:-*	CRLA11------------99
SAVOY, House of	France		Arms:-*	CRLA15----------146
SAVOY, House of	France	Bray descent		CRLA17----------140
SAVOY, House of	France			CRLA18----------177
SAVOY, House of	Europe		Arms:-*	CRLA18----------447
SAWTELL	Eng.	Mass.	Arms:-	CFA4------------15
SAWYER	Eng.	Mass.	Arms:-*	CRLA1----------219
SAWYER	———	———	*(only)	CRLA12-------opp.88
SAWYER	Eng.	Mass./N.H.		CRLA15----------273
SAXE	———	Vt.		PPA------------529
SAXON KINGS of England				CFA27----------230
SAXON KINGS of England				CRLA1----------349
SAXON KINGS of England		Gaunt=French desc.		CRLA1----------549
SAXON Line		Prior to 8th Century		CRLA1----------554
SAXON KINGS of England		Peck=Bowen desc.		CRLA2------------27
SAXON KINGS of England		Warren=Belknap desc.		CRLA2----------183
SAXON Line	Germany	Warren=Belknap desc.		CRLA2----------185
SAXON KINGS of England		Ecgbert		CRLA2----------363
SAXON KINGS of England		Ecgbert or Egbert		CRLA2----------535
SAXON KINGS of England		Schull descent		CRLA5----------112
SAXON KINGS of England		Bray descent		CRLA7----------187
SAXON KINGS of England				CRLA7----------230
SAXON KINGS of England		Haskell descent		CRLA8----------114
SAXON KINGS of England				CRLA9----------383
SAXON KINGS of England		Gaither=Fownes desc.		CRLA11------------44
SAXON KINGS of England				CRLA11----------173

SAXON KINGS of England			Blackiston descent		CRLA11---------383
SAXON KINGS of England		Ecgbert, d. 839	Arms:-*		CRLA15---------182
			Carter=Boynton descent		
SAXON KINGS of England			Ayres=Sheppard desc.		CRLA15---------357
SAXON KINGS of England			Bray descent		CRLA17---------108
SAXON KINGS of England		Egbert	Schrack descent		CRLA17---------392
SAXON KINGS of England					CRLA18---------180
SAXON KINGS of England		Egbert			CRLA18---------268
SAXON KINGS of England			Glendinning=Logan desc.		CRLA18---------329
SAXON KINGS of England			Titus descent		CRLA18------485,490
SAXON KINGS of England			Richardson descent		CRLA19---------213
SAXON KINGS of England		Ecgbert, d. 839			CRLA20---------273
SAXON KINGS of England					CRLA20---------389
SAXONY, Dukes of	Europe				CRLA5----------425
SAXONY, Dukes of	Germany				CRLA7----------218
SAXONY, Dukes of					CRLA11---------100
SAXONY, Dukes of		Ludolf			CRLA17---------204
SAY (de)	Eng.			Arms:-*	CRLA10-----btn.78-9
SAY (de)	Eng.				CRLA12----------20
SAYER	Eng.	Mass.			CFA21---------236
SAYLES	------	R.I.		Arms:-*	CFA4-----------139
SAYLES	Eng.	R.I.		Arms:-*	CFA14----------34
SAYLES	------	R.I.		Arms:-*	CRLA20---------382
SAYLES	Eng.	R.I.		Arms:-*	PBAF-----------68
SAYLES	------	R.I.		Arms:-*	TNEF-----------65
SAYNISCH	Germany	Pa.		Arms:-	AF**-----------99
SAYRE	Eng.	Mass./L.I.,N.Y.		Arms:-	CFA15---------377
SAYRE	------	Mass.		Arms:-	CFA16---------323
SAYRE (Sarish)	Eng.	Mass./L.I.,N.Y.	Arms:-*		CRLA5-----------8
SAYRE	Eng.	Mass.			CRLA14----------59
SCALES	------	N.C.		Arms:-*	CRLA11---------286
SCAMMON	Eng.	Mass./Maine			CFA3-----------85
SCARBOROUGH	Eng.	Va.			CFA17---------377
SCARBOROUGH	Eng.	Va.			CRLA9-----------9
SCARBURG	------	Va.			CRLA2----------120
SCARBURGH=SCARUOROUGH	Eng.	Va.		Arms:-*	CRLA15---------337
SCHAEFFER	Germany	Pa.		Arms:-*	CRLA2----------53
SCHALL	------	Pa.			CRLA11---------343
SCHENCK	------	N.Y.			CFA8-----------42
SCHENCK	Germant/Holland	N.Y.		Arms:-*	AF**-----------480
SCHEPMOES	Holland	N.Y.			CFA11----------46
SCHIEFFELIN	Germany	Pa.			PFU------------350
SCHMELZEL	Germany	N.Y.C.		Arms:-*	AF*------------407
SCHNEBLY	Switzerland	Md.			CRLA7----------452
SCHNEIDER	Germany	Pa.			CRLA9----------461
SCHNEIDER	Germany	Pa.			CRLA11---------352
SCHOOLCRAFT	------	N.Y.			PPA------------167
SCHOONMAKER	Germany?	N.Y.		Arms:-*	CRLA20-----24,30,35
SCHOTT	Germany	Pa.			CFA20---------185
SCHRACK	Germany	Pa.		Arms:-*	CRLA17---------366
SCHREDLEY	Germany	Pa.			CRLA15---------538
SCHRICK	Germany	N.Y.			CFA11----------30
SCHULER	Holland	N.Y.			CFA11----------14
SCHUYLER	Holland	N.Y.			CFA13----------55
SCHUYLER	------	N.Y.			CFA16---------304
SCHUYLER	Holland	N.Y.		Arms:-*	CFA25----------45
SCHWENK	Germany	Pa.			CRLA9----------444
SCOFIELD	------	Mass.			CFA9-----------293
SCOTLAND, Kings of		MacAlpin	Arms:-*		CRLA1----------344
SCOTLAND, Kings of		Kenneth I "MacAlpin"			CRLA2----------36
SCOTLAND, Kings of	Malcolm I	South=Grantham desc.			CRLA2----------530
SCOTLAND, Kings of		MacAlpin	Arms:-*		CRLA5----------427
SCOTLAND, Kings of			Bray descent		CRLA7----------185
SCOTLAND, Kings of		MacAlpin			CRLA7----------226
SCOTLAND, Kings of			Haskell descent		CRLA8----------118
SCOTLAND, Kings of		MacAlpin	Arms:-*		CRLA8----------337
SCOTLAND, Kings of		Hinton descent	Arms:-*		CRLA8----------489

SCOTLAND, Kings of				CRLA9----------359
SCOTLAND, Kings of		Gaither=Fownes desc.		CRLA11-----------46
SCOTLAND, Kings of				CRLA11----------175
SCOTLAND, Kings of		Blackiston descent		CRLA11----------387
SCOTLAND, Kings of	Alpin -834 to Malcolm III			CRLA12----------281
SCOTLAND, Kings of	Carter=Boynton desc.	Arms:-*		CRLA15----------185
SCOTLAND, Kings of		Ayres=Sheppard desc.		CRLA15----------361
SCOTLAND, Kings of	MacAlpin	Schrack descent		CRLA17----------395
SCOTLAND, Kings of				CRLA18----------185
SCOTLAND, Kings of	MacAlpin			CRLA18----------266
SCOTLAND, Kings of		Glendinning=Logan desc.		CRLA18----------334
SCOTLAND, Kings of		Titus descent		CRLA18----------493
SCOTLAND, Kings of		Richardson descent		CRLA19----------213
SCOTLAND, Kings of	MacAlpin			CRLA20----------278
SCOTT	Eng.	Pa.	Arms:-	CFA3------------164
SCOTT	Eng.?	Mass./Conn.		CFA9------------229
SCOTT	Eng.			CRLA1-----------267
SCOTT	Scotland	Va.		CRLA4-----------173
SCOTT	Eng.	N.J.		CRLA8-----------359
SCOTT	Eng.	N.J.		CRLA11----------540
SCOTT		Mass.		CRLA17-----------15
SCOTT	No family data		Arms:-*	CRLA18----------358
SCOTT	Eng.	N.Y.	Arms:-*	AFA***-----------67
SCOTT, see: MARBURY=SCOTT				
SCOTT	Scotland	N.Y.	Arms:-*	PFU-------------335
SCOTTO	Eng.	Mass.	Arms:-*	CFA27----opp.49,176
SCOTTO	Eng.	Mass.		CRLA17----------464
SCOVELL		Pa.?/Ohio		CRLA16----------182
SCUDDER	Eng.	Mass./N.Y.		CRLA8-----------290
SCUDDER		L.I.,N.Y./N.J.		AFA***----------184
SCUDDER	Eng.	Mass.	Arms:-*	AFA***----------385
SCUDDER	Eng.	Mass.		PFU-------------159
SCULL	Ireland	Pa.		CFA6------------284
SCULL	Holland	N.Y./N.J.		CRLA8-------408,418
SCULL	Holland	N.Y./N.J.		CRLA8-----------429
SEABROOK	Eng.	N.Y.	Arms:-*	CRLA18----------542
SEABURY	Eng./Barbados	Mass.		PFU-------------368
SEAMAN		Conn./L.I.,N.Y.		CFA3------------332
SEAMAN	Eng.	L.I.,N.Y.	Arms:-	CFA5------------232
SEAMAN		Mass.		CFA7------------275
SEAMAN	Eng.	Mass.		CFA7------------376
SEAMAN	Eng.	Conn.		CFA10-----------316
SEAMAN	Eng.	Mass./Conn.		CFA16-----------11
SEAMAN	Eng.	L.I.,N.Y.		CFA16-----------34
SEAMAN	Eng.	Mass./L.I.,N.Y.	Arms:-*	CFA18-----------43
SEAMAN	Eng.	Mass./L.I.,N.Y.	Arms:-	CFA18----------218
SEARCY		N.C.		CRLA12----------164
SEARLE		Mass.		TNEF------------165
SEARS	Eng.	Mass.	Arms:-*	CFA4-------------58
SEARS	Eng.	Mass.	Arms:-	CFA21----------183
SEAWELL		Va.	Arms:-*	CRLA15----------332
SEDGWICK	Eng.	Conn.		CRLA16----------127
SEDILOT	France/Canada			CRLA17----------706
SEE		N.Y.	Arms:-	CRLA3-----------181
SEE		N.Y.		CRLA18----------220
SEELEY		Conn.	Arms:-*	CRLA7-----------126
SEELEY		Mass./Conn.		CRLA7-----------539
SEELEY	Eng.	Mass./Conn.		CRLA17----------660
SEELEY		N.J.		AFA***----------328
SEELYE=SEELEY	Eng.	Conn.		CFA26------------75
SEGAR		Mass.	Arms:-*	CRLA20-----------82
SEGENDORF		N.Y.		CRLA7-----------274
SEGRAVE	Eng.			CRLA2-----------457
SEIGNIORIAL Ancestors		Gaither=Fownes desc.		CRLA11-----------55
SEIGNIORIAL Ancestors		Carter=Boynton desc.		CRLA15----------228
SELDEN (or) SELDON	Eng.	Conn.	Arms:-*	CFA1-------------36
SELIGMAN	Germany	N.Y.C.		CFA10-----------292

Surname	Origin	Place	Arms	Reference
SELLECK	Eng.	Mass.	Arms:-	CFA16-----------222
SELLECK	————	Conn.		CRLA13------191,193
SELLECK	Eng.	Va.		CRLA10----------311
SELLERS	Eng.	Pa.		CRLA14-----------37
SELLERS	Eng.	Pa.		CRLA17----------591
SETON	Scotland	N.Y.		CFA6--------------8
SETTLEMIER	————	N.C./Ill.	Arms:-	CRLA3-----------93
SEVERANCE	Eng.	Mass.	Arms:-*	CRLA8-----------46
SEVERANCE	————	Mass.	Arms:-*	CRLA18----------357
SEWARD	————	Va.		CRLA4-----------90
SEWARD	————	Conn.		CRLA19-----------67
SEWALL	Eng.	Md.	Arms:-	CFA3-----------308
SEWALL	Eng.	Mass.		CFA7-----------163
SEWELL	Eng.	Md.	Arms:-	CFA20----------220
SEWELL	Ireland	N.Y. & N.J.		PFU-----------183
SEXTON	Eng.	Mass.	Arms:-*	CFA15----------322
SEYMOUR	Eng.	Conn.	Arms:-*	CFA11----------385
SEYMOUR	Eng.	Conn.		CFA20----------178
SHADE	————	Ohio		CRLA7-----------23
SHAEFFER	————	Pa.		AF***----------168
SHANDS	Scotland?	Va.		CRLA17----------604
SHANNON	————	N.Y.		CRLA6----------482
SHANNON	No family data		Arms:-*	CRLA13----------206
SHARP	Eng.	Mass.		CFA7-----------127
SHARP	Eng.	N.J.	Arms:-*	CRLA9----------310
SHARPLES	Eng.	Pa.	Arms:-*	CFA3-----------194
SHARPLES	Eng.	Pa.	Arms:-*	CFA7-----------200
SHARPLESS	Eng.	Pa.		CRLA17----------244
SHARPLESS	Eng.	Pa.		CRLA17----------359
SHATTUCK	————	Mass.		CFA15----------222
SHATTUCK	————	Mass.	Arms:-*	CRLA6-----------69
SHATTUCK	Eng.	Mass.		CRLA10----------396
SHATTUCK (Chaddock, etc.) Eng.		Mass.	Arms:-*	AF*------------212
SHAW	————	Maine/Mass.		CFA5-----------161
SHAW	Eng.	Mass.		CFA12-----------75
SHAW	Eng.?/Ireland	N.Y.C.	Arms:-	CFA20----------245
SHAW	————	N.Y.		CRLA3----------310
SHAW	————	Mass.		CRLA12----------398
SHAW	Eng.?	Mass.	Arms:-*	CRLA17-----------21
SHAW	Eng.	Mass.		CRLA18-----------75
SHAW	————	Mass./R.I.	Arms:-*	CRLA20-----------38
SHAW	————	Mass.		CRLA20----------207
SHAW	————	Md.		PPA--------------80
SHEAFF	Germany	Pa.		CFA8------------37
SHEAFFE	Eng.	Conn.		CRLA19----------268
SHEARER	————	Pa.	Arms:-*	CRLA17----------361
SHEELEY	————	N.Y.C.		CRLA7----------465
SHEFFIELD	Eng.	Mass.	Arms:-	CFA6-----------89
SHEFFIELD	————	Mass.		CFA10-----------86
SHEFFIELD	Eng.	Mass.		CFA18----------187
SHELDON	Eng.	————		CFA7-----------329
SHELDON	————	R.I.	Arms:-*	CFA8-----------367
SHELDON	————	Conn./Mass.		CFA15----------347
SHELDON	Eng.	Conn./Mass.	Arms:-*	CFA18-----------78
SHELDON	Eng.	Mass.	Arms:-*	CFA18----------133
SHELDON	Eng.	Conn./Mass.		CRLA18----------614
SHELDRAKE	————	Pa.?	Arms:-*	CRLA19----------226
SHELTON	Eng.	Va.	Arms:-*	CFA9-----------207
SHELTON	Eng.	Va.	Arms:-*	CRLA17-----------43
SHEPARD	Eng.	Mass.		CFA2-----------248
SHEPARD	Eng.	Mass.		CFA5-----------376
SHEPARD	Eng.	Mass.		CFA10----------204
SHEPARD	Eng.	Mass.	Arms:-	CFA15-----------99
SHEPARD	Eng.	Mass.	Arms:-	CFA20----------262
SHEPARD	————	N.C.	Arms:-*	CRLA4----------462
SHEPARD	————	Conn./Ohio		CRLA7----------282
SHEPERD	Eng.	Md./Va./W.Va.	Arms:-*	CRLA14-----------86

SHEPHERD	———	N.J.		CRLA9----------178
SHEPHERD	———	———	Arms:-*	CRLA14-------opp.54
SHEPLEY	Eng.?	Mass.		CFA19-----------280
SHEPPARD	———	Md./N.C.	Arms:-*	CRLA15---------341
SHEPPARD	———	N.J.	Arms:-*	CRLA18----------415
SHERMAN	Eng.	Mass.	Arms:-	CFA6-----------288
SHERMAN	Eng.	Mass.	Arms:-*	CFA9-----------167
SHERMAN	———	N.Y.		CRLA6----------178
SHERMAN	———	N.Y.		CRLA6----------496
SHERMAN	Eng.	Conn.		CRLA9----------519
SHERMAN	Eng.	Conn.		CRLA16--------174
SHERMAN	Eng.	Mass./Conn.		CRLA19---------107
SHERMAN	Eng.	Mass.	Arms:-*	AF****----------81
SHERMAN, see: LAUNCE=SHERMAN				
SHERMAN	Eng.	Mass./Conn.		PFU------------186
SHERMAN, Roger	———	Conn.		SDI--------125,126
SHERMAN	Eng.	Mass./R.I.	Arms:-*	TNEF------------27
SHERWOOD	Eng.	Conn.		CRLA2----------236
SHERWOOD	Eng.	Mass./Conn.	Arms:-	AF*------------268
SHIELDS	Ireland	Minn.	Arms:-	CRLA3-----------75
SHINN (Sheen)	Eng.	N.J.		CRLA4----------265
SHIPMAN	Eng.	Conn.		CFA10----------247
SHIPMAN	———	N.J.		CFA20-----------33
SHIPMAN	Eng.	Conn.	Arms:-*	CRLA6----------391
SHIPPEN	Eng.	Pa.		CRLA15---------464
SHIPPEN	Eng.	Mass./Pa.		PFU------------427
SHOEMAKER	Germany	Pa.		CRLA9----------451
SHOEMAKER	Germany	Pa.		CRLA17------288,291
SHORE	———	N.C./Ky./Ill.		CRLA3-----------89
SHORT	———	Va./Ky.		CRLA3----------422
SHORT	———	Conn./N.Y.		CRLA13---------459
SHOTWELL	———	N.J.		ACF------------87
SHOTWELL	Eng.?	N.J.		CRLA17---------309
SHOVE	Eng.	Mass.		CRLA19----------75
SHRYVER	Germany	N.Y.		CFA24-----------49
SHUBRICK	Eng.	S.C.	*(only)	CRLA13---------179
SHULL (Scholl)	———	N.J.	Arms:-*	CRLA5------------1
SHUMAN	———	N.Y.C./N.J.		CRLA19---------165
SHUMWAY	———	Mass.		CFA14----------120
SHUTE	———	Pa.		CRLA14----------34
SIBLEY	Switzerland	Pa.		CRLA9----------151
SIBLEY		Royal Descents & Lineage Outlines		CRLA9-------182,213
SICKLER	———	N.J.	Arms:-*	CRLA11---------442
SIDWELL	———	Md.		CFA23----------152
SILL	Eng.	Conn.		CFA20----------189
SILL	Eng.	Pa.		CFA22----------185
SILL	———	Mass.		CRLA19---------386
SILL	———	Mass.	Arms:-*	CRLA20---------113
SILL	Eng.	Mass.	Arms:-	AF****----------43
SILSBEE	Eng.	Mass.		CFA5-----------367
SILSBEE	———	Mass.		CRLA15---------253
SILVESTER	Eng.	Mass.		CFA19----------285
SIMES	Eng.	N.H.		CFA11----------252
SIMMONS	Holland	N.Y.		CFA14----------367
SIMMONS	———	Md.		CRLA1----------486
SIMMONS	———	Md.		CRLA4----------308
SIMMONS	———	Md./Mo.		CRLA11---------543
SIMMS	———	S.C.		PPA------------343
SIMONDS	Eng.	Mass.	Arms:-	CRLA7----------484
SIMONS	———	Mass.		CFA21----------221
SIMPSON		Va./Miss.	Arms:-	CFA14----------191
SIMPSON	Ireland	N.H.	Arms:-	AF**-----------436
SIMS	———	Va./Conn.		CRLA17---------433
SIMSBURY (City)		Conn. Regional background		CRLA19---------250
SINCLAIR	———	Mich./N.Y.	Arms:-*	AF****---------215
SISSON	———	R.I./Mass.	Arms:-*	CFA4-----------191
SISSON	———	R.I.		CFA12----------102

SISSON	Eng.	R.I./Mass.	Arms:-*	CRLA2-----------252
SISSON	———	R.I.	Arms:-	TNEF------------229
SKELTON	Eng.	Mass.		CFA19-----------51
SKELTON	———	N.J.		CRLA17----------534
SKIFF	Eng.	Mass.		CRLA3-----------36
SKIFF	Eng.	Mass.		CRLA10----------324
SKINNER	Eng.	N.C.	Arms:-	CFA5------------265
SKINNER	Eng.	Conn.	Arms:-	CRLA7-----------39
SKIPWITH	———	Va.		MCS-------------70
SKIPWITH	Eng.	Va.	Arms:-*	PFU-------------470
SKIRVIN	———	Ohio/Mich.		CRLA7-----------558
SKUTE	Sweden	Pa.		CRLA9-----------241
SLADE	———	N.C.		CRLA4-----------454
SLADE	Eng.	R.I.	Arms:-*	TNEF------------17
SLATER	———	N.J.		AF*-------------240
SLATER	Eng.	N.H.		TNEF------------141
SLAUGHTER	———	Va.		CFA5------------293
SLAYMAKER	Germany	Pa.	Arms:-*	CRLA15----------530
SLECHT	No family data		Arms:-*	CRLA18------opp.560
SLECHT	———	N.Y.?	Arms:-*	CRLA20----------25
SLEGHT	Holland	N.Y.		CFA8------------41
SLIDELL	———	N.Y.C.		CFA9------------109
SLINGLUFF	Germany	Pa.		CRLA4-----------1
SLOAN	Ireland		Arms:-*	AF*-------------158
SLOT	Denmark/Holland N.Y.			CFA16-----------71
SMALL	———	N.H.		CFA7------------170
SMALL	Germany	Pa.		CRLA2-----------105
SMART	———	Va.		CRLA9-----------15
SMITH	Eng.	Conn.		CFA2------------116
SMITH	Eng.	Mass.		CFA2------------334
SMITH	Eng.	Mass.	Arms:-*	CFA3------------246
SMITH	———	Mass.?		CFA4------------173
SMITH	Eng.	Mass.	Arms:-*	CFA5------------216
SMITH	Eng.	Mass.		CFA10-----------85
SMITH	Eng.	Conn.		CFA14-----------20
SMITH	Eng.	Mass.		CFA14-----------96
SMITH	Eng.	Mass./Maine	Arms:-*	CFA14-----------143
SMITH	———	N.Y.C.		CFA15-----------306
SMITH	Eng.	Mass.		CFA13-----------343
SMITH	———	Md.		CFA16-----------82
SMITH	———	Mass.		CFA16-----------209
SMITH	———	N.Y.		CFA16-----------301
SMITH	———	Mass.		CFA17-----------327
SMITH	Eng.	Mass.		CFA18-----------88
SMITH	———	Conn.		CFA19-----------60
SMITH	Scotland	Pa.		CFA19-----------185
SMITH	Eng.	Mass.		CFA19-----------241
SMITH	Eng.?	Mass./Conn.		CFA20-----------265
SMITH	Eng.	Mass.		CFA20-----------266
SMITH	Eng.	N.J. or N.Y.?		ACF-------------84
SMITH	———	Mass.		ACF-------------90
SMITH	———	Va.		CRLA2-----------113
SMITH	Eng.	Va.		CRLA3-----------407
SMITH	———	Md.		CRLA3-----------446
SMITH	Eng.	Va.		CRLA4-----------102
SMITH	———	Va.		CRLA4-----------198
SMITH	———	Mass.		CRLA6-----------546
SMITH	———	Maine		CRLA7-----------173
SMITH	Eng.	N.Y.		CRLA8-----------295
SMITH	———	Md.		CRLA8-----------516
SMITH	Eng.	Pa.		CRLA8-----------546
SMITH	Eng.	Mass./N.J.		CRLA9-----------177
SMITH	———	Va.		CRLA10----------34
SMITH	———	N.J./Ohio		CRLA10----------61
SMITH	———	Pa.		CRLA10----------359
SMITH	———	Pa.		CRLA13----------278
SMITH	Eng.	Mass.	Arms:-*	CRLA15----------276

SMITH	——	Va.		CRLA15----------335
SMITH	——	N.J./Pa.		CRLA15----------587
SMITH	Eng.	Mass.		CRLA17----------256
SMITH	——	Mass.		CRLA18----------4
SMITH	Eng.	Va.		CRLA18----------367
SMITH	——	N.Y.		CRLA18----------432
SMITH	——	Mass.		CRLA19----------74
SMITH	——	Mass./N.Y.		CRLA20------6,20,23
SMITH	——	N.J./Mass./Conn.		CRLA20------198,218
SMITH	——	Calif.		AF*--------------6
SMITH	Eng.	Mass.		AF*-------------86
SMITH	——	Mass.	Arms:-	AF*--------175,193
SMITH	Eng.	Mass.	Arms:-	AF****----------87
SMITH	Eng.	Mass./Conn.	Arms:-*	AFA***----------373
SMITH	——	L.I.,N.Y.		PFU-------------464
SMITH	——	Mass.		PPA-------------164
SMITH, James	Ireland	Pa.		SDI---------159,172
SMITH	——	Mass.		TNEF------------164
SMITH, see: HOWARD=SMITH				
SMITHERS	Eng./Canada	N.Y.C.		CFA12-----------356
SMITHWICK	Eng.	N.C.		CRLA4-----------460
SMYTH	Eng.	Mass.		CRLA6-----------355
SNOW	Eng.	Mass.	Arms:-	ACF-------------24
SNOW	Eng.	Mass.		CRLA7-----------442
SNOW	Eng.	Mass.		CRLA10----------355
SNOW	——	Mass.		CRLA15--------50,92
SNOW	Eng.	Mass.	Arms:-*	AFA3------------13
SNOWDEN	——	Md.	Arms:-	CFA3------------291
SNOWDEN	Eng./Wales	Md.	Arms:-	CFA20-----------208
SNOWDEN	——	Md.		CRLA8-----------165
SNYDER	Germany	Pa.		CRLA13----------137
SNYDER	Germany	N.Y.	Arms:-*	CRLA20---------4,21
SOMERS	Eng.	N.J.	Arms:-*	CFA6------------310
SOMERS	Eng.	N.J.	Arms:-*	AFA***----------141
SOPER	——	Mass.		CFA8------------108
SORONDO	Cuba	N.Y.C.		ACF-------------93
SOTCHER	——	Pa.		CRLA2-----------428
SOUDER	Germany	Pa./N.J.	Arms:-*	CRLA18----------576
SOULE	Eng.	Mass.		CFA11-----------302
SOULE	Eng.	Mass.	Arms:-*	CFA23-----------51
SOULE	Eng.	Mass.	Arms:-*	CFA27----38cht.,179
SOULE, George		Mayflower passenger		CFA27-----------207
SOULE	——	Mass.		CRLA12----------413
SOULE	Eng.	Mass.		CRLA13----------245
SOULE	Eng.	Mass.		CRLA17----------462
SOULE	——	Mass.		CRLA19----------78
SOULE	Eng.	Mass.		CRLA19----------147
SOUTH	Eng.	Pa.	*(only)	CRLA2-----------394
SOUTHEY	Eng.	Va.	Arms:-*	CFA10-----------58
SOUTHWICK	Eng.	Mass.		CRLA16----------164
SOUTHWORTH	Eng.	Mass.		CFA8------------264
SOUTHWORTH	Holland	Mass.	Arms:-*	CRLA15----------421
SOUTHWORTH	Holland	Mass.		CRLA19----------149
SOUTHWORTH	——	Mass.		ARSC------------30
SOUTHWORTH	——	Mass.		MCS-------------80
SOWER	——	Pa./Md.		CFA2------------51
SPALDING	Eng.	Conn.	Arms:-	CFA1------------192
SPALDING	Eng.	Va./Mass.		CFA19-----------294
SPANISH Medieval Kings		Wales descent		CRLA13----------79
SPANISH & Other Medieval Kings of Europe through 1700 yrs.				CRLA15----------207
		Carter=Boynton descent		
			Arms:-*	
SPARHAWK	Eng.	Mass.	Arms:-*	CRLA20----------96
SPARKS	Eng./Ireland	Pa.	Arms:-*	AFA***----------21
SPARKS	Eng./Ireland	Pa./N.J.	Arms:-*	AFA***----------307
SPARNECHT	Germany	——		CFA27-----------182
SPAULDING	Eng.	Va.	Arms:-*	CFA6------------52

SPEAKMAN	Eng.	Pa.		CRLA15----------242
SPEER	Ireland	Pa.		CFA6------------334
SPEER	Holland	N.Y./N.J.		CRLA20----------195
SPENCER	Eng.	Mass.	Arms:-*	CFA1------------33
SPENCER	Eng.	Mass./Conn.	Arms:-	CFA1------------263
SPENCER	Eng.	Mass.		CFA7-----------268
SPENCER	———	Va.		CFA16----------161
SPENCER	Eng.	Mass.	Arms:-*	CFA17----------254
SPENCER	Eng.	Mass./Conn.	Arms:-	CFA19---------58,60
SPENCER	Eng.?	Mass.		CFA22-----------94
SPENCER	Eng.	Mass.	Arms:-*	CRLA2----------269
SPENCER	Eng.	Mass./Conn.	Arms:-	AF***----------225
SPENCER	Eng.	Mass./Conn.	Arms:-*	AFA***---------215
SPENGLER	Germany	Pa.	Arms:-*	CRLA3----------393
SPENGLER	Germany	Pa.		CRLA6----------213
SPERRY	Eng.	Conn.		CFA1------------70
SPERRY	Eng.	Conn.		CFA19-----------66
SPICER	Eng.	R.I./N.Y./N.J.		CRLA9----------162
SPICER	———	Va.?/Conn.		CRLA17---------476
SPIER	———	N.J.		CRLA19----------171
SPINK	Eng.	R.I.		CFA17----------293
SPINK	———	R.I.		CRLA19---------289
SPITTALL	Eng.	Pa.		CRLA13---------125
SPONKNABLE	Germany	N.Y.		AF***----------178
SPOONER	———	Mass.		CFA22----------215
SPOTSWOOD	Scotland	Va.	Arms:-*	CFA24------------4
SPOTSWOOD	———	Va.		CRLA2-----------95
SPOTSWOOD	Scotland	Va.	Arms:-*	CRLA4----------118
SPOTSWOOD	Scotland	Va.	Arms:-*	CRLA10---------106
SPOTSWOOD	Scotland	Va.		CRLA18---------368
SPOTSWOOD	Scotland	Md./Va.		CRLA20---------240
SPOTSWOOD	———	Md./Va.	Arms:-	AF**-----------245
SPRADO	Germany	———		CFA27----------183
SPRAGUE	———	Mass.		CFA4-----------173
SPRAGUE	Eng.	Mass.		CRLA9----------433
SPRAGUE	Eng.	Mass.	Arms:-*	CRLA15----------82
SPRAGUE	———	Mass.		PPA------------147
SPRAGUE	———	Mass.		TNEF-----------143
SPRIGG	———	Md.		CFA3-----------296
SPRIGG	———	Md.		CRLA6----------428
SPRIGGE	Eng.		Arms:-*	CRLA18---------551
SPRINGSTEEN	———	———		CFA4-----------175
SPRUYT	Netherlands		Arms:-*	CRLA20----------64
SQUIRE	Eng.	Mass.		CFA10-----------17
SQUIRE	Eng.	Mass.		CFA11----------215
SQUIRE	Eng.	Mass.		ACF-------------50
STAATS	———	N.Y.	Arms:-	CFA12----------239
STAATS	Holland	N.Y.	Arms:-*	CFA25-----------83
STAATS	———	N.Y.	Arms:-*	CRLA7----------271
STACEY	Eng.?	Mass.	Arms:-*	CRLA18----------17
STACKPOLE	Wales	N.H.	Arms:-	CFA15----------200
STACY	Eng.	N.J.		ACF-------------32
STACY	Eng.	N.J./Pa.	Arms:-*	CRLA5----------473
STADELMAN	Germany	Pa.		CRLA19---------346
STAFFORD (de)	Eng.		*(only)	CRLA2----------543
		Jones=Paul=Knight descent		
STAFFORD (de)	Eng.			CRLA2----------561
STAFFORD	Eng.		Arms:-*	CRLA5----------430
STAFFORD (de)	Eng.			CRLA11---------101
STAFFORD (de)	Eng.	Bray descent	Arms:-*	CRLA17---------154
STANDART	Eng.	N.Y./Mass.		CRLA19----------91
STANDISH	Eng.	Mass.	Arms:-	CFA1-----------267
STANDISH	Eng.	Mass.		CFA10----------261
STANLEY	Eng.	Conn.		CFA15----------360
STANLEY	Eng.	Mass.	Arms:-	CFA17----------153
STANLEY	———	Mass.	Arms:-*	CFA27----13cht.,184
STANLEY	Eng.	Conn.		CRLA4----------260

STANLEY	Eng.		Arms:-*	CRLA5----------434
STANTON	———	Mass.		CFA6------------115
STANTON	Eng.	Mass./Conn.		CFA9------------18
STANTON	Eng.	Conn.		CFA10----------281
STANTON	Eng./Ireland Calif./Ill.			CRLA19---------115
STAPLES	———	Pa.	Arms:-*	CRLA8----------260
STAPLES	———	Mass./R.I.	Arms:-*	CRLA17---------481
STARBUCK	———	N.Y.?		CFA20----------312
STARBUCK	Eng.	N.H.		CRLA8----------57
STARBUCK	Eng.	N.H.		CRLA12------267,275
STARBUCK	Eng.?	Mass./N.H.		CRLA18---------354
STARBUCK	Eng.	N.H.	Arms:-*	TNEF------------41
STARIN	Germany	N.Y.	Arms:-*	AFA2------------167
STARKEY	———	Mass.	Arms:-*	CFA9------------248
STARR	Eng.	Mass.		CFA16-----------52
STARR	Eng.	Mass.	Arms:-*	CFA23-----------60
STATON	———	Md./N.C.	Arms:-*	CRLA9----------258
STAUFFER	Germany	Pa.	Arms:-	CFA15----------164
STAUFFER	———	Pa.		CRLA14----------44
STAVELEY	———	———	*(only)	TNEF--------opp.48
STEALEY	———	N.J./Calif.		CRLA10----------98
STEARNS	Eng.	Mass.		CFA6-----------175
STEARNS	Eng.	Mass.		CFA7-----------408
STEARNS	Eng.	Mass.		CFA19-----------80
STEARNS	———	Mass.		CRLA1-----------212
STEARNS	———	Iowa		CRLA3-----------219
STEARNS	Eng.	Mass.		CRLA7-----------378
STEARNS	———	Mass.	Arms:-*	CRLA15-----------39
STEARNS	Eng.	Mass.	Arms:-*	CRLA20----------104
STEBBINS	Eng.	Mass.		CFA7-----------330
STEBBINS	Eng.	Conn.	Arms:-*	CFA27----13cht.,186
STEBBINS	Eng.	Mass.		CRLA18---------623
STEDMAN	Eng.	Mass.	Arms:-*	CRLA19---------395
STEELE	———	N.Y.		CFA10-----------68
STEELE	Eng.	Mass.		CFA11----------187
STEELE	France/W.Indies	Mass./N.J.	Arms:-*	CFA25-----------21
STEELE	Eng.	Mass./Conn.		CRLA16---------117
STEERE	———	———	*(only)	TNEF-------btn.70-1
STEERE, see: PILGRIMS				
STEPHENS	Eng.	Pa.	Arms:-*	AF*------------94
STEPHENS	Eng.	N.H.	Arms:-*	PFU------------292
STERLING	———	Md.		CRLA15---------576
STERNBURG	———	N.Y.	Arms:-*	AF****---------179
STERNES	Eng.	Mass.		CFA15----------356
STETSON	Eng.	Mass.	Arms:-	CFA24----------153
STETSON	———	Mass.		CRLA13---------384
STETSON	Eng.	Mass.	Arms:-*	CRLA20---------332
STEVENS	———	N.H.		CFA6-----------160
STEVENS	———	Maine/Mass.		CFA10----------224
STEVENS	Eng.	Mass.		CFA12----------276
STEVENS	———	Mass.		CFA13----------150
STEVENS	———	Mass.		CFA13----------350
STEVENS	———	S.C.		CFA16-----------41
STEVENS	———	Conn.		CFA16----------211
STEVENS	———	Va./Md.		CFA16----------103
STEVENS	Eng.	Mass.		CFA21----------227
STEVENS	Eng.	Mass.	Arms:-*	CFA27---148cht.,188
STEVENS	———	Conn.		CRLA1-----------156
STEVENS	Eng.	Conn.	Arms:-*	CRLA6----------385
STEVENS	———	———	*(only)	CRLA12-------opp.88
STEVENS	———	Mass.		CRLA13---------276
STEVENS	———	Mass.	Arms:-*	CRLA13---------301
STEVENS	———	Mass.		CRLA15---------379
STEVENS	No family data		Arms:-*	CRLA18---------351
STEVENS	Eng.	Mass.		CRLA19---------200
STEVENS	Eng.	Mass.		CRLA19---------205
STEVENS	———	Mass.		CRLA20----------70

STEVENS	Eng.	Conn.	Arms:-	AF*---------------76
STEVENS	Eng.	Mass.	Arms:-*	AFA***----------381
STEVENSON	------	Mass.		CFA8------------68
STEVENSON	Eng.	N.Y.	Arms:-*	CRLA15----------393
STEVENSON	Eng.	Md.		CRLA17----------417
STEVENSON	Ireland	Pa.	Arms:-*	AF*-------------146
STEWART	Scotland	Mass.		CFA7------------156
STEWART	------	Ky.		CFA10-----------112
STEWART	Scotland	N.Y.C.		CFA20-----------297
STEWART	Ireland	Pa./Md.		CRLA2-----------100
STEWART (Stuart)	Ireland		Arms:-*	CRLA5-----------485
STEWART	Scotland			CRLA8-----------334
STEWART	------	N.Y.		CRLA9-------263,266
STEWART	Eng./Scotland			CRLA9-----------342
STEWART	No family data		Arms:-*	CRLA14-------opp.29
STEWART	------	------		CRLA18------188,192
STEWART	Ireland	Mass.		AF*-------------57
STEWART	Eng.		Arms:-*	AF*-------------163
STEWART	Eng.	N.Y.	Arms:-	AF*-------------236
STEWART	Canada		Arms:-*	AF**------------460
STEWART	------	N.Y.	Arms:-	AF***-----------286
STEWART, see: CARPENTER=STEWART				
STEYMETS	Holland	N.Y.		CRLA12----------433
STICKNEY	Eng.	Mass.	Arms:-*	CRLA3-----------22
STICKNEY	Eng.	Mass.	Arms:-*	CRLA16----------7
STIGER	Germany/Switzerland	Md./N.J.	Arms:-*	CFA24-----------119
STILES	------	Mass.		CFA9------------264
STILLMAN	Eng.?	Conn.		CRLA6-----------263
STITH	------	Va.		CRLA4-----------133
STOCKBRIDGE	------	Mass.		CRLA10----------238
STOCKHAM	Eng.	Pa.	Crest:-*	CRLA13----------256
STOCKING	------	Mass.		CRLA3-----------33
STOCKTON	Eng.	L.I.,N.Y.	Arms:-	CFA12-----------131
STOCKTON	Eng.	L.I.,N.Y.	Arms:-	CFA19-----------174
STOCKTON	Eng.	L.I.,N.Y./N.J.	Arms:-	CFA22-----------245
STOCKTON	Eng.	L.I.,.N.Y.	Arms:-	CFA25-----------136
STOCKTON	Eng.	Mass./N.J.	Arms:-*	CRLA5-----------51
STOCKTON	Eng.	N.Y./N.J.		CRLA11----------257
STOCKTON	Eng.	Mass./N.J.	Arms:-*	CRLA15----------457
STOCKTON	------	N.J.		CRLA17----------301
STOCKTON	No family data		Arms:-*	CRLA18----------272
STOCKTON, Richard	------	N.J.		SDI---------145,152
STODDARD	Eng.	Mass.	Arms:-	CFA3------------72
STODDARD	Eng.	Mass.		CFA6------------299
STODDARD	Eng.	Mass.		CFA15-----------362
STODDARD	------	Conn.		CRLA17----------471
STODDARD	Eng.	Mass.	Arms:-*	AF**------------380
STODDARD	Eng.	Mass.	Arms:-*	AF**------------506
STODDARD	Eng.	Mass.		PFU-------------227
STODDARD	------	Mass.		PPA-------------609
STODDER	Eng.	Mass.	Arms:-*	CFA5------------353
STOKES	Eng.	N.J.	Arms:-*	CRLA2-----------372
STOKES	Eng.	N.J.	Arms:-*	CRLA5-----------24
STOKES	Eng.			CRLA5-----------200
STOKES	Eng.	N.J.		CRLA8-----------353
STOKES	Eng.	N.J.		CRLA11----------531
STOKES	Eng.	N.J.		CRLA15----------447
STOKES	Eng.	N.J.		CRLA15----------550
STOKES	------	R.I.?	Arms:-*	CRLA20----------45
STOKES	------	------	Arms:-*	CRLA20------opp.379
STOKES	Eng.	N.C.	Arms:-*	AFA1------------195
STOLL	Germany	N.Y.	Arms:-	CFA24-----------27
STONARD	------	Mass.	Arms:-*	CRLA20----------39
STONE	------	Mass./R.I.		CFA6------------199
STONE	------	Mass.		CFA12-----------376
STONE	Eng.	Conn.		CFA16-----------221
STONE	Eng.	Mass.		CFA19-----------106

STONE	Eng.	Mass.	Arms:-	ACF--------------18
STONE	Eng.	Mass.		CRLA11---------139
STONE	Eng.	Mass.	Arms:-*	CRLA15----------88
STONE	------	Md.	Arms:-*	CRLA15---------322
STONE	Eng.	Mass.	Arms:-*	CRLA20---------102
STONE	Eng.	Mass./R.I.		AF****---------125
STONE, Thomas	------	Md.		SDI--------189,199
STONEBRIDGE	------	Va.		CRLA19---------181
STORER	Eng.	Mass./N.H.		CFA2-----------295
STORM	------	N.Y.		CRLA9----------435
STOTT	Eng.	Mass.	*(only)	CRLA12----------88
STOUT	------	Mass./W.Indies/N.Y.		CFA10----------296
STOUT	------	Pa.		CRLA9----------456
STOUT	Germany	Pa.		CRLA17---------224
STOUTENBOROUGH	Holland	N.Y.	Arms:-*	AF****----------24
STOUTENBURGH	Holland	N.Y.C.	Arms:-	AF**------------58
STOVALL	Eng.	Va.		CFA16----------146
STOW	Eng.	Mass.		CFA15----------239
STOW	Eng.	Mass.		CFA19-----------59
STOW	Eng.	Mass.		CRLA10---------320
STOWE	Eng.	Mass.	Arms:-	AF*-------------91
STOWERS	------	Mass.		CRLA1----------209
STRAAT	------	------		CFA4-----------176
STRANG	France	N.Y.	Arms:-	CRLA7----------547
STRASSBURGER	Germany	Pa.		CRLA9----------437
STRASSBURGER	Germany	Pa.		CRLA11---------349
STRATTON	Eng.	------		CFA8------------99
STRATTON	------	Mass.		CFA21----------232
STRATTON	------	Mass.	Arms:-	AF****---------235
STRAW	------	Mass.		CFA14----------174
STREAN	Scotland/Ireland	Va.	Arms:-	AF*------------255
STREET	Eng.	Conn.	Arms:-*	CRLA6----------344
STREET	------	N.Y.		PPA------------479
STREETE	Eng.	Mass./Conn.		CRLA19---------107
STRICKLAND	Eng.?	Mass.		CRLA6----------481
STRICKLAND	Eng.	Mass.		CRLA7----------470
STRICKLER	Switzerland	Pa.	Arms:-*	CRLA14----------40
STRINGER	Ireland	N.Y.		CRLA19---------359
STROBRIDGE	Ireland?	Mass.		CRLA7----------412
STRODE	Eng.?	Va.	Arms:-*	CRLA14---------170
STRODE	Eng.	Va.		AF*------------321
STRONG	Eng./Wales	Mass.		CFA11----------355
STRONG	------	Mass./Conn.		CFA15----------350
STRONG	Eng.	Mass./Conn.		CFA15----------346
STRONG	Wales	Mass.		CFA13----------193
STRONG	Wales	Mass.	Arms:-	CFA22----------159
STRONG	Eng.	Mass.		CFA24----------136
STRONG	Eng.?	Mass.	Arms:-*	CRLA3-----------25
STRONG	Eng.	Mass.		CRLA18---------622
STROTHER	Eng.	Va.		CFA5-----------290
STROTHER	Eng.	Va.		CFA10----------115
STROTHER	Eng.	Va.	Arms:-	CFA14----------181
STROUD	------	Pa.		CRLA13---------425
STRUTHERS	Scotland	Pa.	Arms:-	CRLA19---------275
STRYCKER	Holland	N.Y.		CFA7-----------231
STRYKER	Holland	N.Y.		CFA9-----------309
STRYKER	Holland	N.Y.		CRLA8----------288
STUART	------	N.Y.C.		CFA7-----------271
STUART=STEWART	Scotland	------		CFA17----------317
STUART	------	Pa.	Arms:-	CFA22----------251
STUBBS	Eng.?	Pa.	Arms:-*	CRLA1----------134
STUDWELL	Eng.	Conn.	Arms:-	CRLA3----------163
STULL	------	Md.		AF*-------------88
STUMP	Germany	Pa.		CRLA13---------231
STURGIS	Eng.	Mass.		CFA5-----------126
STURGIS	Eng.	Mass.		CFA7-----------353
STURGIS	------	Pa.	Arms:-*	CRLA9----------229

STUYVESANT	Holland	N.Y.	Arms:-	CFA5------------262
STUYVESANT	Holland	N.Y.	Arms:-	CFA13-----------24
STUYVESANT	Holland	N.Y.		CFA25----------113
STUYVESANT	Holland	N.Y.	Arms:-*	CRLA13---------309
STUYVESANT	Netherlands	N.Y.	Arms:-*	HFA-------------133
STYLES	No family data		Arms:-*	CRLA13------opp.450
STYLES	No family data		Arms:-*	CRLA15----------489
SUGDEN	No family data		Arms:-*	CRLA15------opp.271
SULLIVAN (O'Sullivan)	Ireland	Maine	Arms:-*	CRLA8-----------23
SULLIVAN (O'Sullivan)	Ireland	Maine/Mass.	Arms:-*	AFA***----------239
SULLIVAN	Ireland	Maine	Arms:-*	PFU-------------264
SUMMERS	------	N.J.	Arms:-	CRLA6-------------8
SUMNER	Eng.	Mass.		CFA10------------15
SUMNER	Eng.	Mass.		CFA10-----------258
SUMNER	Eng.	Mass.	Arms:-*	CFA14------------23
SUMNER	Eng.	Mass.		CFA13-----------309
SUMNER	Eng.	Mass.	Arms:-	CRLA3-----------263
SUMNER	Eng.	Mass.	Arms:-*	CRLA20----------133
SUMNER	------	Mass.		CRLA20----------214
SUMNER	Eng.	Mass.		PFU--------------76
SUSONG	------	Va.		AF***-----------159
SUTTON	------	Mass.		CFA22------------80
SUTTON	Eng.	Mass.		CRLA13----------366
SUTTON	Eng.	Ohio		CRLA15----------397
SUTTON	Eng.	Pa.	Arms:-*	AF*-------------10
SWAIN	------	------	*(only)	TNEF--------opp.31
SWAIN	------	N.H.		TNEF------------167
SWAINE	Eng.	Mass./Conn.		CRLA18----------226
SWALLOW	------	N.J.		CRLA18----------516
SWAN	------	Mass.		CFA21-----------211
SWAN	Eng.	Mass.		CFA22-----------132
SWAN	Eng.	Mass.	Arms:-*	CRLA16-----------17
SWAN	------	Mass.		CRLA17----------469
SWANN	Eng.	Va.		CRLA11----------310
SWANSON	Sweden	Del.		CRLA1------------37
SWANSON	Sweden	Pa.		CRLA17----------329
SWART	------	N.Y.	Arms:-	CRLA7-------167,175
SWART	------	N.Y.?		CRLA18----------231
SWART, see: BRAY=SWART				
SWARTS	------	Pa.	Arms:-*	CRLA8-----------274
SWARTWOUT	Holland	N.Y.	Arms:-*	CRLA20-----------39
SWARTZ	------	------	Arms:-*	CRLA20------opp.353
SWAYZE	------	L.I.,N.Y.		CRLA19-----------85
SWEDEN, Kings of		Gaither=Fownes desc.		CRLA11-----------60
SWEDEN, Kings of		Blackiston descent		CRLA11----------397
SWEETSER	Eng.	Mass.		CFA2------------148
SWIFT	------	Pa.		CFA11------------38
SWIFT	Eng.	Mass.		CFA12-----------204
SWIFT	Eng.?	Mass.	Arms:-*	CRLA18----------574
SWIFT	Eng.	Mass.	Arms:-*	AFA***----------109
SWINT	------	Pa.		CRLA15----------545
SYKES	Eng.	N.Y.		CRLA13----------235
SYLVESTER	Eng.	N.Y.		CFA4------------223
SYMES	------	N.Y.		CRLA16----------170
SYMONDS	Eng.	Mass.		CFA21-----------236
SYMONDS	Eng.	Mass.	Arms:-*	AFA***--------14,20
SYNG=PHYSICK	------	Md./Pa.		CRLA9-----------521
SYNNOT	Ireland	N.J.	Arms:-*	AFA***----------159

- T -

TABB	Eng.	Va.		CRLA3-----------242

TABER	Eng.	Mass.	Arms:-	CFA15-----------198
TABER	Eng.	Mass.		CRLA18----------392
TABER	-------	Mass.		CRLA20----------190
TABOR	-------	Mass./R.I.		CRLA7-----------307
TAFEL	Austria	Ohio	Arms:-*	CRLA15----------421
TAFT	-------	Mass.		CFA19-----------86
TAILBOYS	Eng.			CRLA15----------147
TAILLEFER, Counts of Angouleme			Peck=Bowen descent	CRLA2-----------33
TAILLEFER, see: ANGOULEME, Counts of				
TAINTER	Eng.	Mass.		CRLA2-----------144
TAINTER	Eng.	Mass.		CRLA15----------85
TALBOT	Eng.	Mass.	Arms:-*	CFA26-----22cht.,27
TALBOT	Eng.			CRLA11----------104
TALBOT	Eng.	Mass.	Arms:-*	CRLA12----------348
TALBOT	Eng.			CRLA18----------473
TALBOT	-------	-------	*(only)	TNEF--------opp.48
TALCOTT	Eng.	Mass.	Arms:-*	CFA9------------201
TALCOTT	Eng.	Conn.		CFA15----------365
TALCOTT	Eng.	Mass.		CFA25-----------37
TALCOTT	Eng.	Mass./Conn.		CRLA13----------189
TALLMAN	Prussia?/Germany	R.I.		CRLA14----------122
TALLMAN	Germany	R.I.		CRLA20----------46
TALMAGE	Eng.	Mass.	Arms:-*	CFA2------------258
TALMAGE	Eng.?	Mass./L.I.,N.Y.	Arms:-	CFA17-----------112
TALMAGE	Eng.	Mass.	Arms:-*	HFA-------------287
TANEY	Ireland	Va.		CRLA4-----------414
TANNER	-------	R.I.		CRLA7-----------320
TAPLEY	-------	Mass.		CFA4------------30
TAPP	-------	Conn.	Arms:-*	PBAF------------133
TAPPAN	-------	Mass.		PPA-------------199
TAPPEN	-------	N.Y.		CRLA12----------430
TARBELL	-------	Mass.		CFA8------------256
TARBELL	-------	Mass.		CFA27-----------192
TARBOX	Eng.	Mass.	Arms:-*	CFA1------------119
TARLETON	-------	Md.		CFA14-----------140
TASH	Scotland/Ireland	N.H.		CFA10-----------359
TATE	Eng.	Maine		CFA6------------243
TATE	-------	Pa./Va.		CRLA3-----------423
TATE	-------	N.C.		AF***-----------147
TATEM	-------	N.J.	Arms:-*	CRLA11----------450
TATLOW	-------	Del.		AFA***----------326
TATNALL	Eng.	Pa.		ACF-------------46
TATNALL	Eng.	Pa.		CRLA15----------597
TAYLOE	Eng.	Va.		CFA9------------141
TAYLOE	Eng.	Va.		CFA19-----------217
TAYLOR	Eng.	Va.		CFA5------------290
TAYLOR	Eng.	Va.		CFA10-----------122
TAYLOR	Eng.	N.J.		CFA12-----------172
TAYLOR	-------	Mass.		CFA8------------337
TAYLOR	Eng.	N.Y.		CFA14-----------280
TAYLOR	-------	Mass.		CFA16-----------268
TAYLOR	Eng.	Va.		CFA17------343,345
TAYLOR	Eng.	N.J.		CFA20-----------145
TAYLOR	Eng.	N.J.		CFA22-----------211
TAYLOR	-------	Va.		CRLA1-----------240
TAYLOR	-------	Mass.		CRLA8-----------34
TAYLOR	Eng.	Pa.	Arms:-*	CRLA8-----------191
TAYLOR	Eng.	Pa.		CRLA8-----------320
TAYLOR	Eng.	Pa.	Arms:-*	CRLA9-----------302
TAYLOR	-------	Md.		CRLA11----------318
TAYLOR	Eng.			CRLA13----------427
TAYLOR	-------	R.I./Conn./Pa.		CRLA15----------455
TAYLOR	Eng./Wales	Pa.	Arms:-*	CRLA17------342,353
TAYLOR	Eng.	Pa.		CRLA17----------633
TAYLOR	Scotland	N.Y.		CRLA19----------151
TAYLOR	-------	Mass.		CRLA19----------262
TAYLOR	-------	R.I.		CRLA20----------161

TAYLOR	Eng.	Va.	Arms:-	AF***-----------103
TAYLOR	------	Pa./N.Y.		PPA-------------597
TAYLOR, George	------	Pa.		SDI--------159,171
TAYLOR	Eng.	Conn.	Arms:-*	TNEF------------83
TEACHOUT	------	N.Y.		AF*------------391
TEACKLE	Eng.	Va.		CFA13----------225
TEACKLE	------	Va.		CRLA2----------114
TEEL	------	Mass.		CRLA4----------360
TEETOR	------	Ind.		CRLA12---------246
TEFFT	Eng.	Mass./R.I.		CRLA12----------84
TELLER	Holland?	N.Y.	Arms:-	AF**------------61
TEMPLE	Eng.	Mass.	Arms:-*	PFU-------------184
TENDERING	Eng.		Arms:-*	CRLA20---------405
TEN EYCK	Holland	N.Y.		CFA10----------302
TEN EYCK	Holland	N.Y.		CFA11-----------47
TEN EYCK	Holland?	N.Y.	Arms:-*	CRLA18---------557
TEN EYCK	Holland	N.Y.	Arms:-*	CRLA20----------66
TENNEY	------	------	*(only)	CRLA12-------opp.88
TERHUNE	------	N.Y.		AF**-----------469
TERRELL	------	Conn.	Arms:-*	CRLA7----------583
TERRY	Eng.	Conn.		CFA2-----------114
TERRY	Eng.	Conn.		CFA8-----------346
TERRY	No family data		Arms:-*	CRLA18------opp.560
TERRY	Eng.	Mass.		CRLA19---------265
TEW	Eng.	R.I.		CRLA17---------445
TEW	------	------	*(only)	TNEF-------btn.78-9
TEW, see: PILGRIMS				
TEWKESBURY	------	Mass.		CFA7-----------160
THATCHER	------	N.J./Pa.	Arms:-*	AF**------------22
THATCHER	Eng.	Mass.	Arms:-*	AFA***---------369
THATCHER	------	Maine		PPA-------------424
THAYER	Eng.	Mass.		CFA7-----------178
THAYER	Eng.	Mass.	Arms:-*	CRLA12----------60
THAYER	Eng.	Mass.	*(only)	CRLA13---------170
THAYER	Eng.	Mass.		CRLA16---------163
THAYER	Eng.	Mass.		CRLA17---------442
THAYER	------	Mass.		CRLA20---------206
THATCHER	------	N.J.		CFA17----------295
THAW	------	Pa.		CFA19----------148
THAYER	Eng.	Mass.		CFA9-----------285
THAYER	Eng.	Mass.		CFA10-----------12
THAYER	Eng.	Mass.	Arms:-	CFA10----------370
THAYER	------	N.H.		CFA11----------220
THAYER	Eng.	Mass.	Arms:-*	CFA24----------142
THEOBALD	------	Va./Md.	Arms:-*	CRLA3----------390
THIBAUT I, see: CHAMPAGNE, Counts of				
THIERN, Vicomtes of	France			CRLA5----------437
THIMBLEBY	Eng.			CRLA15---------148
THISSELL	Eng.	Mass.		CRLA8-----------11
THODEY	------	N.Y.		CFA10-----------69
THOM	Scotland	Va.		CRLA3----------228
THOMAS	Wales	Md.	Arms:-	CFA3-----------294
THOMAS	Wales	Md.		CFA10----------207
THOMAS	Wales	Md.	Arms:-	CFA16-----------82
THOMAS	Wales	Pa.		CFA20-----------91
THOMAS	Eng.?	Md.		CRLA1----------233
THOMAS	Eng.	Va.		CRLA3----------319
THOMAS	------	Ill.		CRLA3----------355
THOMAS	------	Maine	Arms:-*	CRLA3----------385
THOMAS	Wales	Md.		CRLA8----------171
THOMAS	Wales		Arms:-*	CRLA8----------274
THOMAS	------	Pa.		CRLA9----------300
THOMAS	------	Conn.		CRLA13---------456
THOMAS	Eng.	Mass.	Arms:-*	CRLA15----------29
THOMAS	------	Pa.		CRLA15---------232
THOMAS	Wales	Pa.	Arms:-*	CRLA17---------272
THOMAS	------	Pa.		CRLA17---------352

THOMAS	————	Conn.		CRLA19----------105
THOMAS	————	Pa./Va.		CRLA19----------310
THOMAS	————	Ky.		AF***----------233
THOMAS	Eng.	Md.	Arms:-*	AFA***----------393
THOMAS	Wales?	Mass.		PFU------------245
THOMAS	————	Md.		PFU------------316
THOMAS	————	Mass./S.C.		PPA------------408
THOMLINSON	Eng.	Conn.		CFA5------------294
THOMPKINS	————	Va.		CRLA1----------260
THOMPSON	Eng.	Va.		CFA5-------292,295
THOMPSON	————	Conn.	Arms:-*	CFA27----opp.49,195
THOMPSON	Wales	Mass.	Arms:-*	CFA2------------326
THOMPSON	Eng.	N.H./Mass.		CFA6------------235
THOMPSON	————	Ind.		CFA8------------324
THOMPSON	Ireland	Md.		CFA10----------116
THOMPSON	————	N.J.		CRLA5------------65
THOMPSON	————	Pa.		CRLA8----------209
THOMPSON	Ireland	Pa.	*(only)	CRLA13----------340
THOMPSON	————	Conn.		CRLA16----------126
THOMPSON	Eng.	N.J.		CRLA17-----------37
THOMPSON	————	N.Y.	Arms:-*	CRLA18----------578
THOMPSON	Eng.	Mass./Conn.		CRLA19-------93,105
THOMPSON	Eng.	N.C.		AF***----------143
THOMPSON	————	Va.		PPA------------594
THOMPSON	————	Mass.		TNEF------------151
THOMPSON	Ireland	Mass.		CFA19-----------46
THORN	————	S.C.		CFA6------------286
THORNDIKE	Eng.	Mass.	Arms:-*	CFA8-------------97
THORNDIKE	Eng.	Mass.	Arms:-	CFA19-----------93
THORNE	————	Mass.		CFA2------------272
THORNE	Eng.	Mass.	Arms:-*	CRLA17----------313
THORNE	Eng.	Mass.	Arms:-*	CRLA18----------425
THORNE	Eng.?	Va./Mass./N.Y.	Arms:-*	CRLA18----------567
THORNE	Eng.		Arms:-*	AFA***----------113
THORESBY	————	————	Arms:-*	CRLA20------opp.405
THORNTON	————	R.I.		CFA8------------359
THORNTON	Eng.	Va.	Arms:-	CFA14----------183
THORNTON, Matthew	Scotland/Ireland	Maine/Mass./N.H.		SDI----------97,102
THOROUGHGOOD	Eng.	Va.		CFA17----------367
THOROUGHGOOD	Eng.	Va.		CRLA4----------187
THOROUGHGOOD	Eng.	Va.		CRLA9-----------11
THOROWGOOD	————	Va.	Arms:-*	CRLA15----------337
THORPE	————	Mass.		CRLA17----------437
THOURY DE LA CORDERIE (de)	Normandy		Arms:-*	CRLA1-----------42
THRELKELD	Eng.	Md.		CFA17----------365
THROCKMORTON	Eng.	Va.	Arms:-*	CFA10----------116
THROCKMORTON	Eng.	R.I./N.J.	Arms:-*	AFA***----------199
THROCKMORTON	————	R.I.		MCS-------------97
THROCKMORTON	Eng.	Va.	Arms:-*	PFU------------364
THROOP	————	Mass.	Arms:-*	AF****----------176
THROWBRIDGE	Eng.	Mass.		CFA1------------112
THROWER	————	N.C.		AF***----------310
THURSTON	————	R.I.	Arms:-*	CRLA12----------361
THURSTON	Eng.	Va.		CRLA15----------404
THURSTON	————	R.I.	Arms:-*	CRLA20-----------45
THWING	Eng.	Mass.		CFA3-------------13
TIBBETTS	Eng.?	Mass./N.H.		CRLA10----------350
TIDMARSH	Eng.?	Pa.	Arms:-*	CRLA14-----------48
TIENHOVEN, see: COLONIAL DAMES				
TIFFANY	————	Mass.	Arms:-*	CRLA18-----------54
TILDEN	————	Mass.		CFA4------------168
TILESTON	Eng.	Mass.		CFA14----------328
TILGHMAN	Eng.	Md.		CRLA1----------108
TILGHMAN	Eng.	Md.	Arms:-*	PFU------------129
TILGHMAN	————	Md.	Arms:-*	PFU------------170
TILLEY	Eng.	Mass.		CFA6------------353
TILLEY	Eng.	Mass.		CFA7------------361

TILLEY	Eng.	Mass.	Arms:-*	CFA8------------179
TILLEY	———	Mass.		ACF-------------90
TILLEY	———	Mass.	Arms:-*	CRLA18----------604
TILLEY	Eng.?	Mass.		TNEF------------56
TILLEY, see: PILGRIMS				
TILLINGHAST	———	R.I.		ARSC------------25
TILLINGHAST	———	R.I.		MCS-------------32
TILLY	———	———	*(only)	TNEF-------btn.78-9
TILTON	———	Mass.		CFA11-----------335
TILTON	———	L.I.,N.Y.		CRLA9-----------175
TILTON	———	Mass./N.Y.		CRLA18----------565
TINDLE	———	Pa.	Arms:-*	CRLA13----------387
TINGLEY	Eng.?	Mass.		CFA7------------72
TINKHAM	———	Mass.		TNEF-----------243
TITCOMB	———	Mass.		CRLA7----------489
TITCOMB	Eng.	Mass.		CRLA17---------249
TITUS	Eng.	Mass.		CFA2-----------277
TITUS	Eng.	Mass./L.I.,N.Y.		CFA3-----------331
TITUS	Eng.	Mass.		CFA7-----------274
TITUS	Eng.	Mass.		CFA7--------384,385
TITUS	———	N.Y.?		CFA16-----------33
TITUS	Eng.	Mass.	Arms:-	CFA16-----------10
TITUS	Eng.	L.I.,N.Y.	Arms:-*	CFA18-----------45
TITUS	———	Mass.		ACF-------------84
TITUS	Eng.	Mass./N.Y.	Arms:-*	CRLA18------422,428
TITUS	———	Mass./L.I.,N.Y.		AFA***----------50
TOBEY	———	Mass./Maine	Arms:-	CRLA6-----------64
TOBEY	———	Mass.		CRLA6----------279
TOD	Scotland	Conn.		CFA18----------201
TODD	Scotland	N.Y.C.		CFA12----------129
TODD	Eng.	Conn.	Arms:-*	CRLA6----------349
TODD	Scotland/Ireland Pa.			CRLA8----------300
TODD	Eng.	Va./Md.		CRLA8----------517
TODD	Eng.	Conn.	Arms:-	AF**-----------341
TODHUNTER	Eng.	Pa.		CFA22----------186
TOLLEY	———	Md.		CFA5-----------288
TOLLMAN	———	———	*(only)	TNEF--------opp.30
TOLMAN	Eng.	Mass.		CFA9-----------239
TOMES	Eng.			CRLA7----------141
TOMES	———	Conn.		ARSC------------96
TOMLINSON	Eng.	Conn.	Arms:-*	CRLA12------129,132
TOMPKINS	———	R.I.	Arms:-*	CRLA20------------8
TOMPSON	Eng.	Mass.	Arms:-	CFA3------------88
TONE	Ireland	N.Y./Georgetown,/D.C.7		CFA14----------359
TONNERRE, Counts of	France			CRLA5----------439
TONI (de)	Eng.		Arms:-*	CRLA10-----btn.78-9
TONY (de) (Toeni)	Eng.		Arms:-*	CRLA7----------196
TONY (de)	Eng.		Cooley=Twining desc.	CRLA18---------143
TOPPAN	Eng.	Mass.		CFA7-----------356
TONER	Eng.		Arms:-*	CRLA20----------54
TORREY	Eng.	Mass.	Arms:-*	CFA4------------20
TORREY	Eng.	Mass.		CRLA18----------44
TORREY	Eng.	Mass.		CRLA20------169,201
TORREY	———	Mass.		MCS------------40
TORVILLE=de BEAUMONT	Normandy	"before Conquest"		AF*------------43
TOTNES (de)	Eng.			CRLA5----------440
TOTTEN	———	N.Y.		CRLA6----------189
TOUCHET	Eng.		Arms:-*	CRLA5----------440
TOULOUSE, Counts of	France		Gaunt=French descent	CRLA1----------550
TOULOUSE, Counts of	France		Warren=Belknap desc.	CRLA2----------181
TOULOUSE, Counts of	France		Arms:-*	CRLA5----------443
TOULOUSE, Counts of	France			CRLA7----------214
TOULOUSE, Counts of	France	Hinton descent	Arms:-*	CRLA8----------491
TOULOUSE, Counts of	France			CRLA9----------375
TOULOUSE, Counts of	France		Arms:-*	CRLA17---------205
TOULOUSE, Counts of	France			CRLA18---------194
TOULOUSE, Counts of	France			CRLA17---------688
TOURISON	France	Pa.		

TOURNEUR	France	N.Y.		CRLA18----------210
TOURNIER	France/Holland	N.Y.		CFA18------------6
TOUSTAIN	France		Arms:-*	CRLA1-----------47
TOWER	Eng.	Mass.		CFA2-----------361
TOWER	————	Mass.		CFA4-----------51
TOWER	Eng.	Mass.	Arms:-*	AFA***---------377
TOWER	Eng.	Mass.		PFU------------272
TOWNE	Eng.	Mass.		CFA12----------344
TOWNE	Eng.	Mass.	Arms:-	CFA27----------196
TOWNE	Eng.	Mass.		CRLA15---------439
TOWNSEND	Eng.	L.I.,N.Y.		CFA3-----------330
TOWNSEND	Eng.	N.Y.		CFA7-----------273
TOWNSEND	Eng.	R.I./N.Y.		CFA10----------188
TOWNSEND	Eng.	R.I.		CFA16----------33
TOWNSEND	Eng.	L.I.,N.Y.		CFA16----------134
TOWNSEND	Eng.	Mass./L.I.,N.Y.	Arms:-*	CFA18---16,36,40,41
TOWNSEND	Eng.	Mass.	Arms:-	CFA24----------92
TOWNSEND	————	L.I.,N.Y.	Arms:-	CFA26----------85
TOWNSEND	Eng.	Mass./R.I./N.Y.		CRLA4----------332
TOWNSEND	Eng.	Mass.	Arms:-*	CRLA7----------587
TOWNSEND	————	Mass.	Arms:-*	CRLA15---------69
TOWNSEND	Eng.	N.Y.	Arms:-*	CRLA17---------306
TOWNSEND	Eng.	Mass.	Arms:-*	CRLA18----------13
TOWNSEND	Eng.	N.Y.	*(only)	CRLA19----------54
TOWNSEND	————	————	*(only)	TNEF------btn.78-9
TOWNSEND, see: PILGRIMS				
TOWNSHEND	————	Va.		CRLA4----------140
TRACY	————	Mass.		CFA7-----------321
TRACY	Eng.	Mass.		CFA13----------169
TRACY	Eng.	Mass./Conn.		CFA14----------40
TRACY	Eng.	Conn.		CRLA10---------92
TRACY	Eng.	Va.		CRLA12---------418
TRACY	Eng.	Mass.		CRLA17---------454
TRAHAN	Nova Scotia	Pa.		CRLA17---------703
TRAIN	Eng.	Mass.	Arms:-*	CRLA15---------70
TRAIN	Eng.	Mass.	Arms:-	AF**-----------278
TRAINER	Eng.	Pa.		CRLA9----------276
TRAPP	————	Mo.		CRLA7----------543
TRASK	Eng.	Mass.		CFA1-----------141
TREAT	————	Mass./Conn.	Arms:-*	CFA10----------183
TREAT	Eng.	Conn.		CFA16----------179
TREAT	Eng.	Conn.		CRLA2----------287
TREAT	Eng.	Conn.		CRLA7----------443
TREAT	Eng.	Conn.		CRLA13---------59
TREAT	Eng.	Conn.		CRLA18---------612
TREAT	Eng.	Conn.	Arms:-	CRLA19---------297
TREAT	Eng.	Conn.		CRLA19---------420
TREAT	Eng.	Conn.	Arms:-*	PBAF-----------126
TREGO	————	Pa.	Arms:-*	CRLA17---------349
TRENCHARD	Eng.	N.J.		PFU------------112
TRENDALL	————	Va.		CRLA9----------16
TRIMBLE	————	Mass.		CFA7-----------77
TRIMBLE	Ireland	Pa.		CRLA8----------572
TRIPP	Eng.	R.I./Mass.		CRLA16-------66,67
TRIPP	————	R.I.		CRLA19---------73
TRIPP	————	R.I.		CRLA19---------289
TRIPP	Eng.	Mass./R.I.		CRLA20---------189
TRIPP	————	Mass.	Arms:-*	TNEF-----------30
TRIPPE	Eng.	Md.		CRLA2----------187
TRIPPE	————	N.Y.		CRLA8----------326
TROTT	————	Mass.		CRLA13---------413
TROUTBECK	Eng.		Arms:-*	CRLA5----------445
TROUTMAN	Bavaria	Pa.	Arms:-*	CRLA15---------271
TROW	————	Mass.		CFA12----------203
TROWBRIDGE	Eng.	————	Arms:-	CFA5-----------108
TROWBRIDGE	Eng.	Mass.		CFA9-----------276
TROWBRIDGE	Eng.	Mass.		CFA10----------392

TROWBRIDGE	Eng.	Mass.		CFA21-----------242
TROWBRIDGE	Eng.	Conn.	Arms:-*	CRLA7-----------585
TROWBRIDGE	-------	Mass./Conn.		CRLA19----------81
TROWBRIDGE	Eng.	Mass.		CRLA19----------368
TROWBRIDGE	Eng.	Mass.		CRLA20----------209
TRUE	Eng.?	Mass.		CRLA16-----------20
TRUMAN	Eng.	Conn.		CFA9------------22
TRUMAN	Eng.	Conn.		CFA10-----------285
TRUMAN	-------	Conn.		PFU-------------251
TRUMBULL	Eng.	Mass.		CRLA17----------655
TRUMBULL	-------	Conn.		PPA-------------41
TRUSSELL	Eng.		Arms:-*	CRLA5-----------446
TUCK	Eng.	Mass.		CRLA14----------157
TUCKER	Eng.	Vt.	Arms:-*	CFA1------------154
TUCKER	Eng.	Mass.		CFA7------------137
TUCKER	Bermuda	Va.		CRLA11----------124
TUCKER	-------	Mass.		CRLA20----------213
TUCKER	-------	Mass.	Arms:-*	AF***-----------14
TUCKER	-------	Va./Bermuda		PPA-------------40
TUCKERMAN	Germany	Mass.		PPA-------------500
TUDOR	Eng.	Mass.	Arms:-*	CFA4------------72
TUFTS	Eng.?	Mass.		CRLA18----------411
TURNBULL	Scotland	Pa.		CFA13-----------269
TURNBULL	Scotland	Pa.		CFA22-----------129
TURNBULL	Scotland	Pa./Md.		CRLA3-----------284
TURNER	Eng.	Mass.		CFA4------------169
TURNER	-------	Va.		CFA14----------138
TURNER	-------	Conn.		CRLA6-----------346
TURNER	Eng.	Va.		CRLA8-----------551
TURNER	-------	Mass.	Arms:-	AF**------------397
TURNER	-------	Mass.	Arms:-	AF**------------549
TURNER	-------	Mass.		TNEF------------239
TURPIN	Eng.	Va.		CRLA4-----------412
TUTHILL	Eng.	Mass./L.I.,N.Y.		CFA10-----------340
TUTTLE	Eng.	Conn.		CFA2------------355
TUTTLE	Eng.	Mass./Conn.		CFA9------------27
TUTTLE	Eng.	N.H.		CFA10-----------355
TUTTLE	Eng.	Mass.	*(only)	CRLA2-----------324
TUTTLE	Eng.	Conn.	Arms:-*	CRLA6-----------352
TUTTLE	Eng.	Mass./Conn.		CRLA7-----------286
TUTTLE	Eng.	Mass.	Arms:-*	CRLA13----------450
TUTTLE	Eng.	Mass.	Arms:-*	CRLA15----------53
TUTTLE	Eng.	Mass.	Arms:-*	CRLA15----------487
TUTTLE	Eng.	Mass./N.Y.	Arms:-*	CRLA17----------428
TUTTLE	Eng.	Conn.	Arms:-*	CRLA19----------273
TUTTLE	-------	N.Y.		AF***-----------283
TWINING	-------	Mass.	Arms:-	CRLA12------178,181
TWINING	Eng.	Mass.		CRLA13----------261
TWINING	Eng.	Mass.		CRLA18----------535
TWINING	Eng.	Mass.		TNEF------------107
TYBOUT	-------	N.Y.		CRLA9-----------317
TYLER	-------	Md.		CFA15-----------172
TYLER	-------	Conn.		CFA20-----------311
TYLER	Eng.	Va.		PFU-------------255
TYNDALL=WINTHROP	-------	Mass.		MCS-------------11
TYNG	Eng.	Mass.		CFA3------------46
TYNG	-------	Mass.		CRLA1-----------380
TYNG, see: COYTMORE=TYNG				
TYRWHIT	Eng.			CRLA15----------149
TYSON	Germany	Pa.	Arms:-*	CRLA17----------303
TYSON	-------	Pa.?	Arms:-*	CRLA18----------293

- U -

UGAINE MOR, see: IRISH Kings				
UHL	———	N.Y.	Arms:-*	CFA24------------45
UHTRED, Prince of Northumberland				CRLA8-----------332
ULSHOEFFER	———	N.Y.C.		CFA6------------21
UMBAUGH	———	Md.		CRLA18----------584
UNDERHILL	Eng.	Mass.		CFA1------------204
UNDERHILL	Eng.	Mass.	Arms:-	CFA3------------320
UNDERHILL	Eng.	Mass./L.I.,N.Y.	Arms:-*	CFA18------------37
UNDERHILL	Eng.	Mass./N.Y.		CRLA18----------433
UNDERWOOD	———	Mass.		CFA7------------181
UNDERWOOD	Eng.	Mass.		CFA7------------363
UNDERWOOD	Eng.	Va.	Arms:-	CFA17------------343
UNDERWOOD	———	Del.		CRLA17----------65
UPDIKE	Holland	L.I.,N.Y.	Arms:-*	CRLA14----------116
UPHAM	Eng.	Mass.		CFA9------------344
UPHAM	Eng.	Mass.		CFA2------------117
UPHAM	Eng.	Mass.		CFA23------------196
UPHAM	Eng.	Mass.		CRLA13----------465
UPSHUR	Eng.	Va.		CRLA2----------116
UPSHUR	———	Va.	Arms:-*	CRLA15----------335
UPSON	———	Conn.		CFA27------------198
UPTON	———	Mass.		CFA14----------323
UPTON	Eng.	Mass.		CFA19--------77,78
UTLEY	Eng.	Mass.		CFA19----------235
UTTER	———	R.I.		AF****----------124

- V -

VAIL	———	N.Y.		AF*------------317
VAIL	Eng.	L.I.,N.Y.	Arms:-	AF***----------174
VAIL	Eng.	Mass./L.I.,N.Y.	Arms:-*	AFA***----------371
VALE	Eng.	Pa.	Arms:-*	CRLA11----------207
VALENTINE	Eng.	L.I.,N.Y.		CFA10------------192
VALENTINE	Eng.	L.I.,N.Y.		CFA16------------13
VALENTINE	Holland	N.Y.	Arms:-*	CFA18------------1
VALLANDINGHAM	———	Va./Ky.		CRLA3----------391
VALOIS	France	Pa.	Arms:-*	AFA***----------397
VAN ARSDALEN	Holland	N.J.		CFA1------------16
VAN BREESTEDE	———	N.Y.		CFA16------------307
VAN BRUGH	Holland	N.Y.		CFA11------------16
VAN BRUGH	Holland	N.Y.		CFA13------------57
VAN BRUNT	Holland	L.I.,N.Y.	Arms:-	AF**------------101
VAN BUREN	Gelderland	N.Y.	Arms:-*	CFA25----------121
VAN CLEEF	Holland	———		CFA4------------175
VAN CORTLANDT	Holland	N.Y.	Arms:-*	CFA5------------1
VAN CORTLANDT	Holland	N.Y.	Arms:-	CFA13------------29
VAN CORTLANDT	Holland	N.Y.	Arms:-	CFA20----------147
VAN CORTLANDT	Holland	N.Y.	Arms:-*	CFA25----------98
VAN DAM	———	N.Y.		CFA13----------339
VAN DEN BERG	Netherlands	N.Y.		CRLA20----------42
VANDERBILT	Netherlands	N.Y.		CFA2------------53
VANDERBILT	———	———		CFA4------------174
VANDERBILT	Holland	N.Y.		CFA12----------126
VANDERBILT	Netherlands	N.Y.		CFA15----------83
VANDERBILT	———	N.Y.		CFA17----------94
VANDEREECK	———	——— .		CFA4------------174

VANDERHEYDEN	———	Md.		CRLA17----------420
VANDERPOEL	Holland	N.Y.		CFA7------------288
VAN DER POEL	Netherlands	N.Y.	Arms:-*	CRLA20-----------53
VAN DER POEL	———	N.Y.		CRLA20----------186
VANDERSLICE	Holland	Pa.	Arms:-*	AF*-------------383
VANDERSLOOT	Germany	Pa.		CRLA18----------401
VAN DER VEER	Holland	N.Y.	Arms:-*	AFA***----------163
VAN DER VEER	Holland	N.Y.	Arms:-*	AFA***----------351
VAN DEURSEN	Holland	R.I.		CFA14------------63
VAN DE WALKER	———	N.Y.		CFA7------------238
VAN DYCK	———	N.Y.		CFA13-----------336
VAN DYKE	———	N.Y.C.		CFA1-------------17
VAN DYKE	Holland	N.Y.		CFA11------------46
VAN DYKE	Holland	N.Y.	Arms:-*	CFA15------------75
VAN DYKE	Holland	N.Y./N.J.	Arms:-*	CRLA1------------72
VAN DYKE	Holland	N.Y.		CRLA4-------------7
VAN DYKE	Holland	N.Y.		CRLA8-----------232
VAN DYKE	Holland	N.Y.	Arms:-	AF**------------107
VAN DOREN	———	L.I.,N.Y.		AF*-------------267
VAN EPS	———	N.Y.	Arms:-*	CRLA14-----------29
VAN HEYNINGEN	———	N.Y.	Arms:-*	CRLA20-----------63
VAN HORN	Holland	N.Y.		CRLA15----------428
VAN HORNE	———	N.Y.		CRLA12----------434
VAN KEUREN	———	N.Y.	Arms:-*	CRLA20-----------65
VAN KLEECK	———	N.Y.		CRLA12----------436
VAN KOUWENHOVEN	———	L.I.,N.Y.		CFA8-------------41
VAN KOWENHOVEN	Holland	N.Y.	Arms:-*	AF****-----------22
VAN KUREN	———	N.Y.		CRLA12----------431
VAN LEUVENIGH	Holland	Del.	Arms:-*	CRLA1------------76
VAN METRE	Holland	N.Y./N.J.	Arms:-*	CRLA14----------175
VAN NESS	Holland	———		CFA1-------------16
VAN NEST	Holland	N.Y.C.	Arms:-*	CFA16-----------113
VAN NOSTRAND	———	N.Y.		CRLA20-----------56
VAN PELT	Holland	N.Y.		CFA4------------174
VAN PELT	———	N.Y.		CFA11------------46
VAN REED	Holland	Pa.	Arms:-*	AF*-------------381
VAN RENSSELAER	Holland	N.Y.	Arms:-*	CRLA1-----------119
VAN RENSSELAER	Holland	N.Y.		HFA--------------1
VAN SALEE	———	N.Y.		CRLA12----------435
VAN SCHAICK	Holland	N.Y.	Arms:-*	CRLA14-----------31
VAN SCHOONHOVEN	———	N.Y.		CFA2------------281
VAN SCHOONHOVEN	———	N.Y.	Arms:-*	CRLA18----------429
VAN SICKLEN	Belgium	N.Y.		CRLA12----------433
VAN SIPE	———	———	Arms:-*	CRLA20----------353
VAN SLICHTENHORST	Holland	———		CFA11------------14
VAN SLICHTENHORST	Holland	Mass.		CFA13------------55
VAN STEENWICK	———	N.Y.	Arms:-*	CRLA20-----------56
VAN VLIET	Netherlands	N.Y.	Arms:-*	CRLA20-----------64
VAN VOORHEES	Holland	L.I.,N.Y.	Arms:-	CRLA3-----------185
VAN VOORHEES	Holland	N.Y.	Arms:-*	CRLA20-----------60
VAN VOORHAUDT	———	N.Y.?	Arms:-*	CRLA20-----------42
VAN WAGENEN	———	N.Y.	Arms:-*	CRLA20-----------35
VAN WINKLE	Holland	N.Y.		CFA12-----------117
VAN WINKLE	Holland	N.Y.		CFA16------------71
VAN WINKLE	Holland	N.J.	Arms:-	CRLA7------------30
VAN WYCKLIN	Netherlands	N.Y.		CFA7------------232
VAN ZANDT	———	N.Y.		CFA7------------288
VAN ZANDT	Gelderland	N.Y.		CFA11------------46
VAN ZUTPHEN	Holland	N.Y.	Arms:-*	AFA***-----------77
VARICK	———	N.Y.		CFA10-----------301
VARICK	———	N.Y./N.J.		CFA18-----------160
VARLET (or) VERLET	Holland	N.Y./Md.	Arms:-*	CRLA15----------328
VARNUM	Eng.	Mass.		PFU-------------149
VASSALL	Eng.	Mass.		CRLA1-----------433
VASSALL	France/Eng.	Mass.	Arms:-	CRLA8------------42
VAUGHAN	———	Va.		CFA5------------141
VAUGHAN	Eng.	Mass./Maine	Arms:-	CFA6------------210

VAUGHAN	Wales/Ireland	Maine		CFA18-----------184
VAUGHAN	Wales			CRLA18----------206
VAUGHAN	------	Mass./R.I.	Arms:-*	CRLA19----------288
VAUGHAN	Eng.	R.I.		AF****----------135
VAUTIER	France	Pa.		CRLA9-----------236
VAUX	Eng.	Pa.	Arms:-	CFA6------------374
VAUX	Eng.	Pa.	Arms:-*	CRLA5-----------501
VAUX (Vou) (de)	France	N.Y.	Arms:-*	CRLA18------198,219
VAVASOUR	Eng.			CRLA2------------14
VAWTER	Eng.	Va.		CRLA10-----------56
VEAZIE	Eng.	Mass.		CFA13-----------148
VEGHTE	------	N.Y.		CRLA8-----------231
VENABLE	------	Va.		PFU-------------361
VENABLES	------	Va.		CRLA4-----------319
VENABLES (de)	Eng.		Arms:-*	CRLA5-----------448
VENABLES	Eng.			CRLA9-----------175
VENABLES	Eng.		Arms:-*	CRLA11----------176
VERDON (de)		Cooley=Twining desc.		CRLA18----------146
VERE (de), Earls of Oxford	Eng.	*(only)		CRLA2-----------336
VERE (de)	Eng.	Arms:-*		CRLA5-----------450
VERE (de)	Eng.	Haskell descent		CRLA8-----------120
VERE (de)	Eng.	Gaither=Fownes desc.		CRLA11-----------49
VERE (de)	Eng.			CRLA11----------109
VERE (de)	Eng.	Wales descent		CRLA13----------106
VERE (de)	Eng.	Bray desc. Arms:-*		CRLA17------147,151
VERE (de)	Eng.	Vou descent		CRLA18----------246
VERE (de)	Eng.	Titus descent		CRLA18----------513
VERE (de)	Eng.	A.D. 1112-1469		CRLA20----------405
VERLET, see: VARLET				
VERMANDOIS, Counts of	France	descent from Charlemagne		CRLA1-----------375
VERMANDOIS, Counts of	France	Gaunt=French desc.		CRLA1-----------548
VERMANDOIS, Counts of	France	*(only)		CRLA2------------41
VERMANDIOS, Counts of	France	from Pepin, d. 810		CRLA2-----------489
VERMANDOIS, Counts of	France	Arms:-*		CRLA5-----------452
VERMANDOIS, Counts of	France	Haskell descent		CRLA8-----------122
VERMANDOIS, Counts of	France	Hinton descent Arms:-*		CRLA8-----------493
VERMANDOIS, Counts of	France			CRLA9-----------371
VERMANDOIS, Counts of	France			CRLA11----------111
VERMANDOIS, Counts of	France			CRLA11----------178
VERMANDOIS, Counts of	France			CRLA11----------437
VERMANDOIS	No family data	Arms:-*		CRLA15------opp.153
VERMANDOIS, Counts of	France			CRLA18----------195
VERMANDOIS, Counts of	France	descent from Charlemagne		CRLA20----------408
VERMANDOIS (Vernondois), Counts of	France			CRLA7-----------209
VERNON (de)	Eng.	Arms:-*		CRLA5-----------455
VERNON (de)	Eng.			CRLA11----------179
VERNON	No family data	Arms:-*		CRLA11------opp.160
VERNOOY	------	N.Y.	Arms:-*	CRLA20-----------48
VER PLANCK	------	N.Y.		CFA16-----------307
VERPLANCK	Holland	N.Y.	Arms:-	CFA26------------90
VERY	------	Mass.		PPA-------------457
VETCH	Holland	Mass.		CFA13------------32
VICKERS	------	Va./N.C.		CRLA7-----------391
VIERLING	Germany	Mo.	Arms:-	AF***-----------388
VIKING KINGS of Norway, Sweden, The Isle of Man & Orkney				CRLA15----------187
		Carter=Boynton desc. Arms:-*		
VILAS	------	N.H.		PFU-------------280
VINCENT	------	Mass.		CFA4-------------47
VINCENT	------	Mass.	Arms:-*	CRLA7-----------428
VINTON	------	Mass.		CFA7------------314
VINTON	------	Mass.		PFU-------------341
VITRE (de)	France			CRLA5-----------457
VLADIMIR, Prince of Russia	Rurik	Schull descent		CRLA5-----------134
VOORHEES	Holland	L.I.,N.Y.		CFA26------------72
VOSE	Eng.	Mass.		CFA7------------128
VOSE	Eng.	Mass.		CFA7------------138
VOSE	------	Mass.		CRLA20----------211

VOU (de)	France	N.Y.	Arms:-*	CRLA18---------198
VOU, see: VAUX				
VREDENBURGH	------	N.Y.		CFA6------------6
VREDENBURGH	------	N.Y.	Arms:-	AF*-----------258
VREELAND	Netherlands	N.Y.		CRLA20----------15
VROOMAN	Holland	N.Y.	Arms:-*	CRLA7----------178

- W -

WADE	Eng.?	Mass.		CFA10----------268
WADE	Eng.	Mass.	Arms:-*	CFA21----------211
WADE	Eng.	Va.		CRLA1----------274
WADLEIGH	------	Mass.		CRLA7----------488
WADSWORTH	------	Mass.		CFA7-----------323
WADSWORTH	Eng.	Mass.		CFA10----------249
WADSWORTH	Eng.	Mass./Conn.		CRLA19---------400
WADSWORTH	------	Mass.		PFU------------100
WAGGAMAN	Netherlands	Va./Md.		CRLA19---------343
WAGNER	------	Pa.		CRLA6----------147
WAGNER	Germany	Pa.		CRLA17---------270
WAGNER	------	Pa.		CRLA18---------517
WAGSTAFF	Eng.	N.Y.C.		CFA10----------195
WAIT	Eng.	Mass.		CFA9------------50
WAIT	------	R.I.		CRLA6----------179
WAITE	Eng.	Mass.		CFA9-----------252
WAITE	Eng.	Mass.	Arms:-*	CRLA1----------215
WAITE	Eng.	Mass.	Arms:-*	CRLA17---------579
WAITE	Eng.	Mass.	Arms:-*	CRLA18---------408
WAKE	Eng.			CRLA8----------123
WAKELEY	------	Conn.		CFA2-----------288
WAKELEY	------	------	Arms:-*	CRLA20-------opp.18
WAKELEY	Eng.		Arms:-*	CRLA20----------36
WALCOTT	Eng.	Mass.	Arms:-	CFA6-----------363
WALCOTT	Eng.	Mass.		CFA17----------333
WALDO	Eng.	Mass.		CFA8-----------109
WALDO	Eng.	Mass.		CFA20----------258
WALDO	------	Mass.		CRLA12---------155
WALDRON	Eng.	N.H.	Arms:-	CFA3-----------315
WALDRON	Eng.	N.Y.		CFA8-----------340
WALES	Eng.	Mass.		CFA2-----------226
WALES	Eng.	Mass.		CFA11----------225
WALES	Eng.	Mass./Conn.		CRLA13--------28,31
WALES, Kings of Gwynedd		Bray descent		CRLA17---------112
WALES, Kings of Powis		Bray descent	Arms:-*	CRLA17---------131
WALES, NORTH, Kings of	Rhodri Mawr	Vou descent		CRLA18---------260
WALES, Kings of, see: GWYNEDD, POWIS, and RHODRI MAWR				
WALKE	------	Va.		CRLA4----------185
WALKER	Eng.	Mass.	Arms:-*	CFA14----------103
WALKER	------	Mass.	Arms:-*	CFA17----------108
WALKER	------	Pa.		CRLA3----------213
WALKER	------	Va.		CRLA4----------194
WALKER	------	Mass.	*(only)	CRLA6----------286
WALKER	------	Mass.		CRLA13---------362
WALKER	Eng.	Mass.		CRLA19---------383
WALKER	Wales	Pa.	Arms:-*	AF*-----------356
WALKER	Eng.	Ky.	Arms:-	AF**----------109
WALKER	------	Mass.	Arms:-*	AF**----------524
WALKER	------	Mass.		TNEF-----------139
WALL	Eng.	Pa.	Arms:-*	CRLA17---------302
WALLACE	Scotland	Pa.		CFA15----------215
WALLACE	------	N.Y.		CFA24----------135
WALLACE	Scotland	Pa.		CRLA3----------296

WALLACE	Ireland	Pa.	Arms:-*	CRLA8-----------277
WALLACE	———	Ohio		AF**-----------182
WALLACE	Scotland	Va.		PFU------------352
WALLACE	———	Ky./N.Y.		PPA------------551
WALLER	Eng.	Va.		CFA16-----------164
WALLIAMS	Eng.	Del.		CRLA1-----------82
WALN	Eng.	Pa.	*(only)	CRLA2-----------423
WALN	Eng.	Pa.	Arms:-*	CRLA11----------469
WALTER	Eng./Ireland	Mass.	Arms:-*	CFA13-----------370
WALTER	Ireland	Mass.		CRLA20----------211
WALTER	———	Mass.		PPA------------247
WALTON	Eng.	N.Y.	Arms:-	CFA12-----------244
WALTON	Eng.	N.Y.C.	Arms:-*	CFA25-----------89
WALTON	———	Va.		CRLA4-----------411
WALTON	———	Pa.	Arms:-*	CRLA11----------448
WALTON	Eng.	Pa.	Arms:-*	CRLA13----------109
WALTON	Eng.	Mass.	Arms:-*	CRLA15----------64
WALTON	Eng.	Pa.	Arms:-*	AFA***----------23
WALTON, George	———	Va./Ga.		SDI---------239,244
WANTON	———	Mass.	Arms:-	CFA3-----------349
WANTON	———	Mass./R.I.		CFA8-----------365
WANTON	Eng.	R.I.		CRLA14----------72
WAPLES	———	Va./Md.		CRLA9------------6
WARBURTON	Eng.			CRLA9-----------174
WARD	Eng.	Conn./N.J.	Arms:-	CFA16-----------313
WARD	Eng.	Mass.		CFA17-----------247
WARD	Eng.	Mass.		CFA20-----------264
WARD	Eng.	Pa.	Arms:-*	CRLA1-----------39
WARD	Eng.	Mass./Conn.		CRLA1-----------162
WARD	———	Pa./Va.		CRLA4-----------383
WARD	———	Mass.	Arms:-*	CRLA11----------576
WARD	———	Mass.		CRLA12----------29
WARD	———	Md.		CRLA15----------574
WARD	———	Mass.	Arms:-*	CRLA17----------24
WARD	Ireland	Pa.	Arms:-*	CRLA17----------623
WARD	Eng.	Conn./N.J.	Arms:-*	CRLA18------212,229
WARD	Eng.	Mass./Conn.		CRLA19----------422
WARD	———	Mass.		PFU------------161
WARD	Eng.	R.I.		PFU------------233
WARD	———	Maine/Mass.		PPA------------355
WARD	———	———	*(only)	TNEF---------opp.31
WARDELL	Eng.	Mass.		CFA9-----------36
WARDELL	Eng.	Mass.		CRLA15----------453
WARDER	———	Pa.		CRLA5-----------504
WARDWELL	Eng.	Mass.		CRLA4-----------335
WARDWELL	———	Mass./N.H.		CFA19----------288
WARDWELL	———	Mass.	Arms:-	AF*-----------184
WARDWELL	Eng.	Mass.	Arms:-*	TNEF------------15
WARE	———	Va.	Arms:-	CRLA8-----------20
WARE	———	Mass.		PPA------------191
WARENNE (de)	Normandy			CRLA7-----------206
WARENNE (de)	———			CRLA9----------367
WARENNE (de)	Eng.			CRLA20----------396
WARFIELD	———	Md.		CFA2-----------43
WARFIELD	———	Md.		CFA3-----------299
WARFIELD	Eng.	Md.		CRLA1-----------277
WARFIELD	Eng.	Md.	Arms:-*	CRLA8-----------302
WARFIELD	Eng.	Md.	Arms:-*	CRLA11----------18
WARFORD	Eng.			CRLA13----------134
WARHAM	Eng.	Mass.		CFA15----------364
WARING	———	N.Y.		CFA21----------188
WARING	Eng.	Va./Md.		CRLA2----------195
WARNE	Eng.	———	Arms:-*	CFA27----opp.35,199
WARNE	Eng.	N.J.		CRLA13----------407
WARNER	———	———		CFA7-----------330
WARNER	———	Mass.		CFA10-----------83
WARNER	———	Mass.		CFA14-----------94

WARNER	————	Mass.		CFA14-----------269
WARNER	————	Mass.		CFA19-----------272
WARNER	————	Va.	Arms:-	CRLA3-----------109
WARNER	Eng.	Va.		CRLA4-----------39
WARNER	Eng.	Va.		CRLA4-----------112
WARNER	Eng.	Va.		CRLA4-----------222
WARNER	————	Mass.		CRLA7-----------530
WARNER	Eng.	Mass.		CRLA12----------379
WARNER	————	Del.		CRLA20----------145
WARNER	Eng.	Mass.	Arms:-*	AF**------------323
WARREN	————	Mass.		CFA5------------118
WARREN	Eng.	Mass.		CFA7------------350
WARREN	————	Mass.		CFA7------------359
WARREN	————	Mass.		CFA8------------393
WARREN	————	Mass.		CFA9------------210
WARREN	Eng.	Mass.		CFA12-----------109
WARREN	————	Mass.		CFA15-----------357
WARREN	Eng.	Mass.		CFA17-----------196
WARREN	————	Mass.		CFA19-----------295
WARREN	Eng.	Mass.	Arms:-*	CFA23-----------46
WARREN (de)	Eng.	from Rollo, Duke of Normandy		CRLA1-----------366
WARREN (de)	Eng.	Gaunt=French desc.		CRLA1-----------547
WARREN	Eng.	Mass.	Arms:-*	CRLA2-----------141
		Earls of Warren & Surrey		
WARREN	Eng.		*(only)	CRLA2-----------334
WARREN	————	Maine		CRLA4-----------338
WARREN	Eng.		Arms:-*	CRLA5-----------460
WARREN	————	Mass.		CRLA7-----------482
WARREN, Earls of	Eng.			CRLA8-----------341
WARREN	Normandy/Eng.			CRLA11----------113
WARREN (de)	Eng.		Arms:-*	CRLA10-----btn.78-9
WARREN	Eng.	Mass.	Arms:-*	CRLA10------297,344
WARREN	Eng.		Arms:-*	CRLA11----------181
WARREN	————	Mass.	Arms:-*	CRLA12------119,123
WARREN	————	Mass.	Arms:-*	CRLA13----------442
WARREN	Eng.?	Mass.	Arms:-*	CRLA15--------51,65
WARREN	————	Mass.	Carter=Boynton desc.	CRLA15----------93
WARREN	Eng.			CRLA15----------150
WARREN	————	Mass.	Arms:-*	CRLA15----------480
WARREN (de)	Eng.			CRLA17----------207
WARREN	Scotland	Mass./Conn./N.Y. Arms:-*		CRLA18----------598
WARREN	————	Va./W.Va.		CRLA19----------124
WARREN	Eng.	Mass.	Arms:-*	CRLA20----------190
WARREN (de)	Europe/Eng.	Mass.	Arms:-*	TNEF----------90,91
WARRINER	————	Mass.		CFA15-----------329
WARRINGTON	Eng.	————		CFA7------------400
WARTON	————	Pa.	Arms:-*	CRLA17----------288
WASHABAUGH	Germany	Pa.		CRLA13----------229
WASHBOURNE	Eng.	Mass./L.I.,N.Y.		CRLA17----------504
WASHBURN	Eng.	Mass.	Arms:-*	CFA1------------53
WASHBURN	Eng.	Mass.		CFA10-----------252
WASHBURN	Eng.	Mass.	Arms:-*	CFA12-----------69
WASHBURN	————	Mass.		ARSC------------93
WASHBURNE	Eng.	Mass./Conn./L.I.,N.Y.		CFA18-----------57
WASHBURNE	————	Va.	Arms:-*	CRLA15----------319
WASHBURNE	Eng.	Mass./Conn./N.Y.		CRLA18----------457
WASHINGTON	Eng.	Va.	Arms:-	CFA23-----------182
WASHINGTON, George	Eng.	Va.	Arms:-	CRLA3-----------106
WASHINGTON	Eng.	Va.		CRLA4-----------136
WASHINGTON, George	Eng.	Va.		CRLA4-----------218
WASHINGTON	Eng.	Va.	Arms:-*	CRLA4-----------482
WASHINGTON, George	Eng.	Va.	Arms:-*	CRLA10----------120
WASHINGTON	Eng.	Va.		CRLA11----------130
WASHINGTON, James	Eng./Holland		Arms:-*	AFA1------------17
WASHINGTON	————	Va.		MCS-------------27
WASHINGTON	————	————	*(only)	TNEF---------opp.45
WASHINGTON	————	————	Arms:-*	TNEF------------48

```
WASHINGTON, see: READE=WASHINGTON
WATERBURY          Eng.          Mass.          Arms:-*        CFA22------------97
WATERBURY          Eng.          Mass./Conn.                   CRLA13----------190
WATERBURY          ----          Mass./Conn.                   AFA3------------163
WATERMAN           ----          Mass.                         CFA9------------213
WATERMAN           Eng.          Mass.                         AF****----------126
WATERMAN           ----          ----           *(only)        TNEF-------btn.78-9
WATERMAN, see: PILGRIMS
WATERS             Eng.          Mass.          Arms:-*        CFA1------------133
WATERS             ----          Conn.                         CRLA3------------32
WATERS             Eng.          Va.                           CRLA6-----------465
WATERS             Eng.          Mass.                         CRLA17----------441
WATKINS            ----          Va.                           CFA5------------142
WATSON             Eng.          Conn.                         CFA11-----------386
WATSON             Scotland      N.Y.C.                        CFA22---------85,86
WATSON             Eng.          Pa.                           CRLA2-----------426
WATSON             ----          Mass.                         CRLA12----------398
WATSON             Scotland      N.Y.                          CRLA19-----------90
WATTS              Scotland      N.Y.           Arms:-         CFA20-----------233
WATTS              Eng.                                        CRLA11----------486
WATTS              Eng.          Pa.                           CRLA20----------301
WAUCHOPE           Europe                                      CRLA9-----------341
WAY                Eng.          Mass.                         CFA4------------165
WAY                Eng.          Mass./Conn.                   CFA9-------------28
WAY                Eng.          Mass.                         CFA11-----------248
WAY                ----          Pa.            Arms:-*        CRLA17----------347
WAYDELL            Holland       N.Y.                          CFA15------------77
WAYNE              Eng.          Pa.            Arms:-*        CFA20-----------102
WAYNE              Eng.          Pa.                           CRLA11----------185
WEAVER             ----          Pa.            Arms:-*        CRLA8-----------247
WEAVER             Eng.          R.I.                          CRLA13----------460
WEAVER             Eng.          R.I.                          CRLA17----------434
WEAVER             ----          Pa./N.Y./etc.  Arms:-*        AF****----------201
WEBB               Eng.          Mass.          Arms:-*        CFA17-------------1
WEBB               ----          Va.                           CRLA4-----------107
WEBB               Eng.          Va.                           CRLA4-----------154
WEBB               ----          N.Y.                          CRLA10----------391
WEBB               Eng.          Md.            Arms:-*        CRLA17----------414
WEBBER             Holland       N.Y.           Arms:-         AF**-------------65
WEBSTER            Eng.          Mass.          Arms:-         CFA6------------150
WEBSTER            ----          Va./Del./Md.                  CFA7------------395
WEBSTER            Scotland/Eng. Mass.          Arms:-         CFA8------------254
WEBSTER            Eng.          Conn.                         CFA15-----------358
WEBSTER            Scotland/Eng. Mass.          Arms:-*        CFA18-----------125
WEBSTER            Eng.          Mass.          Arms:-*        CRLA3-----------279
WEBSTER            Eng.          Mass.                         CRLA13-----------51
WEBSTER            Eng.          Mass.          Arms:-*        CRLA16-----------18
WEBSTER            ----          N.J.           Arms:-*        CRLA17----------312
WEBSTER            Eng.          Mass.          Arms:-*        CRLA18------591,613
WEBSTER            Eng.          Mass.                         CRLA19------402,405
WEBSTER            Eng.          Conn.          Arms:-*        CRLA20----------181
WEBSTER            ----          Pa.                           CRLA20------294,296
WEDDLE             ----          Pa.            Arms:-         AF*-------------413
WEED               Eng.          Mass.                         CFA9---------62,63
WEED               ----          Mass./Conn.    Arms:-*        CFA27----13cht.,200
WEEDEN             ----          ----           *(only)        TNEF-------btn.78-9
WEEDEN, see: PILGRIMS
WEEKS              Eng.          Mass.                         CRLA18----------539
WEIR               Ireland       S.C.                          CRLA6-----------553
WEIR               ----          ----           *(only)        TNEF---------opp.31
WEISER             Germany       Pa.                           CRLA20----------368
WEITZEL            Germany       Pa.                           CRLA8-----------528
WELBY              Eng.                         Arms:-*        CRLA15-----------40
WELBY=FARWELL      ----          Mass.                         MCS--------------13
WELCH              ----          N.Y.                          CRLA6-----------489
WELCH              Eng.          N.Y./N.J./Pa.                 CRLA17----------228
WELCH Princes, see: RHODRI MAWR
```

WELCOME (Ship)		Mass.	Knight=Walton	CRLA13----------126
			passenger descent	
WELD	Eng.	Mass.		CFA8------------294
WELD	Eng.			CFA12-----------280
WELD	————	Mass.		CFA12-----------293
WELD	Eng.	Mass.		CFA20-----------259
WELD	Eng.	Mass.		CFA21------------76
WELD	Eng.	Mass.		CRLA19-----------95
WELD	————	Mass.		CRLA20----------213
WELDON	No family data		Arms:-*	CRLA13------opp.488
WELLER	————	Conn./Mass.		CFA11-----------328
WELLES	Eng.	Conn.		CFA9-------------25
WELLES	Eng.	Conn.	Arms:-*	CFA9------------200
WELLES	————	Mass.		CFA9------------205
WELLES	Eng.	Conn.		CFA15-----------365
WELLES	Eng.	Conn.		CRLA7-----------138
WELLES	Eng.	Conn.		CRLA10----------215
WELLINGTON	Eng.	Mass.		CFA19------------73
WELLINGTON	Eng.	Mass.	Arms:-*	CRLA12----------117
WELLINGTON	Eng.	Mass.	Arms:-*	CRLA20-----------72
WELLES	Eng.	Mass./Conn.		CRLA16----------148
WELLS	Eng.	Conn./L.I.,N.Y. *(only)		CRLA2-----------317
WELLS	————	R.I.		CRLA15----------284
WELLS	Eng.	N.Y.	Arms:-*	AFA***----------375
WELLS	Eng.	Mass.	Arms:-*	CFA5------------218
WELLS	Eng.	L.I.,N.Y.		CFA10-----------339
WELLS	Eng.	Mass.		CFA19-----------272
WENDELL	Holland	N.Y.	Arms:-*	CFA3-------------54
WENTWORTH	————	N.H.		CFA8------------215
WENTWORTH	Eng.	N.H.	Arms:-	CFA13------------92
WENTWORTH	Eng.			CRLA15----------153
WENTWORTH	————	N.H.		MCS--------------64
WENTZ	Germany?	Pa.	Arms:-*	CRLA11----------456
WERT	————	N.J./Ohio	Arms:-	AF***-----------236
WESSELS	————	N.Y.		CFA8-------------41
WESSON	————	Mass.		CFA6------------357
WEST	Eng.	Va.		CFA5------------298
WEST	————	Pa.		CFA5------------320
WEST	Eng.	Mass.		CFA8------------231
WEST	Eng.	Va.	Arms:-*	CFA24------------16
WEST	————	Va.		CRLA2-----------118
WEST	————	N.H.	Arms:-*	CRLA3-------------8
WEST	————	Va.		CRLA4------------71
WEST	Eng.	Va.	Arms:-*	CRLA4-----------121
WEST	————	Del.?/Ill.		CRLA4-----------409
WEST	————	Mass.	Arms:-*	CRLA8------------16
WEST	————	Va.		CRLA9-------------9
WEST	Ireland	Pa.		CRLA9------------18
WEST	————	Va.	Arms:-*	CRLA15----------336
WEST	Eng.	Va.		CRLA18----------371
WEST	Eng.	Va.	Arms:-*	AF*-------------106
WEST	————	Va.		MCS--------------9
WESTCOTT	Eng.	Mass./R.I.		CRLA15----------281
WESTCOTT	Eng.	Mass./R.I.	Arms:-*	CRLA18----------343
WESTCOTT	Eng.	Mass.		AF****----------122
WESTERVELT	Netherlands	N.J.		CRLA12----------421
WESTFALL	Germany	N.Y.	Arms:-*	CRLA16-----------25
WESTON	Scotland	N.Y.		CRLA13----------437
WESTON	Scotland	N.Y.	Arms:-*	CRLA15----------469
WESTON	————	Mass.		TNEF------------240
WESTWOOD	Eng.	Mass./Conn.		CFA15-----------361
WESTWOOD	Eng.	Mass.		CRLA19-----------48
WETHERALL	Eng.	N.J.	Arms:-*	PFU-------------164
WETHERBEE	Eng.	Mass.		CFA14-----------123
WETHERBY	————	N.J.		CRLA20----------197
WETHERILL	Eng.	N.J.		CRLA8-----------145
WETHERILL	Ireland	Pa.	Arms:-*	CRLA9-----------280

WETHERILL	———	N.J.		CRLA11----------593
WETHERILL	Eng.	N.J./Pa.		CRLA17------398,408
WETHERILL	———	N.J.		MCS-------------67
WETMORE	Eng.	Conn.		PFU-------------436
WHALEY	Eng.	Va./R.I.	Arms:-	AF*-------------397
WHARTON=BICKLEY	———	———		CRLA17------589,590
WHARTON	Eng.		Arms:-*	PBAF------------186
WHEATLEY	Eng.	N.Y.	Arms:-*	AFA***----------169
WHEDON	Eng.	Conn.		CRLA17-----------8
WHEELER	———	Mass.	Arms:-	CFA4------------10
WHEELER	Eng.	Mass.		CFA7------------131
WHEELER	———	Mass.		CFA16-----------214
WHEELER	———	Mass./Conn.		CFA19-----------92
WHEELER	Eng.	Mass./Conn.	Arms:-	CFA27----------202
WHEELER	———	Mass.?		CRLA4-----------374
WHEELER	———	Pa.		CRLA11----------470
WHEELER	———	Mass./Conn.	Arms:-*	CRLA12----------363
WHEELER	Eng.	Mass.		CRLA13----------205
WHEELER	Eng.	N.H.		CRLA13----------277
WHEELER	Eng.	Mass.	Arms:-*	CRLA16-----------13
WHEELER	Eng.	Mass.		CRLA16----------203
WHEELER	———	Mass.		CRLA17----------250
WHEELER	Eng.	Mass./Conn.		CRLA17----------474
WHEELER	Eng.	Mass.	Arms:-*	AF*-------------66
WHEELER	———	N.Y.	Arms:-	AF*-------------225
WHEELER	Eng.?	Mass.	Arms:-*	AF**------------419
WHEELER	Eng.	Mass.	Arms:-*	TNEF------------11
WHEELER	Eng.	Conn.	Arms:-	AFA3------------41
WHEELWRIGHT	Eng.	Mass.		CFA7------------151
WHEELWRIGHT	Eng.	Mass.		CRLA1------------52
WHEELWRIGHT	Eng.	Mass.		CRLA9------------21
WHELDON	———	Mass.	Arms:-*	CRLA10----------291
WHELPLEY	———	N.Y./Mich.		CRLA12----------174
WHILLDIN	———	Mass./N.J.		AFA***----------150
WHIPPLE	Eng.	Mass./R.I.		CFA5------------45
WHIPPLE	Eng.	R.I.		CFA10-----------19
WHIPPLE	Eng.	Mass.	Arms:-	CFA17-----------131
WHIPPLE	———	R.I./N.Y.		CRLA18----------613
WHIPPLE	Eng.	Mass.	Arms:-*	PBAF------------148
WHIPPLE, William	———	Mass./N.H.		SDI-----------97,100
WHIPPLE	———	———	*(only)	TNEF-------btn.70-1
WHITAKER	———	Mass./N.J.		CRLA10----------206
WHITAKER, see: BOURCHIER=WHITAKER				
WHITE	Eng.	Mass.	Arms:-*	CFA3------------40
WHITE	———	Mass.		CFA4------------126
WHITE	Eng.	Mass.		CFA8------------59
WHITE	Eng.	Mass.		CFA9------------280
WHITE	Eng.	Mass.		CFA11-----------361
WHITE	Eng.	Mass.		CFA13-----------199
WHITE	Eng.	Mass.		CFA20-----------336
WHITE	Eng.	Mass.	Arms:-	CFA22----------168
WHITE	———	Mass.	Arms:-*	CFA23-----------54
WHITE	Eng.	Mass.		CRLA4-----------373
WHITE	———	Ky.		CRLA6-----------515
WHITE	Eng.	N.Y.C./Pa.		CRLA8-----------433
WHITE	———	Pa.		CRLA8-----------526
WHITE	Eng.	Mass.		CRLA10----------235
WHITE	———	Va.		CRLA12----------170
WHITE	———	Mass.	Arms:-*	CRLA12------359,368
WHITE	Eng.	N.J.		CRLA14-----------81
WHITE	Eng.	Mass./Conn.	Arms:-*	AFA***----------263
WHITE, see: RAVLIN=WHITE				
WHITENACK	———	N.J.		CRLA13----------401
WHITESIDE	———	R.I.		AF****----------105
WHITEFIELD	———	N.Y.		CFA10-----------223
WHITIN	Eng.	Mass.		CFA24-----------66
WHITING	Eng.	Mass.	Arms:-	CFA1------------43

WHITING	————	Mass.		CFA3--------------4
WHITING	Eng.	Conn.		CFA9-----------313
WHITING	————	Mass.		CFA10----------102
WHITING	————	Mass.		CFA13----------281
WHITING	Eng.	Mass.	Arms:-	CFA19---------61,83
WHITING	Eng.	Va.		CRLA2----------391
WHITING	————	Va.		CRLA4----------349
WHITING	————	Mass.	Arms:-*	CRLA15----------91
WHITING	Eng.	Mass.		CRLA19----------96
WHITING	Eng.	Mass.	Arms:-	AF**-----------416
WHITING	Eng.	Mass.	Arms:-*	TNEF------------85
WHITLEY	————	N.C./Va.		CFA14----------136
WHITLOCK	————	N.Y.		CFA18----------238
WHITMAN	Eng.?	Mass.		CFA5-----------183
WHITMAN	————	Warwick, _____		CFA10------------8
WHITMAN	————	Mass.		CFA13----------174
WHITMAN	————	Ind./N.Y.		CRLA8----------373
WHITMAN	————	N.Y.	Arms:-*	CRLA17----------317
WHITMAN	————	R.I.	Arms:-*	PBAF-----------101
WHITMARSH	Eng.	Mass.		CRLA17-----------25
WHITMIRE	Germany	Pa./S.C.		CFA14----------133
WHITMORE	Eng.	Mass.		CFA17----------124
WHITMORE	Eng.	Mass.	Arms:-	CRLA3----------347
WHITNEY	Eng.?	L.I.,N.Y.		CFA10----------238
WHITNEY	Eng.	Mass.		CFA11----------217
WHITNEY	Eng.	Mass.		CFA11----------237
WHITNEY	Eng.	Mass.		CFA18----------225
WHITNEY	Eng.	Mass.		ACF-------------52
WHITNEY	Eng.		Arms:-*	CRLA5----------464
WHITNEY	————	Mass.	Arms:-*	CRLA10----------412
WHITNEY	Eng.	Mass.	Arms:-*	AFA***---------225
WHITNEY	Eng.	Mass.		PFU------------330
WHITNEY	Eng.	Mass.		TNEF-----------180
WHITNEY	Eng.	Mass.		TNEF-----------205
WHITON	Eng.	Mass.	Arms:-*	CRLA20----------333
WHITON	Eng.	Mass.		PFU------------171
WHITSON	————	L.I.,N.Y.		CFA3-----------331
WHITSON	————	L.I.,N.Y.		CFA7-----------274
WHITSON	————	L.I.,N.Y.		CFA16-----------33
WHITTEMORE	Eng.	Mass.		CFA7-------------5
WHITTEMORE	Eng.	Mass.	Arms:-*	CRLA20----------125
WHITTIER	Eng.	Mass.		CFA19----------283
WHITTIER	————	Mass.		PPA------------389
WHITTINGTON	————	Va.		CRLA9-----------15
WHITTINGTON	Eng.	Va.	Arms:-*	CRLA15----------334
WHITWELL	Eng.	Mass.	Arms:-*	CRLA11----------197
WHITWELL	Eng.	Mass.		PFU------------472
WICK	————	N.J.	Arms:-*	CRLA18----------549
WICKES	————	Conn.		CFA3-----------276
WICKES	Eng.	Mass.		CFA10----------190
WICKENDEN	————	Mass.		CFA10-----------25
WICKHAM	Eng.	Conn.		CRLA20----------226
WICKHAM	Eng.	Conn.	Arms:-	AF**-----------227
WIDUKIND, Saxon Leader	Europe			CFA27---opp.236,238
WIEDERSHEIM	Germany	Pa.		CRLA8----------413
WIGGIN	————	N.H.		CFA7-----------174
WIGGINS	————	N.C.		CRLA4----------425
WIGGINS	————	Va.		CRLA4----------451
WIGGINS	————	N.Y.		CRLA7----------172
WIGHT	————	Mass.		CRLA1----------229
WIGGLESWORTH	Eng.	Mass.		CFA7-----------360
WIGHT	Eng.?	Mass.		CFA13----------300
WILBORE (or) WILBUR	Eng.	Mass.		CFA1------------14
WILBUR	Eng.	Mass./R.I.	Arms:-*	CRLA20-----------37
WILCOX	————	Md.	Arms:-*	CRLA1----------510
WILCOX	————	N.H./Vt./Conn.		PPA------------184
WILCOXSON	————	Mass./Conn.		CRLA7----------161

WILDBORE (Wilbur)	———	Mass.		CRLA20----------188
WILDE	———	N.Y.		CRLA11----------573
WILDE	Ireland	Md.		PPA-------------123
WILDER	Eng.	Mass.		CFA13----------153
WILDER	Eng.	Mass.		CRLA1------206,224
WILDER	Eng.	Mass.		CRLA18----------389
WIGHTMAN	Eng.	R.I.		CFA5------------46
WILHOIT	———	Va.		CRLA6----------291
WILKERSON, see: PILGRIMS				
WILKES	———	Mass.		CFA12----------360
WILKES	Eng.			CRLA20----------69
WILKINS	Wales	N.Y.C.		CFA6------------13
WILKINS	———	Mass.		CFA21----------233
WILKINSON	———	Mass.		CFA7-----------373
WILKINSON	Eng.	R.I.	Arms:-*	CFA10-----------22
WILKINSON	Eng.	R.I.	Arms:-	AF****----------181
WILKINSON	———	———	*(only)	TNEF-------btn.78-9
WILLARD	Eng.	Mass.		CFA2------------93
WILLARD	Eng.	Mass.		CFA8-----------333
WILLARD	Eng.	Mass.	Arms:-*	CFA13------214,220
WILLARD	Eng.	Mass.	Arms:-	CFA21----------228
WILLARD	Eng.	Mass.		CRLA6----------113
WILLARD	Eng.	Mass.	Arms:-*	CRLA7----------159
WILLARD	Eng.	Mass.	Arms:-*	CRLA15-----------36
WILLARD	Eng.	Mass.		CRLA15----------273
WILLARD	Eng.	Mass.		CRLA19----------114
WILLARD	Eng.	Mass.		AF****----------266
WILLARD	Eng.	Mass.	Arms:-*	HFA------------298
WILLCOCKS	———	N.Y.C.		CFA24----------182
WILLCOX	Eng.	Pa.		CRLA15----------518
WILLCOX	Eng.	Mass./Conn.		AF*------------115
WILLET	Eng.	Mass.		CFA25-----------36
WILLETS	Eng.	Mass./L.I.,N.Y.	Arms:-*	CFA3-----------327
WILLETS	Eng.	L.I.,N.Y.		CFA7-----------272
WILLETS	Eng.	L.I.,N.Y.		CFA7-----------380
WILLETS	———	L.I.,N.Y.		CFA16-----------14
WILLETS	———	N.Y.		CFA16-----------32
WILLETS	Eng.	L.I.,N.Y.	Arms:-*	CFA16----------131
WILLETT	Eng.	N.Y.		CRLA14----------75
WILLEY	———	Mass.		CFA1------------35
WILLEY	Eng.	Mass.	Arms:-	CFA27----------204
WILLEY		Md.		CRLA15----------574
WILLIAM THE CONQUEROR	Normandy/Eng.			CFA25-----------11
WILLIAM THE CONQUEROR	"	Drake descent		CRLA1----------300
WILLIAM THE CONQUEROR	"	through Sir John de Grey		CRLA1----------463
WILLIAM THE CONQUEROR	"	Gaunt=French descent		CRLA1----------542
WILLIAM THE CONQUEROR	"	Peck=Bowen desc. *(only)		CRLA2-----------23
WILLIAM THE CONQUEROR	"	Warren=Belknap desc. Arms:-*		CRLA2----------166
WILLIAM THE CONQUEROR	"	Rambo descent		CRLA2------230,233
WILLIAM THE CONQUEROR	"	Ludlow=Brewster descent		CRLA2----------325
WILLIAM THE CONQUEROR	"	South=Grantham descent		CRLA2----------439
WILLIAM THE CONQUEROR	"	Warner=Washington=Lewis desc.		CRLA3----------131
WILLIAM THE CONQUEROR	"	Schull descent Arms:-*		CRLA5-----------98
WILLIAM THE CONQUEROR	"	Haskell descent Arms:-*opp.488		CRLA8-----------66
WILLIAM THE CONQUEROR	"			CRLA8----------380
WILLIAM THE CONQUEROR	"	Gaither=Fownes descent		CRLA11-----------32
WILLIAM THE CONQUEROR	"	Blackiston desc. Arms:-*		CRLA11----------374
WILLIAM THE CONQUEROR	"	Richardson descent		CRLA11----------599
WILLIAM THE CONQUEROR	"	Wales descent		CRLA13-----------67
WILLIAM THE CONQUEROR	"	Childs descent		CRLA13----------196
WILLIAM THE CONQUEROR	"	Carter=Boynton desc. Arms:-*		CRLA15----------153
WILLIAM THE CONQUEROR	"	Smith descent Arms:-*		CRLA15----------301
WILLIAM THE CONQUEROR	"	Ayres=Sheppard descent		CRLA15----------355
WILLIAM THE CONQUEROR	"	**Bray** descent		CRLA17--------86,89
WILLIAM THE CONQUEROR	"	Cooley=Twining descent		CRLA18-----------91
WILLIAM THE CONQUEROR	"	Glendinning=Logan descent		CRLA18----------298
WILLIAM THE CONQUEROR	"	Titus descent		CRLA18----------449

```
WILLIAM THE CONQUEROR Normandy/Eng.      Richardson descent    CRLA19----------210
WILLIAM THE CONQUEROR    "               Ludlow descent        CRLA20----------285
WILLIAM THE CONQUEROR    "               Lindsay=Spotswood desc. CRLA20--------290
WILLIAM THE CONQUEROR    "               Warren descent        TNEF----------92,93
WILLIAMS              Eng./Wales  Mass.                         CFA2------------146
WILLIAMS              Eng.        Mass.          Arms:-*        CFA4------------140
WILLIAMS              ------      Mass.                         CFA7------------179
WILLIAMS              ------      N.Y.                          CFA7------------380
WILLIAMS              Eng.        Mass.                         CFA8------------288
WILLIAMS              Wales       Conn.                         CFA9------------148
WILLIAMS              Eng.        Mass.                         CFA13-----------307
WILLIAMS              Eng.        Mass./R.I.     Arms:-*        CFA14------------35
WILLIAMS              Eng.        Mass.                         CFA15-----------361
WILLIAMS              Eng.        Mass.                         CFA19------------91
WILLIAMS              ------      Pa.                           CFA22-----------233
WILLIAMS              ------      Ohio                          CFA23-----------144
WILLIAMS              Eng.        Conn.                         CFA26------------44
WILLIAMS              Wales/Eng.  Mass.                         CRLA6-----------359
WILLIAMS              Eng.        Mass.                         CRLA7-----------301
WILLIAMS              Wales       Del.           Arms:-*        CRLA11----------220
WILLIAMS              Wales       Pa./Md.                       CRLA15----------442
WILLIAMS              Eng.        Pa.            Arms:-*        CRLA17----------265
WILLIAMS              Eng.        Mass.                         CRLA17----------491
WILLIAMS              Eng.        Mass.                         CRLA19-----------92
WILLIAMS              Eng.        Mass.          Arms:-*        CRLA20-----------88
WILLIAMS              Eng.        Mass./R.I.     Arms:-*        CRLA20----------383
WILLIAMS              ------      N.C.                          AF***-----------268
WILLIAMS              ------      Mass.                         AFA***----------114
WILLIAMS              Eng.        Mass.          Arms:-*        PBAF-------------93
WILLIAMS, William     ------      Conn.                         SDI---------125,130
WILLIAMS              ------      ------         *(only)        TNEF-------btn.70-1
WILLIAMSON            Eng./Ireland Pa.                          CFA18-----------258
WILLIAMSON            Scotland    Va.                           CRLA15----------414
WILLIAMSON            ------      N.Y.                          CRLA16-----------60
WILLIAMSON            Ireland     Pa./S.C.                      CRLA17----------609
WILLING              Eng.        Pa.                            CRLA15----------463
WILLIS               Eng.        L.I.,N.Y.                      CFA7------------383
WILLIS               Eng.        Pa./L.I.,N.Y.                  CFA8-------------47
WILLIS               Eng.        L.I.,N.Y.                      CFA16------------13
WILLIS               ------      Mass.          Arms:-         AF*-------------271
WILLIS               ------      Maine/Mass.                    PPA-------------371
WILLITS              Eng.        Mass./N.Y./N.J.                CRLA17----------499
WILLOUGHBY           ------      Mass.                          MCS--------------68
WILLS                Eng.        N.J.           Arms:-*        CRLA5------------58
WILLS                Ireland     Pa.            Arms:-*        CFA8------------274
WILLSIE              ------      N.Y.                           CFA24------------41
WILLSON              ------      Md.                            CFA16------------84
WILMARTH             ------      Mass.                          AF****-----------91
WILMOT               ------      Mass.                          CRLA7------------60
WILMOT               Eng.        Conn.                          CRLA19----------102
WILMOTT              Eng.        Conn.                          CFA19------------67
WILSON               Eng.        Mass.          Arms:-*        CFA4-------------21
WILSON               Eng.        ------                         CFA7-------------19
WILSON               ------      Ohio/Iowa                      CFA8------------325
WILSON               ------      N.Y.C.                         CFA8------------338
WILSON               ------      N.Y.                           CFA18----------222
WILSON               Scotland/Ireland  Pa.                      CFA22------------59
WILSON               ------      Mass.                          CFA26-----------120
WILSON               Eng.        Mass.          Arms:-         ACF--------------79
WILSON               ------      Pa.            Arms:-*        CRLA1------------55
WILSON               ------      Ohio                           CRLA3------------63
WILSON               ------      Pa./Mo.        Arms:-         CRLA3-----------351
WILSON               Eng.        Va.                            CRLA4-----------317
WILSON               Eng.                       Arms:-*        CRLA5-----------472
WILSON               Eng.        Mass.                          CRLA6-----------376
WILSON               ------      Conn.                          CRLA7------------73
WILSON               ------      N.Y.                           CRLA7-----------255
```

WILSON	———	Va./Del.		CRLA8----------212
WILSON	———	Pa.		CRLA8----------402
WILSON	———	Del./Ohio		CRLA10---------348
WILSON	———	Mass.		CRLA11---------590
WILSON	———	Pa.		CRLA14----------42
WILSON	———	Va.	Arms:-*	CRLA15---------410
WILSON	———	Va.		CRLA17----------17
WILSON	Scotland	Pa.		CRLA17---------498
WILSON	Eng.	Mass.	Arms:-*	CRLA18----------35
WILSON	Eng.	Mass.		CRLA20---------201
WILSON	———	Pa.	Arms:-	AF*------------89
WILSON	Ireland	Pa.	Arms:-	AF**-----------184
WILSON	Eng.	Mass.	Arms:-*	AF**-----------422
WILSON	Scotland	Ill.	Arms:-	AF***----------402
WILSON, James	Scotland	Pa.		SDI--------159,166
WINANS	Holland	Conn./N.J.	Arms:-	CFA18----------279
WINBORN	———	Mass.		CRLA8-----------61
WINCH	———	Mass.		CFA19-----------76
WINCHELL	Eng.?	Mass./Conn./N.Y.		CRLA16-------83,88
WINCHELL	Eng.?	Conn.		CRLA19---------261
WINCHELL	Eng.?	Conn.	Arms:-	AF**-----------285
WINCHELL	Eng.	Mass./Conn.	Arms:-	AF***----------222
WINCHESTER	Eng.	Mass.	Arms:-*	CRLA20----------84
WINDEBANKE	Eng.		Arms:-	CRLA3----------113
WINDECKER	———	N.Y.		CRLA16---------102
WINDER	Eng.?	Va.?/Md.	Arms:-*	CRLA14---------125
WINDSOR	Eng.			CRLA2----------324
WINDSOR	———			CRLA15---------573
WINDSOR (City)		Conn.	Regional background	CRLA19---------240
WING	Eng.	Mass.	Arms:-*	CFA5-----------269
WING	Eng.	Mass.	Arms:-*	CFA7------------25
WINGATE	Eng.?	N.H.		CFA24----------440
WINGFIELD	Eng.			CFA10-----------67
WINGFIELD	Eng.			CRLA20---------108
WINGFIELD	———	Va.		MCS-------------20
WINGFIELD	———	Va.		MCS-------------21
WINSHIP	Eng.	Mass.		CRLA20----------99
WINSLEY	———	Mass.		CRLA14---------168
WINSLOW	Eng.	Mass.	Arms:-*	CFA1------------56
WINSLOW	———	Mass.		CFA6-----------351
WINSLOW	Eng.	Mass.		CFA7-----------305
WINSLOW	———	Mass.		CFA9------------23
WINSLOW	Eng.	Mass.		CFA10----------269
WINSLOW	Eng.	Mass.		CFA10----------286
WINSLOW	Eng.	Mass.	Arms:-	CFA15----------196
WINSLOW	Eng.	Mass.	Arms:-	CFA22----------216
WINSLOW	Eng.	Mass.	Arms:-	CRLA3----------343
WINSLOW	Eng.	Mass.		CRLA13---------376
WINSLOW	Eng.	Mass.	Arms:-*	CRLA15----------49
WINSLOW	Eng.	Mass.		CRLA19----------96
WINSLOW	Eng.	Mass.	Arms:-*	PFU-------------90
WINSOR	———	Mass.		CFA7-----------183
WINSOR	———	R.I.		CRLA19-------11,13
WINSOR	———	———	*(only)	TNEF-------btn.70-1
WINSTON	Eng.	Va.		CFA17----------318
WINTHROP	Eng.	———		CFA18-----------36
WINTHROP	Eng.	Mass.	Arms:-*	CRLA13---------304
WINTHROP	No family data		Arms:-*	CRLA17------opp.344
WINTHROP	———	———	*(only)	TNEF-------btn.78-9
WINTHROP, see: TYNDALL=WINTHROP				
WINTHROP, see: PILGRIMS				
WISE	———	Mass.		CFA6-----------180
WISE	———	Va.		CRLA4----------133
WISE	Eng.	Va.		CRLA9------------8
WISTAR	Germany	Pa.		CFA5-----------343
WISTAR	———	Pa.		CFA5-----------350
WISTAR	Europe	Pa.		CFA6-----------380

WISTAR	Germany	Pa.	Arms:-*	CRLA5-----------492
WISTAR	Germany	Pa.		CRLA11----------517
WISTER (Wuster)	Germany	Pa.	Arms:-*	CRLA11----------117
WISWALL	Eng.	Mass.		CRLA19----------372
WILTSIE	------	N.Y.		CRLA3-----------192
WITHERBEE	Eng.	Mass.	Arms:-*	AF****-----------74
WITHERILL	Eng.	N.J./Pa.	Arms:-*	CFA2------------128
WITHERS	Eng.	Va.	Arms:-	CFA2-------------23
WITHERSPOON, John	------	N.J.		SDI---------145,148
WITMER	Switzerland	Pa.		CRLA19----------233
WITTER	------	Mass.		CRLA17----------473
WITTER	Eng.	Mass.		CRLA17----------583
WOLCOTT	Eng.	Conn.	Arms:-*	CFA21------------38
WOLCOTT	Eng.	Mass.	Arms:-*	CFA23------------71
WOLCOTT	Eng.	Mass./Conn.	Arms:-	CFA26-----------110
WOLCOTT	Eng.	Mass./Conn.		CRLA1-----------150
WOLCOTT	Eng.	Conn.		CRLA4-----------262
WOLCOTT	Eng.	Conn.		CRLA7------------95
WOLCOTT	Eng.	Mass./Conn.		CRLA14----------667
WOLCOTT	Eng.	Conn.		PFU-------------152
WOLCOTT, Oliver	------	Conn.		SDI---------125,128
WOLF	No family data		Arms:-*	CRLA13------opp.298
WOLFE	------	Pa.	Arms:-*	CRLA17----------538
WOLFORD	------	Mass.		CFA19-----------277
WOLSELEY	Eng.	------		CFA9------------138
WOLVERTON	------	N.J.		CRLA10----------251
WOLVERTON	------	N.J.		CRLA12----------375
WONDERLY	------	Pa.	Arms:-*	CRLA8-----------261
WOOD	------	Va.		CFA5-------------35
WOOD	Eng.	Mass.		CFA7------------130
WOOD	Eng.	Conn./L.I.,N.Y.	Arms:-*	CFA14------------10
WOOD	Eng.	Mass.		CFA16-----------291
WOOD	Eng.	Mass.		CRLA2-----------299
WOOD	------	N.Y.		CRLA3-----------194
WOOD	------	Md./Va.		CRLA4-----------283
WOOD	------	R.I./N.J.	Arms:-*	CRLA5------------34
WOOD	Ireland	Pa.		CRLA9-----------537
WOOD	------	N.Y.		CRLA10----------389
WOOD	------	N.Y./Pa.	Arms:-*	CRLA13----------391
WOOD	------	N.J.		CRLA14-----------58
WOOD	------	Va.		CRLA14----------115
WOOD	Eng.	Mass.		CRLA15-----------64
WOOD	------	R.I.?	Arms:-*	CRLA19----------287
WOOD	------	Mass.?/N.Y.		AF*-------------183
WOOD	Eng.	Mass.	Arms:-*	AF**------------122
WOOD	------	Pa.		AFA***-----------40
WOOD	------	Pa.		AFA***----------168
WOOD	Eng.	Pa.	Arms:-*	AFA***----------207
WOOD	------	Mass.		TNEF------------102
WOODBRIDGE	Eng.	Mass.		CFA12-----------213
WOODBRIDGE	Eng.	Mass.		CRLA8-----------538
WOODBRIDGE	Eng.	Mass.		CRLA15----------605
WOODBURY	Eng.	Mass.		CFA5------------192
WOODBURY	Eng.	Mass.		CFA8------------103
WOODBURY	Eng.	Mass.		CFA25-----------128
WOODBURY	Eng.	Mass.	Arms:-*	CRLA8---------47,48
WOODBURY	Eng.	Mass.	Arms:-*	CRLA12-----------26
WOODCOCK	------	N.Y.		CRLA2-----------378
WOODCOCK	------	Mass.		CRLA19-----------89
WOODCOCK	Eng.	Pa.	Arms:-*	AFA***----------235
WOODFORD	Eng.	Mass.		CFA15-----------340
WOODFORD	Eng.	Mass.	Arms:-*	CFA18------------81
WOODFORD	Eng.	Mass.		CRLA18----------626
WOODHALL	Eng.	------	Arms:-	CFA4-------------23
WOODHALL	Eng.	------		CFA7-------------23
WOODHULL	Eng.	L.I.,N.Y.	Arms:-*	CRLA11----------195
WOODHULL	------	N.Y.		MCS--------------99

WOODHULL	Eng.	L.I.,N.Y.		PFU------------110
WOODMAN	Eng.	Mass.		CFA19-----------53
WOODMAN	Eng.	Mass.	Arms:-	CRLA10----------180
WOODMAN	Eng.	Mass.	Arms:-*	CRLA15----------16
WOODMAN	Eng.	------	Arms:-*	AF*-------------12
WOODRUFF	Eng.	Conn.		CFA12-----------17
WOODRUFF	Eng.	L.I.,N.Y.	Arms:-	CFA20-----------229
WOODRUFF	------	Conn.	Arms:-*	CRLA6-----------340
WOODRUFF	------	Conn.		CRLA19----------82
WOODRUFF	Eng.	L.I.,N.Y.	Arms:-*	AF***-----------37
WOODRUFF(E)	Eng.	N.Y.	Arms:-*	AFA***----------291
WOODROW	------	Pa.		CRLA17----------57
WOODS	Eng.	Mass.		CFA12-----------94
WOODS	------	Ky.		CRLA6-----------488
WOODS	------	------		PFU-------------424
WOODSIDE	------	Pa.		CRLA8-----------436
WOODSON	Eng.	Va.	Arms:-	CRLA3-----------371
WOODSON	Eng.	Va.		CRLA4-----------322
WOODSON	Eng.	Va.	Arms:-	CRLA6-----------452
WOODSON	Eng.	Va.	Arms:-*	CRLA10----------21
WOODSON	Eng.	Va.	Arms:-	AF***-----------398
WOODWARD	Eng.?	Mass.		CFA6------------196
WOODWARD	Eng.	Mass.		CFA12-----------374
WOODWARD	Eng.	Mass.		CFA15-----------350
WOODWARD	Eng.	Md.	Arms:-*	CFA16-----------106
WOODWARD	Eng.	Mass.	Arms:-	CFA18-----------144
WOODWARD	Eng.	Mass.	Arms:-*	CRLA2-----------273
WOODWARD	Eng.	Mass.	Arms:-*	CRLA3-----------27
WOODWARD	------	Mass.	Arms:-*	PBAF------------153
WOODWORTH	------	Mass./N.Y.		PPA-------------105
WOOLEY	------	Mass.?		CFA21-----------240
WOOLLEN	Eng.	Pa.		CRLA2-----------51
WOOLLEY	------	R.I./N.J.		CRLA14----------80
WOOLMAN	Eng.	N.J.		CRLA17----------280
WOOLRICH	Eng.	Pa.		CRLA5-----------508
WOOLRICH	Eng.	Pa.	Arms:-*	CRLA17----------345
WOOLWORTH	Eng.	Mass./Conn.	Arms:-*	CFA18-----------59
WOOSTER	Eng.	Conn.	Arms:-*	CRLA12----------106
WOOTEN	Eng.	Va.		CRLA4-----------97
WOOTTEN	------	Del.	Arms:-*	CRLA15----------567
WORCESTER	Eng.	Mass.		CFA21-----------221
WORCESTER	------	Mass.		CRLA14----------166
WORCESTER	Eng.	Mass.	Arms:-*	AF**------------411
WORDEN	------	Mass.		CRLA13----------359
WORDEN	Eng.	Mass.		CRLA19----------168
WORLEY	------	Tenn./N.C.	Arms:-	AF***-----------87
WORRELL	Eng.	Pa.	Arms:-*	CRLA2-----------134
WORRELL	------	Pa.	*(only)	CRLA2-----------404
WORTH	Eng.	Mass.		CFA1------------180
WORTH	Eng.	Mass.		CFA20-----------21
WORTHAM	------	Va.		CFA10-----------77
WORTHINGTON	------	Md.	Arms:-	CFA2------------43
WORTHINGTON	Eng.	Md.	Arms:-	CFA3-----------305
WORTHINGTON	Eng.	Md.	Arms:-	CFA5-----------287
WORTHINGTON	Eng.	Md.	Arms:-	CFA16-----------94
WORTHINGTON	Eng.	Mass.	Arms:-*	ACF-------------1
WORTHINGTON	------	Md.		CRLA1-----------287
WORTHINGTON	Eng.	Conn.		CRLA16----------133
WRAY	Ireland	Pa.	Arms:-*	CRLA18----------295
WRIGHT	Eng.	Md.		CFA3-----------296
WRIGHT	Eng.	Mass.	Arms:-*	CFA5-----------146
WRIGHT	Eng.	Mass.		CFA8------------56
WRIGHT	Eng.	Mass.		CFA11----------358
WRIGHT	Eng.	Mass.		CFA13----------196
WRIGHT	Eng.	Mass.	Arms:-*	CFA14-----------107
WRIGHT	------	Mass.		CFA15----------324
WRIGHT	Eng.	Mass.	Arms:-*	CFA18-----------23

WRIGHT	Eng.	Mass.	Arms:-	CFA22-----------163
WRIGHT	Eng.	———	Arms:-	ACF-------------77
WRIGHT	———	Md.		CRLA3-----------232
WRIGHT	———	Pa.		CRLA8-----------312
WRIGHT	Eng./Ireland	Mo./Miss.		CRLA11------544,552
WRIGHT	———	Mass.		CRLA12-----------44
WRIGHT	Eng.	Pa.	Arms:-*	CRLA14-----------45
WRIGHT	———	Va.	Arms:-*	CRLA15----------330
WRIGHT	Eng.	Mass.		CRLA16----------145
WRIGHT	———	N.J.	Arms:-*	CRLA18----------292
WRIGHT	Eng.	N.Y.	Arms:-*	CRLA19-----------51
WRIGHT	Eng.	Mass.		CRLA20-----------98
WRIGHT	Eng.		Arms:-*	CRLA20-------31,379
WRIGHT	Eng.	Mass.	Arms:-*	AF***-----------28
WRIGHT	———	S.C.		MCS-------------33
WRIGHT	———	Vt.		TNEF-----------179
WURTS=DUNDAS	Switzerland	N.J.	Arms:-*	CRLA8-----------127
WYATT	Eng.		Arms:-*	CRLA1-----------183
WYATT	Eng.			CRLA1-------268,271
WYATT	Eng.	N.J.	Arms:-*	CRLA5-----------498
WYATT	Eng.			CRLA7-----------100
WYATT	———	Mass.	Arms:-*	CRLA15-----------14
WYATT	———	Conn.		ARSC-------------43
WYATT	———	Va.		MCS-------------58
WYCHE	———	Va.		MCS-------------50
WYCKOFF	Netherlands	N.J.		CFA1-------------15
WYKOFF	Netherlands	N.Y.	Arms:-*	AF**-----------311
WYMAN	———	Mass.		CFA20-----------64
WYMAN	Eng.	Md.		CRLA3-----------251
WYMAN	Eng.	Mass.		CRLA11----------591
WYNDESOR	Eng.			CRLA1-----------249
WYNGAART	———	N.Y.		CRLA13----------160
WYNKOOP	———	N.Y.	Arms:-*	CFA25-----------125
WYTHE, George	———	Va.		SDI--------201,212

- Y -

YALE	Wales	Conn.	Arms:-*	CFA12------------8
YALE	Eng.	Conn.		CRLA19----------109
YALE	Eng./Wales	Conn.	Arms:-*	AF**-----------394
YALE	Wales/Eng.	Conn.	Arms:-*	AF**-----------546
YARDLEY	———	Va.		CRLA2-----------119
YARDLEY	Eng.	Va.		CRLA4-----------190
YARNALL	Eng.	Pa.		CFA7-----------397
YARNALL	Eng.	Pa.	Arms:-*	CRLA18----------205
YARNALL	Ireland	Pa.	Arms:-*	AF*------------358
YEAGER	Germany	Pa.		CRLA9-----------460
YEAGER	Germany	Pa.		CRLA11----------351
YERKES	———	Pa.		CRLA11----------274
YERKES	———	Pa.		CRLA11----------485
YERKES	———	Pa.		CRLA20----------299
YONGE	Eng.	Va.	Arms:-*	AFA***-----------9
YOST	France	Ohio		CFA24-----------25
YOUNG	Wales	Pa.	Arms:-*	CRLA8-----------273
YOUNG	Ireland	Va.		CRLA11----------312
YOUNG	———	Pa.		CRLA11----------335
YOUNG	Eng.	N.Y.		CRLA19----------165
YOUNG	Eng.	Mass.	Arms:-	AF***-----------74
YOUNG	———	Pa.		AF****----------101
YOUNGES (Youngs)	Eng.	Mass.	Arms:-*	AFA***----------327
YOUNGS	Ireland	Iowa		CFA12-----------365
YOUNGS	Eng.	Mass.	Arms:-*	CFA1-------------6

YOUNGS   Eng.   Mass.   CFA16------------14
YOUNGS   Eng.   Mass./N.Y.   CRLA12---------207

- Z -

ZELLER   Austria/Switzerland   Pa.   Arms:-*   AFA***------395,399
ZIEGLER   Germany   Pa.   CRLA9-----------446
ZIEGLER   ————   N.J./Pa.   Arms:-*   CRLA15---------466
ZIELIE   France   N.Y.   CRLA7-----------176
ZIMMERMAN   (see: CARPENTER, of Pa.)   CRLA19---------232
ZIMMERMANN   Germany   N.Y.   CRLA9-----------18
ZOUCHE (le)   Eng.   CRLA1-----------363
ZOUCHE (la)   Eng.   CRLA11----------183
ZOUCHE (la)   No family data   Arms:-*   CRLA15------opp.153